THE FOLLY OF REVOLUTION

The Folly of Revolution
Thomas Bradbury Chandler and the
Loyalist Mind in a Democratic Age

S. SCOTT ROHRER

The Pennsylvania State University Press
University Park, Pennsylvania

Frontispiece: Thomas Bradbury Chandler (1726–1790). Artist unknown; eighteenth century. Oil on canvas, 23.5 × 20 in. Yale University Art Gallery. Gift of Clarence Winthrop Bowen, BA 1873, MA 1876, PhD 1882. Photo: Yale University Art Gallery.

Library of Congress Cataloging-in-Publication Data

Names: Rohrer, S. Scott, 1957– author.
Title: The folly of revolution : Thomas Bradbury Chandler and the loyalist mind in a democratic age / S. Scott Rohrer.
Description: University Park, Pennsylvania : The Pennsylvania State University Press, [2022] | Includes bibliographical references and index.
Summary: "A biography of a leading loyalist named Thomas Bradbury Chandler (1726–1790), exploring his advocacy of monarchy and his criticisms of the American revolutionary movement"— Provided by publisher.
Identifiers: LCCN 2021054261 | ISBN 9780271092195 (hardback) | ISBN 9780271092201 (paper)
Subjects: LCSH: Chandler, Thomas Bradbury, 1726–1790. | Church of England—United States—Clergy—Biography. | American loyalists—Biography. | United States—History—Revolution, 1775–1783. | LCGFT: Biographies.
Classification: LCC E278.C45 R64 2022 | DDC 974.9/03092 [B]—dc23/eng/20211109
LC record available at https://lccn.loc.gov/2021054261

Copyright © 2022 S. Scott Rohrer
All rights reserved
Printed in the United States of America
Published by The Pennsylvania State University Press,
University Park, PA 16802-1003

The Pennsylvania State University Press is a member of the Association of University Presses.

It is the policy of The Pennsylvania State University Press to use acid-free paper. Publications on uncoated stock satisfy the minimum requirements of American National Standard for Information Sciences—Permanence of Paper for Printed Library Material, ANSI Z39.48–1992.

To Anne, the light of my life—a light that went out too soon.

CONTENTS

List of Illustrations *(viii)*
Acknowledgments *(ix)*

Introduction: Authority and Obedience in Revolutionary America *(1)*
1. Disciple: Thomas Bradbury Chandler, Samuel Johnson, and the Making of a High Church Royalist *(17)*
2. Englishman: Church and State in a Chandlerian World *(43)*
3. Time Traveler: The Glorious Revolution and the High Church Cause *(65)*
4. Episcopalian: Chandler and the Bishop's Cause *(88)*
5. Warrior: The Fight for an American Episcopate *(105)*
6. Loyalist: The Defense of British Authority *(128)*
7. Londoner: A Loyalist in Exile *(152)*

Epilogue: A Royalist in a Revolutionary World *(179)*
Appendix: The Library of Thomas Bradbury Chandler *(185)*
Notes *(217)*
Bibliography *(231)*
Index *(243)*

ILLUSTRATIONS

1. Samuel Johnson of Stratford, Connecticut, circa 1761 *(28)*
2. St. John's parish house, 1765 *(46)*
3. Elizabeth Town, New Jersey, during the Revolution *(46)*
4. Benjamin Hoadly, 1741 *(72)*
5. Chandler's *An Appeal to the Public*, 1767 *(99)*
6. Chandler's *What Think Ye of the Congress Now?*, 1775 *(140)*
7. St. James's Palace, London *(168)*

ACKNOWLEDGMENTS

I owe a number of debts for the writing of *The Folly of Revolution*. The manuscript went through a round of peer review during the advance-contract stage and a second round after I submitted the manuscript several years later. The reviews were tremendously insightful, and I have done my best to try to address the reviewers' concerns. I thank the reviewers for all of their excellent suggestions; the book is far better for it.

A generous grant from the Historical Society of the Episcopal Church enabled me to conduct research at the Lambeth Palace Library in London. This research was especially helpful in my interpretation of the Tudor and Stuart eras. The Lambeth library staff made this American expatriate feel at home during my stay. The staff at the Christoph Keller Jr. Library, General Theological Seminary in New York City, was also tremendously helpful. Their excellent holdings on colonial Anglicanism include the Bishop Seabury Collection and pamphlets that Thomas Bradbury Chandler owned at one time.

In addition, I thank the library staff at the Loyalist Collection, University of New Brunswick, as well as the staff at the New Jersey Archives in Trenton. All helped me find material that fleshed out the story of this American loyalist.

The most challenging part of the research involved hunting down the full titles and authors' names in Chandler's library. It was a time-consuming, tedious task that was made possible by the wonders of the internet: I relied primarily on Google Books, the Post-Reformation Digital Library, and WorldCat for my research.

As always, Kathryn B. Yahner, acquisitions editor at Penn State University Press, proved to be a pleasure to work with. I thank her for all her patience and excellent guidance over the past six years. And I thank Nicholas Taylor for his careful copyedit of the manuscript. Finishing this book would have been a lot harder without support from my son, Josh, and his beautiful wife, Alexandra Cople. A dark cloud was hanging over our family during the final months of writing and editing. But their love and help were instrumental in giving me the peace of mind to finish, and Alex took time out of her busy practice to draw Chandler's parish house.

This book is for Anne. I trust she and her bassets are smiling down on my modest accomplishment, and on us.

Introduction
Authority and Obedience in Revolutionary America

In the spring of 1764, an ailing George Whitefield embarked on his sixth preaching tour of the American colonies. Not shy about his abilities despite his declining health, the famed Anglican evangelist from Gloucester, England, reported that the crowds remained large and enthusiastic, and that the invitations for him to preach "come so thick and fast from every quarter, that I know not what to do."[1]

Not all colonists proved so welcoming. After a successful stay in Philadelphia, Whitefield wanted to preach at St. John's Church in Elizabeth Town, New Jersey, where Anglicans and others "bewitched" by the Grand Itinerant were clamoring to hear him speak. St. John's pastor—an irascible Anglican missionary by the name of Thomas Bradbury Chandler—said no.[2]

In the long, controversial career of Thomas Bradbury Chandler, the incident was a telling one, for it said much about the values and beliefs of one of the leading royalist thinkers in British North America. To his critics, Chandler was an "Ecclesiastick," a term of opprobrium they reserved for high church Anglicans who they believed persecuted their religious foes and longed for a pre-1688 world in which a strong monarch ruled.[3] Chandler was, indeed, a royalist. He believed in the union of church and state. He argued, passionately and defiantly, that governmental authority was essential to the smooth functioning of society. He prized hierarchy and abhorred democracy. To Chandler, the evangelical movement threatened to upend this traditional world by attacking the clergy, exalting the power of the laity, and encouraging the reborn to create a new, democratic society atop the rubble of the old, hierarchical one. The mere presence of Whitefield, whom Chandler derided as a "common incendiary," appalled him. The revivals, he explained years later, divided communities and undermined order; they were "productive of divisions and separations without end.... Enthusiasm, like faction, is utterly ungovernable."[4]

Chandler's rejection of Whitefield dismayed his parishioners, even angered them. But he stood his ground, "and after a while the tumult subsided," he reported to his superiors in London. Chandler viewed the incident as a teachable moment during a perilous time in American history. Protests against parliamentary authority were only beginning to stir in the mid-1760s, but Chandler well understood the direction American society was heading. In both the religious and political spheres, democracy was gaining ground and a royalist America was increasingly under assault. Whitefield's proposed visit came at a time when Chandler was already working to strengthen British authority and the Church of England in the colonies by aggressively campaigning for an American episcopate.[5]

Chandler's attempt to bring an Anglican bishop to the colonies in the 1760s, followed by his efforts to stave off American independence in the early 1770s, left him a figure of scorn in radical circles. His powerful tracts in 1774 and 1775 mocking the revolutionary movement, the Continental Congress, and New England were burned by the Sons of Liberty and nearly got him killed. And his full-throated campaign for hated bishops branded him for posterity as a high church crank woefully out of step with his revolutionary times.

The real Chandler, as a result, has been lost to history. We have no biographies of Chandler; instead, in study after study, usually on the bishop's cause, he emerges in brief mentions as a one-dimensional figure—the outspoken Anglican churchman hurling incendiary rhetorical bombs at Whigs and opposing the glorious cause that was the American Revolution.[6]

Chandler deserves a careful reappraisal, and for reasons that go beyond the need to understand the life of an American who pursued unpopular causes during the revolutionary era. Chandler the high church royalist stood at the head of an important segment of the American population that opposed the American Revolution and supported traditional British values. What these beliefs meant, and how Chandler came to hold them, is the subject of this book.

To many Americans today, a Chandlerian world of monarchy and hierarchy, of order and obedience, is little known and understood. In the popular imagination, the founding generation shared a love of individualism and democracy while abhorring monarchy and strong government. In a 2019 book, the erudite George F. Will, a syndicated columnist and influential conservative thinker, portrayed the founding generation as classical liberals devoted to democracy, individual liberty, and limited government—values antithetical to those held by Chandler and other "Friends of Government" (as Chandler and his allies described themselves). The revolutionaries, of course, won both the war and the fight over what kind of society the new nation would become, and with their victory, the alternative vision that Chandler promulgated has receded from historical memory.[7]

In 1775, however, the outcome was very much in doubt. A large part of the American public (possibly a majority on the Revolution's eve) admired monarchy, feared rebellion, and understood the importance of authority to society. Alexander Hamilton—an aide-de-camp to General George Washington during the war, a co-author of *The Federalist Papers*, and the subject of a wildly popular twenty-first-century musical that interprets the revolutionary period through a contemporary lens—was a social conservative who feared democracy and admired monarchy and the British constitution. In 1780, Hamilton proposed creating a monarchical government with republican liberties. "[The monarch] ought to be hereditary and to have so much power that it will not be [in] his interest to risk much to acquire more," he wrote. Hamilton also embraced the Chandlerian view that order was important to good government, and he worried that citizens in a republic might not share the deep respect for law and authority that they did under a monarchy.[8]

This concern with order might seem surprising, but it should not be. Across the political spectrum throughout the eighteenth century, leading Americans—merchants, planters, lawyers, and clergymen—wrestled with the question of how to preserve order and the deference owed to the elite in a democratizing world. The assault on Chandler's beloved hierarchy, with a monarch on top and a mass of commoners on the bottom, was coming from many quarters and had many causes. Extensive geographic mobility in the colonies was undermining community, weakening traditional social bonds, and allowing ordinary people to assume leadership roles, especially in the backcountry. In addition, Protestantism was undercutting the authority of leaders: the Great Awakening and evangelism placed salvation in the hands of the individual, while Presbyterian synods and Congregationalist covenants gave power to laymen in the running of their congregations. In the teeming seaports from Boston to Charleston, merchants enlisted the aid of laborers and seamen in the defense of American rights in the 1760s, but then struggled to keep them in line in the protests and riots that followed the Stamp Act and other British measures. As a leading urban historian noted, merchants came "to fear the awful power of the assembled artisans and their compatriots." The elites' fears of the masses only grew in the 1770s and 1780s as the newly declared United States embarked on its grand republican experiment. They saw ordinary people gaining power and state legislatures kowtowing to popular whims. As one historian said of the 1780s, revolutionary leaders came to believe "that the American Revolution had gone too far. Their great hope was that the federal convention [of 1787] would find a way to put the democratic genie back in the bottle."[9]

It was this fear of democracy that Chandler and other loyalist intellectuals sought to exploit when they campaigned against the revolutionary movement in the 1770s. For their American audience, they phrased the question simply: How could social and political order survive when subjects had the right to challenge authority? The leading voice for this view was Thomas Bradbury Chandler. In a particularly elegant passage summing up Bernard Bailyn's seminal *Ideological Origins of the American Revolution*, historian Robert M. Calhoon, the dean of loyalist studies, neatly captured Chandler's importance to American history: "Bernard Bailyn's groundbreaking analysis of the pamphlets of the American Revolution peeled layer after layer from more than a decade of imperial and constitutional debate until he reached the core of their meaning. He found this meaning *not* in a pamphlet by Adams or Jefferson or Paine, but in a challenge to Whig ideology penned by the high Tory theorist and polemicist Thomas Bradbury Chandler."[10] Bailyn had, indeed, praised "the elegant, scholarly Thomas Bradbury Chandler" as being in the forefront of loyalist writers who attacked the revolutionary movement at its weakest point. Bailyn summed up Chandler's challenge succinctly: "What reasonable social and political order could conceivably be built and maintained where authority was questioned before it was obeyed?"[11]

In his three tracts urging colonists to reject revolution, Chandler warned them about the dangers rebellious subjects posed to government and society. "The bands of society would be dissolved," he wrote in *A Friendly Address to All Reasonable Americans*, "if reverence, respect, and obedience, might be refused to those whom the constitution has vested with the highest authority."[12]

Virtually all loyalist thinkers, from Jonathan Boucher to William Smith and Samuel Seabury Jr., said much the same thing in their denunciations of the revolutionary movement. In June 1775, Smith, provost of the College of Philadelphia, could be found preaching "that without order and just subordination, their [sic] can be no union in public bodies. However much you may be equals on other occasions, yet . . . every individual is bound to keep the place and duty assigned him, by ties far more powerful over a man of virtue and honour, than all the other ties which human policy can contrive."[13]

Chandler's colleague Samuel Seabury Jr., an Anglican minister in New York, maintained that "government was intended for the security of those who live under it—to protect the weak against the strong—the good against the bad—to preserve order and decency among men, preventing every one from injuring his neighbor. Every person, then, owes obedience to the laws of the government under which he lives, and is obliged in honor and duty to support them." If a person has the right to disregard the law, Seabury continued, "*all* have the *same* right; and *then* government is at an end."[14]

High church clergy were not alone in sounding these alarms. In April 1775, Frederick Smyth, chief justice for the colony of New Jersey, lectured the Middlesex County grand jury about the importance of respect for government and the threat posed by "a Tyranny of the People." "Every individual hath an interest in the public tranquility, which once destroyed all private rights will sink and be absorbed," Smyth said. "If Liberty and the Common rights of the Subject are really the objects in view, let it be remembered that Liberty is never more in danger than when it vergeth into Licenciousness—Liberty must ever be founded in Law, and protected by it."[15]

Americans' views of order, obedience, democracy, and rebellion had roots deep in English and Western history. On the Whigs' side, historians since the 1950s have been methodically uncovering the sources of revolutionary thought. Among the most influential remains the work of Gordon S. Wood. In *The Creation of the American Republic*, Wood noted that American revolutionaries drew their inspiration from classical antiquity, British history, and European rationalism. From history, American revolutionaries came to understand how power corrupted rulers and threatened the liberties of the people. Antiquity—a time when Athens and other republics flourished—was a source of inspiration to these budding liberals, while the fall of these ancient republics was equally instructive. British history provided further powerful lessons, especially the seventeenth century, a time when the people triumphantly overthrew Stuart rulers and saved the nation from Catholicism and tyranny.[16]

Numerous historians have also shown how important religious history—especially dissenter history—was in Whig circles. The English Civil Wars of the 1640s, which witnessed the execution of Charles I and the establishment of a Cromwellian protectorate, were particularly searing. The successful rebellion against the Crown, and the accompanying emasculation of the state church and its hated bishops, inspired American radicals. So did a dissenting tradition in the British Isles that saw Puritans and Presbyterians repeatedly challenge Anglican and royal power in the sixteenth and seventeenth centuries. This dissenting tradition, with its deep distrust of the state church and British authority, made the colonists' conspiracy fears of the 1760s and '70s especially intense, as historian J. C. D. Clark has shown.[17]

Clark also demonstrated the ways that the heated religious rivalries of earlier centuries shaped politics and concepts of liberty. "In the rivalry and antagonism of religious sects," he observed, "is to be found a crucial component of imperial politics and a central theme in the history of political thought, hitherto largely the province of church historians, but deserving of a more central place in the historical arena." John Seed made a similar argument, positing that the history of persecution of dissenters in the seventeenth century was a central and shaping force among dissenters in the eighteenth century. The return of the Stuarts and the state church in 1660, accompanied by a crackdown on dissent, left a legacy of distrust and hatred in coming decades that greatly affected politics.[18]

How American loyalists made use of history is another matter. As on the Whig side, many scholars recognize that history played a crucial role in shaping loyalist beliefs. But analyses of this history share a common weakness: historians view the Americans who defended the king in 1775 as a mirror image of their revolutionary counterparts. Loyalists read the same sources and shared the same historical memories as the revolutionaries but came to opposite conclusions. "If republican ideology was a hybrid of classical ideas conceived in a Machiavellian moment, loyalism drew on principles deeply embedded in English politics, philosophy, and literature," observed Jerry Bannister and Liam Riordan. "These principles manifested themselves in an eclectic range of thinkers—from Hobbes and Locke to Burke and Durham—as Britons debated the covenants that bound subjects to their king."[19]

In a 1972 essay, historian Mary Beth Norton presented one of the most powerful cases for this school of thought as she concluded that loyalists, just like their radical American cousins, were Lockeans and Whigs. Loyalists, she explained, were not backward conservatives clinging to a romanticized British past but were in the mainstream of eighteenth-century English Whig thought; American revolutionaries, by contrast, embraced a radical variant of Whiggism discredited in England. "Instead of characterizing the American Revolution as a struggle between Whigs and Tories, I would argue that in ideological terms, it should be seen as a contest between different varieties of Whigs, Whigs whose respective world views brought some of them to become revolutionaries and others to become loyalists," she wrote. Norton's loyalists, in short, cited the same authorities as American radicals. "Copious references to Locke, Hume, Montesquieu, Grotius, and Vattel line the pages of works by Joseph Galloway and other loyal essayists," she observed. In addition, according to Norton, the loyalists argued from Lockean premises. They accepted the constitutional settlement that followed the Glorious Revolution of 1688–89 and rejected the Jacobite movement that sought to return the Stuarts to the throne.[20]

In accounts of radical and loyalist thought, the Glorious Revolution was especially important. Norton and other historians note that both loyalists and radicals accepted the outcome of the constitutional settlement that followed the peaceful overthrow of James II. In the words of Robert Calhoon, "The Glorious Revolution transformed the concept of order throughout the Anglo-American world. It settled once and for all the question of parliamentary supremacy. And by securing the Protestant succession to the throne . . . the Glorious Revolution insured that the absolutism of the kind Louis XIV was then instituting in Catholic France would not develop in the British Isles."[21]

In a study of colonial Anglican clergy during the revolutionary era, Nancy L. Rhoden agreed. "As inheritors of the Glorious Revolution Settlement, which had included provisions for constitutional monarchy and religious toleration," she wrote, "colonial Anglican clergymen of the late eighteenth century did not wish to dispute or unravel the political changes since 1688. Even Anglican loyalists, who affirmed the political superiority of British institutions, wanted to separate themselves from non-juring, and therefore disloyal, doctrines of passive obedience and non-resistance."[22]

The life of Thomas Bradbury Chandler presents a fascinating test of these theses, for he left behind a trove of documentary sources—most importantly, a catalog of his extensive library—that allows us to climb into the mind of a leading loyalist and critic of the revolutionary movement. Like his radical counterparts, Chandler was enthralled by the Glorious Revolution, but not quite in the way Norton and Calhoon posited. Chandler did indeed understand that, after 1688, Parliament reigned supreme in the British constitutional system. Responding to American claims that Parliament had no right to tax the colonies, he argued for parliamentary authority over British North America. But to read these arguments as "acceptance" of the Glorious Revolution distorts, and simplifies, Chandler's beliefs. As his library holdings and life experiences reveal, Chandler's fascination with the Glorious Revolution had little to do with constitutional issues involving parliamentary authority or the fate of the Stuart line. Instead, he studied the various debates surrounding the 1688–1720 period intently—most of them quite obscure and rarely mentioned in analyses of Americans' intellectual heritage—in order to gain a deeper understanding of revolution, governmental authority, obedience, and the importance of episcopacy to a well-functioning state. Chandler's library holdings and his forays into dusty corners of English history help solve key puzzles: Why did Chandler love monarchy so strongly and hate democracy so passionately? Why did he value order so highly? Most of all, why did he see revolution as folly?[23]

Thomas Bradbury Chandler was born in 1726 and raised in a Congregational world, the eldest child in a wealthy Puritan family from Connecticut with roots extending to the Great Migration of the 1630s. The Chandlers were farmers and militia officers, town officials and church deacons. Thomas wanted nothing to do with that world. As an undergraduate at Yale, he converted to Anglicanism and, after graduating in 1745, studied theology under the Reverend Samuel Johnson of Connecticut, a brilliant high churchman and strong supporter of episcopacy. At the conclusion of his studies and after a brief stint teaching school in his hometown of Woodstock, Chandler arrived in the picturesque village of Elizabeth Town near New York City in 1748 to become a catechist and, three years later, minister at St. John's. There, he would spend the next forty-two years, except for a ten-year exile in London during the American Revolution. Despite the Whitefield incident, Chandler was beloved by his parishioners, and he succeeded in building an impressive membership for the struggling church, so much so that St. John's became one of the largest Anglican congregations in colonial New Jersey.[24]

Chandler's personality was far more complicated than his reputation as a high church extremist would suggest. His letters to London could be impudent and impatient, but also reasoned and powerful as he pleaded for an American bishop. His published writings suffered the same flaws and exhibited the same strengths: they were—mostly—calm in an attempt to persuade a "reasonable" public, but they were also peppered with insults so penetrating that his outraged targets labeled Chandler an enemy to the people. In person, he had a kindly, even cherubic face, defined by pencil-thin eyebrows, "uncommonly" blue eyes (in the words of one of his daughters), and an aquiline nose. His health was poor—he struggled with smallpox and had a painful, cancerous nose—but he exuded energy and a capacity for work until his final years. Despite his bookish propensities, Chandler was gregarious, known for a friendly manner and engaging voice. Unlike Samuel Johnson, he enjoyed the demanding social responsibilities of a colonial parson in a small village.

Yet Chandler, the first born in a wealthy family who married into the upper crust of New Jersey society, could be haughty and hot-tempered. In his dealings with his religious rivals, Chandler alternately charmed and insulted his dissenter neighbors. Among the Anglican clergy, he had his share of critics and supporters. Detractors such as William Smith believed Chandler's campaign for an American episcopate was poorly conceived and ill-timed. His supporters felt otherwise. Possessing a first-rate mind and the confidence of someone born into wealth, Chandler was a natural leader. With Samuel Johnson's health failing in the 1760s, Chandler assumed the mantle of leadership as the northern Anglican clergy campaigned for an American episcopate. This coterie of clergy—primarily Charles Inglis, Samuel Seabury Jr., and Myles Cooper—looked to Chandler for guidance. It was Chandler who organized petition campaigns to London, wrote the main tract for episcopacy, and spearheaded the defense of their campaign.[25]

Opponents and supporters alike agreed that Chandler was a scholar of distinction. The patriot clergyman Ezra Stiles—no fan of Chandler and his high church beliefs—praised Chandler's intellect and considered him one of the best-read churchmen in America. Chandler was a serious bibliophile of nearly Jeffersonian ambitions who amassed one of the largest private libraries in early America. After his death in 1790, Chandler's estate put his library up for sale, listing each work and the price. The catalog of Chandler's holdings—a fabulous source that historians have noted but not examined—reveals both the breadth of his interests and the sources of his intellectual thought. It is this library that gives us important insights into what educated colonists read and how a leading loyalist used history to construct a mental world that rejected rebellion.[26]

Chandler is best known for his campaign for an American bishop, but episcopacy was merely the means to an end. Chandler prized order, and he disdained the two biggest threats to order—democracy and revolution. As he saw democracy and the revolutionary movement gaining ground in the colonies, Chandler wanted to better understand the forces at work and to devise ways to counter them. Thus he accumulated an impressive collection of books about the founding of the Church of England in Tudor England, the rise of Puritanism in the sixteenth century, and the debates about obedience and rebellion that followed the Glorious Revolution of 1688–89. For

Chandler, this history reinforced the dangers of democracy and the value of a hierarchical society centered on monarchy and a state church whose mission was to buttress governmental authority.

American revolutionaries knew their history, too, but they focused not on the minutiae of the 1688 period as did Chandler, but on the tumultuous events in seventeenth-century England: Laudian persecution in the 1630s, followed by the Civil Wars of the 1640s, the Restoration of 1660, and the overthrow of James II in 1688. For American Whigs, this history provided valuable lessons on the dangers of a tyrannical king and state church as well as the importance of resistance. Whig heroes included James Tyrrell, whose *General History of England* (a copy of which Chandler owned) defended the rights of the people to rebel, and the greatly admired John Locke, who laid out a contractual society in which government rested on the consent of the governed.

Chandler owned four of Locke's works and likely read him closely, mulling over Locke's views of family and his analysis of order and rebellion, but Chandler never accepted Lockean contractualism. Central to his understanding of rebellion and obedience were two pivotal, and now obscure, events from the Glorious Revolution: the protests of the nonjurors—those Church of England clergy in the British Isles who refused to take the oath of allegiance when William and Mary ascended to the throne in 1689—and the Bangorian controversy, so named because Benjamin Hoadly as Bishop of Bangor sparked a fight over church powers following a sermon he delivered on March 31, 1717. For Chandler, the views of Hoadly were more damning than those of Locke because of the former's attacks on hierarchy and authority.[27]

A critic of religious strife, Hoadly wanted to curb the powers of the institutional church and end the practice of forcing people to worship at the state church. Chandler owned more than ten works by Hoadly and a far large number of tracts by his critics. These critics warned that Hoadly's doctrines would destroy church authority and all laws imposed on matters of faith or conscience. The nonjurors and high church polemicists rejected the idea that ordinary people could be on an equal footing with their superiors. Hoadly's philosophy, they said, would mean that every man had the right to judge Scripture for himself.

For Chandler, the debates surrounding the Glorious Revolution helped him make sense of the growing crisis in Britain's North American colonies. He was concerned about more than the religious divisions in America and the growing violence of street protests, both of which threatened British authority; he worried about what kind of society British North America would become.

Chandler saw individualism rising in both church and state. He saw growing economic prosperity creating a middle-class society. And he saw representative democracy expanding, which undercut deference and threatened the elite's ability to lead. As alarming as the political protests of the 1760s and 1770s were, Chandler was little surprised by what was happening. The trends had been obvious to him for years, and he drew parallels between America of the 1760s and England of the seventeenth century.

Chandler, as a result, was not merely a backward-looking royalist refighting the political battles of earlier centuries. He saw the contest between dissenter and churchmen, between rebellious subject and central authority, as not only ongoing but entering a dangerous new phase in the 1760s that threatened the traditional, monarchical society he loved. This fight was a key reason he wanted a bishop so badly for the American branch of the Church of England. Historians typically portray the bishop's campaign as an outgrowth of the persecution and impotence the northern Anglican clergy felt. As Peter W. Walker observed in a 2016 dissertation on loyalist clergy,

> The [Anglican] missionaries believed that the Church of England was the established church in America—at least in principle. They considered it staggeringly unjust that colonial Dissenters had arrogated that role to themselves. Not only this, the missionaries believed they received worse treatment from American Dissenters than English Dissenters received from the Church of England. In 1759, the Connecticut missionary Samuel Johnson told the Archbishop of Canterbury, "the Church is really in a State of Persecution under them here, where they have, without any warrant from their Charter, pretended to establish themselves."[28]

There is much truth to this interpretation. Chandler and his clerical allies did see themselves in a position of weakness, and they did see themselves as victims, unlike their brethren in the South, where Anglicanism was the established church in Virginia and the Carolinas. Northern missionaries for the Society for the Propagation of the Gospel in Foreign Parts felt surrounded and besieged by their far more numerous rivals, and they complained bitterly about their treatment at the hands of the dissenters and about London's supposed lack of support for northern Anglicans.

But the wellspring for the bishop's campaign ran deeper than the clergy's frustration with their supposedly inferior status. Flowing through Chandler's writings and reform campaign were insights gleaned from the Glorious

Revolution and the ways religion can help prevent revolution and protect monarchy. His campaign for an American episcopate pulled together all the threads in his religious and political thought. The arrival of a bishop, he believed, would strengthen the Church of England in America and the Crown's authority in the fractious colonies, where democracy was gaining the upper hand. For Chandler, his collection of books and tracts on England and Scotland in the seventeenth century provided ample proof that episcopacy was an essential pillar in a monarchical society and that Anglicanism promoted respect for authority and government.

It is striking just how important the 1680–1720 period was to Chandler, and how deeply he read into this period of history. Unlike other American intellectuals, he did not look to the ancient world for guidance. On the radical Whig side, Athens and the Roman republic were a model to emulate and study. On the loyalist side, the ancients provided words of wisdom on the dangers of democracy and how the rule of commoners could lead to anarchy. Aristotle, for one, believed people of low birth or from the mechanical occupations were unfit to rule. If his library catalog is any indication, Chandler's gaze did not go so far back. He instead trained his telescope on Scotland and England in the closing years of the seventeenth century and the early years of the eighteenth. Nor did he look to continental sources for guidance. The Protestant Reformation and religious wars of the early modern period produced a robust body of literature on the importance of obedience, everything from Martin Luther's admonitions to obey earthly rulers to Jean Bodin's *Six Books of the Republic* (1576), which stressed the patriarchal nature of governmental authority. Bodin's work is especially interesting given its parallels to key Chandlerian themes: that a family was most stable when the patriarch exercised absolute authority and thus that a state was strongest when a monarch enjoyed similar authority. Patriarchy and hierarchy were important in Chandler's writings, but it was Robert Filmer (1588–1653)—the leading English apologist for monarchy—and not Bodin who inspired Chandler.[29]

In important ways, Chandler's outlook was also shaped by American conditions. He came away from his Connecticut upbringing with a visceral hatred—and hatred is not too strong of a word—of New England, Congregationalism, and the Great Awakening. As an undergraduate at Yale, he naturally gravitated to the Anglican orbit. The reasons were not hard to find. To an extraordinary degree, the Church of England's values of hierarchy and order were his values, and Chandler reveled in the church's three-century history, even the controversial chapters that Whig foes seized on in an attempt to discredit it. Chandler especially admired Richard Hooker, the famed Anglican theologian and apologist, and defended William Laud, the reviled archbishop who persecuted Puritans in the 1630s and spurred the mass migration that led to New England's founding. The Church of England was a state church that defended monarchy and preached the importance of obedience to, and duty and respect for, one's superiors. Kings and God were conjoined, as the former ruled with the divine blessing of the latter. As the Bible commanded, according to Anglican dogma, subjects owed allegiance to both king and God. As a result, rulers "have a right to be obeyed in all things, wherein they do not interfere with the commands of God: for in obeying them, we obey God, who commands by their mouths and wills, by their laws and proclamations," explained a 1755 edition of the church's primer on obedience, *The Whole Duty of Man*.[30]

Chandler's arrival in Elizabeth Town landed the pugnacious, and proud, young minister in a fierce religious contest pitting "dissenters"—primarily Presbyterians—against Anglicans. He came to Elizabeth at a critical juncture, when the Church of England was working hard to expand in the American colonies. The effort was succeeding, especially in New England. The church grew from 111 parishes in 1700 to 289 in 1750. The expansion was largely the result of an aggressive missionary effort that followed the founding of the Society for the Promotion of Christian Knowledge (SPCK) in 1698 and the Society for the Propagation of the Gospel in Foreign Parts (SPG) in 1701. The former was the brainchild of Thomas Bray, the Bishop of London's deputy in Maryland, who was alarmed by the shortage of Anglican ministers in the colonies. The SPCK published religious literature and established schools, while the SPG supplied missionaries to the colonies who would work among the king's subjects and prevent the spread of infidelity and popery.[31]

But the Church of England still had much work to do in America, especially in the northern colonies. In Elizabeth and its environs, the Presbyterians were dominant and membership at St. John's had fallen off when Chandler arrived in 1747. He worked tirelessly to change that over the next twenty-seven years. Driving him was his belief in the superiority of episcopacy and the state church. As a missionary, Chandler sought to inculcate Anglican values in his parishioners and neighbors. But more than that, he viewed the contest with the dissenters as a battle for a traditional society. Presbyterianism and Congregationalism, he concluded, posed grave dangers to monarchy and hierarchy, and he wanted their expansion slowed and their influence contained.

This battle in Elizabeth Town occurred at the same time as London's authority in the colonies was deteriorating. And for this development, Chandler heaped a good deal of blame on dissenters—they were, according to

Chandler, cantankerous, divisive, and hostile to good government and monarchy. Equally damning in Chandler's view, the dissenters were encouraging individualism. Individuals who followed their own inclinations in church made for disobedient, and potentially rebellious, subjects in the political realm. English Puritans, after all, had been stirring up trouble for the Crown since the days of Queen Elizabeth and Archbishop John Whitgift. Chandler saw similar challenges in the colonies—and specifically in New England, obviously, with its Puritan heritage, democratic ethos, and hostility to Anglicanism. Whitefield and the Great Awakening posed a second serious threat because of evangelicals' questioning of authority. Jonathan Edwards and his *Freedom of the Will*, published in 1754, posed a third.

Edwards, the brilliant theologian and philosopher from the Connecticut River Valley, attempted in his famous treatise to carefully define free will and to account for human sin in a Calvinistic world. An all-powerful God bestowed on his human creations the ability to choose between multiple courses of actions, Edwards reasoned, but they choose within a range of behaviors that God selected. Edwards's purpose was to counter liberal thinkers who maintained that free will resided within individuals and not God. Edwards and other Calvinistic theologians worried that an expansive notion of free will would empower individuals and undercut moral agency.[32]

Edwards's definition of free will was an elaborate compromise between two extremes, but Chandler rejected it anyway because Edwardean free will would give too much power to the individual. Chandler brooded about *Freedom of the Will* and its implications for years after its publication, and he declared in 1768 that Edwards "must be confuted, or submitted to; for I cannot much longer bear the opprobrium of his continuing unanswered."[33]

The fears of the dangers posed by selfish individuals were only one part of Chandler's disdain toward democratic society and what eventually became the independence movement. He hated what the revolutionaries represented. The Continental Congress, Chandler complained, was a "government of unprincipled *mobs*"—a term in English history reserved for the vulgar. He further warned that "ignorant men, bred to the lowest occupations," were guiding political affairs. These ignorant men, Chandler warned, threatened to bring ruin to the colonies, even in the unlikely event the ragtag American forces managed to defeat superior British forces. Both the economy and civil liberties would suffer outside the protection of the empire. The English constitution "has always been the wonder of the world," he reminded Americans. Like other loyalists, he decried the Continental Congress for both circumventing British authority and empowering the people.[34]

The impact of Chandler's three pamphlets on wavering colonists is unclear, but the tracts sold well and succeeded in enraging the revolutionaries, who worried about their effect on public opinion. His non-Anglican neighbors were certainly none too pleased with Chandler's defense of the king—Elizabeth Town was a radical stronghold, home to the revolutionary Governor William Livingston of New Jersey and a base for the Sons of Liberty. Chandler put his life on the line by defending monarchy and Parliament. As did other places throughout the colonies, Elizabeth violently opposed the Stamp Act, but Chandler defended it. The same pattern unfolded in the 1770s. Elizabeth—primarily its Presbyterian residents—backed the revolutionary cause; Chandler and most of his parishioners rejected it. In 1775, Chandler's relationship with his radical neighbors reached a breaking point following the publication of his latest attacks on the revolutionary movement. A large crowd led by the Sons burned Chandler's writings at the courthouse in December 1774, and inebriated militia members marched on his house in early 1775. Chandler became so fearful for his life that he abandoned his family and escaped to New York City in late April 1775. A few weeks later, he took passage to London aboard a British naval ship.

The Folly of Revolution tells this dramatic story by taking the reader deep into a now lost monarchical world. The opening chapter recounts Chandler's early life, the reasons he became a high church Anglican, and Samuel Johnson's influence on his intellectual development. Chapters 2 and 3 describe Chandler's experiences as a missionary and explore his studies of Tudor and Stuart history—two eras that heavily influenced Chandler's views of episcopacy and rebellion. Chapters 4 and 5 examine the central cause of Chandler's life: his effort to create an American episcopate and the firestorm it created in the American colonies. Chapters 6 and 7 look at Chandler's opposition to the American Revolution and his lonely exile in London, which lasted for a decade. An epilogue visits Chandler's final years and the fate of his traditional, British world in the tumultuous decades of the 1780s and 1790s.

A note about terminology and sources. Chandler was a "conservative" in the limited sense that he was defending tradition as he perceived it at the time, but I avoid the term because of the complexity of his thought. Chandler did not oppose change, for example, and he embraced "New Learning"—Samuel Johnson's term for the Enlightenment and the great secrets it was unlocking—and supported religious toleration in the colonies. Chandler *was* a high church royalist whose beliefs were anchored in an Anglo-British value system with roots extending to the reign of Queen Elizabeth. This traditionalism prized monarchy, episcopacy, a state church, and hierarchy, and it shared much with the "high church" values with which Chandler's foes tarred him. The two terms, however, were not synonymous. High church Anglicanism emphasized divine-right episcopacy and sacramental worship, as opposed to the low church emphasis on the evangelical. It also emphasized the close alliance between the Crown and the church.

Loyalism, meanwhile, refers to those Americans who remained true to the king and the British empire. Like Chandler, many loyalists valued monarchy and abhorred democracy and rebellion, and some (but not all) were high church Anglicans. A number of loyalists were moderates who criticized Parliament, including its attempts to tax the colonists, but rejected independence. I do not use the term "Tory" to refer to loyalists because American supporters of independence deployed the term as an insult in an effort to discredit their foes. Likewise, I do not use the term "patriot" because of its bias toward the revolutionaries. The implication was that "patriots" loved America while supposedly unpatriotic loyalists did not. But this was not true; Chandler and other loyalists loved America just as much as the revolutionaries did. They wanted America to thrive, and they were convinced the colonies would fare best by remaining in the empire. In the loyalist mind, it was the revolutionaries who were unpatriotic because they wanted to secede from Great Britain and bring ruin on the colonies.

Primary sources, of course, dictate much of what we can learn about Chandler. When Chandler fled to London in May 1775, his family burned many of his private papers to prevent them from falling into radicals' hands. As a result, we know little about his marriage or his family life. In addition, unlike many other ministers, Chandler did not publish any sermons—with one exception—and his sermon notes are not extant, so it is difficult to know what kind of preacher he was and what he told parishioners as the revolutionary movement gained strength.

The Folly of Revolution rests on the catalog of Chandler's library, which provides an outstanding window into his mind and the British roots of his thought; his extensive correspondence with Anglican colleagues and with London as an SPG missionary; his writings on the bishop's cause and the revolutionary crisis; and a diary he kept in London. Together, these sources enable us to reconstruct Chandler's life and the monarchical world he fought so hard to preserve.

CHAPTER 1

Disciple

Thomas Bradbury Chandler, Samuel Johnson, and the Making of a High Church Royalist

The book was an ode to a man and a cause. A love letter, if you will, to a cherished mentor who had died only months earlier. Written by Thomas Bradbury Chandler over a four-week span in the waning days of 1772, the volume described the life of Samuel Johnson, Anglican minister from Stratford, Connecticut. But *The Life*, as Chandler called it in his correspondence, was more than a biography. It was a portal into a high church world that Chandler loved, and it offered important clues into why he entered it.[1]

Twenty-six years earlier, a year removed from Yale College, a twenty-year-old Chandler studied theology under Samuel Johnson. It was a year that changed the course of Chandler's life, as the two men became close friends and allies in high church causes. Johnson taught Chandler theology and the traditions that informed high church Anglicanism; helped steer him into the ministry; and inculcated a high church view of society that Chandler followed the rest of his life. As critical as all this was, Johnson was important to Chandler for another reason. The religiously conservative Johnson was a liberal reformer in the field of education who criticized the old way of teaching, and he impressed on Chandler the importance of critical thinking and hard work. Thus, under Johnson's tutelage, the erudite Chandler mastered an approach to study and books that served him in good stead the rest of his life.

That Chandler took so readily to Johnson's worldview was not surprising. Chandler, who met Johnson in 1744, had decided to join the Church of England about a year earlier, and his outlook and temperament made him a ready acolyte of Johnson's. Both men were born and raised in Connecticut; both grew up in a Congregational household in a Puritan-dominated colony; both abhorred the Great Awakening and the excesses they associated with radical, and evangelical, Protestantism. They thought alike and even looked alike—two men with kindly faces who easily put on a pound or two after meals of wine and good food. Johnson found himself drawn to Chandler and saw much in this bookish young man who was teaching a "Latin School" in his hometown of Woodstock, Connecticut, in 1746. Chandler possessed a brilliant mind, was pious, and was no admirer of Congregationalism and the New England Way.[2]

NEW ENGLAND UPBRINGING

Before he met Samuel Johnson, before he undertook his intellectual and spiritual journey to the glories of King Henry VIII's church, there was Chandler Hill.

Thomas Bradbury Chandler grew up on his father's thousand-acre estate on the far reaches of Woodstock, an interior town in northeastern Connecticut that bordered western Massachusetts. It was in Woodstock's rolling hills, amid a setting of genteel wealth and family influence, that Chandler's unique personality took shape. The eldest child of William and Jemima Bradbury Chandler, Thomas was a member of the large, successful, and influential Chandler clan.

His great-great-grandparents were William and Annis Chandler, who came to the Massachusetts Bay Colony in 1637 as part of an exodus known as the Great Migration, in which twenty-one thousand religious radicals traveled to America in the hopes that they could build a new religious world, a City upon a Hill, that would shame the rest of Christianity into reforming their corrupt ways. Massachusetts Bay's founders preached a simple but powerful message to their followers: they were a chosen people on a mission to redeem Christendom and the Church of England.[3] After arriving in Massachusetts Bay, William and Annis Chandler, described by one chronicler as "very religious and godly," took their place in this brave new religious world. It was a humble beginning for the Chandler clan. Farmers of modest means, William and Annis settled in Roxbury, Massachusetts, just south of Boston, where they lived on a twenty-two-acre lot. Their heirs, however, thrived in the New World, and quickly, as they parlayed strong business and leadership skills, along with Puritan piety, into lucrative careers in New England. Indeed, the Chandlers excelled in several worlds—the church, the government, the militia, the surveyor, and the farm.[4]

John Chandler (1610–1703)—Thomas Bradbury Chandler's great-grandfather—was the fourth child and youngest son of William and Annis. With five others, he negotiated the purchase of a fifteen-hundred-acre tract from the Mashamoquet tribe in northeastern Connecticut on Massachusetts's western border that became the farming village of Woodstock. It was a lucrative decision on John Chandler's part to move his family to the frontier in 1686. The village was hilly and far from Hartford and the coast, but it was blessed with rich soil and a plentiful water supply fed by several streams, including Muddy Brook and Saw Mill.

From the outset, John and various branches of the Chandler family made their mark on the village, with their names peppering town records from the 1680s well into the eighteenth century. To distinguish between all the John and William Chandlers, family records identified them by their titles: Deacon John, Captain John, Colonel John, Judge John. The Chandler men were prominent in town affairs: in the 1690s alone, Chandlers served as selectman, town clerk, and schoolteacher. John Chandler—Thomas's great-grandfather—became a selectman and served as a deacon in the Congregational church, and he was rewarded for his faithfulness with a pew next to the pulpit stairs in the meetinghouse. With such close ties to the church, he became known as Deacon John.

Thomas Bradbury Chandler's grandfather was Colonel John (1665–1743), eldest son of Deacon John. According to a family chronicler, Colonel John was not well educated, but, as his political career attests, he was talented, hardworking, and driven. He was the first town clerk, and he also served on the town committee in the 1690s and was selectman. His obituary in the *Boston Gazette* described him as gregarious, "a gentleman greatly delighted with conversation." For a brief period at the close of the seventeenth century, John lived in New London, and it was in that coastal town where Thomas Bradbury Chandler's father, William, was born in 1698. After running a "house of entertainment" there, John and his family returned to Woodstock, and John became the town surveyor in 1703—a consequential post because this border town was involved in a long-running dispute with Massachusetts over boundaries. He also represented the town at General Court and was a militia officer, leading twenty men to help defend Worcester in Massachusetts, when, in the words of a family chronicler, "the peace of the country was disturbed by the renewal of hostilities by the Eastern Indians." By 1722, he was assigned the first pew in the new meetinghouse, a reward "for his [high] social standing in the Town." He, too, was known for his piety. The *Gazette* obituary described how he opened his doors to all, "especially the faithful ministers of Christ of all denominations."[5]

John died in 1743, when he was seventy-nine. He left behind a large estate worth £8,699 that was divided among his nine living children. William, Thomas's father, was the third son and did not inherit the homestead. Instead, William's younger brother Samuel got it, along with £3,000 "in Consideration of his great Prudence, Industry and Dutiful Behaviour and application in my Business." If the will was any indication, William was not as close to his father as his brothers were. John's will mentioned William only once, and John selected as executors "my well-beloved Sons, Samuel Chandler and Thomas Chandler," the youngest son.[6]

Nevertheless, William's share of his father's estate was sizable, and his marriage further improved his financial situation. William's wife, Jemima Bradbury of Salisbury, Massachusetts, who was a descendant of Massachusetts governors Winthrop and Dudley, inherited land from her father, Thomas Bradbury, that had been owned by Thomas's grandfather. William, who was a land surveyor, farmer, and militia officer, owned about a thousand acres on the eastern town border, a mile from the meetinghouse, that became known as Chandler Hill. Chandlers were ubiquitous in the neighborhood. William leased farms to two relations, Charles and William B. Chandler, and Chandler Hill was just down the road from Samuel Chandler's place. He also dabbled in the land market. In 1726, for instance, William and Jemima sold a nineteen-acre tract known as Amsterdam Farm, which contained a house and barn, for £650.[7]

The year 1726 marked a milestone in William and Jemima's relationship: on April 26, their first child was born, and they named him after her father. Thomas Bradbury Chandler left no accounts of his childhood. We can only speculate about his life at Chandler Hill. We do know from genealogical accounts that his father was physically imposing, befitting his military background and gentry status, and that his mother was quite intelligent. A newspaper obituary praised her "superior natural and acquired abilities and power of mind." Jemima was literate and a strong student; she excelled at natural philosophy, geography, and, of course, religion. She was, according to the *Worcester Spy*, "of unaffected piety, exemplary in all her paths."[8]

If Thomas's choice of career was any indication, Jemima had a bigger influence on her eldest son than did William. Thomas chose religion and the life of the mind over farming, surveying, and soldiering. Still, some of his father's personality apparently rubbed off on him. Growing up as a member of a wealthy and politically connected clan, Thomas learned all about the exercise of authority, and he emerged from Chandler Hill with the mien of a New England blueblood. He entered Yale near the top of his class because of his Chandler pedigree—Anglican minister Samuel Seabury Sr. approvingly described the Chandlers as "a family of honour and Reputation"—and his views of authority and subordination shaped his writings and informed his approaches to leadership as a minister in the Church of England. Chandler's tracts of the 1770s positively sneered at the ordinary farmers and mechanics who had jockeyed to assume leadership positions in the revolutionary movement. Although Thomas never served in the militia, some of his father's pugnacity rubbed off on him. He enjoyed a good polemical scrap and delighted in hurling insults at his opponents. Chandler could be ferocious in his writings, employing a touch that was more anvil than feather. His upbringing was one reason why. "When I was young I was taught to believe that honesty is the best policy, the truth of which maxim I could wish to see once put to the trial," he wrote in a characteristically blunt letter to Samuel Johnson in 1765 castigating the Church of England for its supposed shortcomings. Such a maxim meant that Chandler was never shy about expressing his opinions to his friends, his enemies, and the church; as he said to Johnson in the 1765 letter, he felt it was his duty to tell people "plainly" what they had "an undoubted right to expect."9

Thus, from an early age, Chandler had a whiff of haughtiness about him. He grew up around wealth and power, and he became used to the idea that the better sort led and inferiors followed. The British world he so admired only reinforced his natural inclinations. From books and personal observation about the ways of the world, young Chandler learned how hierarchy worked in Britain and its overseas dominions. Every British subject—be it a peasant in Scotland, a plantation owner in the Caribbean, or a farmer in Connecticut—owed his allegiance to the king. In such a society, whose origins dated to the medieval period and its carefully defined estates, the king was at the top of the pyramid, and power flowed downward to the African slave at the bottom. Inequality was the glue, and the sinew, of such a society. The mature Chandler believed strongly that British subjects, including American colonists, owed the government its loyalty, even when that government "adopt[s] measures that are wrong or oppressive." The injured "may complain and remonstrate against them in a respectful manner," Chandler explained in one pamphlet, "but they are bound, by the laws of Heaven and Earth, not to behave undutifully." To a certain extent, large numbers of Chandler's fellow American colonists agreed that inequality was natural. As one contemporary observer put it, "Order is Heav'n's first law; and this confest, Some are, and must be, greater than the rest, More rich, more wise." Unlike his friend and rival Thomas Jefferson, John Adams did not believe that all men were created equal. "Inequalities of Mind and Body are so established by God Almighty in the constitution of Human Nature," Adams explained, "that no Art or policy can ever plain them down to a level."[10]

Thomas Bradbury Chandler was a product of this hierarchical world, and he had the good fortune to be closer to the top of the pyramid than the bottom. He was the first born in a wealthy family whose members were expected to lead. This inherent advantage shaped the man and the king's fierce defender he was to become. It was an upbringing quite different from that of two of his closest high church allies, Samuel Seabury Jr. and Charles Inglis. Both of these men were raised in the Church of England. Seabury, who was three years younger than Chandler, was the son of an Anglican minister, a close colleague of Samuel Johnson who had become a member of the Church of England in the "Yale Apostasy" of 1722. Thus, from the cradle, young Samuel learned high church ways. He followed in his father's footsteps by becoming a minister. Inglis, who was born in Ireland in 1734, was also the son of an Anglican rector. He, too, followed in his father's footsteps by taking holy orders. Inglis migrated to the American colonies in 1755 and became a minister in 1758, working in Delaware for a few years before becoming curate at Trinity in New York City in 1765.[11]

Chandler followed a different path to high church Anglicanism. He did not grow up in an Anglican household; he grew up in a Congregational one. In a great irony given Chandler's later views toward rebellion (he opposed it) and authority (he defended it), Thomas had to declare his independence from the family faith and the pathways earlier Chandlers had taken. In the patriarchal world of the eighteenth century, fathers typically expected their sons to follow in their footsteps. Farmers taught their sons farming; craftsmen passed on the skills of their trade to their progeny; rectors Seabury and Inglis imparted the ways of the Lord to their sons, who became ministers as adults.

Chandler's father was a farmer, surveyor, politician, and Congregational communicant. Thomas became none of those things. First he rejected the family faith by joining the Church of England while at Yale. Then, after graduation, he rejected the family businesses of farming, surveying, and politics. This declaration of independence in spiritual affairs was more than an act of rebellion against his father, who was a Congregationalist in good standing, as his admission to communion beginning in 1728 attests. Thomas was also rejecting Woodstock, the colony of Connecticut, and Congregational New England. One surviving letter from 1764 that Chandler wrote hinted that he was estranged from at least one member of his family—a sister whom Thomas used to consider "sensible, discreet and grateful." But her new husband "never favored me with a line to inform me of his marriage, or of anything else." Chandler clearly did not approve of him. He accused the husband of spoiling his sister, and "I have much reason to suspect him of bigotry, if the Connecticut Hobbism may be called bigotry"—likely a dig at the suitor's selfishness for keeping the marriage a secret from Chandler.[12]

As his later writings made clear, Chandler detested the New England Way. He savaged the region his family had called home since the 1630s and denounced its leaders as fanatics. Chandler joined a church that preached obedience to authority and believed in measured, reasonable worship; he turned his back on his parents' church, which was built on conversion, covenantal theology, and laymen's rights.

THE YALE YEARS

A precocious learner, Thomas left Chandler Hill in 1741 at age fifteen for New Haven. But the next four years were not happy ones for Chandler: He was disappointed with his classes and the religious climate he encountered on campus. Yale remained a Puritan stronghold in the mid-eighteenth century, run by a Congregational minister who wanted his charges to become Congregational ministers, and key textbooks were Puritan classics that no high church Anglican much liked. Chandler and Samuel Johnson believed the college, which was founded in 1701, was intellectually backward. Both men viewed Yale's early years as an educational Dark Age because the curriculum was so closely tied to outdated books that did not encompass the latest discoveries of Newton and other Enlightenment thinkers. While things had improved by the 1740s when Chandler attended Yale, the college was still struggling to make the transition from the centuries-old ways of learning to the new, of which Johnson was an ardent champion.[13]

Thanks to several gifts by private donors, the college library had grown to 2,600 books by midcentury, and its holdings on Enlightenment discoveries were slowly expanding. Chandler partook of this bounty. "He was a great Reader at College," his classmate Ezra Stiles recalled, "chiefly of Poetry, belles Lettres & Histy—a pretty good Classic Scholar, indifferent in the Sciences."[14]

Yale's freshmen studied the grammar of three ancient languages: Latin, Greek, and Hebrew. By the end of the year, their tutor expected them to be able to translate biblical passages from the original. Sophomores studied logic; juniors "natural philosophy" (basic sciences, such as physics, astronomy, and biology) and math; seniors "metaphysics" (the study of the "existence of things, their natures and causes"). Several subjects were constants all four years: theology, ethics, and oratory. A tutor taught lower-level classes while college president Thomas Clap handled the seniors. Instruction consisted mainly of recitations in assigned textbooks. During Chandler's time in New Haven, three Yale graduates served as tutors: Chauncey Whittelsey, who taught the freshmen; Noah Welles, who taught the sophomores; and John Whiting, who handled the juniors.[15]

Much of the curriculum was standard for the time, similar to the classes a student at Harvard or Oxford took. Nevertheless, Chandler had to contend with the matter of Puritan orthodoxy. Yale was a Congregational bastion. New Haven did not gain an Anglican church until 1752, seven years after Chandler left, and at least one of his tutors—Noah Welles—was an ardent foe of episcopacy. Students were required to attend services at the Congregational meetinghouse, conducted during Chandler's time by Joseph Noyes, whom one historian described as "reputedly the dullest preacher of his generation." The Westminster Confession of Faith—the English Civil War–era document of 1646 that high church Anglicans saw as Reformed blasphemy—was recited weekly, as were the teachings of Puritan divines that grated on any good Anglican. Saturdays at Yale were devoted to "the Study of Divinity," according to college rules, "and the Classes Shall during the whole Term recite the Westminster Confession of Faith received and approved by the Churches in this Colony, Wollebius, Ames Medulla, or any other System of Divinity by the Direction of the President."[16]

The references to Wollebius and Ames spoke loudly about Yale's religious bent. Johann Wollebius (1589–1629) was a leading Reformed theologian. William Ames (1576–1633) wrote *Medulla Theologiae* (*The Marrow of Sacred Divinity*), a primer on Puritan theology. Both Ames and Wollebius emphasized traditional Calvinist themes and reinforced the covenantal teachings of Puritanism. Chandler detested Calvinism, believing it unbiblical and abhorrent to an inclusive state church, and he rejected the covenantal underpinnings of the Congregational faith as producing nothing but trouble.

Equally upsetting to Chandler was his classmates' embrace of the Great Awakening. In his *Life of Samuel Johnson*, Chandler described the Awakening as "a strange, wild enthusiasm, introduced by Mr. [George] Whitfield, and propagated by his followers throughout the country." In Chandler's and Johnson's view, the Great Awakening's crimes were many, and Chandler succinctly listed them. For one, it represented an attack on the Church of England, as well as on reason and common sense. Second, it was led by "ignorant lay-exhorters, uttering the most horrid expressions concerning God and religion." Third, Chandler said, these ignorant exhorters sought to scare people into converting. "Their night meetings in particular, at some of which Mr. Johnson was present in disguise, exhibited the wildest scenes of confusion and uproar," Chandler complained.[17]

For once, Chandler was not exaggerating: The Great Awakening *did* divide congregations and churches throughout the thirteen colonies, especially in New England, as it sought to rekindle religious passion in a Protestant world that had grown seemingly stale in its efforts to revitalize Christianity. Whitefield and his followers did attack established ministers as unregenerate, and they did deliver hours-long, fire-and-brimstone sermons that sought to scare people into turning to Jesus Christ. Whitefield's tactics were especially effective. A mesmerizing and powerful speaker, Whitefield embarked on preaching tours in the 1740s that became must-see events, drawing huge crowds, sometimes as large as twenty thousand people. He converted thousands and sparked a revival of religion that put the established churches and their ministers on the defensive.[18]

The Great Awakening's effects were equally momentous at Yale. Clap, a stern, old-school Puritan, at first welcomed Whitefield's arrival in New Haven, hoping he would be an ally in the great cause of converting sinners and in inspiring students to study theology more diligently. But like Chandler, Clap was soon decrying the Awakening's excesses and the divisions it was producing. He fined students who followed Gilbert Tennent on his preaching tour and missed class. He denounced students and others—including the exhorter James Davenport—who attacked ministers as unregenerate. Clap and the Yale trustees voted on September 9, 1741, "that if any Student of this College shall directly or indirectly say, that the Rector, either of the Trustees or Tutors are Hypocrites, carnall or unconverted Men, he Shall for the first Offence make a publick Confession in the Hall, and for the Second Offence be expell'd." He was good as his word: one unfortunate student was expelled when he said his tutor had no more saving grace than a chair.[19]

Thus Yale was in an uproar over the Great Awakening when Chandler took his place in New Haven in September 1741. The campus was riven by dissension as pro- and anti-revival students and faculty hurled insults at each other, and Clap was trying to regain control of events. The tumult likely played a role in Chandler's decision to join the Church of England during his final year as an undergraduate. The revivalists' methods and beliefs appalled him, and he turned to a church that in his opinion offered sanity and reason. Chandler was not alone in his views. As he put it years later, the Church of England grew impressively during the Awakening because "large numbers of cool and considerate people, finding no rest among the dissenters, betook themselves to the church, as the only ark of safety."[20]

Yale's religious life likely annoyed Chandler for another reason: it was designed to produce *preaching* ministers who possessed the ability to think and speak on their feet—skills that Whitefield, Davenport, and other preachers were using to great effect during the Awakening. These were skills that Chandler (and Johnson) decried. Johnson, Chandler explained in *The Life*, "looked upon [extempore praying and preaching] as the great engines of enthusiasm."[21]

At Yale, Chandler also got a heavy dose of Isaac Watts, the English hymnist and Whiggish theologian, who was another Congregational favorite and a staple in classes. Chandler and his classmates read Watt's *Logick* (1725) and other works ranging from Scripture to astronomy. Chandler, as a result, left Yale in 1745 with a hatred of Congregationalism, a commitment to the Church of England, and an understanding that he had much to learn about theology and the episcopal church he favored.[22]

Chandler's rejection of Congregationalism was quite a contrast to some of Yale's eminent graduates in the eighteenth century, including Jonathan Edwards and Ezra Stiles. Edwards, who earned his bachelor's and master's degrees, was at Yale from 1716 to 1722. His coursework differed little from Chandler's. Both young men underwent spiritual conversions during their time on campus. Chandler, of course, abandoned his childhood faith for Anglicanism; Edwards, the son of a Congregational minister and a grandson of the famous Puritan pastor Solomon Stoddard, fell seriously ill his senior year and wrestled with his mortality and with existential questions about God and the afterlife. Like other evangelicals, Edwards struggled to achieve a new birth and even questioned his Calvinist faith during a mildly rebellious youth. But during his time at Yale he made peace with his God and his faith and went on to a legendary career as a theologian and a catalyst of the Great Awakening in the 1730s in the Connecticut River Valley. His evangelical values were a polar opposite of Chandler's.[23]

Stiles, meanwhile, graduated a year after Chandler. He shared his classmate's intellectual curiosity and burning desire to learn. His scholarly abilities matched Chandler's—possibly exceeded them—and like Chandler he had a disdain for the Great Awakening. Stiles's father, Isaac, was an Old Light minister who opposed the Awakening and was a close friend of Yale President Clap. His son was close to Clap as well during his time in New Haven. At Yale, Chandler decisively committed to Anglicanism; Stiles needed years to work out his religious values. He flirted with Arminianism and deism and at several points considered joining the Church of England: the Anglican church at Newport, Rhode Island, tried to recruit him as its pastor. Eventually, after years of indecision, Stiles rejected the law and settled on a ministerial career, accepting the pastorship of a Congregational church in Newport. His politics drifted leftward as well. While Chandler remained moored to conservatism, Stiles absorbed a Whiggish view of history, taking the un-Chandlerian position that politics and religion must remain separate.[24]

STUDYING UNDER JOHNSON

Samuel Johnson was at the height of his powers and influence in 1746 when Chandler, who at the time was a schoolteacher in Woodstock, came under his guidance. Fifty years old, Johnson was on a mission to strengthen the Church of England in Connecticut and the northern colonies. For all the divisions of the Great Awakening, and all the handwringing over the supposed loss of piety among later generations of Puritans, Congregationalism remained the dominant religious force in New England. In Connecticut, it was the established church. But Johnson and the Society for the Propagation of the Gospel nevertheless believed conditions were ripe for the Church of England to expand in the region. SPG secretary David Humphreys wrote that "great Numbers of Inhabitants were exceedingly desirous of worshipping GOD after the Manner of the Church of *England*." When supplicants in a community petitioned for an Anglican missionary, Humphreys said, the SPG did its best to send one.[25]

But the SPG needed missionaries, and Johnson took it on himself to recruit talented young churchmen to the Anglican ministry. More than forty young men studied with him over the years. "For near fifty years there was not, I believe, a single candidate for holy orders in the colony who did not apply to him for his advice and direction . . . or who did not owe his success, in a great measure, to his patronage," Chandler recalled. "To those of them

FIG. 1 Thomas McIlworth, portrait of Samuel Johnson of Stratford, Connecticut, circa 1761. He trained more than forty young men, including Thomas Bradbury Chandler, for the ministry. Photo: Sotheby's (Wikimedia Commons).

who needed pecuniary assistance for the voyage to England, he gave generously and cheerfully, in proportion to his abilities."[26]

Johnson was, in Chandler's estimation, a mix of steely resolve and benevolent kindness. He was tall and corpulent, and "there was something in his countenance that was pleasing and familiar, and that indicated the benevolence of his heart." Johnson liked to carry on a good conversation, according to Chandler, "enlivened and rendered more pleasing by the natural cheerfulness of his disposition." But he also was a bookish scholar who was more comfortable teaching theology to Yale graduates than he was delivering sermons from the pulpit or sharing hearty laughs with parish members during pastoral visits. Johnson was not a good public speaker, and the warmness he exuded in private seemed to desert him in a public setting, where Chandler described his manner as "grave and composed." In Chandler's estimation, Johnson was a talented teacher, possessing broad "knowledge of the affairs of the world. . . . He was not only a good classical scholar, but well versed in all the liberal arts and sciences. He knew, and could explain with precision, their respective boundaries and limits, their connections with each other, and in what manner they are conducive to the happiness of man."[27]

The steely part of Johnson's personality came in his dealings with his religious foes. Despite the SPG's efforts—which Johnson complained were inadequate—Connecticut remained a Congregational stronghold in the 1740s. As "dissenters," members of the Church of England were in a humiliating position. They had to register as Anglicans at their local county court and were forced to pay taxes to support the resident Congregational minister. Those Anglicans who refused to pay the religious tax were jailed, as happened to church members in Newtown and Fairfield in 1724. The Church of England had only six congregations in 1736; the Congregationalists had more than one hundred.[28]

Johnson's anger had been further stoked by his experiences during the 1720s, when the Church of England assigned him to Stratford—for a brief time the only Anglican congregation in Connecticut. He was not only isolated; he also "found himself on all sides surrounded by bitter adversaries," Chandler said. "He was generally considered and treated as a schismatic and apostate." His enemies, Chandler continued, wanted nothing more than to drive him out of the country.[29]

Johnson seethed at the injustice of the situation: the king's church, so powerful and respected in England, was a detested, albeit growing, sect in New England, on par with lowly Quakers and Baptists. In dispatches, petitions, and letters, Johnson informed British authorities of the church's rude treatment in Connecticut, but he said his appeals for help were met with shrugs of indifference. Thus, in the 1730s, Johnson began trying to build the church's strength in Connecticut on his own. One step was to bring Connecticut's five Anglican ministers together in occasional confabs so they could discuss their problems and formulate strategies to overcome them. Johnson also worked to raise the church's profile in the colony. Anglicans were few in number in Connecticut and scattered; moreover, the church suffered from a shortage of ministers. Lacking clergymen, the church could neither tend to the cares of its flock nor expand into new territories. And ordaining ministers was time-consuming, expensive, and dangerous because qualified candidates had to cross the Atlantic Ocean to London, an ordeal that took months.[30]

In a mark of Johnson's desperation, this Anglican theologian who believed so strongly in proper ordination procedures hit upon the expediency of lay preaching. He recruited young men and sent them to an area that seemed open to Anglican proselytizing. While there, the recruit preached to interested hearers, worked to build membership, and studied divinity. Those who excelled were sent to England for ordination upon completion of their theological studies.[31]

Starting in 1732, Johnson had begun a parallel effort: he worked directly with promising young Yale graduates who seemed like good candidates for ordination. In a letter to the Society for the Propagation of the Gospel, he explained that he was "putting the Young Men Bred there [at Yale] upon reading of Good Books, in directing their studies and leading them into a good affection to our Excellent Church."[32]

During a more than yearlong course of study with Johnson, Chandler read. He not only could pick Johnson's brain but could draw on his impressive library. According to Chandler, Johnson made it "his practice to recommend, and then lend to them [his students] the most useful books, of which he had a large and valuable collection." Like Chandler, Johnson was a prodigious reader. He listed each volume he read between 1719 and 1756 and the date he finished reading it. It was a long list: he averaged one book a week for nearly forty years (and, presumably, beyond), and the subjects ranged from classics of Western literature such as Shakespeare and *Paradise Lost* to history.[33]

Working with this Anglican bibliophile must have been a happy experience for Chandler, especially after his frustrating course of study at Yale. It was a chance to read deeply and widely, and to learn from a high church master. Indeed, Chandler continued to lean on Johnson for books after 1746. In 1753, Chandler could be found borrowing volumes from Johnson and describing the great satisfaction this gave him.[34]

Especially important was Chandler's readings in theology and church history. Knowledge was power, Johnson lectured. While the leading lights of the Great Awakening emphasized a proper conversion based on feeling, not education, Johnson taught Chandler the importance of study, for, at heart, a minister was a teacher who instructed his flock in the mysteries of the Lord's ways. But before one could become a good teacher, one had to study. Johnson led by example, Chandler said—he was a lifelong learner who "seldom lost an hour through carelessness, and never through indolence." Expanding the mind, Johnson stressed to Chandler and his other students, was in Chandler's words "the duty of all men, of whatever station or character; as it enlarges the mind, and consequently increases a man's ability to do." But this was especially true for a minister, Chandler said. "He that undertakes to instruct others ought not to be a novice himself" was Johnson's philosophy. To be a successful minister required constant study, even after one's formal schooling was over. Learning was essential to teach and to rebut "the various tribes of [Christianity's] opposers," Chandler explained.[35]

Johnson also introduced Chandler to church history and the high church conception of society. Suffering in the Congregational stronghold of Connecticut as a dissenter, Johnson had long been thinking about, and reading deeply into, such thorny issues as authority, religious uniformity, and the role of the state church in British society.

Johnson's high church notions of religious uniformity rested on the time-honored English dictum that there could be only one truth, and that this truth was indivisible. In the spiritual realm, such a belief meant that only one church possessed the correct answers, and those who deviated from the truth were in error. Church authorities and the state had a solemn obligation to uphold the truth and to reclaim those misguided souls who wandered from it. Authorities, in other words, had the duty to crack down on heresy and would be negligent if they did not enforce religious uniformity. Persecution, from this vantage point, was good: Crackdowns against dissent would save the deluded from eternal damnation. And crackdowns would also save society—religious pluralism threatened political and social stability by increasing strife and risked undermining true religion because God would punish those who pursued false doctrines. As Archbishop of Canterbury John Whitgift put it in 1572, the devout—and civil and religious authorities—must not tolerate dissent, for "it is every faithful man's part to suppress errors, to convince heresies, and to main[tain] the truth." St. Augustine offered a more pithy justification for religious uniformity (and persecution): "What death is worse for the soul than the freedom to err? It is better to love with severity than to deceive with indulgence."[36]

Chandler drank up this history, reading the leading works of its practitioners. It was his years in New England and with Johnson that saw Chandler develop his hostility to democracy and his distrust of a pluralistic society. His hostility arose from his readings into church history, his gentrified upbringing, and his revulsion at the unruliness of American society, including the pandemonium of the Great Awakening and Puritanism's embracing of the laity. As this young man studied Anglicanism and drew closer to its tenets, Chandler identified ever more closely with all things British. It was another lesson he learned from Johnson. When Johnson went to London for ordination, he was enthralled by all that he saw, from the soaring spires of Canterbury Cathedral to the intellectual earnestness of Oxford and Cambridge. "I can scarce speak of Oxon [College at Oxford] without raptures," Johnson recalled, "for I must allow that throughout the whole course of my life, I never spent ten days with half the pleasure which I had during the little time I was there." Like

Chandler a half century later, Johnson was awed by London and the sophistication of British culture. The sprawling size of the metropolis. The majesty of its political and religious life. The sophistication of its society.[37]

Not that Johnson and Chandler were alone in their love of British ways. More colonists identified with Britain as the eighteenth century wore on, thanks to a burgeoning patriotism during the Seven Years' War and an expanding economy. As their wealth grew, Americans began aping British and European fashion, architecture, and society. Boston mansion or southern plantation house, it mattered little. Learned and cultivated Americans aspired to the finer things Britain had to offer. As one historian noted, "The changes in America were a variant of changes occurring in all the British provinces at roughly the same time. With the houses went new modes of speech, dress, body carriage, and manners that gave an entirely new cast to the conduct and appearance of the American gentry."[38]

But as in other things, Johnson and Chandler carried their love of Britain further than other Americans, a love that went well beyond clothes and Georgian architecture and culture. These two high church Anglicans deeply admired the British union of church and state. Careful study of history, especially sixteenth- and seventeenth-century history when the Church of England was founded and strengthened, taught them the superiority of a monarchical government allied with an episcopal state church.

Chandler and Johnson were also moved by the beauty and solemnity of Anglicanism's liturgical services. For both men, the contrast between Congregational and Anglican services was stark. Like Chandler, Johnson had grown up attending the Congregational church where his parents worshiped and was "educated under strong prejudices against the Church of England, of which he knew but very little [about]," Chandler recalled. Congregationalism bothered Johnson. He detested its "enthusiasm"—its shallow displays of emotion during church and among individual hearers that, in his view, held no deep commitment to God. He especially disliked two close relatives of experiential religion: long, impromptu prayers and sermons that were delivered spontaneously based on what the speaker was feeling at the moment. Both men saw James Davenport and his ilk as wild, uncouth ranters who defiled houses of worship.

Because Connecticut had no Anglican churches during his youth, Johnson learned of Anglican ways through a chance encounter with a book. In 1715, Johnson found a kindred spirit in a Church of England archbishop in Dublin named William King who wrote a volume which proved that "public worship carried on in the extempore way, was wrong and unscriptural," Chandler said. King's treatise called for structure, for well-defined liturgy in church services. Then, a year later, came an even bigger discovery when Johnson read the Book of Common Prayer for the first time—a transforming experience, according to Chandler. First published in 1549 during the short, ill-fated reign of the boy king Edward VI, the prayer book laid out the forms of service for daily and Sunday worship in the Church of England, including morning and evening prayer, the litany, and holy communion. The liturgy and its structure struck a chord with Johnson; he found its order and regularity soothing and its language beautiful. As he explained years later, "Nothing can be devised or imagined more conducive to promote Devotion and Holiness, than that most excellent, that most devout and comprehensive Form of publick Devotion." Enthralled, Johnson joined the Church of England and took holy orders a few years later—a decision that stunned the Yale community where Johnson was a tutor and a Congregational minister. Johnson's conversion was part of the "Yale Apostasy" of 1722, a dispute over ordination procedures. Seven Congregational ministers, including Johnson, informed Yale's trustees of their decision that September to resign their posts and to join the Church of England. This apostasy shocked and shook up the Congregational world.[39]

Johnson's study of religious history deepened his commitment to the Church of England. He invested a great deal of time in the mid-seventeenth century, especially the years immediately following the English Civil War. He looked intently at the latitudinarians, a late seventeenth-century group of academics at Cambridge who also were known as "Cambridge Platonists." Led by Ralph Cudworth and Henry More, the latitudinarians sought to bring reason and rationality to religion. Apostles of moderation, latitudinarians had words of criticism for almost all Christian movements because of their supposed excesses. They rejected Calvinism over its harsh, inflexible predestination tenets; criticized Puritans for their argumentative and nonconformist ways; and condemned those Anglicans whose excessive zeal led to ugly crackdowns on dissenters. Like their Elizabethan forebears who espoused via media, they wanted a middle way.[40]

Johnson was a keen student of this movement, and Chandler became one, too. Two authors stood out for Johnson. The first was Edward Stillingfleet (1635–1695), who was dean of St. Paul's, a chaplain in ordinary to the king, and a prolific author. The second was Daniel Whitby (1638–1726), a harsh critic of Calvinism. Both men strongly defended Anglicanism, arguing that an established church and religious uniformity were vital for an orderly society. The debate fascinated Johnson, according to Chandler, and he made it a point to examine both sides of the argument. Johnson read those Puritans who attacked episcopacy and denounced the Church of England constitution as unbiblical, and he carefully studied the Anglican response, concluding, in Chandler's words, that his church came "nearest to purity and perfection of the first ages of Christianity."[41]

Chandler drew two lessons from all this. One was the superiority of Anglican arguments that the Church of England and its episcopal government were grounded in biblical truth; the lay-dominated Congregationalism of its Puritan enemies was not. And second was the importance of study, of carefully examining the two sides of an argument. In his *Life of Samuel Johnson*, Chandler's admiration of Johnson's approach to learning was evident. He especially appreciated the way his mentor immersed himself in a debate, approaching it in the same manner as an Enlightenment-era scientist seeking to accumulate all the facts before drawing a conclusion. "Johnson carefully compared together what was offered by Hoadly and Calamy in their long controversy on the subject [of church government]," Chandler said in describing one key debate that occupied his mentor. "They put into the opposite scales Sir Peter King's *Inquiry* and Slater's *Original Draught*.... The effect was, that from the facts in scripture, compared with those of the primitive church, it appeared plain to them that the episcopal government was universally established by the Apostles."[42]

Johnson, in short, taught Chandler the importance of critical thinking, of looking skeptically at conventional wisdom and contemporary society. As Chandler phrased it, Johnson "laid aside the prejudices of his education, one after another; giving up opinions which he had received as properly established." Critical thinking, Chandler noted, led Johnson to the Church of England and allowed him to quit 'the rigid predestinarian notions for those which appeared to be more rational and scriptural doctrines."[43]

As Chandler's 1790 library catalog shows, he followed these lessons throughout the course of his life. Chandler accumulated a large collection of dueling works—of Whitby and Hoadly, of Stillingfleet and Clarke. Chandler wanted to understand what his intellectual foes thought, and why. A close reading of their arguments strengthened his own. For this insight, he owed an intellectual debt to Johnson. He first read many of these authors under Johnson, and then acquired more of their works and placed them on his library shelves at his glebe house in Elizabeth Town.

As alike as these two men were in personality, temperament, values, and beliefs, they had their differences. Johnson had a philosophical bent to him;

Chandler did not. Although Chandler read church history assigned by Johnson with relish, he exhibited less interest in Johnson's other academic interests. Chandler had begun his studies with Johnson at a particularly interesting point in his hero's intellectual development: Johnson was putting the finishing touches on his great ethical system, including *A General View of Philosophy* in the 1730s and his *System of Morality* in 1746. These and other works were Johnson's attempt to make sense of a rapidly changing intellectual world. Johnson was obsessed with understanding the New Learning of the Enlightenment. Contemporaneous with Johnson's New Learning was his attempts to better understand critical thought and how an individual learned.[44]

Johnson's journey to the New Learning started long before 1746, when Thomas Bradbury Chandler began his theological studies with the minister from Stratford. As a student at Saybrook, where Yale was then located, Johnson found himself puzzling over the French humanist Petrus Ramus (1515–1572), a staple of the college curriculum, who devised a system of logic that made the universe orderly and intelligible, consisting of graspable principles that governed the world God had created. In 1543, Ramus published the landmark *Aristotelicae Animadversiones*, which criticized the old logic, and *Dialecticae Partitiones*, which outlined his theories of science. In the latter Ramus outlined the use of summaries, headings, citations, and examples, in which all experience could be reduced to arguments and subdivided into "invention" and "judgment." Johnson found Ramist logic confusing and arbitrary. He wanted to do better.[45]

And then in 1715, Johnson stumbled on Francis Bacon's *Advancement of Learning*, which outlined the empirical methods of the scientific revolution, and he bought the book—a startling purchase, Chandler recounted, because it was "perhaps the only copy that was then in the country." (There probably were about twenty-five copies in the American colonies at the time.)[46] Bacon's great work shook Johnson up and caused him to reassess everything he had been taught at Yale. "In short," Chandler said, "every thing appeared new to him, and he seemed to himself like a person, to use his own expression, 'suddenly emerging out of the glimmer of twilight into the full sunshine of open day.'"[47]

What made Bacon so revolutionary to Johnson and others was his assault on the medieval conception of learning, the belief that education was a quest to find the uniform principles in a world created by an all-powerful deity; it was not about accumulating facts. In the medieval scheme, God ruled the cosmos, including all its planets, and he had formulated a divine plan that assigned a role for every person, animal, and thing. It was the task of the scholar and his "sciences" to deduce what that plan was. Science was not about conducting experiments to understand the physical workings of the world; it was about studying nature in an attempt to unlock the mysteries of the supernatural.

Absorbing all these advances, and thinking deeply about how students should be taught, Johnson devised a new educational system. He broke learning down into two categories, led by "'Philogy,' or 'the Study of Words and other Signs,' and II. 'Philosophy.' Or the Study of the Things signified by them," Johnson wrote in his *General View of Philosophy*. Philosophy was crucial in Johnson's complex schemata. "Philosophy is the Study of true Wisdom, or the Study of Truth and Right, in order to the attainment of true Happiness," Johnson explained, "in the Knowledge of things as being that they really are, and in acting or practising according to that Knowledge." And true happiness, he continued, "consists in that Pleasure which attends the Contemplation of all things that come within the Compass of our Knowledge." And happiness was "the great End ultimately pursued through all the Arts and Sciences."[48]

For Johnson, all this was a Baconian approach to learning, where deductive reasoning would lead the seeker to the proper answer. "It is plain, that the whole of our Happiness, and consequently the whole of Philosophy consists in the Cultivation & Improvement of our Rational powers and Faculties," Johnson wrote, "and in the Contemplation of things as being what they really are, both in the Natural & Moral World."[49]

Johnson preached to Chandler and his other students that rational philosophy provided a way to "learn the Rules and Means of cultivating & improving our Rational powers of Thinking & Speaking, that we may find the Truth our selves, & convey it in the best manner to each other." Logic was also important for another reason, according to Johnson: "Logic, or the Art of Thinking, leads us into our own minds and gives us an exact Knowledge of our Intellectual powers with their Objects and the Signs we make use of to enlarge our knowledge and communicate our Thoughts, and to excite and direct our exertions."[50]

In *The Life*, Chandler did not dwell on the metaphysical aspects of Johnson's intellectual journey. Certainly, he appreciated the ethical system's insights into critical thinking, but he seemed to care little about Johnson's attempts to improve education, and philosophy held little attraction for Chandler. Instead, Chandler focused on the religious dimensions of Johnson's ethical system. For Chandler, Johnson's system of morality was all about "checking the progress of enthusiasm, and counteracting the absurd doctrines that were perpetually propagated throughout the country." Chandler was correct that Johnson wanted to curb emotion in religion. But his philosophical system went way beyond that. Johnson's ultimate purpose was to understand God's—and the human—mind. Johnson argued that an individual's knowledge came through God's "intellectual Light or intuitive Evidence." From that conclusion, Johnson elucidated a method for educating children and improving their ability to reason. This involved teaching them morality and religion. His 1746 tract *A Short System of Morals* posited that all ethical principles could be reduced to "that grand ancient principle of true wisdom, Know thyself; which must imply, not merely the knowledge of ourselves, highly considered, but also in all the relations where we stand; for this is the knowledge of ourselves in the whole."[51]

Chandler did allow that Johnson's speculations on moral philosophy were about "the nature of man, his excellence and imperfections . . . and the end of our being, with the natural proofs of a future state." But Chandler did not elaborate on the significance of this. In *The Life*, he moved quickly on to safer topics, including the cause dearest to his heart—the need to establish an episcopate in the colonies.[52]

In writing *The Life*, Chandler relied heavily on Johnson's autobiography for his material and in numerous places he accepted uncritically Johnson's interpretation of events. Such was the case with Chandler's handling of one of the more embarrassing episodes in Johnson's academic career—his embrace of a discredited scholar by the name of John Hutchinson (1674–1737).

Hutchinson wrote *Moses's Principia*, in which he argued that all knowledge was contained in the Hebrew version of the Old Testament. In Hutchinson's opinion, God had revealed himself to the prophets, who in turn wrote them down in Hebrew. At the Tower of Babel, however, God punished man for his many moral failings by, in the words of one historian, "burdening him with a multiplicity of languages that prevented him from understanding the Hebrew truths." God's word was lost as the number of Old Testament translations grew. To recover God's revelations, Hutchinson studied Hebrew and its grammar; more-accurate translations, he believed, would bring believers closer to God and to an understanding of how the natural world worked. In the end, his *Moses's Principia* rejected science and the assertion of Newton, Bacon, and others that nature, and not the Bible, held the keys to understanding the world. Hutchinson's thesis intrigued Johnson, specifically the parts about Hebrew grammar. For him, it made perfect sense that an exercise in grammar—through the power of study and hard work—could bring one closer to God. Johnson was an outlier on Hutchinson; most scholars did not take *Moses's Principia* seriously. Joseph Ellis, the leading historian of Johnson's thought, concluded that Johnson's embrace of Hutchinson was "a sad, misguided phase of a generally distinguished career."[53]

Drawing on Johnson's own account, Chandler had a quite different take in his *The Life* than did Ellis. For him, the episode was another example of his mentor's talents as a scholar and his willingness to question conventional thinking. Johnson, Chandler wrote, read Hutchinson's works "over and over again; he studied them with the utmost care and attention." This careful study, Chandler said, meant that Johnson approached Hutchinson with a critical and skeptical eye. Johnson, according to Chandler, was "greatly disgusted at the superciliousness of [Hutchinson], who treats the great names of Sir Isaac Newton and Dr. Clarke contemptuously." Yet Johnson admired Hutchinson's "profound and stupendous genius." Hutchinson succeeded in weakening "the principles of the Newtonian philosophy, showing its inconsistency in several points; and that he had proved that the only right system of philosophy is taught in the Bible." Johnson also concluded that "Mr. Hutchinson had discovered some very important ancient truths . . . particularly with respect to the divine names." So for Chandler, Johnson offered up a nuanced and balanced account of a controversial scholar whose work "made such a noise in the learned world."[54]

A HIGH CHURCH CONVERT

In October 1746, Johnson informed church officials in London that Chandler wanted to enter the ministry, and the competition began quickly for his services. Anglican ministers—especially *talented* ministers—were in short supply in the colonies. Because of his youth, Chandler was not old enough to become a minister; he would to have serve first as a catechist, which involved reading prayers and a sermon and visiting congregation members. But Chandler had several options in New York, including at North Castle and Bedford, and one possibility in Elizabeth Town, New Jersey.

Johnson encouraged Chandler's plans to become a minister. And Chandler had other supporters as well. One of the most enthusiastic was the Reverend James Wetmore, an Anglican minister in Rye, New York. Wetmore was a Yale graduate (class of 1714) and a colleague of Samuel Johnson's who had served at West Haven. He wrote several letters of recommendation on Chandler's behalf, and he wanted him as a catechist in New York. In February 1747, Wetmore told the SPG that he had met "a very worthy Young Gentleman Mr.

Thomas Bradbury Chandler, educated at Now-Haven Colledge who has lately declared himself a Conformist to our Church, and has desired me to profest his Duty to the Honorable Society and request that his Name may be recommended among the Candidates for Holy Orders."55

Another important ally was the Reverend Samuel Seabury Sr., father of Samuel Jr. The elder Seabury reported to SPG officials in London that Chandler's abilities, including his "Learning, Prudence Gravity Sincere piety and good Temper," made him an excellent candidate for the ministry. Seabury also recommended Chandler to the vestry at St. John's Church in Elizabeth Town, which was searching for a minister in the wake of its pastor's death.56

On the advice of Seabury and others, St. John's Church recruited Chandler heavily. On December 26, it informed the Society for the Propagation of the Gospel of its intention to hire him. It also asked Johnson to write the SPG, and he obliged on January 12, 1747, telling the Society that St. John's "desire[s] earnestly" that Chandler succeed the Reverend Edward Vaughan. Johnson said Chandler and St. John's were a good match. Both sides wanted each other, Johnson wrote, and "he on that Account, may be very likely to do much good there." Johnson also praised Chandler as a human being and a scholar. "He was bred at this College, and I have known him three years, at least[;] he appears to me a truly valuable person, of good parts and competent Learning," Johnson said, adding that Chandler is "of good Morals & Virtuous Behaviour" and is held in "good Estimation of all that know him."57

Weighing his options carefully, Chandler decided to leave Connecticut for St. John's in Elizabeth Town. The determining factor, according to Wetmore, was St. John's promise that Chandler could succeed Vaughn as minister when he was old enough. But it was not an easy decision, and Chandler wavered during the courtship. Chandler at one point asked Wetmore if he could serve as catechist at New Bedford and North Castle, and Wetmore obliged by sending him an offer letter. But, according to Wetmore, Chandler made him wait "some time" before accepting—and then Chandler changed his mind, likely because of the entreaties by St. John's. The indecision disappointed SPG officials in London and must have displeased Wetmore, although he continued supporting Chandler's efforts to become a minister. Chandler understood his mistake. He had Wetmore write to the SPG that he "hopes his Declining [the appointment] will be excused, as it is a blow of being more useful in a Situation that will be more agreeable to him." Chandler, Wetmore hastened to add, was determined "to devote his best Services to Religion and in the Communion of the Church of England."58

With the strong backing of Johnson, Seabury, and the ever patient Wetmore, Chandler's appointment was approved, but bad feelings over the affair remained. In the letter informing him of his appointment, the SPG secretary scolded Chandler, telling him that "the Society were not pleased with your refusal of the Catechist's place under Mr. Wetmore, which had been granted at your own request." With his appointment confirmed, Chandler in May 1748 began working at St. John's as a catechist. His salary was a paltry ten pounds a year. (The SPG promoted Chandler to missionary two years later, and in June 1751, at age twenty-five, he went to England to receive his holy orders.) Chandler's decision to go to Elizabeth Town raised the congregation's spirits. Chandler reported that he was "kindly received by the People upon my first Arrival, & their Fondness for me has not decreased." Others were also heartened by his arrival. Chances were strong that the struggling congregation will increase "considerably under the care of a Zealous & discret missionary," wrote Henry Barclay, "and such a one I have reason to Believe Mr. Chandler will approve himself, and most Especially from the Excellent Character given him by Dr. Johnson and Mr. Wetmore."[59]

But what kind of minister was St. John's getting?

Apparently one with some speaking abilities as a preacher, for Seabury in his letter of recommendation praised Chandler's "able Voice." Events would also show that Chandler was a tireless missionary in New Jersey for the Church of England; he traveled extensively throughout the colony in an attempt to build the king's church in a place that was overrun by Presbyterians, Lutherans, Baptists, Quakers, and other (in Chandler's eyes) detestable sects. He regularly preached in places lacking an Anglican minister, including at Woodbridge, about ten miles from Elizabeth Town. In 1762, Chandler claimed he had ridden more than three thousand miles in recent years and "preached near two hundred Sermons, besides doing other Duties." He also was extremely loyal to St. John's. After settling in at Elizabeth Town, Chandler reported in 1754 that he had received "Invitations to other Places, but the Inclinations & wants of the People made too Strong an Impression on me, & I consented not to leave them."[60]

Yet the defining characteristic of Chandler's ministry would prove to be his high church values. After concluding his studies with Johnson, Chandler carried to New Jersey deeply traditional views of church and state. The bedrock high church principle for Chandler was his commitment to episcopal government and bishops. It was a commitment forged by a rabid opposition to Congregationalism, complete disdain toward New England, and deep study of religious history.

The New England Way was based on the Cambridge Platform, the Puritan attempt to erect a church on biblical precedents. Compiled by a synod of ministers in 1648, it placed the congregation at the center of the church, and it defined the church as "being a company of people combined together by covenant for the worship of God." Only the congregation had the power to call and ordain a minister, a power "that the churches exercised . . . in the presence of the Apostles," according to the synod, and a power that it likened to the election of a magistrate. It further said that no church had authority over another, and that when a minister left the church, his ministerial authority left with him. He would not be a minister again until a congregation hired him and reordained him through the "Imposition of Hands."[61]

Thus, in the Puritan scheme of things that Chandler so detested, community gained strength from the commitment and participation of the many. A church government of the few, headed by a monarch and bishops, was unwise. New England Congregationalists were not alone in preaching these beliefs. They were merely trying to implement what their radical forebears had sought two centuries earlier. The Puritan movement arose during the late sixteenth century out of opposition to the Church of England under the Tudor monarchs, and one important reason was reformers' rejection of episcopal government led by two archbishops (Canterbury and York) and twenty-six bishops. Reformers, including Thomas Cartwright (ca. 1535–1603), called for eliminating the episcopal office and replacing it with a government led by ministers, deacons, and lay elders. Two *Admonition to the Parliament* stated the case most powerfully, with the first *Admonition* calling episcopacy "antichristian and devilish, and contrary to the scriptures." Throughout Europe, including in Scotland and England, reformers were seeking the elimination of ecclesiastical structures.[62]

Thus high church Anglicanism defended episcopacy against the attacks of enemies who wanted to end it. In the American colonies, Samuel Johnson taught future Anglican ministers, including a rapt pupil named Thomas Bradbury Chandler, this history and the high church values that defined a church led by bishops. Johnson saw numerous problems, both biblical and practical, with a Congregational system, and Chandler's *Life of Samuel Johnson* neatly summarized them. When ordinary people have influence, Chandler wrote of Johnson's beliefs, they become conceited, and "the natural consequence" of conceitedness is "censoriousness and uncharitableness." And censoriousness leads to "virulent separations and schisms," which in turn leads to laymen seeking "private revenge." All this bickering undercuts discipline and harms the church as injured members quit and form their own rival congregations.

The threat of schism, Chandler and Johnson believed, was even greater in the colonies, "where every individual seemed to think his own judgment infallible," than it was in England. In the end, Congregationalism would crumble under the weight of schisms caused by squabbling congregations—an argument Archbishop Whitgift and other Church of England defenders made repeatedly in the 1580s and 1590s.[63]

Thus Johnson, and Chandler, found the Church of England and its ecclesiastical structure a powerful answer to democratic chaos. The bishops led, and laymen followed. For both men, this hierarchal scheme made perfect sense. One only had to look to New England to see the merit of their position. But they also believed they had history, and the Bible, on their side. Johnson's favorite author on the subject, according to Chandler, was John Potter, who wrote *A Discourse of Church Government: wherein the rights of the church and the supremacy of Christian princes are vindicated and adjusted*, which was first published in 1707. Potter, the son of a linen draper, was Archbishop of Canterbury from 1737 until his death in 1747 and was an articulate high churchman. Johnson praised Potter's conclusions on episcopacy as unassailable. When he was done reading *A Discourse of Church Government*, "the effect was that, from the facts in scripture, compared with those of the primitive church, it appeared plain to [Johnson and his colleagues] that the episcopal government was universally established by the Apostles wherever they propagated Christianity," Chandler recalled, and "through the first order of the ministry, called Bishops, the power of the priesthood was to be conveyed from the great head of the church."[64]

Church history, they believed, was clear on this count. "Christ and his Apostles did actually establish a certain form and order of government in the church," Chandler said of Johnson's view, "which, as to all its essential parts, was to continue 'to the end of the world.'" No one, Johnson believed, had the authority to alter it. He found the Congregational position impossible; power simply could not rest with the congregation.[65]

Or so Chandler was taught from a high church master. He arrived in Elizabeth Town in 1748 convinced that episcopacy was superior to Congregationalism, and that the New England Way was the wrong way. Further study and experience only strengthened this belief.

CHAPTER 2

Englishman
Church and State in a Chandlerian World

When Thomas Bradbury Chandler took up his duties as a catechist in 1748, he was only twenty-two years old. Excited to be working for the king's church, he exuded a mix of enthusiasm and confidence, tempered by a dash of realism. The road ahead, Chandler well knew, would be hard. St. John's was not the dominant church in Elizabeth Town; the Presbyterian church was. Moreover, East Jersey was overrun with "dissenters." The Anglican missionary Thomas Wood of Brunswick, who helped out at St. John's in the years before Chandler was ordained, lamented just how badly outnumbered Anglicans were in Elizabeth. The village had at least a thousand dissenters to only two hundred Anglicans or so, and "5 Meetinghouses [were] within 5 or six miles of ye town." Worse, Wood and Chandler fretted, and with good reason, that a Presbyterian-dominated college would soon open in Elizabeth, as its inhabitants under the direction of "a very rigid Presbyterian" were busy raising money for buildings. Chandler warned Samuel Johnson that the college was "one great part of their design . . . to have an engine to play against the Church; and indeed the suppression of the Church seems to be aimed at every shape in these parts."[1]

Yet during these first years in Elizabeth Town, Chandler was cautiously optimistic that through hard work and a superior message, better days lay ahead for the Church of England in New Jersey. Besides reading prayers and a sermon every Sunday, "[I] have made it my Business to frequently visit the people of every Condition," Chandler informed the Society for the Propagation of the Gospel in 1749, and "I have had the good Fortune to keep them together." The challenge was twofold, he explained. St. John's has "been now above a Year & Half without a Shepherd," and "so many Arts [have] been used by the Dissenters to gain them over to that Interest." Nevertheless, Chandler said, members "still remain hearty & stedfast in the Principles of the Established Church. They form a full, steady Congregation, behave with much Decency & Regularity in time of Divine Service." Chandler, along with Wood and other missionaries, was confident that many more would come once St. John's had a regular minister.[2]

Chandler's situation, however, was ripe with irony. The Church of England's minority status in East Jersey greatly bothered Chandler and violated everything he believed in. To this high church Anglican, dissenters should be the ones in the minority. Chandler held strong views about a properly functioning society and the role of the state church in it. England was his model. There, king and prelate worked together to inculcate reverence for God and monarchy. Laws required people to attend Sunday service or face fines. Dissenters were few and barely tolerated. Taxes supported the king's church and provided handsome livings for its bishops, who sat in Parliament and carried themselves with the mien of princes, befitting their high station in society.

Chandler was fascinated by, and envious of, this English world. As he settled into his new life and made himself at home in the recently acquired parsonage, he became immersed in an Anglican colonial community, cultivating allies, forming friendships, and becoming a leader of the northern clergy. Chandler, meanwhile, continued his studies begun under Samuel Johnson and brooded about the weaknesses of the king's church in the colonies. He wanted to understand the origins of the Puritan movement in Tudor England and how the Elizabethan church confronted the challenge posed by this upstart Protestant reform group. During the 1748–69 period, as a result, Chandler undertook two tasks: He worked hard as a missionary, laboring to strengthen the Church of England in the middle colonies. And he read deeply, refining his views of episcopacy, church and state, church powers, dissenter rights, and revolution itself. A royalist and traditionalist at heart, Chandler became an expert on English political and theological history. He partook of the library at nearby King's College in New York City, borrowed tracts from friends, and painstakingly built up his own sizable collection of books.

As he crisscrossed East Jersey preaching to and praying with anyone who would listen, Chandler increasingly became convinced that the events of the sixteenth and seventeenth centuries contained important lessons for eighteenth-century British North America, where the Crown's hold on the colonies was weakening and upstart sects were gaining the upper hand in the contest with the Church of England.

SETTLING INTO THE MINISTRY

St. John's did all it could to make its talented young catechist feel at home. After heavily recruiting Chandler in 1748, it went out and purchased a fine house on the banks of Elizabeth Creek for him to live in as a parsonage. Elizabeth by then had grown into New Jersey's largest town in 1750 with two hundred to three hundred houses and one of its wealthiest. It was an attractive place, peppered with shingled houses and well-tended gardens and orchards. A Swedish visitor praised its well-built houses and stone buildings, while an English diplomat described the village as "rich and thriving." Especially striking were the two steepled churches built by the village's Presbyterians and Anglicans. Chandler himself pronounced Elizabeth, which looked out from Newark Bay to Staten Island, a bustling place, being "situated on a very Public Road in the most populous and thriving part of the Province." The Presbyterian-dominated village had a genteel flavor, so much so that a young, impressionable Alexander Hamilton, who spent part of 1774 in Elizabeth, reported having a "strong prejudice" for the British view and monarchism while he was living in the village.[3]

For Chandler, the parsonage's location on a four-acre glebe met both his intellectual and social needs. His house was near New York City and the library at King's College, and it was close to the town center. Nearby was the Presbyterian Church, the courthouse, and a school known variously as the Presbyterian or Elizabeth Academy. Also nearby were numerous mansions, including what became known as Boxwood Hall, built in 1750 by the village mayor and later owned by Elias Boudinot, a revolutionary leader who befriended a young Alexander Hamilton newly arrived from the Caribbean. Chandler's parsonage was constructed circa 1696 by Andrew Hampton, who came to Elizabeth sometime in the 1680s. The house was one and a half stories and likely brick, and it featured double-gable chimneys and three dormers. St. John's Church acquired the house in 1749 from John Emott, and Chandler moved into the new parsonage in 1750. He praised the congregation for its purchase of "an agreeable Parsonage," although his new home apparently was too small for his tastes. In 1765, presumably at Chandler's request, congregation members took up a subscription that enabled Chandler to construct a

FIG. 2 The St. John's parish house in 1765, after the west wing was added. The addition contained Chandler's library and dining room. Drawing by Alexandra Cople.

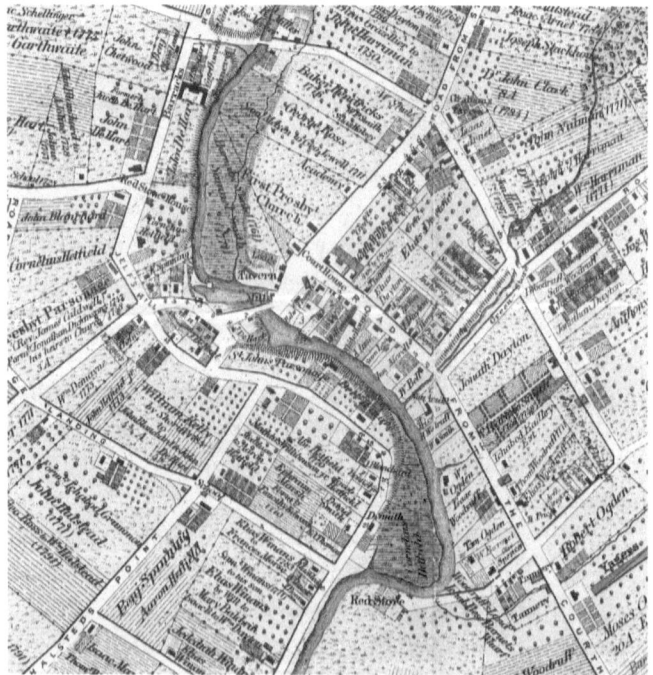

FIG. 3 A map of Elizabeth Town, New Jersey, shows the St. John's Church parish on Elizabeth Creek, with orchards and gardens. Ernest L. Meyer and J. Schedler, *Map of Elizabeth Town at the Time of the Revolutionary War* [...] (New York: J. Schedler, 1879), detail. Geography and Map Division, Library of Congress, Washington, DC.

wing on the west side for a study and dining room. A grateful Chandler complimented St. John's for its beneficence, saying "they have been as generous as I could well desire."[4]

Chandler gained more than a house when he moved into the parsonage. In 1750 he married Emott's daughter Jane (1733–1801), and the couple went on to have five daughters (two of whom died young) and a son during a forty-year marriage. The union cemented Chandler's membership in the town's upper crust: Jane's mother was a Boudinot, and the Emotts themselves had money, high social standing, and close ties to St. John's Church, which was founded in 1706 and became an incorporated parish in 1762. The Emott family's roots extended into the colony's earliest days. James Emott was a French Huguenot who came to New Jersey from England in about 1682 and served as secretary of the province. He married Mary Carteret, a daughter of New Jersey governor Philip Carteret (1639–1682); Philip was a fourth cousin of Sir George Carteret, who was proprietor of the colony. When James Emott died in 1713, Mary Carteret Emott inherited £2,000, a princely sum for the times. She promptly married Anglican missionary Edward Vaughan, Chandler's predecessor at St. John's. The match brought Vaughan money, a house, and a nine-acre lot on Point Road, which he willed to the Society for the Propagation of the Gospel upon his death in 1747.[5]

With the parsonage an easy stroll to both St. John's Church and the village center, a gregarious Chandler was well placed to entertain the citizens of Elizabeth and his congregation. One near contemporary recalled that Chandler "lived with such a degree of ease and comfort, and with such a free and unlimited hospitality as are remembered by many who are still living, both with wonder and pleasure. I have scarcely ever met with any aged person belonging to our Church who had visited Elizabeth Town, that did not delight in recalling the many happy hours which he had spent in that agreeable family, and at that hospitable board." Indeed, Chandler lamented to Samuel Johnson that he could hardly call Elizabeth "a place of retirement, for I am necessarily exposed to too much company."[6]

The parsonage's proximity to New York City was also important. Although it was still overshadowed by Philadelphia to the south and Boston to the north, New York City was growing in the mid-eighteenth century, with its population approaching twenty thousand by 1766. The seaport and burgeoning commercial center was home to King's College, the stately Trinity Church, and other important Anglican institutions, and was a convenient place for Chandler to meet with Samuel Seabury Jr., Myles Cooper, and other clerical allies.

Unlike Samuel Johnson, the bookish Chandler enjoyed the social obligations of his ministry and from his first arrival saw pastoral visits as an important part of his job. By visiting the "more distant parts of this Town," Chandler believed he could keep members loyal to St. John's. He criticized his predecessor as indolent. Vaughn's lethargy, Chandler feared, allowed the dissenters to outstrip St. John's in popularity. By the 1730s, the Anglican church was contending with five other rivals, including the Quakers, whose membership nearly matched St. John's. Chandler moved aggressively to improve St. John's position, and he made considerable progress. Within six years of his arrival, eighty-five families were members and communicants totaled ninety. Membership grew so impressively in his early years that Chandler told the Society for the Propagation of the Gospel in May 1752 that because the "congregation has visibly increased . . . we find it necessary to erect a new Gallery on the South Side of the Church."[7]

Chandler spent a significant amount of time outside of Elizabeth, especially at Woodbridge, "a Country Town, large & populous," that he estimated was "Ten Miles distant" from Elizabeth. Presbyterians and Quakers were his chief rivals, and both were doing well, according to Chandler. The Presbyterians had fifty congregations in New Jersey in the prerevolutionary period—the most in the colony—and the Quakers were second with forty. The Church of England, by contrast, had thirty congregations. The Dutch Reformed, Baptists, German Lutherans, and Methodists also were numerous, and a sprinkling of Moravian and other sects could be found in New Jersey as well. This religious diversity was a reflection of the colony itself, which, like neighboring Pennsylvania, was home to large numbers of Dutch, Germans, Swedes, Scots, Scots-Irish, Welsh, Irish, and others. By 1750, New Jersey had a population of about sixty thousand, up from fifteen thousand in 1700.[8]

Surveying this complex landscape, Chandler was determined to go anywhere where he might be able to do some good. One such place was another Presbyterian stronghold, Whippany, about twenty miles from Elizabeth in Morris County, which was the domain of a talented minister named Jacob Green who would become an ardent revolutionary when war with Great Britain came. Chandler vowed to "spend as much of my Time at these Places as I can, consistently with my Duty at Home, which I must regard in the first Place." Presbyterians and other rival churches certainly took notice of his ambitions. "Some of the Dissenters at Woodbridge wonder that I take so much Pains to come there," Chandler reported, "& think I have no Right, imagining that I am limited by the Society to Eliz. Town."[9]

Chandler prided himself on his ability to get along with the dissenters. In 1764, he reported that "I have always lived upon good Terms with my dissenting neighbors, & with some of them I have cultivated a considerable Degree of Friendship." Nevertheless, Chandler viewed them as rivals, even enemies. Letter after letter to London portrayed dissenters—and he always referred to them as dissenters, a term of opprobrium in his high church world—as threats to the Church of England and monarchical society. Unlike in Europe, Chandler explained, Catholics posed little threat to Protestants in New Jersey. "We have none in this Province," he said. "The chief Enemies of ye Church are ye English dissenters of different Denominations, who are thrice as numerous as its Professors, & more active against us than our Friends are for us." In the Protestant world, evangelicals and pietists stressed the need to bring sinners to Christ by encouraging them to undergo a new birth. The Moravians, one of the largest pietistic sects in the eighteenth century with missions around the world, espoused heart religion in which the Bible and a love of the Savior would bring converts to Jesus. Other evangelicals, including the Anglican George Whitefield, embraced revivalism and saw the Great Awakening as a powerful tool to reinvigorate Christianity.[10]

Chandler brought a different mindset to his pastoral duties than did his dissenting neighbors. He rejected revivalism, going so far as to deny Whitefield's request in 1764 to preach at St. John's, to the great disappointment of his flock. Chandler viewed his fellow Anglican as a renegade and his behavior as "undutiful & schismatical." In a letter to Samuel Johnson, Chandler reported "that enthusiasm begins to spread very fast within the borders of my mission. There are many instantaneous conversions going on, and I apprehend it will require much care and prudence to guard my flock." To strengthen the Church of England in America and fend off the dissenter and evangelical menaces, Chandler wanted to teach people about authority and the proper role of the state church in a monarchical society. His sermons, he fretted, were having little effect. In fact, "to dwell much on ye foregoing Subjects in ye Pulpit might have a bad Effect upon some." Instead, he wanted to inculcate proper values in his charges through carefully chosen books on church and state and the dangers of schism. Books, Chandler explained in a letter to the Society, held two key advantages over sermons: they can be read at leisure, and they possessed the ability to reach those people who did not attend church regularly. Without books, he said, "I find it very difficult to remove ye Prejudices which generally prevail in this Country." By "prejudices," Chandler meant colonists' annoying habit of questioning authority and the status of the Church of England as the established church in England.[11]

Throughout the 1760s, Chandler repeatedly asked the Society in London to send him books that he could distribute to church members and others. In one letter alone he requested copies of William Fleetwood's *The Reasonable Communicant: Or, an Explanation of the Sacrament of the Lord's Supper*; John Leland's *A View of the Principal Deistical Writers*; Edward Weston's *The Englishman Directed in the Choice of His Religion*; and the "invaluable" sermons of the late Bishop Thomas Sherlock (1678–1761), "which thro' ye Bounty of a Royal, & of a right Reverend Benefactor are common here, will prove ... a sufficient Antidote against Infidelity."[12]

It was an interesting list to say the least, demonstrating Chandler's willingness to read authors of widely differing views and backgrounds because of the lessons he could extract from them. Fleetwood (1656–1723) was Bishop of St. Alsaph and later of Ely—and an ardent Whig who supported the Glorious Revolution and countenanced rebellion in certain situations. Despite Fleetwood's shaky political pedigree, he wrote an influential primer on the Anglican liturgy, *The Reasonable Communicant*, published in 1704, which went through more than sixteen editions. For someone of Chandler's beliefs, John Leland (1691–1766) was even more dubious than Fleetwood—he was an English Presbyterian who became an Arian in his final years. But the inclusion on the list of Leland's *A View of the Principal Deistical Writers* indicates that Chandler feared deism was becoming a threat to traditional Christianity. Weston (1703–1770) was the son of an Anglican bishop who wrote a series of how-to books, including *The Country Gentlemen's Advice to His Neighbours* (1755). His *The Englishman Directed in the Choice of His Religion* was a Lockean treatise that used reason to, Weston said, assist "those who are willing to make a rational Enquiry into Things, and to be set right in the Religion which they should live."[13]

Most tellingly, Chandler requested a tract on the nature and constitution of the church that he said would explain the "Necessity of Authority." Besides the dissenter threat, Chandler was confronting a broader, and equally serious, challenge to governmental authority and hierarchy in Elizabeth and its environs. A decade of land riots that had begun in 1745 had left their mark in Chandler's home county of Essex in the 1750s and 1760s. The cause of the unrest was proprietorial claims for land in East Jersey that placed farmers' holdings in jeopardy. When Samuel Baldwin of Newark, whose land title was based on an Indian purchase, was arrested on trespassing charges and jailed, a mob of about 150 men armed with clubs and other weapons freed him on September 19, 1745. The mob threatened to return with a larger force if authorities made any additional arrests. Riots continued over the next ten years in Essex and several nearby counties, including Morris and Bergen, where authorities arrested landholders on trespassing or rioting charges. The farmers also assaulted proprietary agents and chased off tenants on proprietorial lands in Elizabeth and other villages.[14]

For Chandler, such unruliness was appalling: Authority, he believed, was under assault. Lacking the imprimatur of the established church, the Church of England was struggling to hold back the dissenter and democratic tides in the colonies. Chandler's response to these challenges said everything about his values and views of church and state: he wanted to teach his parishioners about obedience and the role of the state church in a properly functioning society. To impart these lessons, Chandler drew on his growing knowledge of Tudor history, a period that greatly interested him because of the founding of the Church of England and its defense of episcopacy.

THE TUDOR ROOTS OF CHANDLER'S THOUGHT

In Chandler's voluminous library was a small but important collection of approximately twenty-five books on the Tudor era, including works on the most important controversies of the period written by or on the leading figures, such as Thomas Cranmer, Thomas Cartwright, John Whitgift, and Richard Hooker. The Scottish philosopher David Hume (1711–1776) wrote an epic eight-volume history of England; Chandler owned volume 5—on the Tudor period. During the bishop's campaign in the 1760s and early 1770s, Chandler repeatedly referenced Tudor history. He admired the controversial Archbishop of Canterbury Whitgift and his successor, Richard Bancroft, calling them "Men of eminent Abilities, of invincible Integrity, of undissembled Piety, and zealous Advocates for the Protestant Religion." And he cited the work of Bishop John Jewel (1522–1571) when defending episcopacy, saying "everyone understands [Jewel] to have written the real, undisguised Sense of the Church in England, in his celebrated *Apology*." Thus the Tudor period was a small but telling part of Chandler's library. The reasons for this interest were not hard to find: in the late sixteenth century, defenders of the Elizabethan church effectively laid out the high church case for episcopacy, authority, and obedience as they battled a dangerous new reform movement known derisively as Puritanism.[15]

When she became queen in 1558, Elizabeth wanted a strong and unified state church that would have broad appeal throughout her kingdom. Achieving these ambitious goals required Elizabeth to move forcefully but carefully because her predecessor, Mary (1516–1558), had restored Catholicism as the national religion during her five years on the throne. The forceful part of Elizabeth's mission came quickly. Parliament passed the 1559 Act of Supremacy, ending papal authority over the English church and making the queen supreme governor. The act required all clergy, magistrates, and royal officials to take an oath of allegiance acknowledging Elizabeth as the head of the church. Hume noted that through the act, Elizabeth was "vested with the whole spiritual power" and had the authority to "repress all heresies." The act also empowered the queen to form a court of ecclesiastical commission, which, Hume observed, "assumed large discretionary, not to say arbitrary powers [to stamp out heresy], totally incompatible with any exact limitations in the constitution."[16]

The delicate part came in how Elizabeth returned the English church to Protestantism. The new queen did not want to alienate those English who still preferred the ancient Roman church over English-style Protestantism. The new state church, as a result, designed a communion service that was theologically bland enough to encourage Catholic participation, and it used the vestments that predated the reforms of Elizabeth's brother, King Edward VI (1537–1553). By retaining some Catholic forms and ceremonies, the queen managed "to reconcile the catholics to the established religion, and at the same time struck out every thing that could be offensive to them in the new liturgy," Hume wrote.[17]

But a sizable minority of English Protestants were unhappy with these compromises because they preserved too many Catholic practices. The most radical of them believed the church needed a complete overhaul, and they argued that Elizabeth's halfway measures did not go far enough. The state church, they said, was rotten at the core, a godly institution staffed by ungodly people. When Elizabeth came to the throne in 1558, 10–15 percent of benefices lacked a minister, and she moved quickly to fill the vacancies by placing whomever the church could find. The church struggled to attract qualified candidates because the ministry paid so poorly: two thousand out of thirteen thousand parishes supplied livings of only eight pounds a year. With reason, reformers complained loudly, and for years, that the clergy was corrupt, uneducated, and uninspiring. Few parsons knew how to deliver a sermon that could lift people's hearts and bring more sinners to Christ. Worse, many could barely read the Book of Common Prayer, the mainstay of the Anglican service. The lax morals of the clergy further offended the Puritans. The bishops' courts, they said, were too lenient with offenders who committed such grave crimes as blasphemy, sexual licentiousness, and usury.[18]

Vestments were another sore point with the reformers. The 1559 Act of Uniformity, in its elaborate attempts to achieve conformity, prescribed how the clergy should dress. One purpose was to achieve dignity and decorum in the queen's church, goals that Elizabeth embraced. "Her love of state and magnificence," Hume noted, "inspired her with an inclination towards the pomp of the catholic religion." But the clergy's regal, Catholic-like clothing outraged Puritan reformers; they likened fancy vestments to "monkery, Popery and Judaism." Puritans saw knee-length tunics as "a filthy popish rag" and demanded they be banned. The clergy should dress plainly and sensibly, they said, because they wanted ministers to be of the people and not of the priesthood, as in Rome, where the clergy stood apart from, and above, their parishioners. Surplices were a flashpoint in this heated debate over "monkery"; following the lead of Protestant reformers in Geneva and elsewhere, Puritans fought to institute simpler services that eliminated all vestiges of Mass that were led by priests who dressed in ceremonial robes.[19]

The Puritan protests over dress and ceremony annoyed Elizabeth and Whitgift, but they were far more alarmed that reformers were challenging the heart of the English state church—its episcopalian governing structure. At Trinity College in Cambridge, Cartwright lectured on the need to eliminate the episcopal office and replace it with a church government led by ministers, deacons, and lay elders. The two *Admonition to the Parliament* were, in part, an emotional plea for the queen and Parliament to discard this unbiblical and Catholic system of governing. The first *Admonition* urged Elizabeth and the Parliament to "take away the Lordship, the loitering, the pompe, the idlenesse, and the livings of bishops." This battle over church structure had international dimensions as well. In Geneva, John Calvin had long advocated eliminating ecclesiastical structures and replacing them with lay elders. It was a cause Protestant radicals were taking up everywhere in the sixteenth century, including in Scotland.[20]

For Chandler, the ensuing contest between high church defenders of episcopacy and conformity and upstart Protestant dissenters was a feast for the mind as England's greatest religious intellectuals, including Richard Hooker, Thomas Cartwright, and John Whitgift, laid out their visions of church and state. Chandler learned from all three, but the one whose temperament was closest to his own was Archbishop Whitgift, who resided at Lambeth Palace in London from 1583 until his death in 1604. The two men shared a temper, a biting disdain for democracy and the participation of ordinary folks in governing, and a love of episcopal government. Whitgift—a bear of a man with a thick beard and fierce eyes—was the queen's battering ram in the fierce campaign against dissenters in the 1580s and 1590s.

Whitgift and Cartwright first clashed at Trinity College in the late 1760s where Whitgift was master (and later vice chancellor) and Cartwright was the Lady Margaret professor of divinity. Cartwright used his professorship to attack the Elizabethan church, including its episcopal structure and its use of surplices. At Trinity, the two antagonists engaged in verbal combat that goaded Whitgift into taking increasingly extreme positions backing royalism. Whitgift argued for the divine right of kings and denounced Cartwright's assertion that church and state should be separate.[21] In March 1574, for instance, in a sermon he delivered at Greenwich with Elizabeth in the audience, Whitgift condemned not only Puritan reformers but their followers. Common people were easily misled, Whitgift warned: "they are so much delighted with novelty, so ready to embrace any strange and new kind of doctrine." They were, in other words, an easy mark for Puritan reformers and their "invented opinions," he said; only the better sort can be trusted. Whitgift had no patience for those who dared to challenge authority; such people were "unlearned tongs," he said on another occasion, and "I doe with all my harte hate contention and strife." When reformers criticized the Book of Common Prayer, Whitgift responded that "singular learned men" compiled it and that it was perfect because of that. Whitgift saw reformers as selfish individuals who were out to promote their own ends and not the good of society. In one sermon, he reproved those whose religion consisted "in contention, not peace; in contempt, not in obedience; who under the pretence of zeal, sought their own liberty . . . and with the shadow of reformation, cloaked and covered their usury, their minds desirous to spoil the Church."[22]

For Whitgift, no reformer was more dangerous and selfish than Cartwright, and he tried to persuade him to recant his presbyterian views. When Cartwright refused, Whitgift suspended him from lecturing and then deprived him of his professorship. When Cartwright still refused to end his campaign for reform, Whitgift in September 1572 expelled him from Trinity.[23]

All of this was a preliminary to their duels in the 1570s over the *Admonition to the Parliament*, written by John Field and Thomas Wilcox in 1572, advocating the abolition of episcopacy and the institution of a presbyterian government.

When those two reformers were jailed for their impudence, Cartwright took up their cause in a *Second Admonition to Parliament*; Whitgift replied with *An Answere to a Certen Libell*, to which Cartwright responded in 1573 with *A Replye to an Answere*. Whitgift then published *A Defence of the Ecclesiastical Regiment in Englande defaced by T.C. in his Replie against D. Whitgift*. Chandler owned copies of the latter two books, both of which were massive works that laid out the debate in exacting detail.

In his *A Replye to an Answere*, Cartwright once again attacked episcopacy by appealing to biblical history. He conceded that bishops were present in the early church, but argued that the meaning of the term was quite different then. The office was not the powerhouse it became in the Catholic Church, Cartwright said. It was synonymous with "minister," with power that was carefully circumscribed. "In the councel of Carthage, holden in Egyptians time, it appeareth that no bishop had authority over another, to compell another, or to condemne another," Cartwright wrote. Bishops, in other words, had authority over only one church. For Cartwright, the growth of episcopal power was blasphemous, the work of Satan. Its unbiblical origins meant that a church built on an episcopal edifice was rotten at its core. Creators of the bishop's office "sought nothing else but an ambitious and stately Lordship over those which had not that title," Cartwright complained. "And what intolerable presumption is this, to change the institution of God." The office of archbishop was even more offensive to Cartwright than that of bishop because its power was so extensive.

Episcopal power produced pomp and princely livings, Cartwright continued. The early church, by contrast, was all about simplicity and sacrifice, Cartwright said; it was about putting the love of God and Jesus first. Indeed, the councils of Carthage, Cartwright said, had even "decreed that the bishops should have a little house neare unto the church" and were to live humbly. In Tudor England, a bishop's residence was "a princely palace . . . whose chambers shine with gilt." The English church under Elizabeth contained all the faults of the Roman church, Cartwright concluded. Its episcopal structure was as rotten as Rome's, and this Protestant church differed little in practice from it.[24]

In scathing and sarcastic prose that Chandler would employ, Whitgift offered up a stirring defense of episcopacy and authority and attacked Puritan pleas for equality. To the reformers' arguments that the episcopal office was unbiblical in origin, Whitgift dismissed them with his own lesson in Old Testament teachings. "It is without all doubte," Whitgift declared, that the office of bishop predated the Nicene Council, the fourth-century ecumenical gathering that established Christianity's statement of faith. It is also without doubt, he continued, that the archbishop's office "is the chief and principall office" whose task is "to keepe unitie in the Churche, to compounde contentions, to redresse heresies, schisms, factions." Biblical history showed one bishop was chosen "to rule over the rest." Such superiority was important, Whitgift explained, because one must person must lead. Otherwise, he wrote, you would have "an armie of souldiers without a Captaine, a ship without a master, a flocke of sheepe without a shepherd."[25]

Whitgift compared the Puritan reformers to Anabaptists and "Libertines"—the ultimate insult. Anabaptists and libertines rejected episcopal authority in favor of governing structures that were democratic. Remove bishops from the church, Whitgift warned, and commoners would lead, leaving the church with a "barbarous confused societie without order." In actuality, Puritan reformers during the Tudor era were only arguing for equality among ministers, but Whitgift correctly foresaw where Puritan beliefs were headed. The whole thing "smelleth of plaine Anabaptisme," he said. "Surely if you had once made an equality, (such as you phansie) among the Clergie, it would not be long [until] you attempted the same among the laytie."[26]

Whitgift conceded that in the time of the apostles, "the peoples consent was in many places required in the appointing of ministers: But I say, that in the whole of Scripture, there is no commandment that it should be so." He believed commoners should not govern and that their piety did not compare to that of the ancients, who were "virtuous and godly." In Elizabeth's England, the archbishop said, "the church is full of hypocrites, dissemblers, drunkerds, whoremongerers."[27]

For Whitgift, the conclusions were obvious: The episcopal office was both biblical and necessary. Bishops represented power and authority and order, and their leadership represented the natural order of things. "There always hathe bene and muste be degrees and superioritie," he exclaimed, "for the Church of God is not a confused congregation, but ruled and directed as well by discipline and pollicie in matters of regimente."[28]

Elizabeth saw the Puritan reform movement and its attacks on episcopacy as a challenge not only to the church but to her rule. She had turned to the stern Whitgift in the first place because his predecessor, Edmund Grindal, who was Archbishop of Canterbury from 1576 to 1583, was too timid in meeting the Puritan threat. She needed a stronger, more loyal lieutenant than the passive Grindal. Elizabeth felt besieged in 1583 when she turned to Whitgift for help: her finances were shaky, she had no heir, she faced a constant stream of Catholic plots and provocations, and Protestant reformers were growing more aggressive.

When the Puritans began holding "prophesyings"—conferences of ministers who met to hear a discourse on Scripture—Grindal had looked the other way. Elizabeth feared these gatherings would allow the Puritans to create a national network that would enable them to radicalize the ministry and challenge her authority. She ordered Grindal in late 1576 to suppress the prophesyings. He refused, and did so in a highly offensive letter that questioned the queen's judgment and outraged Elizabeth.[29]

Whitgift worked hard to undo the mistakes of the Grindal era by clamping down on sedition and enforcing conformity. In September and October of 1583, he and the bishops drew up a series of twenty-four articles that, with the blessing of Elizabeth, required all ministers in the church to subscribe to the 1563 Articles of Religion, royal supremacy, and the Book of Common Prayer. Whitgift's decree was detailed and pointed, and its target was those Puritans who wanted to undo the Elizabethan settlement and rid the Church of England of its episcopalian structure. The majority of the articles sought to bring dissenting ministers into line and to ensure no troublemakers would be admitted into the ministry. The fifth article, for instance, declared "that none be admitted to preach or interpret the Scriptures, unless he be a Priest, or Deacon at the least, admitted thereunto according to the laws of this realm." But Whitgift also wanted "all preaching, reading, catechizing, and other such like exercises" held in private places to be "utterly extinguished." This article was aimed at stopping private meetings that allowed Puritans and other dissenters to plot and scheme against the state church. Whitgift further sought to rein in reformers by including an article stating "that none be permitted to preach, read, and catechize in the church or elsewhere, unless he . . . minister the sacraments according to the Book of Common Prayer" and preached at least four times a year.[30]

Subscription to the Thirty-Nine Articles of 1563 was also important to the archbishop and his conformity campaign; this set of articles laid the foundation for a more moderate Elizabethan church by rejecting the Protestant radicalism of Edward and of the Continent. The articles retained numerous Catholic elements, including episcopacy, cathedrals, and medieval-style worship, complete with elaborate ceremonies, solemn liturgy, and soaring music. The articles valued sacraments and ritual over preaching, and rejected predestination and Reformed views of salvation. In requiring subscription to the

Thirty-Nine Articles, Whitgift was forcing the state church's ministers to reject reformers' dreams for a Protestant church free of bishops and ceremony.[31]

Most crucially, Whitgift rejected critics' charge that compulsion cannot achieve unity. Compulsion brought order and structure, and it enabled men of wisdom and learning to lead, he argued. How would these laudable ends "be procured," the archbishop asked, "if a fewe person[s] so meanly qualified" were allowed to challenge clergy?[32]

Whitgift did not see himself as a tyrant or persecutor but as a person of high principle doing the Lord's work. "I have taken upon me the defence of Religion and rights of this Church of England, to appease the Sectes of Schimse therein to reduce all the ministers there to uniformitie," he wrote, "and to due obedience herein I intende to be Constant and not to waver with everie minde." Whitgift also stressed that the conformity drive was both lawful and fair, and he never wavered in this belief that ministers who refused to conform were justly punished. These are "the most troublesome persons in all that country," he said.[33]

Whitgift preached these principles repeatedly. People had to obey their magistrate: "Obedience is of necessity; and . . . all Christians ought to obey," Whitgift declared on November 17, 1583, when he gave his first sermon as archbishop. Wise and strong leaders, he continued, must encourage the godly and punish the wicked; the dissolute were a "plague" who undermined good order and the church. "Saith Our Saviour: *Every kingdom divided against itself cannot stand*," Whitgift said.[34]

The archbishop defined obedience as all-encompassing: "In doing, in praying, in honouring, in believing." It was not enough to merely declare obedience, he said; deeds must match words. The obligation to obey was deeply rooted in history and the origins of Christianity, Whitgift continued. Jesus himself preached that it was "lawful to give tribute unto Caesar," this at a time "when the church was in her virginity, in persecution, and the Christians so few in number; how much more needful is it to be taught in these our corrupt days, so full of disobedience."

Whitgift also believed princes were owed reverence, and princely authority rested on a mixture of honor and fear. Both were necessary if a prince was to effectively lead: "It is said, My son, give fear and honour to whom it is due." But what should a loyal subject do when a prince is corrupt or tyrannical? "Shall we obey the magistrate in all things without exception?" Whitgift asked. "This question is common; and the answer easy, and without question. The commandments of magistrates, being not against the word of God, bindeth in conscience, and are to be kept upon pain of damnation." But if the magistrate "commandeth anything against the law of God, answer with the apostle; . . . 'It is better to obey God than men.'" Princes, he added, "serve Christ, in making laws for Christ." Two of the biggest threats to their rule were Anabaptists because they would "take obedience clear away. For they would have no magistrates at all"; and "papists," who seek their destruction by proclaiming the pope superior to the prince.[35]

As important as Whitgift was to Chandler's understanding of obedience and authority, the writings of another Church of England stalwart from Tudor England—Richard Hooker (1554–1600), the era's leading religious intellectual—loomed just as large because of Hooker's influential defense of episcopacy and hierarchy. Chandler's library contained a copy of Hooker's magnum opus, *Of the Laws of Ecclesiastical Politie*, and a biography of Hooker by English writer Izaak Walton. The Oxford-educated theologian, who served as Master of the Temple, was the polar opposite of Whitgift: measured, reasonable, careful—a calm voice to the archbishop's volcanic eruptions. Hooker was a true believer in via media, a bookish man who was appalled by the religious strife of the late sixteenth century and wanted to end the fighting among English Protestants. Thus, in the final decade of his life, Hooker wrote *Of the Laws of Ecclesiastical Politie*, which consisted of eight books and was published in stages beginning in 1594.

In it, Hooker argued for a broad, tolerant state church that would encompass a variety of views. But more important to Chandler was Hooker's eloquent defense of the church, its episcopal structure, and its hierarchy. Chandler certainly had nothing but praise for *Of the Laws of Ecclesiastical Politie*, calling it Hooker's "immortal Work." "The whole System of Church-Government is examined from its first Principles," Chandler wrote with admiration, "and the Church of England, particularly its Hierarchy, is defended with such Force of Argument and Perspicuity of Method, as are an Honour even to the Age in which he wrote."[36]

In *Of the Laws of Ecclesiastical Politie*, Hooker stressed the theme that Chandler repeated as he campaigned for an American episcopate: episcopacy was superior to congregationalism. Even "Mr. Calvin himself, though an enemy" to episcopacy, recognized that the early church needed someone in charge "in every city, to whom they appropriated the title of bishop, lest equality should breed dissension," Hooker observed. By dissension, Hooker meant synods were nothing more than a cacophony of voices that resulted in chaos and indecision. To get anything done, synods must have someone in charge. As he succinctly put it, "Can their pastoral synod do any thing, unless they have some president amongst them?"[37]

By contrast, episcopacy created clean lines of authority, headed by "a minister of God" who acted as a "judge in Christ's stead." Hooker noted that the word "bishop" came from Greek, defined, in his words, as "one which hath principal charge to guide and oversee others." The office grew quickly "to signify such episcopal authority, alone as the chiefest governors exercised over the rest." Such a structure, he argued, was essential to maintaining a strong church and a properly functioning society. Constitutions and laws can accomplish only so much, Hooker said. For these legalistic tools to work, the church "dependeth most upon the vigilant care of the chiefest spiritual governors." Lay governors lacked both the learning and the authority bestowed by God to fill the supervisory role.[38]

This power gave the bishops another advantage, Hooker continued: Prelates alone possessed the stature and authority to deal with the aristocracy. Ministers and lay elders did not. And this bald fact was so plainly obvious, "no judicious man will ever make any question or doubt." Hooker's larger point was that episcopacy was a key thread in the fabric that was the English constitution and a society resting on separate estates headed by the Crown. Pull on this thread, and the whole thing would unravel. Hooker likened hierarchy to "a threefold cable, consisting of the king as a supreme head over all, of peers and nobles under him, and of the people under them." Bishops resided in the second "wreath of that cable," equal to the nobility. Indeed, their stature as equals meant that Puritan crusades to abolish episcopacy were absurd and impossible, according to Hooker, because bishops and temporal lords were so "twined together, how can it possibly be avoided, but that the tearing away of one must needs exceedingly weaken the other, and by consequent impair greatly the good of all?" Eliminating bishops would lead to catastrophe by fatally damaging the careful balances of the English constitution. Bishops served as a check, providing guidance to the nobility and "correct[ing] such excesses in them" as needed. Bishops were important to the other end of the social scale as well—those clergy ministering to the lower orders. Bishops provided crucial support to ministers' efforts to support and strengthen the church. Prelacy, as a result, was "the glue and soder of the public weal, the ligament which tieth and connecteth the limbs of this body politic."[39]

The episcopal office was so important to the body politic, and bishops were ranked so highly in English society, that Hooker dismissed reformers' criticisms of their lavish lifestyle. The greater the office, the greater the compensation to which a man was entitled—even those serving God, Hooker argued. Because of their extensive responsibilities, bishops deserved "a state of wealth proportionate" to their abilities. Making them poorer would only "make them of less account and estimation than they should be." Worse, Hooker warned, returning the church and its bishops to the poverty of the early church would destroy the beauty and majesty of the Church of England. Meager livings would undermine the bishops' power; "paganism and extreme barbarity" would follow.[40]

Like Whitgift and other high church acolytes, Hooker thus presented a worldview opposite that of the Puritans and Presbyterians. While Hooker and his compatriots revered the early church of apostolic times, they did not see it as definitive. Hooker did not view the Church of England's governing structure as invalid because it could not be found in Scripture. Presbyterians and Puritans put way too much stock in Scripture, Hooker believed. It was a guide, albeit an important one, but only a guide, and Christians had to use their God-given reason to decide what should be followed and what should be discarded to meet the needs of a modern society. Because the Bible was silent on the details of church governance, Hooker wrote, Christians were free to work out the details, a view that he shared with Whitgift. But he also echoed the archbishop's rejection of the idea that individuals' interpretation of Scripture was as valid as a minister's. Such a belief, Hooker wrote in book 2, only leads to "gross and palpable errors." Scholars and the church leadership were the ones best qualified to unravel the deep mysteries of Scripture. And Hooker shared Whitgift's fear that Congregationalism and lay power would mean the end of the established church and everything associated with it, including episcopacy and the alliance between church and state.[41]

CHANDLER AND TUDOR ENGLAND

For Chandler, the writings of John Whitgift, Richard Hooker, and others held invaluable lessons about episcopacy and its critical role in supporting monarchy, hierarchy, and authority. The Elizabethan church laid out the dangers of democracy and the need for authority. Chandler drew extensively on these arguments when he composed his tracts on episcopacy in the 1760s and the revolutionary movement in the 1770s, and he approved of much of what Whitgift, Bancroft, and others sought to accomplish during their battles with their Presbyterian and Puritan enemies. Living and working in the cacophonous middle colonies, he wanted his fellow colonists to understand this history. Thus, in his writings and likely his sermons, Chandler could be found arguing for the importance of episcopacy and order.

Chandler's championing of Tudor-era values proved controversial with the descendants of Whitgift's foes—Puritans and Presbyterians—and with American Whigs. Chandler's opponents reviled Whitgift and a seventeenth-century successor, William Laud, Archbishop of Canterbury during the reign of Charles I, who did as much as anyone to spark the Puritan exodus to Massachusetts Bay in the 1630s. As we shall see in chapters 4 and 5, New England Congregationalists and middle colony Presbyterians blocked Chandler's plans for an American episcopate, because they feared he was attempting to implement Tudor- and Stuart-style tyranny in the colonies. Pastor Charles Chauncy of Boston's Congregational First Church and other enemies of episcopacy cited the Church of England's long history of persecution, pointing to "the days of those hard-hearted Archbishops, Parker, Bancroft, Whitgift, and Laud."[42]

Chandler responded that critics did Whitgift and Laud an injustice by dismissing them only as "rigorous Exacters of Conformity." They laudably intended to strengthen the state church and religion, he declared. The Test Act of the seventeenth century, which barred nonconformists and Catholics from public office, "was to prevent the Enemies of the Church from getting Power to destroy Her," he said. Chandler also defended the Uniformity Act of 1662, rejecting Chauncy's complaint that it led to the dismissal of many qualified ministers. Quite the contrary—it actually improved the ministry by raising standards, Chandler wrote. As proof, he cited an authority who reported that the ejected consisted of "not a few Mechanicks, and Fellows bred to the meanest Occupations; many more who had seen neither of the Universities; several Troopers and others who had served in the Rebels Armies."[43]

Thus Chandler made no apologies for his admiration of the Elizabethan church and the stern measures of Tudor and later periods. All of these acts, in his view, deserved praise because they sought to strengthen the Church of England. And Whitgift and other archbishops had every right to impose conformity, Chandler said. In fact, the Puritans would have done the same thing if they were in power. "There was not a Puritan in the Kingdom at that Time," he wrote in 1769, "that if he had been armed with the like Power, he would have pressed Conformity to his own System, with as unrelenting Zeal, as either of those Prelates."[44]

Chandler's embrace of conformity and Elizabethan values had its limits, however. The America of 1760 was not the Tudor England of 1560, and Chandler did not see conformity as practical in the colonies. Dissenters made up three-quarters of the population in the thirteen colonies; in England, they made up fewer than one-tenth. In addition to large numbers of Presbyterians and Congregationalists—the two key dissenting groups in England—Germans and other Europeans, who possessed their own peculiar brand of Protestantism, were numerous in the colonies.[45]

The relative weakness of the Church of England in New Jersey and the middle colonies influenced Chandler's thinking as well. Dissenters dominated the religious scene in these colonies, putting Chandler on the defensive in the fight for an American episcopate and leading him to champion toleration in British America. Dissenters liked to cite the history of Tudor and Stuart England to explain why they would never agree to the seating of an Anglican bishop in the colonies. Chandler wondered how dissenters could ignore the flip side of this religious history—the rise of toleration in the seventeenth history. He repeatedly cited this history, asking a simple question of his episcopal foes: If dissenters had the right to practice their faith in the colonies, why should not the Church of England? It was only fair, Chandler argued, that the Anglican minority in the northern colonies be accorded the same rights that dissenters enjoyed in England.

Thus, despite his defense of conformity and Elizabethan church life, Chandler embraced toleration. He may have praised Whitgift and admired his principles, but Chandler stressed that he was "no Friend to Fines and Imprisonments on a religious Account." In 1774, he could even be found defending the Quebec Act, which among other things guaranteed that Roman Catholics could practice their faith in Canada and which removed the Protestant faith from the oath of allegiance to the Crown. The Quebec Act outraged American Whigs and Protestant dissenters, because they feared it was part of a British plot to strip Americans of their liberties and to establish the Catholic faith in Canada and points south. Chandler scoffed at these fears. He denied the Quebec Act established the Catholic church and he defended toleration for a Christian church that, in Protestants' views, had a long history of persecution and thus was outside the pale of seventeenth- and eighteenth-century notions of toleration.[46]

In the end, English religious history played a complex, and at times contradictory, role in shaping Chandler's mental world. The values of Tudor England undergirded his views of episcopacy, authority, and hierarchy, and they supplied him with the arguments he needed when composing his tracts in the 1760s and 1770s. During the bishop's campaign, he repeatedly cited the Tudor-era church to buttress his arguments on the importance of episcopacy to both society and the Crown.

His reading into Tudor history and later periods also meant that Chandler saw Puritans and Presbyterians as enemies who wanted to harm the king's church. Dissenters, in Chandler's mind, were cunning foes whose motives were nearly always suspect. Hence, Chandler believed Presbyterian plans to open a college in Elizabeth Town were part of a nefarious plot to suppress Anglicanism in the region. (Presbyterians and Congregationalists were just as paranoid about the Church of England because of *their* readings into Tudor and Stuart history.)

But dissenter history was valuable to Chandler in other ways: he liked to accuse his foes of hypocrisy because they favored toleration for English dissenters but not for American Anglicans. To his opponents, Chandler was the inconsistent one, because he defended conformity and praised Whitgift and Laud while urging toleration. They saw the two things as incompatible, and Chandler's full-throttled embrace of episcopacy told them all they needed to know about his values and motives. English history in the sixteenth and seventeenth centuries amply taught Congregationalists and Presbyterians about the tyranny of Anglican bishops and the established church.[47]

Chandler's foes were not far off the mark. As his library holdings and writings attest, Chandler's heart lay with these earlier periods. With the important exception of toleration, Tudor values were largely his values. And Chandler worked hard in the 1760s to teach American colonists about episcopacy, authority, and the value of a state church in a hierarchical society. This task, of course, proved to be a steep hill to climb in the years before the American Revolution, for he was up against powerful democratizing forces. More ominously for "Friends of Government," sterner challenges to British rule were fast coming.

CHAPTER 3

Time Traveler

*The Glorious Revolution and
the High Church Cause*

In Boston on the night of August 26, 1765, a mob infuriated by the Stamp Act descended on the mansion of Lieutenant Governor Thomas Hutchinson. Armed with axes, the rioters ripped the wainscoting from the walls, destroyed much of the furniture, and made off with anything they could carry, including £900 in cash and the Hutchinson family's clothes. By the time they were done in the morning, the mansion was in ruins. The attack, according to one observer, represented "savageness unknown in a civilized world."[1]

About two hundred miles south, in New York City on October 31, 1765, a crowd of laborers, artisans, and mariners broke windows and threatened to pull down the houses of those who supported the Stamp Act—the tax on printed paper passed by Parliament on March 22, 1765. An even bigger crowd the next day accused the governor of being the "Chief Murderer of their Rights and Privileges." They strung up an effigy of the governor, complete with a stamped paper in his hand, and gutted the home of British Major Thomas James, commander of the Sixtieth Regiment of the Royal Artillery, who had vowed to enforce the legislation by cramming the stamps down New Yorkers' throats.[2]

As such riotous scenes were repeated throughout the colonies, Thomas Bradbury Chandler worried that royal America itself was under assault. A spirit of rebellion was gaining in the colonies in the 1760s, and a dangerous new group called the Sons of Liberty was forming. The violence and the street protests were upsetting enough to this high church Anglican. But from his perch as a missionary for the Society for the Propagation of the Gospel,

Chandler saw something deeper and more alarming at work: the challenges to parliamentary authority and the spread of radicalism were symptomatic of a broader societal illness that bordered on madness, he believed.

"The duty of a missionary in this country," he informed the SPG in January 1766, has "now become more difficult than ever.... Such an universal spirit of clamor and discontent, little short of madness—and such an opinion of oppression, prevails throughout the colonies, as I believe was scarcely ever seen on any occasion in any country on earth." From Halifax to Georgia, he continued, the colonists were "determined never to submit to what they esteem so great an infringement of their essential rights, as some of the late Acts of the British Parliament."

Chandler believed shortsightedness in both Whitehall and Lambeth were contributing to the American crisis. Parliament was too aggressive in its efforts to collect revenue and ensure the colonists paid their fair share of the empire's defense; it should "relax of its severity," he wrote, which he conceded "will be no easy thing, after such provocations" on the colonists' part. Good policy, he instructed, would go a long way toward avoiding "a dangerous extremity." But church leaders had an opposite problem. They were too lethargic, Chandler complained; their failure to properly support the American branch of the Church of England was stoking the flames of colonial rebellion. "If the interest of the Church of England in America had been made a national concern according to the policy of all other nations, who had colonies," he explained, "by this time a general submission to the parent country ... might have been expected." But the leadership was continually refusing to send an American bishop. As a result, "who can be certain that the present rebellious disposition of the colonies is not intended by Providence as a punishment for that neglect?"[3]

Despite these criticisms, Chandler was unhappiest with his fellow colonists. Rioting was simply unacceptable. Subjects have the right to raise objections in a "respectful manner," Chandler conceded, "but they are bound, by the laws of Heaven and Earth, not to behave undutifully, much more not to behave insolently and rebelliously." As his readings, actions, and letters show, the tumult of the 1760s was causing Chandler to think deeper about the connections between religion and revolution and whether subjects have the right to rebel against government.[4]

To answer these important questions, Chandler again looked to English history, this time to the Glorious Revolution and its aftermath. For as important as Tudor England was to Chandler's intellectual development, the 1690s and early 1700s loomed even larger in his mind. Scattered throughout the shelves of Chandler's nearly two-thousand-volume library was a substantial collection of Whig and Tory writings on the Glorious Revolution and two tempests that followed King James II's exile: the protests of the nonjurors—the Church of England clergy who refused to take the oath of allegiance owed to William and Mary—and the Bangorian controversy. These episodes were central to Chandler's understanding of power and allegiance, and they infused his thinking on episcopacy, church-state relations, revolution, and the rights of dissenters.

He collected more than one hundred books and pamphlets on the Bangorian controversy and nonjurors' protests alone. Nearly as impressive was the number of Whig writings he acquired, including the works of John Locke and James Tyrrell, who in his *General History of England* defended the rights of the people to rebel. Chandler owned fourteen books by Benjamin Hoadly, a hero to American Whigs for his stand on individual conscience, and possessed at least another thirteen books answering Hoadly's arguments. Another one-hundred-plus books dealt with church powers, dissenters, and related controversies.[5]

Thus, like a time traveler, Thomas Bradbury Chandler visited the dramatic events of 1688 and 1689 from the comfort of his parsonage in Elizabeth Town. These studies, and the conclusions he drew from the Glorious Revolution about religion and revolution, went to the heart of the man, his monarchical beliefs, and his rejection of revolution and democracy.

THE GLORIOUS REVOLUTION

The subject of Chandler's fascination was a dramatic rebellion that began in the late fall of 1688.

On November 5—the eighty-third anniversary of the Gunpowder Plot, when Catholic conspirators tried to blow up Parliament—William of Orange came ashore at Torbay in Devon, England, bearing the banner "For liberty and the Protestant religion." With him were some fifteen thousand soldiers, four thousand cavalry, and nearly five hundred ships and troop transports, an invasion fleet four times larger than the Spanish armada a century earlier.[6]

With good reason, James II trembled, and not just out of fear of the Dutch invaders. William was in England at the invitation of the Catholic king's opponents, and the loyalty of James's army was uncertain after his three tumultuous years on the throne. Indeed, English defections to the Protestant William, a dour Calvinist who was a bitter foe of France, began almost immediately, grew steadily, and came to include James's youngest daughter, Anne, who detested her father's Catholic beliefs and did not want to see her younger half brother inherit the throne. With his support among the English populace crumbling, and his army and navy unwilling to fight for him, James lost his nerve. Under darkness on December 11, disguised as a servant, James and a Catholic supporter named Sir Edward Hales rode a skiff down the Thames, where the king threw the Great Seal of England into the river. They then made their way to Faversham, where some sailors recognized Hales (but not James) and took the small party into custody. Their captors delivered the two men to the Queen's Arms inn. There, someone realized that Hales's companion was no mere servant, and the king was returned to London. Nearly two weeks later, with the connivance of William, who wanted his rival gone and his path to the English Crown cleared, James "escaped" again and sailed for France and the protection of his powerful Catholic cousin Louis XIV.

Thus, in a few short weeks, William and his English conspirators successfully overthrew a monarch in a nearly bloodless rebellion that history has praised as a Glorious Revolution. The drama thrilled Whigs and their American supporters. The people, in their view, had triumphed over a tyrannical Stuart monarch, and the horror of a Catholic dynasty was averted. Conservatives had a different view. They were aghast that a traitorous Dutch usurper—William was James's son-in-law—had driven a lawful English monarch out of the country, and they considered William III an illegitimate king. Passive obedience, they pointedly reminded their Whig opponents, required subjects to submit to their monarch. For the next twenty years or so, they engaged Whigs in debate over the legality, and meaning, of the Glorious Revolution. This debate turned on two critical questions: When was it permissible for subjects to rebel? And was revolution ever justified?[7]

In a flood of books and pamphlets, the two sides poured out their answers. Some of England's greatest minds participated, including John Locke and Benjamin Hoadly on the Whig side and Henry Sacheverell and Francis Atterbury on the Tory. Through long, learned treatises that ranged from the witty to the dull, they stated their cases about obedience, the rights of subjects, the duties of a king, and revolution.

The seeds of this revolution were planted when Charles II died in 1685. Upon his passing, his younger brother James, the second son of Charles I, became king. James inherited the worst instincts of his Stuart forebears: he was an inept politician who possessed the singular ability to antagonize Parliament.

He sought to reassert absolute monarchy by divine right—the Stuarts' motto was "Not by the desires of men but by the will of God"—appointed Roman Catholics to government positions, demanded a larger army, and pressed for toleration for dissenters and Catholics.

The latter cause was especially offensive to high church Anglicans. Anti-Catholicism remained strong in England at the end of the seventeenth century, and James's brother, Charles II, had done much to enflame it by pursuing pro-Catholic policies during his twenty-five years on the throne. He wanted to align England's foreign policy with Catholic France, and he tried to create an alliance of dissenters and Catholics that would have the power to check the Church of England and its supporters. English Protestants still feared Catholics even though the Church of England was nearly two centuries old in 1700. England's enemies, especially France and Spain, represented popery and absolute monarchy, and Protestants worried that the Stuarts—Charles II, a reputed Catholic, and James II, a true Catholic—wanted the same for England. Parliament, as a result, in the early 1680s debated who should succeed Charles as it considered passing a bill that would exclude a Catholic from inheriting the throne. But the choices were problematic. James was Charles's son and was Duke of Marlborough, but he was illegitimate and a Catholic. Given the lack of alternatives, Parliament felt it had no right to intercede; if it did, it might plunge the country into a new civil war. And so the exclusion bill failed and James became king in 1685 upon the death of his brother. Nevertheless, the succession problem remained a subject of dispute, and the pressures continued to build as James pursued his Catholic and absolutist aims.

When James's wife, Mary, gave birth to a Catholic son who would be first in line to become king, Anglicans feared the worst. The horror of "bloody" Mary Tudor's reign in the mid-sixteenth century remained fresh in Protestant memory, and Anglicans worried that England would face a period of unlimited Catholic rule. Seven leading Protestants, including the Bishop of London, urged William of Orange—who was married to James's daughter Mary—to invade England, and assured him that his intervention would enjoy wide support. William agreed to for reasons he did not specify, but Dutch officials stressed the importance to Holland of keeping England a Protestant nation and in the anti-France coalition that William was leading. Lacking support in Parliament, among the public, and in the army, James barely put up a fight and scurried to France at the earliest opportunity. William became king, with Mary as his queen.

Most Englishmen celebrated James's ouster as glorious because no kingly heads were lost, unlike in 1649 when parliamentary forces executed Charles I. England had been saved from popery. But a vocal minority of Englishmen disagreed. They protested that the ouster of James II and the meddling of Parliament were wrong, even illegal. The ensuing controversies over these events fascinated Chandler because the debate raised momentous questions about monarchy, revolution, the rights of subjects, and the state church's place in society.

The first controversy involved the "nonjurors," Latin from *juro* meaning to swear an oath. The origins of this controversy lay in what, exactly, transpired when a defeated James withdrew to France. Did he abdicate the throne, leaving it vacant for someone to fill? Or did the king flee with the intention of returning to England to fight another day and reclaim his crown? James's foes, of course, believed he had abdicated and that Parliament had the right to appoint a new monarch. Tories disagreed. James's flight, the Earl of Pembroke explained, was no "more than a man's running out of his house when on fire, or a seaman's throwing his goods overboard in a storm, to save his life, which could never be understood as a renunciation of his house or goods." The two chambers of Parliament called a convention on January 22, 1689, to decide how the kingdom should proceed with James on the European continent. Six days later, the Commons passed a resolution declaring that King James, having subverted the constitution on "the advice of Jesuits and other wicked persons . . . and having withdrawn himself out of this kingdom, has abdicated the government; and that the throne is hereby vacant." But the Tory-dominated House of Lords was not convinced that James had abdicated. For Tories, a parliamentary declaration that the Crown was vacant would violate the laws of hereditary succession. Worse, letting Parliament choose a monarch would turn England into an elective kingdom. Convention members also spent considerable time debating whether Parliament should offer the Crown to William or Mary, or to both. As the convention pondered these issues of state, and with William and his large army in England, France declared war on the United Provinces, and William became impatient with the slow pace of the discussions. He wanted the convention to make a decision quickly so he could secure England's help in fending off a possible French invasion of Holland. William thus told a small gathering of peers that he wanted to be king and would not act as a mere consort to Mary; he also warned the peers that he would return to Holland with his army if Parliament did not accede to his demands, leaving England exposed to attack. (This was no empty threat;

Whigs feared that if the Dutch troops left, France would attack England in a bid to restore James to the throne.) To soften this ultimatum, William agreed to share the Crown with his wife. The convention promptly voted in February that James had abdicated, and that William and Mary were to rule jointly as king and queen, although William would hold the real power.[8]

Conservatives were upset with the convention's decision, believing that no parliamentary body had the right to appoint a monarch. Only God, through hereditary succession, could. The coronation of William and Mary on April 11, 1689, presented them with a terrible moral dilemma. They had sworn oaths of allegiance to James and believed they could not in good conscience swear new oaths to monarchs who had come to the throne in such a devious manner. The first Stuart king, James I, explained as well as anyone why an oath was binding: "The duty and alleagance, which the people sweareth to their prince, is not only bound to themselves, but likewise to their ... lawfull heires.... No objection ... may free the people from their oath-giving to their king, and his succession." Parliament tried to assuage the nonjurors' concerns by having Bishop Thomas White of Peterborough draw up an oath of allegiance that did not require the swearer to declare that William and Mary were the "rightful and lawful" rulers. Instead, they merely had to promise to be faithful to the king and queen. The parliamentary bill approving this language required all clergy, schoolmasters, and university faculty to take the oaths by August 1, 1689. If they did not, they would first face suspension and then loss of office.[9]

Nine Anglican bishops, including White, refused to take the compromise oath, with one nonjuror lambasting it as a "Party Crime" imposed by "the pretended Authority." A watered-down oath, in their view, could not gloss over the fact that William and Mary had invaded England, had driven off the reigning king, and were occupying Whitehall illegally. These nine bishops, all members of the high church wing of the Church of England, were joined by about four hundred other clerics, a majority of bishops in Scotland, and one bishop in Ireland. Supporters of William and Mary saw their refusal to support the Crown as both illegal and treasonous, given the convention's decision that James had abdicated the throne, and they deprived them of their livings. Their ouster spawned further controversy as the combatants argued over the legality of the move and whether the nonjurors' replacements were themselves legitimate. The controversy dragged on into the eighteenth century when a number of Anglican clergy refused to accept the accession of the Hanoverians in 1714.[10]

FIG. 4 William Hogarth, *Benjamin Hoadly, Bishop of Winchester*, 1741. Hoadly had sparked the Bangorian controversy years earlier with his sweeping attacks on the powers of the institutional church and the exaltation of the laity. Photo © Tate.

Both sides published lengthy pamphlets, and a "Jacobite" party arose, whose goal was to return the Stuarts to the English throne. At least fifty of these books on the nonjurors, including works by the leading combatants, found their way onto Chandler's shelves. Two of the most important authors were Benjamin Hoadly (1676–1761) and Charles Leslie (1650–1722).

Hoadly was an Anglican reformer and latitudinarian who opposed the high church's efforts after the Stuart restoration in 1660 to crack down on dissent. He wanted "comprehension"—to recast the Church of England as a truly national church that would embrace all Protestants rather than excluding those who refused to conform to its liturgy and doctrines. He supported the Glorious Revolution and believed in Parliament's right to install—or depose—a monarch. The nonjurors' rejection of subjects' right to rebellion, and their defense of passive obedience, offended him.[11]

In 1709, Hoadly, Leslie, and others debated the nature of authority. Leslie was a nonjuror who defended divine-right monarchy and passive obedience. In his *Constitution, Laws, and Government of England, Vindicated*, Leslie ridiculed the idea that subjects and their representatives in Parliament had the right to anoint a monarch. "You Set up the Crown like the Goal to Prison-hase, the best Runner carries it," Leslie wrote. "That if a *Jack Straw* with his *Mob* should Surprize *Whitehall*, Seize the King, and Usurp the Government, it is all his own." Leslie then laid out the high church view of English political and constitutional history to demonstrate that the king was supreme over Parliament and its mobs. From the nation's earliest days, Parliament existed only at the king's forbearance, Leslie stated. Parliaments "were Call'd by *Kings*, and all the *Authority* that they have is Deriv'd wholly and solely from the *Crown*." Milton, Locke, Sydney, and other theorists "who place the *Original* of *Government*, in the *People*" mistakenly claimed that the House of Commons was original and essential to the constitution—a "blasphemous" idea, Leslie declared. Although the Lords and Commons were an accepted part of the Constitution by 1700, they had not always been. "The *Lords* are all made by the *King*, and were his *Great Council* long before the *Commons* were taken in."[12]

In an argument that rebellious Americans would have to grapple with in the 1770s, Leslie maintained that sovereignty could not be divided. If supreme authority rests with the Crown, "then can it not be *Limited* by *Parliament*.... Allegiance is due to the *King*, and to him *Alone*. [There] can be no Sharing of this *Supremacy*." Leslie sneered at the idea that Parliament could act as a judge over the supreme authority, the monarchy. When it did such a thing at various points in English history, it did so illegally in violation of the constitution. A prominent example occurred during the commonwealth, when the Commons killed not only Charles I but the constitution by illegally seizing power. "The Prevailing *Faction* in that House of *Commons*, having first *Grabled* their own *House* . . . got the first of the three Estates, the *Bishops*, turn'd out of the *House* of *Lords*. And soon after Discarded, by their own Authority, all the *Temporal Lords*, and took the whole *Government* into their own Hands, thus totally subverting the *Constitution*."[13]

From there, Leslie turned to his main point: Parliament, acting on behalf of the people, cannot place someone on the throne. Such a thing was unnatural, and against all reason, in a divinely ordered universe. "GOD made *Kings*, and *Kings* made *Parliaments*," he said. William and Mary's supporters said the new monarchs were owed allegiance because they had successfully overthrown the reigning monarch and thus extinguished the Stuarts' claim to the throne. But that was impossible, Leslie responded. A de facto king, placed on the throne by the people and holding it by force, was a "usurper" who was *not* owed allegiance because his accession was illegal.[14]

Mere possession of the throne, as some of William's supporters argued, does not make it legal, Leslie continued. "The Relation betwixt *King* and *Subject* is not to be Dissolved barely by *Possession*, more than that of *Parent* and *Child*," Leslie wrote. Children owe allegiance to their parents under all circumstances, and subjects owe their king allegiance for the same reason. In fact, Leslie said, kings' claims to allegiance are even greater than parents' because of the monarchy's divine origins. "*Kings* Represent the person of *God* to Us more than our Natural *Parents*, who are not call'd *Gods*, and the *Anointed* of *God*, as *Kings* are." Again turning to biblical and English history, Leslie said authority was both paternalistic and patriarchal; it flowed downward from God to the king, not upward from the people.[15]

Leslie's arguments echoed those of other nonjurors, whose views in turn rested on high church notions of patriarchy and monarchy. Such notions owed much to a preeminent theorist of royal absolutism, and a favorite of Chandler's and other loyalists, the Cambridge-educated baronet Robert Filmer. For Filmer, monarchical authority was an outgrowth of the natural authority that parents, specifically fathers, held over children, and he said this God-ordained authority had been handed down since the earliest days of human existence.

Filmer laid out his case in his classic, but controversial, *Patriarcha: or the Natural Power of Kings*, which he reportedly began writing in the 1620s and finished shortly before the first Civil War broke out in 1642; the book was published posthumously in 1680, was embraced by Leslie and other high church advocates, and drew fierce counterattacks from John Locke, Algernon Sydney, and others. Its premise was twofold: "The greatest Liberty in the World (if it be duly considered) is for a people to live under a Monarchy," and monarchy was the only viable form of government. Filmer built his argument on biblical history, beginning with Adam, whom he considered the first king. God created Adam first, before Eve, and the timing was crucial, Filmer said: "If Adam and Eve had been both created at once, it could not have been known which of these two were to command, and which to obey," he wrote. "For Adam's strength would have given him no authority.... And when they had Children betwixt them; the Children could as little have told which of the Parents they should have obeyed." But God created Adam first, Filmer said, and from Adam came Eve. As the Apostles noted, Filmer said, God made Adam superior to Eve: "She was made in a state of subjection to her Husband, and he very well understood it when he gave her a Name, which was a mark of his Sovereignty and Dominion."

Male dominion, specifically patriarchal dominion, over women and children flowed from this moment, as did something more elemental, according to Filmer. Children must obey their fathers; inferiors must obey their superiors. Kings, he continued, were the fathers of their people, and as the supreme father, he has a natural right to lead society. So for Filmer, there was but one conclusion: "This subjection of Children [was] the Fountain of all *Regal Authority*, by the Ordination of God himself."[16]

The natural rights of a father were the exact same as those of a king, Filmer continued, "but only in the Latitude or Extent of them: as the Father over one Family, so the King as Father over many Families extends his care to preserve, feed, Cloath, instruct, and defend the whole Commonwealth." Monarchy, he declared, reflected the natural order of things and was God's will: "God shewed his Opinion, when he endued not onely Men, but all Creatures with a Natural Propensity to Monarchy," he wrote. And "do we not find, that in every Family, the Government of One Alone, is most Natural?"[17]

Monarchy was so superior to other forms of government, Filmer continued, that it must be absolute. Otherwise, the alternative was democracy, a chaotic form of governance that bred mischief, disorder, and violence. "No Government can be maintained where the party governed hath a right to resist his Superior or Governor," he said. To those who believed the king's subjects possessed the right to resist a tyrannical ruler, Filmer responded that human nature made rebellion a nonstarter because "the Nature of all People is, to desire Liberty without Restraint." A mixed government, with the people represented in a parliamentary body, was unworkable for the same reason, he said. "The Vanity of this Fancy is too evident, it is a meer Impossibility or Contradiction," he wrote, "for if a King doth but once admit the People to be his Companions, he leaves to be a King, and the State becomes a Democracy."[18]

Sovereignty, as a result, cannot be divided, Filmer said. The monarch must be supreme, and Filmer relegated parliaments to advisory roles—legislative bodies that "but only do deliberate and advise their Supreme Head, who still reserved the Absolute power in himself."[19]

Hoadly heatedly disagreed with Leslie and Filmer. In his *The Original and Institution of Civil Government*, Hoadly denied that monarchy was "*absolute* and *uncontrollable*, not to be forfeited by any Misbehavior; not to be resisted or opposed on any Account" simply because the institution was made by God himself.[20]

Hoadly said the entire patriarchal edifice built on the story of Adam and Eve was unscriptural, even silly, and he called the nonjurors' rejection of rebellion morally indefensible. If power rested only in male hands, Hoadly asked, what do we make of biblical admonitions for children to obey their parents, plural, and not their parent, singular? "Why, as it hath been decreed already, in this *Scheme* that *Honour thy Mother* shall signify no more than *Honour thy Mother* as far as thy *Father* will command, or permit thee," Hoadly wrote.

Thus the husband's power was not absolute, nor was Adam's, and Jesus and St. Paul never spoke of their power as absolute.[21]

Hoadly also ridiculed the idea that subjects owed unlimited obedience to good and evil rulers alike, and that God had supposedly sanctioned both. "Can any one say, that a *Prince* cannot have Authority to do Good without having *Authority* to do Mischief? Whence can he have this *Authority*?" Hoadly wondered. "Not from *God*, because He cannot commission to anything that is Evil." Hoadly argued that civil authority rested on the consent of the governed, and the governed can withdraw this consent: "*Active Obedience* cannot possibly be intended to signify *absolutely*, or extend to *all* Cases," he exclaimed. For Hoadly, the implication was clear: resistance to unlawful authority was legitimate.

In making such arguments, Hoadly was relying on John Locke (1632–1704) and Richard Hooker, the Tudor-era theologian who maintained that government was a voluntary compact between people and ruler. Locke wrote his famous *Two Treatises of Government* (published in 1689), which Chandler owned, as an angry response to Filmer's arguments. Locke, too, ridiculed Filmer's assertion that parental authority was the basis of regal power, and that parental authority rested only on patriarchal power. But Locke was equally contemptuous of Filmer's championing of monarchy and absolute power. Such views could mean only one thing, Locke wrote: "We are all born slaves, and we must continue so," because Filmer placed a ruler above the law, beyond challenge from his subjects. After attacking Filmer's *Patriarcha* line by line in book 1, Locke in book 2 laid out his famous views of natural rights and contract theory that proved to be so influential with Whigs (but not with Chandler and other high church Anglicans).[22]

Hoadly and his allies thus drew on the arguments of Locke and Hooker to make their case that the Glorious Revolution was legitimate and William and Mary wore their crowns lawfully. The nonjurors, Hoadly concluded, were the ones acting unlawfully because they denied the authority of a government sanctioned by the parliamentary convention and ultimately English society.[23]

The nonjurors' protests went beyond the accession of William and Mary. They also were unhappy that the Glorious Revolution spawned a growing toleration of dissenters both within and outside the Church of England. In 1689, Parliament approved the Toleration Act, permitting all Christians but Roman Catholics to have their own houses of worship, ministers, and teachers. Dissenters still could not hold political office, and they were still required to take oaths of allegiance, but the passage of the Toleration Act signaled a historic shift in British society toward more religious diversity.[24]

Hoadly was a leader in a post-1689 latitudinarian movement that pressed for comprehension within the Church of England. In 1703, he published a book that occupied an important spot on Chandler's shelves: *Reasonableness of Conformity to the Church of England*, an impassioned plea for the established church to be more welcoming to Protestants of divergent beliefs. The state church should not divide into warring wings or camps over petty disputes involving doctrine; it should be tolerant of a variety of views, Hoadly argued. He wanted the church to embrace adiaphora—an understanding that some things were of little consequence and not worth arguing over. Such a welcoming position, he believed, would strengthen, not weaken, the Church of England by encouraging dissenters to worship in its chapels instead of breaking away to form their own congregations.[25]

Such thinking appalled the nonjurors. Henry Sacheverell (1674–1724), a high church cleric, was the most forceful opponent of toleration, seeing such permissiveness as both harming the cause of state religion and encouraging resistance to authority. In an explosive sermon delivered on November 5, 1709—the anniversary of the 1605 Gunpowder Plot and the landing of William at Torbay in 1688—Sacheverell derided Hoadly and the latitudinarians as "schimismatical impostors" and "False Brethren" who were traitors to their church. He called comprehension in the Church of England a "Spurious, and Villainous Notion, which will take in Jews, Quakers, Mahometans, and anything as well as Christians." The end result, Sacheverell warned, would be to "Undermine the very Essential Constitution of Our Church."[26]

Because of latitudinarians' treasonous behavior, Sacheverell continued, the Anglican Church had seen its "Pure Doctrine . . . Corrupted and Defil'd; her Primitive Worship and Discipline Profan'd and Abus'd; . . . Her Altars and Sacraments Prostituted to Hypocrites, Deists, Socians, and atheists."

Sacheverell traced these evils to the Glorious Revolution and the damning beliefs of Whigs and latitudinarians that resistance to authority was legal. "The Grand Security of our Government, and the very Pillar upon which it stands," he said, "is founded on the steady Belief of the Subject's Obligation to [an] Absolute, and Unconditional Obedience to the Supreme Power in All Things Lawful, and the utter Illegality of Resistance upon any Pretence whatsoever." Consider what would happen if "the People [were allowed] to Judge and Dethrone their Sovereigns, for any Cause they think fit," Sacheverell told his audience. No monarch, and no constitution, would be safe from the "Vipours in our Bosom," he warned.[27]

Sacheverell's sermon posed a serious challenge to the latitudinarians. He delivered it at St. Paul's Cathedral, the seat of the Bishop of London and the heart of Anglican power. The sermon sold widely—some forty thousand copies. Its popularity, combined with Sacheverell's fierce attack on the Glorious Revolution and an increasingly moderate Church of England, forced Hoadly and other Whigs to respond, as did the House of Commons itself, which impeached Sacheverell for his impertinence. His trial in the Lords lasted nearly a month, as the opposing sides debated the doctrines of comprehension, resistance, and obedience. The vote to convict was relatively close, sixty-nine to fifty-two. But the Lords did not send Sacheverell to prison or fine him. Instead, they ordered his sermons burned and suspended him from the pulpit for three years. Whigs were outraged at this show of leniency and high church Tories were ecstatic. Emboldened, the latter burned Hoadly in effigy and forced a parliamentary election in the waning months of 1710. The Tories won, boosted by a nine-county tour that Sacheverell undertook on the party's behalf.[28]

As with the nonjuring controversy, the debate interested Chandler for an obvious reason: the trial of Sacheverell focused on the issues of passive obedience, resistance to civil power, and toleration, three core interests of Chandler's. Hoadly, again, was a key combatant, writing twelve tracts about Sacheverell and pressing his claim that religious toleration and unity were essential if Britain were to escape Jacobitism and Catholicism and if the Church of England were to thrive in the new century. Sacheverell's defenders excoriated Hoadly for championing democracy in which the people would be "the source of power and justice." American radicals were also intensely interested in the Sacheverell affair. For them, the episode was another appalling example of high church extremism and the dangers that Anglicanism posed to religious freedom and republicanism.[29]

Chandler had a far different, and more nuanced, view of the debate than did his American Whig rivals. Living a half century after this intellectual duel, in a fractious colony overrun by dissenters, he well understood the dangers that Sacheverell highlighted. A cacophony of voices led to religious strife and to challenges to episcopal authority. Dissenters on both sides of the Atlantic, Chandler understood all too well, wanted nothing to do with bishops. Thus he believed that Sacheverell's argument was indisputable. Nevertheless he *was* sympathetic to Hoadly's pleas for comprehension. Chandler wanted a bigger and stronger Church of England in the colonies, one that would be home to a variety of Protestants. As a missionary in New Jersey, he was working hard to try to make that happen. Chandler, however, envisioned a limited comprehension that, while welcoming more people into the state church, would preserve bishops' powers and keep laymen in their place. He agreed with the nonjurors that Hoadly's arguments would ultimately empower ordinary worshipers and weaken the institutional church. Chandler feared the same of John Locke's treatises, which were so popular among Whigs in England and America. Locke posited that individuals possessed the ability to interpret Scripture for themselves and to achieve salvation on their own. Weakened religious institutions necessarily followed in a religious world populated not by a single state church led by powerful bishops but by laymen seeking their own answers about God. For Chandler, these were dangerous arguments that had to be refuted.[30]

THE BANGORIAN CONTROVERSY

Hoadly's duels with the nonjurors over the meaning of the Glorious Revolution did not settle the question of when inferiors could challenge their superiors. Nor did it settle the question of comprehension in the state church. Instead, the fight grew even more intense after Hoadly delivered a sermon on March 31, 1717, that his opponents viewed as an all-out assault on episcopal authority and the Church of England. An outpouring of pamphlets and broadsides followed; in July 1717 alone, seventy-four tracts were published on the Bangorian controversy. One Anglican bishop looking back at the debate reduced the thousands of pages spilled to a simple division—one side "was for liberty, however they would [choose] to employ it; and the other for power however they would come at it." Other observers were not so kind about this expenditure of ink and paper. In 1727, John Wesley, the future founder of Methodism, found much of the debate tedious, especially the duel between Hoadly and high church champion Francis Atterbury. Wesley confessed that he tried to read up on the controversy but had to "break off in the middle, I could not conceive the dignity of the end was at all proportioned to the difficulty of attaining it." Chandler heartily disagreed, as his extensive library holdings on the Bangorian controversy attest. The issues raised were worthy of intense study.[31]

Despite years of debate over the Glorious Revolution and the nonjurors' rejection of rebellion, Hoadly's sermon elicited shock because of his sweeping attacks on the powers of the institutional church and the exaltation of the laity. The sermon began innocently enough. The Bishop of Bangor examined the meaning of "the Church of Christ." At one time, Hoadly said, the phrase referred only to those believers who followed Jesus. Now, he said, it meant that Jesus was "the sole law-giver to his subjects, and himself the sole Judge of their behavior in the affairs of conscience and eternal salvation." Jesus, Hoadly continued, "left behind no visible human authority; no viceregents who can be said properly to supply his place; no interpreters upon whom his subjects are absolutely to depend." Jesus, in other words, left no organizational body—no church institution—to act in his place. For Hoadly, Christ's individual followers and not the institutional church were the best judges of the Bible and of Christ's teachings. "All his subjects, in what station so ever they be, are equally subjects to Him," Hoadly declared. Hoadly's argument that individuals were perfectly capable of interpreting the Bible themselves meant that the institutional church did not necessarily possess superior wisdom in divining God's teachings. Hoadly then carried this insight to its logical conclusion: a church's claim that its creeds, liturgy, and doctrines were superior to those of its rivals was incorrect.[32]

Hoadly attacked the power of the state church from a second direction through his doctrine of "sincerity," which posited that the state church—or any "visible" church for that matter—cannot coerce people into coming to Jesus Christ, nor could it force individuals into being righteous. Spiritual beliefs, he said, had to be genuinely felt; worshipers had to possess an inner sincerity in matters of faith and in their commitment to God. Thus, said Hoadly, it was wrong for overbearing state churches to compel attendance and to enforce doctrinal purity on members with different beliefs. Instead, he advised, visible churches should be warm, welcoming places that embraced people who held differing theological views of baptism, salvation, and other core Christian beliefs. This argument built on his earlier calls for comprehension, adiaphora, and peaceableness; the state church should not divide into warring wings over petty disputes involving doctrine.[33]

The high church wing of the Church of England was horrified anew by Hoadly's latest arguments, and the first retaliatory strikes against Hoadly came from Alexander Innes and Andrew Snape. The latter, who was headmaster of Eton, homed in on Hoadly's assertion that mere humans did not have the power to impose penalties on spiritual issues. In Hoadly's misguided view, "Christ's kingdom is not of this world," Snape wrote, "and none of the 'engines of this world' are to be employed either for or against his subjects."

As a result, Snape warned, Hoadly's doctrines would destroy church authority and all laws imposed on matters of faith or conscience, including those aimed at the Catholic Church. Hoadly, in turn, reacted with indignation to Snape's line of reasoning, claiming that Snape and others were twisting his words. "I not only do not own such consequences, but I really do not see them," he said in denying that he wanted to destroy the Church of England. But Hoadly did not back down on the importance of individual faith: "As for the Church of England [and its doctrines], I regard it as a noble claim of the right of Christians to judge for themselves."[34]

The nonjuror William Law, who refused to declare allegiance to George I in 1714, was one of Hoadly's fiercest foes in the Bangorian controversy and a defender of Snape. Law wrote in a letter to the Bishop of Bangor that Snape was hardly alone in his interpretation of Hoadly's writings. "When Dr. Snape represents your Lordship as no friend to the good Orders, and necessary Institutions of the Church," Law said, "you complain of the ill arts of an adversary, who sets you out in false colours. . . . But, my Lord, in this Dr. Snape only thinks with those who would be counted your best Friends, and would no longer be your Friends, but they conclude you have declared against the Authority of the Church."[35]

Law published *Three Letters to the Bishop of Bangor* in which he called Hoadly's views on sincerity a threat to both the Church of England and Christianity itself, for "not only sincere Quakers, Ranters, Muggletonians, and Fifth Monarchy-Men, are as much in the Favour of God, as any of the Apostles; but likewise sincere Jews, Turks and Deists." Law warned of a second consequence of Hoadly's view of sincerity: "If the Favour of God equally follows every equal Degree of Sincerity, then it is impossible there should be any difference, either as to Merit or Happiness, between a sincere Martyr and a sincere Persecutor; and he that burns the Christian, if he be but in earnest, has the same Title to a Reward for it, as he that is burnt for believing in Christ."

Law reminded Hoadly that he was a bishop in the Church of England and was betraying his own institution. "You openly expose our Communion, and give up all the advantages of it, by telling all sorts of People, if they are but sincere in their own Way, they are as much in God's Favour as anybody else," Law scolded. "Is this supporting our Interest, my Lord?"

Like other nonjurors and high church polemicists, Law rejected the idea that ordinary people could be on an equal footing with their superiors. In fact, the very idea horrified Law because if one carried Hoadly's sincerity doctrine to its logical conclusion, any believer would be equal to a bishop or minister, and all differences between the two would be erased. "For if Regularity of Ordination and Uninterrupted Succession be mere Trifles, and nothing," Law explained, "then all the Difference betwixt us and other Teachers, must be nothing: for they can differ from us in no other respects."

To dispense with apostolic succession, Law wrote, would mean that Hoadly's servant could ordain a minister or baptize an infant. Could anything be more absurd? Law asked. "Should a private Person choose a Lord Chancellor, and declare his Authority good; would there be anything but Absurdity, Impudence and Presumption in it?" Law certainly grasped an important implication of Hoadly's philosophy: his belief that every man had the right to judge Scripture for himself led to the views of Thomas Paine, who declared in *The Age of Reason* in 1794 that "my own mind is my own church," and of Robert Bellah, a sociologist of religion who argued in a 1985 book that individual conscience is the standard for religious truth.[36]

The debate between Law and Hoadly thus transcended arguments over ecclesiastical government. Law defended hierarchy in church and state, divine right for the Crown, and episcopal authority for the visible church. For him, lay rights was an oxymoron, as was the notion that the church was a voluntary body consisting of devout individuals. Hoadly, of course, argued the opposite. Like the Puritans, he saw the church as a community of believers. Compulsion held no place in Hoadly's world. Church participation was voluntary, and a person should attend only because he or she believed. Nor did Hoadly have any patience for hierarchy and the extensive powers for the church that the high church wing claimed. Hoadly believed Law's vision was obsolete in a post-1689 world. Kings no longer ruled by divine right, Hoadly pointed out.

A committee appointed by the church's Lower House of Convocation agreed with Law, concluding that Hoadly wanted to do away with ecclesiastical authority and church government. The committee saw Hoadly's sermon and writings as a direct attack on the episcopal structure of the Church of England. Moreover, the committee worried that Hoadly's stance would also undercut royal supremacy and Parliament's right to intervene in church matters. The result of all this, the committee warned, would mean there were "no governors left" in the church and the kingdom of Christ would be "reduced to a mere state of anarchy."[37]

Hoadly, however, had a powerful ally in a powerful position: King George I, who held Hoadly in high regard because of his rejection of the nonjurors' arguments and his impassioned defense of the Hanoverians, who came to power in England in 1714 when Queen Anne died without issue and the Stuarts challenged the accession of this German-based dynasty. George prorogued the convocation in November 1717 and again in February 1718 before it could approve the committee's report. The silencing of the convocation did not end the Bangorian controversy, however. High church members remained fearful of the threat posed by Hoadly and the Whigs to the Church of England, and the pamphlet war ground on.[38]

Francis Atterbury considered Hoadly the most detested clergyman in England—which was true enough among high church Tories but not among Whigs. Hoadly was a hero to many colonists in British America, especially in New England. One admirer was Jonathan Mayhew of Boston, a Harvard graduate and radical Congregational preacher, who recalled that while growing up in Massachusetts, Sydney, Milton, Locke, and Hoadly inculcated the "doctrines of civil liberty" in him. When Mayhew was writing his 1750 tract justifying resistance, *Discourse Concerning Unlimited Submission*, he drew on the arguments Hoadly used against Leslie. Americans of a radical bent thus saw Hoadly as an ardent champion of democracy and a determined foe of hierarchy, centralized religious authority, and religious persecution.[39]

Hoadly's views also influenced many of Chandler's fellow American Episcopal clergy, men who in 1775 blanched at the prospect of taking up arms against the king. Jacob Duché (1737–1798), rector of Christ Church in Philadelphia whom Chandler knew, embraced the individualist strain in Hoadly's philosophy. A benevolent God, Duché believed, gave individuals the free will to think for themselves, and this free will made individuals responsible to God for their actions. He wanted *via media*—a middle way between extremism and anarchy, dogmatism and deism.[40]

The printer, inventor, and Enlightenment thinker Benjamin Franklin, too, embraced a middle way in religion that merged rationalism and traditional Christianity. Like Hoadly, Franklin saw religion as something very personal. In his "Silence Dogood" essays, he mocked state-supported churches and "hypocritical pretenders to religion" that he believed such established churches produced. By the mid-eighteenth century, many of Hoadly's views were advancing in British America. Faith was an individual decision between man and his God, and religion could not be coerced, Enlightened thinkers believed. "The legitimate powers of government extend to such acts only as injurious to others," Thomas Jefferson observed in his *Notes on Virginia*. "But it does me no injury for my neighbor to say there are twenty gods, or no God. It neither picks my pocket nor breaks my leg." In short, said Jefferson and other intellectual heirs of Hoadly, "reason and free inquiry" must replace coercion.[41]

Such thinking alarmed Chandler. His takeaway from his study of the Glorious Revolution, including the Bangorian controversy, was that a pre-1688 world was superior to what Jefferson, Hoadly, and others wanted: Kings led, and subjects followed. The church, overseen by bishops, supported the state, and the king supported the church. Dissenters worshipped at the forbearance of the state establishment. Order reigned, and the people knew their place. The individualism that Benjamin Hoadly championed in the wake of the Glorious Revolution had little place in Chandler's world. And adiaphora posed dangers because it could undercut the true church—the Church of England—although Chandler understood that tolerating theological divisions (along with a carefully defined comprehension) had the potential to bring in more worshipers to Anglicanism.

Chandler's extensive review of the 1688–1720 period refined his views on church-state relations and the importance of hierarchy. He agreed that Hoadly went too far in placing so much power in the hands of the laity. In a 1771 sermon, Chandler reminded his listeners that "surely something more must be due to the clergy than to Christians of the lowest degree; for as has been observed, they are the most important members of the mystical body of Christ, without whose functions the body must soon perish." Chandler lamented that such a view was an unpopular one in the colonies. "We [ministers] are not forward to speak on this subject, nor to say what we esteem to be our just rights," Chandler exclaimed, "in an age wherein the least intimation of our claiming superior respect or kindness, on account of our stations in the church, is so liable to be treated as priestcraft."[42]

Chandler's views of patriarchy and authority owed a particularly large debt to Robert Filmer. In *The American Querist*, Chandler asked "whether some degree of respect be not always due from inferiors to superiors, and especially from children to parents, and whether the refusal of this on any occasion, be not a violation of the general laws of society, to say nothing here of the obligations of religion and morality?" From there, Chandler concluded that the relationship of Great Britain and the colonies was that of parent to child, and no parent "can put up with such disrespectful and abusive treatment from children, as Great-Britain has lately received from her colonies."[43]

Among his clerical colleagues, Chandler was not alone in his admiration of Filmer, the monarchist whom Whigs reviled. Jonathan Boucher defended Filmer against Locke's attacks, saying "I have lately perused the book [*Patriarcha*], and did not find it deserving of all that extreme contempt with which it is now the fashion to mention." In language similar to Chandler's, Boucher stated that Filmer's views made perfect sense. "Filmer's opinion is, that every human being is born the political subject of some other human being; that infants, the moment they are born, are the natural subjects of their parents; and that the State, or supreme power of any country, is the parent, or in the place of a parent, to all who are born within its jurisdiction, entitled to their allegiance, but bound to provide for their guardianship."[44]

Chandler, however, in his writings neither endorsed the Glorious Revolution nor rejected it. He knew that it had broad support among American colonists and that its achievements by the mid-eighteenth century were almost universally accepted throughout the English-speaking world. Given this popularity, Chandler chose his words carefully. He, for example, defended the state's right to establish a national church, but qualified it by adding that the Crown must protect the rights of dissenters. "Establishments, without a toleration of Dissenters, are intirely out of the Question," Chandler proclaimed. Nevertheless, "the Magistrate has a Right to give some peculiar Countenance and Encouragement, to what he esteems to be the true Religion.... And I will venture to add, that he was a Right to shew *as much* Favour to his Religion, as is necessary to support it, and is consistent with a full and free Toleration." In another instance, Chandler called King William III, whom the nonjurors rejected as an illegitimate monarch, "the immortal and true patron both of civil and ecclesiastical liberty."[45]

But such gracious praise of William came only in 1775, when Chandler was trying to head off a rebellion against the king. In his published writings, he wanted to appear reasonable so that he could win over public opinion. Chandler's clerical allies, too, were mindful of the great popularity of the Glorious Revolution—and of the unpopularity of high church principles among Whigs. When Charles Inglis anonymously published a tract condemning Thomas Paine's *Common Sense* in 1776, he denied that he was an Anglican clergyman or a "tory." He assured readers "that I am none of your *passive obedience and non-resistance men*. The principles on which the glorious Revolution in 1688 was brought about, constitute the articles of my political creed."[46]

In addition, Chandler distanced himself from Jacobitism, another discredited political movement that dated to the Glorious Revolution. When he campaigned for an American episcopate in the 1760s, his Whig foes warned that "Nonjuring Jacobite bishops" would arrive in the colonies, as they claimed had secretly happened in 1723 and later. Chandler denied that any "Jacobite Bishops have arrived in the Colonies ... in any disguise; and I sincerely wish and pray that such Bishops may never Visit us." Whigs on both sides of the

Atlantic saw those Britons who were trying to return the Stuarts to the throne as traitors to the house of Hanover and the British nation because they were trying to undo the 1688–89 political settlement. Chandler agreed. His interest in the nonjurors had nothing to do with Jacobitism; he never questioned the legitimacy of the Hanoverians. Instead, Chandler read the nonjurors closely because of their insights into rebellion and authority.[47]

The importance of the nonjurors and high church conservatives from the 1680–1720 period to Chandler's thinking was incalculable. His library catalog shows he read relatively little on the English Civil Wars of the 1640s, a staple of Whig libraries. American radicals of the 1770s were drawn to the era because of the thunderous debates on democracy that took place; for them, the Levelers, Diggers, and others who challenged monarchy were heroes who offered insights into current battles with King George III and Parliament. But not so for Chandler. His shelves were barren of works by Levelers like John Lilburne, who attacked kingship; by more moderate thinkers like Henry Parker, a lawyer, or minister Philip Hunton, who both declared that a nation's foundation rested on the people's consent and that monarchy existed only at the forbearance of the people; by Richard Overton, another Leveler, who condemned Parliament and helped radicalize Cromwell's New Model Army. (One important exception: Chandler owned a copy of John Milton's *Eikonoklastes*, a 1649 tract that opposed Charles I's absolutist claims for monarchy and denied that a king's right to rule came from God.) Nor did Chandler own any works from the 1640s by Charles's defenders, writers such as Michael Hudson, an ardent champion of monarchy whose *The Divine Right of Government* maintained that monarchy was the only plausible form of government.[48]

Exactly why Chandler spent so little time studying this period is unclear. His deep disgust with the Civil Wars, the execution of Charles I, the prominence of Puritan reformers in the tragedy, and the emergence of Cromwell likely factored in. The violence of the period may have been too difficult for this lover of government and authority to contemplate. Instead, Chandler gravitated to a more peaceful revolution that debated church-state relations, rebellion, and authority in fascinating depth. For Chandler, conservatives like Filmer and Leslie in the post–Civil War period helped lead him to an inescapable conclusion: regardless of a government's transgressions, rebellion was wrong. This theme emerged most powerfully in his tracts of the 1770s opposing the revolutionary movement. In *A Friendly Address to All Reasonable Americans*, for example, Chandler spelled out the dangers of rebellion, portraying resistance to government as an unpardonable sin. "The ill consequences of open disrespect to government are so great, that no misconduct of the administration can justify or excuse it," Chandler wrote in 1774. "The guilt of [disrespect] is so aggravated, that Christians are required, under the heaviest penalty to avoid it."[49]

In Chandler's view, the revolutionary movement was "abusive" and "disrespectful" to the Crown and Parliament. Colonists, in essence, were talking out of turn by challenging their "parent." The American Whigs' protests of the 1760s and later offended Chandler's sense of hierarchy and loyalty, and they ran counter to the Tory ethos of the 1680–1720 period that he so closely studied and admired. His deep reading into the Glorious Revolution ordered his mental world and made him increasingly uncomfortable with the direction of colonial society in the 1760s and early 1770s.

High church defenders of the seventeenth century, including the nonjurors and Robert Filmer, taught Chandler that monarchy was the natural order of things and that democracy represented chaos. His experiences in New England and New Jersey reinforced those lessons. No government could survive if inferiors were allowed to participate in governance. Chandler detested New England for that very reason. Its inhabitants were "Republicans" with a long history of rebellion on both sides of the Atlantic. Republicans rejected the patriarchy of Filmer; they embraced the individualism of Hoadly.

The Glorious Revolution and its debates over revolution and obedience, in the end, did not turn Chandler into a Lockean liberal, as it did for so many of his American compatriots. Quite the contrary. He remained a monarchist. This time traveler looked longingly and approvingly at a glorious English past, when monarchy rested on divine right and democracy did not yet exist.

CHAPTER 4

Episcopalian
Chandler and the Bishop's Cause

As the Church of England and the Crown struggled to assert their authority in British North America in the 1760s, Chandler proposed a seemingly simple solution to their problems: bring one or more Anglican bishops to the thirteen colonies. A stronger church, he reasoned, would lead to a stronger state. British history and the Glorious Revolution, after all, had taught him that episcopacy was a bulwark for the Crown. "Episcopacy and Monarchy are, in their Frame and Constitution, best suited to each other," Chandler observed near the end of *An Appeal to the Public*, his controversial 1767 tract urging the adoption of an American episcopate. "Episcopacy can never thrive in a Republican Government, nor Republican Principles in an Episcopal Church." King and church, he continued, "are mutually adapted to each other so they are mutually introductive of each other. He that prefers Monarchy in the State, is more likely to approve of Episcopacy in the Church, than a rigid Republican."[1]

This connection between episcopacy and monarchy, of course, was what made Chandler's campaign to bring bishops so problematic for those colonists worried about their civil liberties. They, too, had studied English history, and it taught them that bishops posed grave dangers to their Whiggish values. Since the days of Thomas Cartwright and John Whitgift, "dissenters" had attacked episcopacy as unbiblical and a blight on Christianity. Presbyterian and Puritan radicals believed bishops were unholy agents of the state. Their views of episcopacy did not change when they came to the New World in the seventeenth century. Puritans and Presbyterians were determined to keep the hated bishops an ocean away, in Europe, and noted that their ancestors had fled England, Ireland, and Scotland to escape episcopal tyranny.

Chandler thus had his work cut out for him in the 1760s as he worked to bring a bishop to British North America. History, his high church values, and a legacy of failure shaped his campaign. The first serious attempts to establish an American episcopate dated to the days of Queen Anne in the first decade of the eighteenth century, and archbishops from the 1720s on had periodically tried to gain approval to send one or more bishops to the colonies. All had failed. To have any chance of success, Chandler well knew he had to overcome this history, and he tailored his initial arguments accordingly, downplaying his high church views of society and stressing that an American bishop would have spiritual powers only. An American bishop would not haul miscreants into spiritual courts, sit in Parliament, or oversee estate probates.[2]

Chandler's campaign consisted of two components. Drawing on his years of study, he wrote four long tracts that laid out the most powerful, reasonable arguments he could muster to make his case that dissenters could not deny an episcopal church the right to appoint bishops. In making this seemingly reasonable request, Chandler sought to turn history and long-held Whig beliefs on dissenter rights and adiaphora to his advantage. The second component was tactical. Chandler oversaw an ambitious lobbying campaign consisting of petitions and addresses that pressured Parliament and the ministry to back an American episcopate. He also worked with his fellow clergy on a series of newspaper columns that sought to win over Americans to their side. This lobbying effort included visits by Chandler, Charles Inglis, and other northern clergy to the southern colonies in an attempt to persuade their Anglican brethren to back an episcopate.

The bishop's campaign brought out the best and the worst in Chandler. The fight for such a goal—the most important in his career—energized him. Samuel Johnson, the most influential Anglican minister in the northern colonies, was old and in poor health in the 1760s and he passed leadership of the bishop's campaign on to Chandler. Chandler eagerly accepted this responsibility. St. John's rector was the most enthusiastic warrior for the cause, and the most learned. The campaign allowed Chandler to flex his considerable leadership skills. This scion of the wealthy Chandler family from Connecticut was comfortable exercising authority and rallying his fellow clergy to follow his lead. Samuel Seabury Jr., by contrast, was quiet and lethargic (in Chandler's view) while Inglis was a late comer to America who looked up to Chandler as a mentor and turned to him for guidance.

The vehicle Chandler used to assert his leadership was an annual convention of New Jersey Anglican clergy that he had begun convening in 1758 and which met fifteen times over the next seven years before merging in 1767 with the convention of New York. These conventions were opportunities to talk, strengthen the clergy's missionary work, deal with disputes within parishes, and socialize. Most of all, the conventions were a way to plot strategy on the campaign for an American episcopate. Chandler used the gatherings to keep the clergy united behind his campaign at a time when William Smith, provost of the College of Philadelphia, was pressing for a compromise that involved sending commissaries—representatives of the Bishop of London, who was in charge of the American church—to the colonies in place of bishops.[3]

But the campaign also brought out the worst in Chandler. Despite his efforts to downplay, and even hide, his high church values, he opened his most important tract, *An Appeal to the Public, in Behalf of the Church in America*, with a vigorous defense of divine-right episcopacy, a concept loathed by Congregationalists and Presbyterians, and he could not resist lecturing readers about a proper society based on the antidemocratic principles of Robert Filmer and other defenders of hierarchy. In follow-up writings, he praised not only monarchy but many of the church's repressive tactics in earlier centuries, including the Test Act. Such views only gave more ammunition to his foes and confirmed their worst fears that high churchmen were plotting to steal their liberties. Chandler, meanwhile, could not keep his temper in check as he faced withering attacks on his character and on his beloved episcopacy. He was especially angry that those colonists thwarting his campaign were primarily Presbyterians and Congregationalists from New England—the two groups he most detested, from a region he loathed.

THE 1760S CAMPAIGN FOR A BISHOP

Believing the timing was propitious for a renewed episcopal campaign, Chandler had high hopes in 1764 that the American church could finally gain a bishop. "I trust, from observing the signs of the times, that in due season we shall, by divine permission, have bishops in America," he told Samuel Johnson in an August 20 letter that year. An American episcopate, Chandler confidently asserted, had the support of the king, the ministry, and the bishops themselves. Thomas Secker, a close ally of Johnson's and a strong backer of an American bishop, had become Archbishop of Canterbury in 1758, and in the summer of 1764, Secker and Archbishop of York Robert Hay Drummond formally asked the ministry to approve a bishopric. This development excited Chandler, who believed Secker was in a position to secure it. Chandler was so confident of success, in fact, that he wrote, "I shall almost tremble to hear the name of the person appointed."[4]

Secker was certainly a valuable ally. The new archbishop wanted to strengthen the Church of England in the colonies and understood that American Anglicans needed a resident bishop to do so. For all its gains in recent decades, the church was still struggling in the northern colonies. A ministerial shortage especially made expansion difficult. Secker had a political goal as well: Strengthening the church would strengthen the British empire by creating colonists and Indians who were more loyal to the Crown. Besides trying to convert Native Americans to Anglicanism, Secker wanted the church to more aggressively evangelize among those whites who were ignorant of the church's teachings and of religion in general. America, he complained in a sermon a decade earlier, had become a dumping ground for "Malefactors." Secker thus wanted to build a colonial church with a strong missionary outlook that would extend the Church of England's influence to hostile places—not only Indian territory but Congregational-dominated New England. After moving into Lambeth in 1758, Secker reached out to Johnson for his advice on how to achieve these goals and to learn more about the state of the colonial church, according to Chandler's *Life of Samuel Johnson*. Johnson had long been pressing London for an American episcopate, and he repeated his arguments to Secker. The archbishop readily agreed on the need for American bishops. The presence of bishops, combined with the opening of Anglican colleges, would allow the Church of England to supply more ministers to the frontier and to dissenter-dominated regions. In addition to executing Secker's vision for a grand missionary effort, a bishop would bring proper leadership to the colonial church. Secker assured Johnson that he would give the bishop's cause all his attention "in the best Manner that I can."[5]

Besides gaining Secker's support, Chandler was hopeful that the political stars were aligning. George III had become king on October 25, 1760, sparking a surge of patriotism throughout the empire and optimism in Britain's future. Victory over the French and Indians in the Seven Years' War further fueled confidence in Britain's greatness. Among Chandler and his high church allies, the ministry's promise to pursue imperial reforms and tighten control over the colonies presented tantalizing possibilities because they believed that a strong state church went hand in hand with a strong imperial government. The so-called era of "Salutary Neglect" was ending.[6]

But first, Chandler had to get the Anglican missionaries in the northern colonies behind him. William Smith and Samuel Auchmuty, who was rector of Trinity Church in New York City and an ally of Smith's, urged the delegates at the November 1764 New Jersey convention to back Smith's commissarial plan, but Chandler countered that the plan was unworkable because the commissaries were so weak they could not meet the American church's needs. Seabury agreed, and the convention sided with Chandler. "Unalienable episcopal power, and not commissarial power, is the thing" the delegates wanted, Chandler reported to the Bishop of London. When the New Jersey convention met a year later, joined by clergy from New York and Connecticut, the attendees unanimously resolved to petition British authorities for an American episcopate. Chandler would write the most important addresses—those to the king, the two archbishops, the Bishop of London, and the Society for the Propagation of the Gospel. Myles Cooper agreed to draw up the petitions for Oxford and Cambridge universities. Chandler simultaneously would use the awarding of his doctor of divinity degree to curry favor with church leaders in England—the two archbishops, three leading bishops, and Oxford University's vice chancellor—to introduce himself and begin a correspondence on American episcopacy.[7]

Events, however, were moving fast, and Chandler recognized that the political climate was not nearly as fortuitous as it appeared to be only a few years earlier. The Sugar Act of 1764 and the Stamp Act of 1765 outraged the colonists, and London did not want to further enflame American opinion by approving something so politically unpopular as an American episcopate. Secker lamented to Johnson that before the Stamp Act's passage, "a bishop or bishops would have been quietly received in America." Facing fierce American opposition to new taxes, Parliament would not act now on bishops.[8]

Chandler agreed that the Stamp Act represented a setback to their campaign, but he was also frustrated that Parliament's approval for an internal church matter was even needed. He viewed the situation as an irritant arising from the Glorious Revolution, which cemented the King-in-Parliament concept and ensured that a new bishopric would require a parliamentary act. "I do not know that we ever desired them to do anything. What reasons can there be for consulting the Parliament?" Chandler complained in a 1766 letter to Johnson. "How in the name of goodness does it concern them, whether such a bishop as we have requested be sent us any more than whether an astronomer or a poet should come over to America; for he is to receive no powers nor perquisites from them."[9]

Chandler by this time had also become disenchanted with what he considered the timidity of the church leadership, including Secker. "I fear [the archbishop] will think it not prudent and good policy to push the affair, as it may be disagreeable to many persons," he told Johnson. "I cannot say I wish to see him a Laud or a Sixtus Quintus [the pope during Queen Elizabeth's reign], in all respects, but if he had a little more of their resolution, I imagine it would not hurt the Church. The good Bishop of London appears from his answer . . . to be of the same timid disposition with his Grace." Secker, too, was frustrated with the political situation, but he said in his defense that an aggressive campaign would only backfire. He repeatedly cautioned Chandler and his allies to avoid antagonizing Parliament and the ministry—advice that Chandler ignored.[10]

Despite the seemingly hopelessness of their position in 1765, Chandler and his clerical allies decided not to give up or to wait until conditions changed. "It appears to us that bishops will never be sent us, until we are united and warm in our application from this country—and we can see no reasons to expect a more favorable time by waiting," Chandler explained to Johnson. Chandler believed patience had gotten advocates of an American episcopacy nowhere in the past six decades; Seabury, Cooper, and Chandler's other allies in New York and New Jersey agreed. So did Johnson. The aging minister sent an emotional plea to Secker in May 1766, asking if "our dear mother country [will] have no bowels of compassion for her poor depressed, destitute children of the established church (a million of them) dispersed into these remote regions?"[11]

Not surprisingly, the initial volley of petitions and appeals to London was having little effect, according to Samuel Auchmuty, who reported in June 1766 that he had received a cache of letters from London. One letter writer said that despite King George's support for an American episcopate, the bishop's campaign was "ill timed, as it is impossible to pursue such a measure at present with any success." Like Chandler, Auchmuty was disappointed with Secker. "Why does not the Archbishop take him at his word and push the affair?" Secker, however, pointed out that George's support was not enough: Although "the king hath expressed himself repeatedly in favor of the scheme," Secker told Johnson, the petitions from New Jersey, Connecticut, and New York were "postponed to a fitter time," presumably because of parliamentary opposition.[12]

If the bishop's campaign was to succeed, Johnson was convinced that Chandler needed to publish a major pamphlet on episcopacy. He urged

Chandler over the summer of 1766 to write something. Chandler responded, disingenuously, that he was unfit for the task but added that he would undertake it if no one else would. The convention that met that fall at Shrewsbury, New Jersey, discussed what to do. Attendees agreed the convention should prepare an address for the public and left the writing of the pamphlet to a committee, but the committee made little progress. Chandler would have to write it, as Johnson had wanted all along, and he began exchanging ideas with Johnson, who according to Chandler sent a plan for the pamphlet.[13]

Chandler needed little guidance. He had long been thinking about what such a pamphlet should say and who his audience should be—London or his fellow colonists. Unlike Auchmuty, Chandler believed the petitions had done some good in England; the American episcopate had the support of the king, the ministry, and the bishops, he said. They were, in Chandler's words, "convinced already of the usefulness of our proposal." (Samuel Johnson's son William Samuel Johnson, who represented Connecticut in London, disagreed. He told his father in 1767 that opposition to bishops in London was "universal, and the common sentiment of all the leaders of all the parties.") The challenge, Chandler explained to Samuel Johnson, was to get the southern clergy "heartily" behind an episcopate—a challenge "sufficient for an Hercules, and yet it must be accomplished before success can be expected." Otherwise, Parliament will never agree to an American episcopate and the ministry and English bishops will do nothing. Only by presenting a united front in America, Chandler said, can advocates of a bishop hope to change the political climate in England. "I have for a long time been convinced of the necessity of it [a pamphlet], in order to bring the Dissenters and some of the Church people, and perhaps some of our clergy into a just way of thinking on the subject," he wrote in early September 1766.[14]

Although Chandler decided to aim his *Appeal to the Public* at an American audience, he also wanted to pressure London officials anew. Thus in late 1766, Chandler prepared new addresses to the Bishops of London and Oxon, as well as the Dean of Gloucester, and he unsuccessfully tried to get some colonial clergy to write to other leaders. These addresses were long, sometimes overly emotional pleas for an American episcopate. Never known for his tact, Chandler at times let his frustration and anger about the lack of progress show. The address to the Bishop of London, dated December 1766 and mailed on January 19, 1767, said that while the American clergy have "the highest veneration for the wisdom of our superiors, . . . we are very unhappy, and we know not how to be silent, while it [the American church] continues to suffer in such an unprecedented manner." Chandler also defended the campaign's timing, and took seven quarto pages to do so. The clergy did not mean to "throw difficulties in the way of government," he told the bishop. "When we signed our addresses it was impossible to foresee that the disturbances which soon followed would arise to so great a height."[15]

Chandler worked hard to rally his fellow ministers, and he traveled to New York to show them the addresses and get their "approbation." All the consultation came at a cost, however. He lamented to Johnson in January 1767 that "I have been plagued in being concerned with committees, by which means we have been three months in doing what one person might have as well done in a fortnight." And the writing of the pamphlet that became *An Appeal to the Public* was going slowly. In January, Chandler only had a title page to show Johnson, indicating that the bulk of the writing took place during the spring. By the end of June, the tract was finished and the dedication was written.[16]

In the middle of the most important campaign of his career, Chandler agreed to visit Maryland in May and early June 1767, where the Coventry parish on the Eastern Shore had an opening for a minister and wanted Chandler to fill it. This New England–born clergyman was curious to see the place, which was one of the original Anglican parishes in this southern colony. When Chandler visited, the parish remained an Anglican stronghold; the main church—a one-story brick structure in the town of Rehoboth on the Pocomoke River—was the center of a vibrant Anglican community consisting of more than two hundred communicants, far larger than St. John's. More importantly, Chandler viewed his trip as an excellent opportunity to seek support for an American episcopate in a region that generally was lukewarm to his campaign. Unlike in the northern colonies, the Church of England was established in the South and dissenters were the ones in a position of weakness. Most of the southern clergy were low church and felt no need for bishops, especially since their relations with the powerful gentry were generally good. Virginia had a commissary from 1689 to 1776 who took care of some of the administrative tasks Chandler wanted, such as recruiting ministers. (The commissary, though, did not have power to ordain or confirm, and Chandler opposed such a position for that very reason.) Chandler and his colleagues, however, viewed Maryland with promise.[17]

But Chandler's visit did not go well. "You may be sure that they are averse to an American episcopate, and they are much averse to having their numbers increased or their vacancies supplied from the northward," he recounted in a letter to Johnson upon his return. Leading parish Anglicans thought highly of

Chandler. In March, the vestry had sent two members to Elizabeth Town to recruit Chandler, and "after a long entreaty of many days," Chandler agreed to visit. He preached several sermons to large audiences, and the vestry told Governor Horatio Sharpe that "after hearing him and being acquainted with his General good Character he appeared to have the Unanimous consent of the whole parish in his favour." But Chandler's appointment became entangled with local politics. Some "ill-disposed persons," in the vestry's words, campaigned against him; they instead successfully persuaded the governor to ignore the vestry's recommendation and choose a candidate of his liking. Chandler blamed "Presbyterians in that neighborhood, by mere dint of falsehood and misrepresentation," for this turn of events.[18]

The whole episode bothered Chandler. The promise of a large salary had tempted him in the first place because he would be better able to care for his family, and he believed he could "do much more good there, than all the good I can do here." But he understood from the outset what a difficult situation he was entering. Chandler considered the previous minister "undoubtedly the very worst" in the province and a "traitor" to the Anglican cause. Once in the parish, Chandler's opinion of the place did not improve. He described the region as impoverished: the land was flat and swampy and "the soil poor and miserably uncultivated, excepting some spots which they plant with tobacco." To his northern eye, the farmers were backward and towns were few and far between. As a result, Chandler reported, "a man may be obliged to make a day's journey to find a smith, or to send his wife's shoe a dozen miles to be heel taped."[19]

On the positive side, Chandler praised the inhabitants as "zealous churchmen, without any tincture of enthusiasm. They have no Roman Catholics and but few dissenters to plague and torment them." Finding the people to be devout Anglicans, Chandler must have felt some hope that he could gain support for his episcopal campaign. Thus he took his case for an American bishop to parish members and Governor Sharpe (1718–1790), an Anglican and a former British military commander. Chandler found Sharpe to be polite and pleasant. Nevertheless, the governor let Chandler know he would not get the Coventry appointment, "although His Excellency... was pleased to say that he should be glad of my residence in the province." Sharpe was so cordial that Chandler felt emboldened to discuss his effort to secure an American episcopate. This also did not go well. "I made some little opening on the subject of bishops, but had little opportunity as I unluckily fell in with the provincial court, the public Bans, Balls, Assemblies, and the devil knows what," Chandler reported. "All that I was then able to obtain was a promise that he would not oppose us and that he would transmit any representation we should make on the subject, to the proprietor. He appears never to have thought or heard much on the subject; and I hope Messrs. Cooper and McKean (whom I met at Newcastle on their way to him) will be able to make some good impressions upon him."[20]

Safely back in New Jersey, Chandler finally was able to finish his pamphlet. He sought feedback during its composition from Seabury but got none. Samuel Johnson, however, did provide guidance, although Chandler did not elaborate on his mentor's suggestions. By the end of August, Chandler reported that *An Appeal to the Public* was at the printer but had run into delays because James Parker had gout. As he waited for Parker to recover and finish printing his pamphlet, Chandler was thinking about his next steps. He decided to prepare an advertisement for the *Appeal* and line up endorsements. He also asked Johnson to write a preface, as he was convinced a preface from someone as distinguished as Johnson "would give more weight to the publication." Chandler was again optimistic that conditions were improving. Bishop Robert Lowth of Oxford had sent "a most polite, obliging and friendly letter" in answer to the address of the previous convention as well as a private one to Chandler. "I am now fully satisfied that our petitions and remonstrances have had this good effect, that the attention of our superiors is engaged to the state of the American Church, and their eyes opened with regard to its interests, in connection with those of the nation; and although nothing can be done for us immediately, yet as soon as affairs will admit of it, bishops *will* be granted us."[21]

Confidence was so high that Chandler and Johnson had a candidate in mind to serve as the first American bishop: George Berkeley Jr. Berkeley was the son of the noted philosopher and Bishop of Cloyne. He also was a Secker protégé and an enthusiastic advocate for an American episcopate. Johnson wanted to bring Berkeley to America in hopes this would pave the way for him to become bishop. Chandler liked the idea, telling Johnson in 1770 that the "Residence of a Clergyman, of his Character and Disposition, for some Time in this Country, will certainly tend to forward an Episcopate." Inglis agreed as well, but nothing came of this idea.[22]

THE *APPEAL TO THE PUBLIC*

After all the petitioning and distractions, *An Appeal to the Public* finally appeared in print in the fall of 1767. Parker, presumably over his gout, finished the job in September. The pamphlet was one of the most important pieces Chandler ever wrote, and he worked extremely hard on it. But given his belief that the prize was within reach, he was curiously dubious about what it would accomplish. At the end of October, Chandler sent a copy of his pamphlet to the Bishop of London with a cover letter attached. "The most that I can say in Favor of the Performance," Chandler wrote, "is, that it expresses the Opinion of the Clergy in most of the Colonies," and he hoped it "may have some good effect here."[23]

The likely reason for Chandler's lack of enthusiasm was that *An Appeal to the Public* was a political document. He wrote it to sway American critics of episcopacy, or at least to try to temper their opposition. Chandler was up against the long, virulent hatred of bishops and all they represented to their foes, as well as fears in England that an American episcopate would revive the bitter religious hostilities of earlier centuries. This unhappy situation forced Chandler to water down the authority of an American bishop and to make the fateful decision not to more directly confront the anti-episcopal history that dissenters constantly cited. Chandler admitted as much in his letter to the Bishop of London. Chandler said that in laying out his case, he had to leave out "other Facts and Reasons, which could not be prudently mentioned in a Work of this Nature, as the least Intimation of them would be of ill Consequence in this irritable Age and Country." The sadness for Chandler was that an honest, full-throated case for episcopacy would have presented the high church conception of the state church in a strong, monarchical government. He was enough of a high church acolyte to believe that his vision of society, based on all he had learned about Tudor and Stuart England, would have won over those in England who supported the Church of England in America. "But," he told the Bishop of London, "I must content myself with having proposed those only which could be mentioned safely, and leave the Event to Divine Providence."[24]

An Appeal to the Public ran 118 pages, plus an appendix, and was divided into eleven sections. Throughout the tract, Chandler did all he could to answer every objection foes of episcopacy could muster. He downplayed the powers an American bishop would possess, asserting the colonial office would be merely administrative providing two main tasks: ordaining ministers and disciplining them once in office. Chandler promised that American bishops "shall have no Authority, but purely of a Spiritual and Ecclesiastical Nature, such as is derived altogether from the Church and not from the State." But Chandler could not resist trumpeting the superiority of episcopacy over presbyterianism

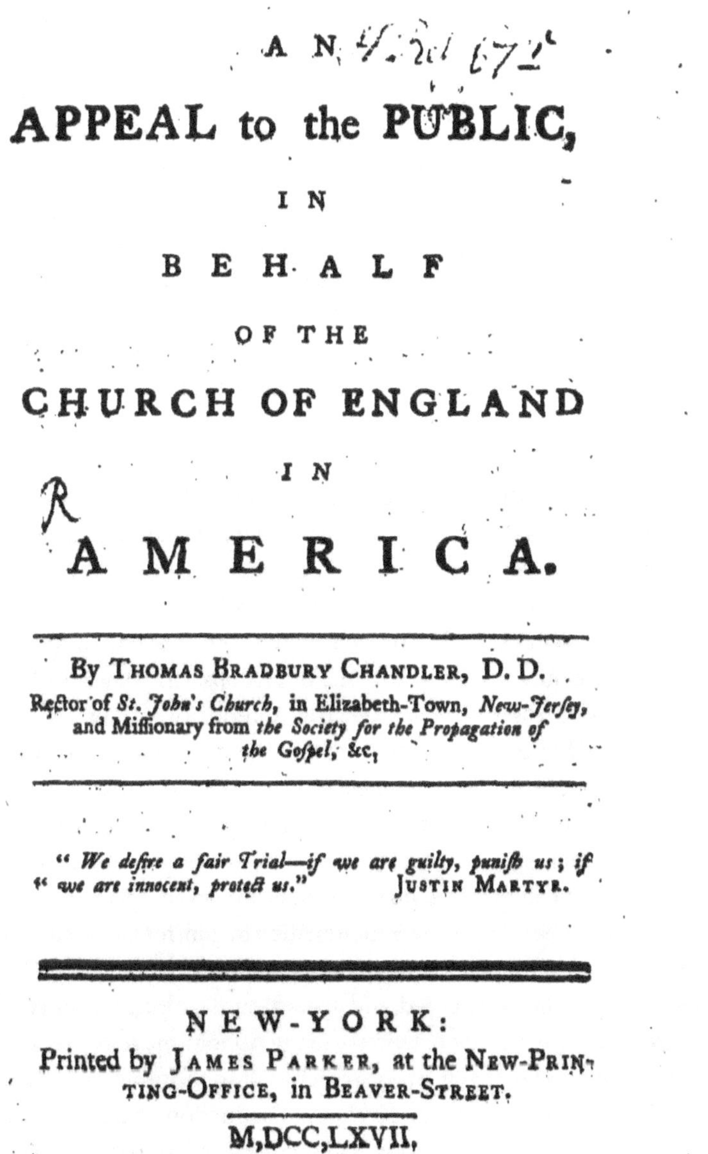

AN

APPEAL to the PUBLIC,

IN

BEHALF

OF THE

CHURCH OF ENGLAND

IN

AMERICA.

By THOMAS BRADBURY CHANDLER, D.D.
Rector of *St. John's Church*, in Elizabeth-Town, *New-Jersey*,
and Missionary from *the Society for the Propagation of
the Gospel*, &c.

" *We desire a fair Trial—if we are guilty, punish us; if
we are innocent, protect us.*" JUSTIN MARTYR.

NEW-YORK:
Printed by JAMES PARKER, at the NEW-PRIN-
TING-OFFICE, in BEAVER-STREET.
M,DCC,LXVII.

FIG. 5 Title page of Chandler's *An Appeal to the Public*, 1767, which sold widely in the colonies, including in Boston, and sparked intense controversy.

and lecturing readers on the importance of obedience. Refuting dissenters' version of biblical history, he asserted the episcopal office was of divine origin and sanctioned by the apostles. Given its origins, Christians could not tamper with the episcopal structure. "The Government of the Church is as much a positive Institution as the Christian Sacraments," he wrote, "and the Laws relating to it bind us as strongly, as the Laws which oblige us to receive Baptism or the Holy Eucharist." Moreover, Chandler continued, the evidence from the second and third centuries was overwhelming that the early Christians venerated episcopacy and considered it superior to presbyterianism. Indeed, even "Rejecters of Episcopacy" conceded "that Episcopal Government obtained very early in the Church."[25]

The office grew in importance and power over the centuries, Chandler continued, benefiting in many nations from an alliance between church and state. But he said episcopal authority remained constant, no matter its territorial size or relationship to the state. "As worldly Prosperity or Adversity does not affect the Nature of the Office, so neither does the Location nor Limitation of it with Regard to Place. He who has a small Diocess, has the same Episcopal Powers, as he that has a large one."[26]

And those powers, he stated, were threefold: ordination, confirmation, and government. As with monarchy in the secular realm, the episcopal office stood above others in the spiritual. For bishops, "the Power or Right of Government is necessarily included in the Superiority of their Office," Chandler explained. "For in every Society, where there is a Subordination of Offices, that which constitutes the highest Office is the legal Possession of the highest Power; and the superintending and governing Power, being superior to all others, must of Consequence belong to the highest office."[27]

A bishop can delegate power to inferiors, even presbyters, "but in such Cases, it must be exercised in Subordination to him, for he can never divest himself of his controlling and superintending Authority," Chandler said. Ordination rested with bishops, he noted, and it was absurd for Puritans and Presbyterians to argue otherwise. "For to whom can the Appointment of inferior and subordinate Officers belong, in every Society, but to those who govern it? Besides, the same Arguments which prove the Distinction of Bishops from Presbyters, prove also that Ordination is an Office peculiar to the former." Scripture showed that presbyters had no power to ordain, he said. History, too, demonstrated this truism as well, and for further proof Chandler directed readers to one of his favorite writers from the Tudor period—Richard Hooker—and to one from the 1688 era—John Potter, author of *Discourse of Church Government*.[28]

Lacking bishops, the American branch of the Church of England was rudderless, Chandler wrote: the American church was in "wretched Condition... for want of Bishops." An American bishop would serve as the stern hand who would provide structure, wisdom, and guidance to the clergy and the laity. Lurking over all this was Chandler's pre-1688 belief in a sovereign power where authority must reside. "When it is said, that the Church of England in America, without Bishops, must be without Government," he explained, "this is to be understood in a qualified Sense. For where there is absolutely no Government at all, there can be nothing but Disorder and Confusion."[29]

With no bishops present, the laity simply had too much freedom to do as it pleased. "The State of the Church in America is, at present, really this," Chandler explained. "The Clergy are independent of each other, and have no Ecclesiastical Superiors to unite or control them; and the People are sensible of their Want of Power, and find themselves free from all Restraints of Ecclesiastical Authority." Lacking a head, Chandler said, the church body was weakened as church discipline broke down. Broader societal conditions were contributing to this problem, Chandler lamented. In an age dominated by reason and the questioning of authority, the reverence for nobility and hierarchy was weakening: "A Man would be generally esteemed to be either wrong-headed, or mean-spirited, or both, who should profess much Reverence for Ecclesiastical Authority," Chandler said. "The Charge of Priest-Craft... would be sure to fall upon the Clergy, should they have Courage to speak up in Defence of it."[30]

Chandler conceded, however, that lay power was so advanced in the colonies that an American bishop could not reverse it and would not even try. "In this State of Things," he reassured his American readers, "the Restoration of the primitive Discipline seems to be a Matter rather to be wished for and desired, than to be rationally attempted by those in Authority. Accordingly no Attempts of this Nature will be made under an American Episcopate; the Discipline of the Church, so far as it relates to the private Members, will be left as it is, and nothing farther will be done than refusing the Communion to disorderly and scandalous Persons."[31]

Instead, bishops would concentrate on reforming the clergy. With a bishop in residence in America, wayward clergy would be easier to discipline, unlike in the present situation where the supervising bishop was three thousand miles away in London and responsible for overseeing an impossibly large diocese. "A Bishop residing in the Country can suspend [a clergyman acting in an open and scandalous Manner] immediately," Chandler said, "and if upon

Trial the Case shall be found to deserve it, he can proceed to deprive him of his Benefice."[32]

For Chandler, another major practical consideration was the difficulty of ordaining American candidates for the ministry. Without a bishop nearby, they had to cross the Atlantic Ocean to reach London at great expense and danger. Ship's passage, in Chandler's reckoning, averaged £100 sterling per person. "To Men of Fortune this is an inconsiderable Sum; but Men of Fortune must not be expected to devote themselves to the Service of the Church in America." Taken together, the cost and the danger of an Atlantic voyage contributed greatly to the shortage of Anglican clergy in America: "In the Province of New-Jersey there are Twenty-one Churches and Congregations; Eleven of these are intirely destitute of a Minister, and there are but Five Clergymen to do the Duties of the other Ten," Chandler noted. But even when candidates did hazard the ocean crossing, "another glaring Disadvantage, to which the Church in America is manifestly subject, arises from the impossibility that a Bishop residing in England, should be sufficiently acquainted with the Character of those who go Home from this Country for Holy Orders."[33]

The arguments for episcopacy were both simple and overwhelming, Chandler believed. An episcopal church without bishops was not episcopal. He also argued that it was a matter of fairness. The Church of England in America was only asking for the same right as other churches—the freedom to run its church in the manner it saw fit. These arguments were not new; episcopal advocates, ranging from Edmund Gibson in the 1720s to Johnson and Secker in the 1750s, had made them before, as had the Bishop of Landaff in a sermon he delivered shortly before publication of *An Appeal to the Public*. Chandler, however, was not seeking originality; he wanted a plainly written tract that would educate ordinary Americans supposedly ignorant of church history about the essential role of episcopacy in a properly functioning church government. The pamphlet's calm tone was carefully designed to head off attacks by opponents who loathed all things episcopal. Chandler hoped fair-minded Americans would see episcopacy in a new light, as a benign institution that would merely allow the Church of England to function in America. Thus from the title page on, Chandler strove for reasonableness. He included a short quote from Justin Martyr underneath his byline that simply said, "We desire a fair Trial—if we are guilty, punish us; if we are innocent, protect us." He followed that up on the frontis with a longer quote from one of his favorite authorities on episcopacy, Bishop Gilbert Burnet, that, in a few words, covered many of the objections to a bishopric. Burnet asserted the office was biblical and was important for "propagating and preserving the Christian Religion."[34]

Despite his attempts to appear reasonable, Chandler's bitterness occasionally surfaced. A bishopric was needed, he claimed, to stave off the ruin of the church in America, whose enemies were so successfully persecuting it. The church's condition deserved compassion and pity. "The Church has been long struggling under such an increasing Load of Difficulties, and is now in such a State of Oppression, as to deserve the Compassion of the whole Christian World," he wrote in words that would invite the ridicule of his American enemies. The ruin of the American church, he warned, would lead to the ruin of the Church of England itself, with dire consequences for the British empire at large. The interests of the state coincided with the interests of the church. This combination of pity and fear led to his famous declaration that "Episcopacy and Monarchy are, in their Frame and Constitution, best suited to each other." The demise of the monarchy during the English Civil Wars of the 1640s led to the demise of the church, he noted. And "the Resurrection of the one, afterwards closely attended the Restoration of the other; and he that has a Regard for the Happiness of either, can never wish to see the Experiment repeated, either in England or her Colonies."[35]

Presbyterian-dominated Scotland further taught Chandler what happened to a society when democratic forces ran amuck and undercut strong church government by eliminating bishops. When William of Orange invaded England in late 1688, Scottish Presbyterians moved quickly to end episcopacy in Scotland and restore those Presbyterian ministers who had been deprived of their livings after the restoration of Charles II in 1660—demands that William reluctantly went along with in an effort to secure the loyalty of his northern kingdom. The Scots then began a campaign to evict Church of England clergy from their livings, a campaign that proved so successful that by 1720, the Presbyterians had gained control of all churches in Scotland.[36]

The abolition of the bishop's office and the ejection of episcopalian clergy led to a pamphlet war, with Church of England members accusing the Presbyterians of persecution and tyranny. Chandler owned eight pamphlets on these Scottish controversies, and he marked key passages as he read them, thus providing a tantalizing glimpse into his thinking and the issues that animated him during this period.[37]

The annotations were heaviest in three tracts that vividly described Presbyterian persecution of Scottish Anglicans. In *A Late Letter Concerning the Sufferings of the Episcopal Clergy in Scotland*, Chandler highlighted an incident where soldiers "went to Ministers Houses, abused their Persons, spoiled their Furniture and Books, and banished them from their Charges and Livings." In addition to decrying these episodes as barbaric, the pamphlet described what would happen if a presbyterian system replaced episcopal government; Chandler focused on a passage that argued when presbyterianism becomes the mode of church government, "Anarchy and Confusion [will follow] in the State," with the Civil Government [being] as confused and tumultuary, as Presbytery in the Church." The pamphlet defended the episcopal office as biblically sound; Chandler highlighted the passage recalling how James I, "that wise Prince," restored in Scotland "that truly Ancient and Apostolical Government of the Church by Bishops, which out of all our impartial Historians, will sufficiently appear to any unprejudged Readers."[38]

Another pamphlet Chandler marked up extensively attacked presbyterianism as oppressive. "The Church of Scotland is at this time under the Claw of an inraged Lion; Episcopacy abolished, and its Revenues alienated; the Clergy routed," the tract lamented. "Some by a form of Sentence, and others by violence and popular Fury; their Person and Families abused, their Houses ransack'd, their Gowns torn to pieces, with many Injuries and Indignities done them."[39]

Chandler did not directly reference Scottish history in his writings. He instead deployed imagery that he knew would resonate most powerfully with Protestants of all stripes: Catholic persecution of Protestants during the Spanish Inquisition and later. Nevertheless, his study of Scotland reinforced his support of monarchy, his fears of democracy, his distrust of presbyterianism and lay rights, and his belief in episcopal government.[40]

Deprive the American church of bishops, and society will end up like Scotland—or New England, Chandler warned. New England's fatal flaw, Chandler believed, was that the region valued democracy over monarchy and congregationalism over episcopacy. As he explained in 1774, "Many of the first settlers [in New England] imported with them an aversion to the *regal* part of our Constitution and were thorough-pierced Republicans. To every species of monarchy they were as inveterate enemies as any of their brethren, whom they left behind them in England." Those original settlers, Chandler continued, passed on their anti-monarchal principles in "an uninterrupted succession, from father to son, and from generation to generation, to the present day."[41]

Because of these larger issues, Chandler saw the stakes in his campaign as exceedingly high: the fate of monarchy and governmental authority in America. His enemies agreed the stakes were momentous, but for vastly different reasons.

CHAPTER 5

Warrior

The Fight for an American Episcopate

Thomas Bradbury Chandler was no prophet. On January 22, 1768, he reported to Samuel Johnson that "My Appeal circulates but slowly, and the difficulties are great that attend the dispersion of copies to the southward." In fact, the pamphlet was circulating widely, especially in America's three most important cities—Philadelphia, New York, and Boston. Dissenter foes of episcopacy were avidly reading it, as were leading political figures who distrusted British intentions in the colonies. In Boston, both John Adams and his cousin Samuel Adams had read Chandler's pamphlet and were appalled. In late May 1768, John Adams told readers of the *Boston Gazette* in a column signed "Sui Juris" that "every Friend of America" ought to be alarmed by *An Appeal to the Public*. In three essays he published in April 1768 as "A Puritan," Samuel Adams also attacked Chandler's tract.[1]

Over the winter and spring, Chandler came to realize that his pamphlet was indeed being read, but it was no cause for celebration. Instead, he was horrified at the political storm he had kicked up and angered at the vitriol that was being hurled at him. He derided one anonymous attack as "abusive" and "low nonsense, and it is much inferior to high nonsense, which [at least] has some cleverness." He lashed out at another attack as "an impudent blundering performance, and must be answered."[2]

In the fight to win over the American public, Chandler and his high church allies were up against some of the finest minds in the colonies. Spearheading the attack against Chandler's campaign was William Livingston, Chandler's future neighbor and the governor of New Jersey during the American

Revolution. Livingston was a Presbyterian, wealthy lawyer, and prominent member of the powerful Livingston clan in New York. He had long opposed Anglican projects in New York, including the chartering of King's College as an Anglican institution, and published extensively on Whig causes in the *Independent Reflector*. Livingston was a talented writer whose barbs continually annoyed Chandler and other Anglican clergy. Indeed, Chandler sarcastically referred to one of Livingston's essays as being written "in his high prancing style."[3]

Amid the ugly insults hurled by both sides, Chandler's pamphlet and the accompanying campaign for an American episcopate unleashed a serious debate about the meaning of English history and what kind of society the colonies would become. For American Whigs, Chandler's campaign threatened American liberties—they saw it as the nefarious twin of Parliament's efforts to enslave the colonies. Livingston and others turned to lessons of the past to warn about the dangers of ecclesiastic bondage. This intense assault on Anglican values, in turn, forced Chandler and his high church allies to fight back, and fight back they did. Led by Chandler, they wrote newspaper essays, organized new petition campaigns, lobbied their southern Anglican brethren, and published tracts defending episcopacy and demanding an American bishop. This effort required a great deal of collaboration and effort. Although it ultimately failed, the bishop's campaign brought Chandler, Seabury, Inglis, and others closer together as they fought for their vision of American society.

THE ANTI-EPISCOPAL CAMPAIGN

William Livingston did not want Chandler's *An Appeal to the Public* to go unanswered, because he worried that British authorities could mistake silence as acquiescence to an American episcopate. But instead of countering *An Appeal* with a long pamphlet, Livingston believed publishing weekly newspaper essays would reach a broader audience than would a tract sold by a printer that relatively few would bother to read. In early February, he told Noah Welles, a friend and colleague, that he planned "to engage a few Friends of Liberty to furnish their quota of such weekly Papers: and as soon as a competent Number is provided, to begin the Business. By this means the Dissenters here, will be alarmed; and the Ministry intimidated."[4]

To help him in his effort to discredit Chandler and his *Appeal to the Public*, Livingston recruited his old chums who formed the New York Triumvirate: John Morin Scott and William Smith Jr., as well as Noah Welles, Charles

Chauncy, and a few others. The result was the *American Whig*, a series of essays that debuted on March 14, 1768, in the *New-York Gazette*, published ironically by James Parker, the printer of the *Appeal*. Besides recruiting writers, Livingston persuaded Parker to print the essays for at least a year, lined up subscribers to support the project, and solicited allies in other cities. On March 26, Livingston told Samuel Cooper, a Boston Congregational minister, that "a Number of Gentlemen will shortly open the Ball in Philadelphia." He asked Cooper to find writers in Boston to attack the *Appeal*. Cooper demurred, telling Livingston, "Your Plan and the Execution so far as I have seen is well adapted to rouse and awaken ... and I hope will soon be universal."[5]

In Philadelphia, Francis Alison, John Dickinson, and George Bryan teamed to produce the *Centinel*, which first appeared on March 24, 1768, in the *Pennsylvania Journal*. *Whig* and *Centinel* proved to be a potent combination, and Chandler was soon complaining about "the furious and outrageous attack of the *American Whig* and his fellow laborers." He scurried to New York in late March to meet with Myles Cooper, Samuel Seabury, and others to coordinate a response. These Anglican leaders agreed to answer the *Whig* and the *Centinel* with *A Whip for the American Whig*, written by "Timothy Tickle." Chandler wrote the third *Whip*, but he left the bulk of the writing to the others. Chandler preferred to concentrate his energies on preparing another pamphlet, which he felt would more effectively answer the various attacks than would a newspaper essay. The twenty-three "Tickle" essays, which first appeared in April 1768 and ended in September of that year, had two goals: to defend Chandler and to discredit his newspaper foes. While Chandler's pamphlets mostly exuded reasonableness in an effort to sway fair-minded colonists, Timothy Tickle felt no such compunction. The essays matched *Whig* and *Centinel* in vitriol, and they repeatedly argued that Chandler's foes were meeting reason with scurrilous attacks, all in an effort to discredit episcopacy and divide American Anglicans. Civility was not Timothy's watchword. One essay, for instance, lampooned *Whig* as "a long-nosed, long chin'd, ugly looking fellow."[6]

Believing Livingston and his allies were badly distorting Chandler's arguments and misleading a gullible public, New Jersey Attorney General Cortlandt Skinner, an ardent royalist, urged Chandler to reprint the *Appeal* in the newspapers. Chandler, however, demurred because he said it would undercut sales of his pamphlet. "I will publish it [later] in all the papers between Nova Zembla [in Canada] and Cape Horn, provided I can do it without any expense to myself," he said. "This method will drive it through the southern colonies."[7]

Despite Chandler's dismissal of his enemies' responses as crude, the essays by *Whig* and *Centinel* were well written, expertly highlighting the vulnerabilities in Chandler's case. Chandler's opponents knew their English history nearly as well as he did, and they repeatedly turned to the past to warn about the risks that bishops posed to American liberties. In *An Appeal to the Public*, Chandler ignored much of this history in an effort to present episcopacy in the most favorable light. His strategy failed. By skimming over English history and downplaying the established church's abuses of earlier centuries, he left himself open to attack and was forced in his rebuttals to engage the Whig version of events.

The attacks were comprehensive, lambasting virtually everything Chandler and high churchmen valued. In twenty-six essays that ran between late March and September 5, 1768, the *Whig* argued that Chandler was trying to place the colonies in "ecclesiastical bondage." The first essay expressed shock and disappointment at the *Appeal*'s timing. Given the colonists' recent clashes with Parliament over the Stamp Act, "is this a time to think of episcopal palaces, of pontifical revenues, of spiritual courts, and all the pomp . . . and regalia of an American Lambeth?" *Whig* asked.[8]

In an attempt to discredit Chandler, *Whig* turned to church history in his third essay, portraying high churchmen as persecuting extremists who could not be trusted. He also questioned their Protestant bona fides, dismissing them as closet "papists" who were never really committed to reform. *Whig* traced this fatal flaw to the Church of England's founding: Henry VIII undertook an English Reformation not out of concern for building a true Protestant church but as a way to divorce Catherine of Aragon and marry Anne Boleyn. The Church of England, as a result, was rotten from its inception, *Whig* said, and most Englishmen in the Tudor period did not feel passionately about their new church. When Queen Mary I returned the kingdom to Catholicism in 1553, most Englishmen complied. They were no more sincere when Elizabeth became queen in 1558 and returned the nation to Protestantism, *Whig* continued. "Many who were really papists in their hearts yielded to the times and conformed out of self-interest." High church adherents, he argued, were half Protestants who resisted further reforms and were "always mighty sticklers for pomp in religious worship; for rites and ceremonies, and the uninterrupted line of succession." The high church and its bishops, in short, did nothing to build a true Protestant church based on faith and commitment to the gospel.

"From the beginning," he wrote, the English Reformation rested on force, with high churchmen persecuting those who tried to reform the church or who refused to conform. Ecclesiastical abuses only grew under the Stuarts—a "weak and tyrannical race of princes," *Whig* exclaimed. The high churchmen "intoxicated those monarchs with the most fulsome flattery, assuring them, that as vicegerents of God, they were not accountable to men, and that subjects must obey on pain of damnation. The kings in return promoted those sycophants to great riches and dignity, and permitted them to gratify their cruel and popish spirit, by persecuting their fellow protestants."

Whig also attacked the high church for opposing the Glorious Revolution and William III's reign. "They greatly disturbed the peace and comfort of that excellent prince, by many plots and conspiracies." The high church continued its rebellious ways during the reigns of George I and II. "And who are now so earnestly desirous of having Bishops introduced into the colonies, to lord it over them?" *Whig* asked. "Who indeed but the High Churchmen." For *Whig*, Chandler and his allies were "the true, if not the only, descendants and approvers of Arch-Bishop Laud's principles and measures." Low churchmen, by contrast, embraced the Reformation out of conscience and tried to advance it while supporting dissenters' civil liberties. These low churchmen, *Whig* said, were the "worthy part" of the church, and he had no quarrel with them. "They are sincere friends to their country; and pity it is, that the Missionaries do not learn moderation and candour from them."[9]

The *Centinel*, meanwhile, attacked Chandler from another angle: his embrace of the state church and continual use of the term "dissenter." Noting that Chandler's conception of the church drew on the nonjurors and the arguments they raised in the years following the Glorious Revolution, the *Centinel* accused him of wanting to extend the Church of England's privileges to the colonies. Chandler, in short, wanted to make the Church of England in America the established church. *Centinel* made that claim based on Chandler's use of language—the minister from Elizabeth Town presented the Church of England in America as *the* church, according to the *Centinel*. Chandler and his allies used the term "to distinguish themselves and their followers, while with an air of arrogance and superciliousness, they call other denominations of Christians, Dissenters." *Centinel* said that Chandler well knew from history that terms like the Church, divine right, and uninterrupted succession were terms of opprobrium for Congregationalists, Presbyterians, and other Protestant groups. "The Doctor cannot have read so little either of civil or ecclesiastical history," *Centinel* noted, "as not to know the magic of words, and the blind devotion paid to names and sounds." The *Centinel* also wondered why Chandler equated episcopacy with "national religion" and asked why "episcopacy alone [is] honored with that name? Is it because it is established by law in England? Is not Presbytery also established by law? And was it not established in 1707, a more enlightened age surely than that in which Episcopacy was established at the reformation? If the one is a national church, because established in England, why not the other, because established in Scotland? But what is this to us in America?"

The *Centinel* was equally dismissive of Chandler's claims that he was not seeking to create an established church in America. "Can there be no Bishops without establishments . . . ?" That would be almost impossible, *Centinel* said. For that reason, as well as the long ugly history of episcopal tyranny, Chandler "will find that the prejudices and objections of most of our Colonies are too deeply rooted and too well founded, for them to ever submit quietly to an American Episcopate." Bringing bishops to the colonies "would be to destroy their charters, laws, and their very constitutions." *Centinel* complained that Chandler and his fellow missionaries were abetting the Greenville administration "and those Enemies of America, who are exerting their utmost to strip us of our most sacred, invaluable and inherent Rights; to reduce us to the state of slaves."[10]

Like the *Whig*, *Centinel* used comparisons to the post-1688 period to try to discredit Chandler. *An Appeal* argued that the Church of England in America was in danger for want of bishops—a scare tactic, *Centinel* said, that nonjurors and the high church used during the "never-to-be-forgotten period of the *English* history, when the very persons who raised it and kept it up, were laboring to introduce Popery, the pretender, and arbitrary power." The high churchmen, *Centinel* continued, awakened all these fears so they could enflame the people's passions and direct them "against the friends of liberty, religion, and their country. In short such men as Tillotson, Tennisson [sic], Hoadly, Burnet, the shining Lights and greatest ornaments of their own Church, were vilely misrepresented as betrayers of the same."

And like the *Whig*, *Centinel* criticized Chandler's assumption that the Church of England was the true church. "He takes it for granted the Episcopalians are the *American Church,* and that his associates the missionaries are the *Clergy*: all other denominations of Christians he treats as Dissenters, Schismatics, and Sectaries."[11]

Centinel drew on powerful historical memory to remind his readers about the dangers lurking in Chandler's plan to bring bishops to America. Ecclesiastical history was filled with the "follies, absurdities, frauds . . . and cruelty of spiritual tyrants; who practiced every artifice to persuade, or cajole, the temporal rulers to support their measures." The result, *Centinel* said, was persecution—"the most dreadful evil"—and the belief that dissenters were "disaffected to government and dangerous to the state." By asserting that episcopacy encouraged loyalty to the state, Chandler was promoting that very same spirit, according to *Centinel*. "This spirit would beyond all doubt," he wrote, "carry the abuse of ecclesiastical domination, as high as ever *Laud* and his brethren did, or as far as Doctor *Sacheverell* contended for."

As history showed, the presence of bishops in the colonies would hurt the cause of reformation, *Centinel* argued, because high churchmen have long opposed innovations in the church. "Generally the body of the established Clergy, instead of promoting [reformation], violently opposed it, by the help of those very emoluments and advantages which had been granted for the support of religion.... Bishop Burnet very pleasant says... 'we acknowledge our Church liable to err in in the general, but when you come to particulars we are always in the right.' Under the specious pretence of keeping out dangerous innovations and errors, no mistakes or corruptions, however hurtful or disgraceful, are allowed to be corrected."[12]

Such a history meant the bishops and high churchmen could not be trusted. "Although the wings of these high-flyers have been cropt, and their exhorbitant powers limited in some degree, by the salutary restraints of some modern statutes; yet we know it was much against their wills, that such merciful laws were made," *Centinel* wrote. The word of "their advocate Doctor Chandler" was not enough "before we can believe, that the spirit of persecution is not yet alive in that Church."[13]

Neither Chandler nor his fellow missionaries could be trusted, *Centinel* concluded. The Society for the Propagation of the Gospel was "formed under the specious pretence of propagating Christianity in foreign parts." But "for every proposal, there may be assigned a *specious* reason and a *true* reason; the specious reason here alleged was the conversion of the Indians in America.... The true but latent reason, as it seems, was to prepare the way for Episcopal dominion."

Whig certainly agreed with *Centinel* about the threat that bishops posed to American liberties. The two-century drive for conformity, as well as the intolerance shown for Christians who held different beliefs, was simply wrong. "As a Whig, I am utterly opposed to the irrational and execrable practice of punishing people for opinions in no degree hurtful to civil society," *Whig* declared, "and if the scheme which the author of the Appeal so ardently espouses, portended no evil to others, I should bid it *good speed*."[14]

These attacks left Chandler fuming because he believed they were grossly unfair. In the *Appeal*, he had stressed that he was not accusing American dissenters of disloyalty when he proclaimed that monarchy and episcopacy were perfect partners. And he asserted ad nauseam that bishops would respect the rights of other churches and be a burden to no one. After the appearance of *Whig*'s first essay, he took out a long advertisement, which he wrote on March 16 and published in the *New-York Gazette* on March 21, vowing to set the record straight. Chandler portrayed himself as the victim. "I make it a general rule to myself, to treat all persons with as much notice and respect as they deserve," Chandler wrote. "Upon this principle I propose to conduct myself towards the *American Whig*; so that what treatment he is to receive from me, will depend greatly upon his future behaviour." But Chandler could not resist insulting *Whig*. He panned the *Whig*'s essays as being "penned altogether in a ludicrous strain; it is thickly bespangled with drollery, it frequently flashes with witticisms (but observe *gentle reader*, they are of a spurious breed,) and in short, ridicules the general subject of the Appeal and its various parts."

Chandler was also angry that *Whig* was publishing his essays anonymously, seeing it as unsporting. Chandler noted that he stood fairly "upon open ground" while his opponent hid behind a mask. "An engagement by two persons under such different circumstances," Chandler pointed out, "would afford to the public an odd spectacle. While I should risque my own character and reputation in the fray, I know not until I can discover the real features of my antagonist, whether he has any reputation and character to risque. For this reason it has been generally esteemed base and ungenerous, for a writer who disguises or conceals himself, to attack an author who stands fairly upon open ground."[15]

Despite disdaining newspaper essays, Chandler did write one, and it was as vitriolic as those penned by his foes. After calling them fools, he came to his real purpose: attacking the *Whig* as a hypocrite. Bishops were not the persecutors; the dissenters were for denying an American episcopal church the right to a bishop. "Whilst he, and his brethren of the faction, have the word, *moderation*, in their mouth, they act the part of furious persecutors," he wrote. "They betray their intolerant principles, and desire to enslave others, amidst clamorous outcrys for liberty." It was a tactic he would employ a few years later when he savaged Continental Congress and American radicals, especially New Englanders, as the worst kind of hypocrites.[16]

The most serious attack on the *Appeal* came not from the *Whig* or *Centinel* but from Charles Chauncy. Chauncy was pastor at Boston's Congregational

First Church and a lifelong foe of episcopacy. Ironically, he had a few things in common with Chandler. Chauncy, too, was a scholar and serious bibliophile. His biographer reported that he spent up to fifteen hours a day studying theology and Scripture. Both men despised the Great Awakening because of its emotional excesses and rejected the evangelical conversion experience. And both men came from distinguished New England families whose forebears crossed the Atlantic in the 1630s. Chauncy's great-grandfather, an Anglican minister of Puritan leanings, refused to heed Archbishop Laud's call to read the Book of Sports—a decree that banned recreational activities such as country festivals—and was deprived of his living. To escape Laud's crackdown, he came to New England in 1638 during the Great Migration.[17]

Charles Chauncy wrote his first anti-episcopal tract in 1734 after his brother-in-law Addington Davenport quit his Congregational church and became a lecturer at King's Chapel in Boston. Davenport defended episcopacy, arguing that it was the proper form of church government since the time of the Apostles. This heretical stance led Chauncy to take up the study of church history and episcopacy. As a good Puritan, he opposed divine-right monarchy and episcopal church government.[18]

Chandler's crusade in the 1760s to bring a bishop to the colonies alarmed Chauncy, and he needed little coaxing from William Livingston to take up his pen against the *Appeal*. Given his great-grandfather's experience and what he considered a history of episcopal persecution, Chauncy never believed Chandler's claims that extending episcopacy to America was a minor bureaucratic adjustment. After all, none other than William Laud had tried to bring a bishop to New England in 1638, and in the eighteenth century English bishops and Anglican clergy had made life difficult for New England Congregationalists. Chauncy was well familiar with some of the recent examples: In 1725, the Bishop of London and Boston's Anglican clergy had helped defeat a plan by Massachusetts Congregationalists to have their synod officially recognized. Thirty-seven years later, Anglican clergy successfully blocked Congregationalist plans to obtain a charter for a missionary group that the Anglicans feared would have rivaled, and hurt, the SPG.[19]

Upon Jonathan Mayhew's passing in 1766, Chauncy became the leading foe of episcopacy in New England. Publication of *An Appeal* prompted Chauncy to dust off the arguments he employed in his 1734 tract, which had never been published because of the lack of subscribers. His answer to Chandler came quickly, in 1768, and ran 205 pages. In great detail and learned prose that answered each section of *An Appeal* almost line by line, Chauncy pulled together all the arguments he raised three decades earlier, as well as the themes that *Whig* and *Centinel* were stressing: Chandler's claim that bishops would have only ecclesiastical and spiritual powers was simply impossible. Bishops were an extension of the state. Once safely settled in America, bishops would seek to obtain the powers that their brethren enjoyed in England.[20]

Publication of Chauncy's tract only added to Chandler's headaches. By this time, he must have felt under siege with the newspaper war raging and the learned Dr. Chauncy taking shots at him. Chandler spent 1768 stewing and preparing his response to Chauncy and the newspaper attacks. The product of his year's labor was *The Appeal Defended: Or, the Proposed American Episcopate Vindicated, in Answer to the Objections and Misrepresentations of Dr. Chauncy and Others*, published in 1769 by Hugh Gaine. This defense ran 268 pages—63 pages longer than Chauncy's pamphlet and a staggering 150 pages longer than *An Appeal to the Public*. Chandler had a lot to get off his chest. Once again, he could not contain his anger. Chauncy, the *Whig,* and *Centinel* "have endeavoured to place the whole Matter in Dispute in a ludicrous Light, and have condescended to act the Part of Buffoons, for the Amusement, rather than of sober Reasoners, for the Instruction, of the good-natured Reader," Chandler exclaimed. But what really outraged Chandler was that his foes "have used all their Address to engage the Prejudices, and inflame the Passions, of the Populace, against the Residence of Bishops in America."[21]

The enflaming of passions forced Chandler to finally confront the Whig version of history that denounced bishops as tyrants. He would not repeat the mistake he made in *An Appeal to the Public* in which he ignored this history. First, he revisited the growth of religious toleration in the seventeenth century—a favorite Whig topic—to show that Chauncy and his allies were being ideologically inconsistent in opposing an American bishop. In pushing the case for adiaphora, Whigs and Protestant radicals in this earlier century had maintained that the Church of England and others should tolerate religious differences and that good people of faith could interpret Scripture in their own way. Bitter fights over arcane points of theology were unnecessary and counterproductive, Bishop Benjamin Hoadly and others argued.

Chandler now seized on this history to point out that American Anglicans' plea for bishops "depends not upon the absolute Truth, but upon our belief of the Truth, of those Principles. The Plea of Dissenters for a Toleration in England, was never founded, I presume, on the absolute Truth and Certainty of their respective Tenets." Surely then, Chandler reasoned, Presbyterians and Congregationalists were wrong to oppose a Christian doctrine that

Episcopalians believed in. "It is sufficient that Men *believe* the religious Systems they have adopted to be true, and that they hold no Doctrines that are inconsistent with the Safety of the State, to intitle them to a Toleration from the civil Government," Chandler wrote. "Toleration implies, in the very Notion of the Word, a Liberty for Men to enjoy the free, open and undisturbed Use of such Methods of public Worship, and such Forms of ecclesiastical Government, as belong to their religious Systems." Christian liberty could mean only one thing, Chandler declared: "the Church of England in the American Colonies has a Right to be tolerated . . . [and] she has Right to an Episcopate."[22]

But this line of argument went only so far for Chandler. He also had to counter Chauncy's attacks on the episcopal office itself and his assertion that early English reformers were not Episcopalian but Presbyterian. Chandler's defense of episcopacy entailed a careful, methodical review of the Tudor period in which he attacked Chauncy's use of sources and the conclusions the Boston minister drew from them. Here, Chandler's extensive reading from his large library shone through. His key points were that English Protestants' beliefs had evolved over the sixteenth century and that Chauncy was cherry-picking quotes to buttress his case.

For all the gyrations of the period—a mild Protestantism under Henry, followed by a radical Protestantism under Edward VI, and a brief return to Catholicism under Mary—the Henrician Church of England rested on two bedrock beliefs, according to Chandler: Archbishop Thomas Cranmer (1489–1556) and other English Protestant leaders agreed the Roman Catholic Church was "grossly corrupted," and that a thorough religious reformation was needed in England. "But how *far* either was the Case, was the Work of Time to determine," he said. The sixteenth century, in other words, was a time of experimentation, and "it is no Wonder that we meet with some crude Expressions, relating to Episcopacy," Chandler said. "The Prepossessions of a *Popish* Education still operated in the Minds of these honest Searchers for Truth."[23]

Chandler accused Chauncy of blindly following Edward Stillingfleet's *Irenicum*, a treatise on church government published in 1659. Chandler considered it a flawed work and noted that Stillingfleet himself later repudiated it. Like a graduate student analyzing the historiography of a topic, Chandler reviewed the Tudor era's key writings, including the *Institution of a Christian Man*, the classic 1537 statement of the newly formed Henrician Church of England. His purpose was to show how Cranmer and others came to strongly support an episcopal church. Chandler argued that the sermons and writings of church leaders made clear that the church by Edward's reign was episcopal. A later church historian and bishop named White Kennett (1660–1728) came to the same conclusion, and Chandler quoted him admiringly: the "superiority of Bishops is one of the Two distinguishing Principles of our Reformation."[24]

Chauncy had argued that after Mary's death, Queen Elizabeth had reestablished a Protestant church government on the basis of "God's word" and not on the episcopal principles under Henry and Edward. He also asserted that the "notion of the right of Bishops to govern and ordain, as being officers in the Church, superior to Presbyters by Divine Appointment, was, as the excellent Mr. J Owen says, 'first promoted in the Church of England by Arch-Bishop Laud.'" The point was critical to Chauncy, because he wanted to show that bishops' extensive powers were a later invention of the hated Laud, and a tyrannical one at that.[25]

Chandler the historian scoffed at these arguments. The evidence was overwhelming, he said, that Elizabeth reestablished a Protestant church on episcopal principles—doctrine that had been "fairly settled by the venerable Reformers of King Edward's Reign, without a particular Re-examination." During Elizabeth's nearly forty-five years on the throne, John Whitgift and other church leaders "vigorously defended" the divine appointment of bishops in answer to Puritan attacks on the office that began in 1572 with the publication of the *Admonition to the Parliament*. As proof, Chandler cited Whitgift's own words: "'We make no Doubt,' says the Archbishop, 'but that the episcopal Degree, which we bear, is an Institution apostolical and divine.'" This defense of episcopacy, according to Chandler, was met with "great Approbation and Applause," and Richard Hooker and other contemporary writers made similar arguments. Chandler noted that even the *Centinel* in his twelfth essay acknowledged that the early Church of England recognized that bishops were of divine right and an order superior to presbyters.[26]

In reviewing Tudor history to bolster his case for American bishops, Chandler revealed his high church values, which he had tried to mask in *An Appeal to the Public*. Foremost was his love of monarchy and appreciation for the special relationship it enjoyed with the state church. Chandler praised the thirty-seventh of the Thirty-Nine Articles, the Church of England's statement of faith that was finalized in 1571 after undergoing several revisions in earlier decades. The monarch was supreme in all matters, he wrote: the doctrine "is expressed with great Clearness and Precision in her 37th Article," which stated that Elizabeth was the main power "unto whom the chief Government of all

Estates of this Realm, whether they be ecclesiastical or civil, in all Causes doth appertain." Chandler, however, did not claim unlimited authority for the Crown—a claim that would go too far for his American audience. "More Power than this, we give not to our Princes," he stressed, "and less, I believe, is not claimed by the supreme civil Governors of any Kingdom or Republic upon Earth." The church, Chandler continued, kept control over the "ministering of God's Word" and the sacraments, although the queen "should rule all Estates and Degrees committed to their Charge by God." Needless to say, Chandler did not cite the more harsh sections of Article 37, such as the one that proclaimed, "The Laws of the Realm may punish Christian men with death, for heinous and grievous offences."[27]

On balance, Chandler approved of the monarch's special relationship with the Church of England. The king or queen was the head of the church, and he described the Crown's role in Filmer-like terms: a kingdom resembled a large family, Chandler said; the king was the political father of this family and was supreme to all other elements in society. "And without his Consent or Authority, no Bishop or ecclesiastical Person can lawfully officiate within his Dominions. But the giving this Authority by Commission, or in any other Way, does not convey to any Man his sacred Character."[28]

Chandler's high church values meant he also took on the Whig belief that the Church of England unfairly persecuted its enemies. Thus Chandler defended two of the most hated measures of Restoration England: the 1662 Act of Uniformity mandating adherence to Anglican liturgy, and the 1673 Test Act imposing a religious test on officeholders. Both acts, he said, were necessary measures in troubled times. The Test Act was especially important "to prevent the Enemies of the Church from getting Power to destroy Her," Chandler wrote. And its enemies were not Catholics but fellow Protestants. As proof of this shocking fact, Chandler quoted a historian named Paul de Rapin (1661–1725), a Presbyterian of Whiggish beliefs who wrote a massive ten-volume history of England. In it, according to Chandler, Rapin warned, "'Tis certain, if the Presbyterians can ever act without Controul, they will not be satisfied till the Hierarchy of the Church of *England be intirely demolished.*"[29]

But such a defense of monarchy, church power, and orthodoxy merely confirmed American Whigs' suspicions about Chandler and high churchmen. "The spirit of high churchmen is absolutely incompatible with that of our excellent constitution," *Whig* noted in his twelfth essay. "Was their power equal to their wishes, they would neither eat nor sleep before they had turned a limited monarchy, into an absolute one. Whenever they boast of their attachment to monarchy, they mean an unlimited monarchy, which they love, because it would assist them to render the church absolute."³⁰

Centinel, with merit, considered Chandler a church apologist. The many "instances of episcopal tyranny, which should fill every reader with horror," *Centinel* wrote in his fourth essay, "extort from the Doctor himself, notwithstanding his fondness for ecclesiastical power, the modest softened concession, 'that there have been formerly some instances wherein the power of our bishops has been strained too high.'" Indeed, Chandler excused the Act of Uniformity and other excesses as a product of the times, according to *Centinel*, "in which neither the natural rights of men, nor the religious rights of Christians, were so well understood, as in the present age." But even then, *Centinel* continued, Chandler argued that "the spirit of the church of England, like that of the gospel, was *more peaceable, gentle, and easy to be intreated*, than that of any other national church."³¹

Chandler, as a result, was walking a fine line as he attempted to defend the Church of England's behavior in earlier centuries while simultaneously denying it had a persecuting spirit. He praised Whitgift's conformity drive but defended religious liberty in other contexts. He said repeatedly that his foes were persecutors and hypocrites. He extolled monarchy but was not above using Lockean language when it suited him. In one instance, for example, he complained that Chauncy did not understand the term natural rights. "Natural rights, when the Expression is used properly, can signify nothing less than such Rights as Men are born to—such as they are intitled to upon the common Footing of Humanity, without any Distinction of Christian or Pagan, Protestant or Papist," he wrote.³²

Chandler was sounding so Whiggish because he wanted the "dissenters" to concede that American Anglicans had the right to practice their religion in peace. Thus, Chandler added, "Whatever therefore is the natural Right of one Many, is the natural Right of another." All could assert this right, including "Papists, Jews and Mahometans; . . . and, I may add, the Members of the established Church."³³

In the spirit of adiaphora, Chandler denied that he and his allies saw episcopacy as superior to other forms of church government. But this denial was hardly convincing, because he could not resist asserting Anglicanism's superiority over its rivals. "The Religion of the Church of England, is evidently the purest and best *in the national Opinion*, or it would never have been received as such, and established at Home," he explained. "But *is Religion, in none of the other Forms, to be regarded?* In my Judgment of the Matter, Religion under every Form ought to be regarded, in a greater or less Degree, as perhaps the worst Form of it is better than none at all; and under all Forms it ought to be tolerated, as far as consistent with the public Safety."[34]

One of the most powerful criticisms Chandler had to grapple with was the Whiggish, and very American, fear of power growing over time. Chauncy, *Centinel*, and others repeatedly said the toothless American bishops under Chandler's plan would at some point seek all the authority and prestige the office enjoyed in England. Chandler replied that such a risk applied to "all Sorts of Men," including presbyters. Nevertheless, power's potential growth was so amorphous, so inchoate that Anglicans should not be denied the right to bring bishops to America, Chandler argued. "Who knows whether the New-Englanders will not hang Quakers and Witches again?" he wondered. "But why should either be suspected? The clergy of England are in general Friends to religious Freedom: The People of England, Whigs and Tories, are unfavorable to clerical Power; and a far greater Danger, than the Doctor's imaginary one, is that of their laying aside all Regard to the Christian Ministry, in every Shape, and to Christianity itself."[35]

Not surprisingly, Chauncy did not find Chandler's defense persuasive. He drew up a nearly two-hundred-page tract in response that was published in 1770. Most of his arguments repeated those in his earlier pamphlet. Chauncy again spent considerable time attacking his opponent's view of episcopacy and arguing for the superiority of the presbyterian system. And history again took center stage, as Chauncy criticized Chandler's interpretation of Tudor and Stuart England. "He is grossly mistaken in the idea he has given of the sentiments of the men he has named [from these two eras]," Chauncy declared. "They were, it is true, Episcopalians upon the foot of divine right, in a qualified, mitigated sense; but not in the sense in which Laud and the Doctor, plead for this right." Laud, Chauncy insisted, was the first to contend "for the superiority of Bishops over Presbyters, by divine appointment . . . as I am able to produce abundant evidence to the contrary." All of Chandler's cited authorities, Chauncy continued, agreed that "beyond denial that their notion of Episcopacy, upon the *jure divino-ship* plan, was so qualified as to be consistent with an intire change in the exercise of governing and ordaining power."[36]

> Now, let it be particularly remembered, the Doctor has told us, (p. 41) he has "proved, that the doctrine of the Bishops and Clergy, in the reign

of Queen Elizabeth, must have been agreeable to the Queen, and to the principal persons about her court." If so, Whitgift, Bancroft, and other episcopal writers in this reign, were not for ordination by Bishops, so as to nullify ordination by Presbyters; nor could they disown any as LAWFUL ministers of the church of England MEERLY because they had been ordained by Presbyters only.[37]

Chandler had been bracing for Chauncy's response, according to Charles Inglis, and the latter had confidence Chandler would best his dissenter rival. Chauncy's tract, Inglis confided to a colleague, "will be much such another as his former Productions, weak, sophistical & impertinent." He added that he had no doubt that "Our Brother Chandler . . . will acquit himself with reputation." Chandler's rejoinder came in 1771 in *The Appeal Farther Defended; in Answer to Farther Misrepresentations of Dr. Chauncy*. The debate was sputtering to an end at last, the two combatants having already fired off their best shots. Brevity was not the watchword. Nor was originality. Chandler's latest effort weighed in at 240 pages—a response nearly as long as *The Appeal Defended*. The tract ranged over familiar ground, revisiting the controversies of the Tudor and Stuart periods. It defended anew the state's right to establish a national church as long as the rights of dissenters were secured. "Establishments, without a toleration of Dissenters, are intirely out of the Question," Chandler said. But "the Magistrate has a Right to give some peculiar Countenance and Encouragement, to what he esteems to be the true Religion. . . . And I will venture to add, that he was a Right to shew *as much* Favour to his Religion, as is necessary to support it, and is consistent with a full and free Toleration."[38]

Over the long, frustrating campaign, Chandler's mood had swung wildly from optimism to despair and back again. But in his final skirmish with Chauncy, Chandler concluded on a hopeful note, stressing that the episcopal cause was just. As always, his high church values surfaced as he praised monarchy one last time. American advocates of episcopacy "consider our gracious Sovereign as their Defender and Patron, by Duty as well as by Inclination," he wrote. "They cannot therefore but flatter themselves that, notwithstanding the unreasonable and malicious Opposition they have met with, an Episcopate will be granted them on the Plan that is proposed." Inglis, meanwhile, believed episcopacy's advocates emerged victorious: "Our Paper War with the Dissenters is now over," he wrote in August 1769. "They retired from the Field of Controversy with much Ignominy."[39]

THE SOUTHERN REACTION

Most Anglican clergy in the southern colonies refused to support their northern brethren in the campaign for an American episcopate. One exception was Maryland. "The Maryland Clergy are very zealous [for episcopacy], & have even offered to contribute to the Support of a Bishop," Inglis reported in November 1770. Ministers there "earnestly" petitioned the king, the two archbishops, and others in well-written addresses, according to Inglis, and Chandler and Inglis were encouraged enough by the response that they collaborated on a circular letter to send to "the principal Clergymen" in Virginia and the Carolinas.[40]

In Virginia, the debate over an American episcopate had simmered in Williamsburg's newspapers since publication of *An Appeal to the Public*. Supporters of Chandler's plan, including Virginia's commissary, agreed a bishop could help maintain discipline among the clergy and strengthen the Church of England's position in Virginia at a time when dissenters, including upstart Baptists, were gaining adherents at the expense of the established church. But these allies were a minority; most clergy in the colony did not see the necessity of a resident bishop because of the Church of England's status as the established church and its close ties to the overwhelmingly Anglican gentry.

When Commissary James Horrocks called for a May 4, 1771, convention of Virginia Anglican clergy to discuss backing an American episcopate, only twelve out of one hundred ministers showed up. Hoping for a better turnout, Horrocks rescheduled the session for June 4, but again only twelve came. The commissary decided to press on over the protests of Samuel Henley and Thomas Gwatkin, who argued the convention was in no position to recommend anything because of the sparse turnout. Eight ministers voted to petition the king for an American bishop, but they agreed not to send it unless a majority of clergy within the colony supported the campaign. Henley and Gwatkin, ordained Anglican ministers who taught at the College of William and Mary in Williamsburg, also argued that any petition would need the backing of the governor, Privy Council, and Burgesses since the church was the colony's established church—backing that was not forthcoming. On July 12, 1771, the House of Burgesses declined to support the episcopal campaign, stating that the introduction of bishops would lead to "much Disturbance, great Anxiety, and Apprehension . . . among his Majesty's faithful *American* subjects."[41]

Learning of this maneuvering in Virginia and the newspaper debate it spawned in Williamsburg, Chandler composed an emotional appeal to his

"Friends and Brethren" that was endorsed by seven other northern clergy, including Seabury, Inglis, Cooper, and Auchmuty, and published as a pamphlet in 1771 by Hugh Gaine. Chandler shared an advance copy with Inglis, who praised it as being "written with great Temper & Strength of Argument."[42]

The tract expressed the hope that Virginia's opposition to the bishop's cause was a "misunderstanding" and not "a Want of Fidelity to that Church of which you are Members." To educate his southern brethren about the campaign, Chandler laid out a detailed history of efforts to secure an American episcopate, stressing the importance of bishops to the church and the innocuousness of the proposal. Episcopacy's supporters, Chandler said, have no "Design against your Liberty or Property." He also reassured the Virginians that episcopacy would not weaken colonial ties to the mother country—and added, unwisely, that American bishops would actually strengthen ties to Britain.[43]

For all his soothing words, Chandler characteristically could not avoid sending a few barbs the Virginians' way. Ignoring the Church of England's complicated standing in this gentry-dominated colony where Anglicanism was the established religion, he expressed his disappointment that Virginia's Episcopalians were not supporting a bishopric. The Burgesses' July vote especially disappointed him. The members of this august legislative body, Chandler noted, were devout members of the Church of England. "And yet, these *professed Friends* to Bishops, have declared their Abhorrence of them, unless at the Distance of 3000 miles; calling the Plan for introducing them ... a *pernicious Project*." By opposing the bishop's cause, he warned, Virginia was aiding and abetting the church's enemies, and true friends of episcopacy would view this betrayal with "Grief and Shame." He pleaded with the Virginians to give the northern clergy's arguments a fair hearing and asserted that, contrary to popular belief, a majority of Virginia's clergy actually supported an American episcopate. "Out of a *Hundred* Clergymen belonging to Virginia, *Four* have publickly opposed an Application for American bishops, we can consider as no Proof of the general Aversion of the Inhabitants to such an Appointment."[44]

Inglis had high hopes Chandler's tract would win over the opposition, but the mimetic appeal rehashed arguments he had made many times before and showed little understanding of conditions in Virginia. In a short but biting response, Gwatkin took full advantage of these shortcomings, laying out a host of objections in rapid succession. For starters, Gwatkin said, Chandler's plan never grappled with the fact that Anglicanism was the established church in Virginia. As a result, "you propose a Species of Episcopacy with which our Constitution is totally unacquainted." Chandler wanted a resident bishop to have the power to ordain and to discipline the clergy, but in Virginia the secular and religious authorities are intertwined: "the Clergy connected themselves with the *Civil Powers*, placed the Church under their Protection, and consequently have given up all Right . . . of making Alterations without [the civil powers'] express Approbation and Consent." For example, according to Gwatkin, the General Court doubled as "an Ecclesiastical Court, and claims an entire and complete Jurisdiction over the Clergy of this Province." To implement Chandler's vision for resident bishops would mean overturning the Virginia constitution—an impossibility, Gwatkin said, without the Crown's approval. Moreover, bringing a bishop to the colony would force "his Majesty to exercise a *suspending Power*, by making an Appointment which must clash with the Laws of this Country [Virginia], or else refer the Affair to British Parliament and thus renew the unhappy Controversy concerning the Right of that Body to make Regulations for the *internal Government of America*."[45]

Gwatkin also dismissed Chandler's proposal for a limited American bishopric as "a Mongrel Episcopate, unknown to the Constitution of England, or the Laws of Virginia." Because Virginia's constitution was a copy of England's, he continued, a bishop in Virginia would have to sit on the Privy Council, just as English bishops are required to serve in the House of Lords. And under canon law, he argued, a colonial bishop would have the right to convene spiritual courts and thus also would hold sway over the laity, contrary to Chandler's plan. These difficulties and others, Gwatkin complained, highlight "your Ignorance of the Constitution of this Province . . . [while] your sinister Endeavours to overturn the Constitution of our Church is unpardonable."[46]

In addition, Gwatkin's address revealed a fundamental divide between the northern and southern branches of the Church of England. Unlike in the North, Virginia's laity was used to exercising power through the vestry, power that it would be loath to relinquish if a bishop took up residence in the colony. "The Experience of above a Thousand Years is sufficient to convince us that popular Elections of Ministers, and a resident Diocesan Episcopacy are incompatible with each other," Gwatkin wrote. Because the laity, especially the gentry, were used to running things, Gwatkin foresaw clashes between the vestry and the bishop. "Suppose our Bishop were to deprive a Clergyman, and the Vestry thought proper to rechoose him," he wondered, "what is to be the consequence? If a Vestry make Choice of a Heretick, must the Bishop be obliged to admit him?"[47]

Gwatkin defended the "patriotic" Burgesses' decision to reject the episcopal campaign. "They foresaw its mischievous Tendency," he said. The presence of a powerful, and independent, bishop would strengthen the clergy and lead to conflict with civil rulers and others. "They wisely considered that a Clergy dependent upon Nobody besides their Bishop, and that Bishop unconnected with the Civil Government of the Colony, would be a ... Means of inducing them to form an Interest separate from that of the rest of the Community, and consequently laying an everlasting Foundation for future disturbances."[48]

In the end, *An Appeal to the Public* and Chandler's vigorous defense of it failed to win over Gwatkin and other American skeptics. Indeed, College of Philadelphia Provost William Smith considered the entire campaign a mistake, maintaining that it succeeded only in raising "a great Flame" against the Church of England in America. Bishop of London Richard Terrick agreed, writing in 1772 that Chandler's crusade had worsened the political climate on both sides of the Atlantic and made efforts to win an American episcopate "doubtful." The campaign's timing was horrid, because it heightened Whigs' apprehensions about British intentions at a time when the Crown and Parliament were trying to tighten their control over the American colonies and political tensions were rising. A series of agitations followed the Boston Massacre on March 5, 1770, and Chandler's plea for an American episcopate became increasingly tangled up with the broader debate over parliamentary authority. Boston freeholders, for instance, published a list of "infringements" on their rights in November 1772. After complaining about Parliament taxing them without their consent and about the power of the admiralty courts, the Bostonians warned of the grave dangers the bishop's cause posed to American liberties. Only Massachusetts's General Court, and not London, had jurisdiction over the colony's religious life, the freeholders agreed. "We think therefore that every design for establishing the Jurisdiction of a Bishop in this Province, is a design both against our Civil and Religious rights." Writing years later, John Adams said that the episcopal campaign had spread a "universal alarm against the authority of Parliament. It excited a general and just apprehension, that bishops, and dioceses, and churches, and priests, and tithes, were to be imposed on us by Parliament."[49]

Chandler, however, did have his defenders, especially in England, where high churchmen viewed his writings as a tour de force for episcopacy and a traditional world that prized order and hierarchy. The Hutchinsonians—a movement that took its name from John Hutchinson (1674–1737) and whose purpose was to defend Trinitarian orthodoxy against Arianism and deism—and other old-guard clergy in England praised him. In this rotund American from a colonial backwater, they had found a kindred spirit. Chandler's values were their values. Both the Hutchinsonians and Chandler revered the memory of an earlier England when King Charles I and Laud, as heirs to Queen Elizabeth and Archbishop Whitgift, presided over a powerful Church of England that put dissenters in their place. After publication of *An Appeal to the Public* and the defense of it, an episcopal foe reported that "every one now understands [that Chandler] speak[s] the real, undisguised sense of Dr. Secker." Chandler's years-long campaign brought him into a network of Hutchinsonians and other conservatives, including Secker, Robert Lowth, George Berkeley Jr., and Thomas Newton. Among Chandler's friends were Lowth, Glocester Ridley, and Josiah Tucker.[50]

Chandler stayed in touch with his British correspondents in the early 1770s and monitored developments in England. The chances of obtaining an American episcopate remained slim, of course. With great reason, the ministry in the early 1770s was even less inclined to back Chandler's cause than it was in 1767 because of the growing American political revolt. But like a smoldering fire not yet extinguished, the episcopal debate blazed anew in England for an ironic reason: Archbishop Secker, the most fervent British supporter for American bishops, had died in August 1768. His passing at age seventy-four meant that his allies could posthumously publish a letter Secker had written nearly twenty years earlier in response to a note of May 29, 1750, from Horatio Walpole, brother of Sir Robert, disputing the need for American bishops. Secker's detailed response defended plans to send two or three bishops to the American colonies and argued it would pose no threat to civil liberties. A year after its publication in 1769, the Archdeacon of Cleveland in rural Yorkshire, England, Francis Blackburne, responded by publishing *A Critical Commentary*. Blackburne was a Lockean and a critic of the established church who denounced subscription and other staples of the Anglican church. Besides rebutting Secker's arguments on episcopacy, Blackburne accused the SPG of manipulating Chandler and his allies into advocating for American bishops. He also defended English dissenters who had sided with their American cousins in opposing plans to send bishops to America, citing the long history of episcopal abuse and the ongoing threat of "Jacobites and toryism." Dissenters well "knew the hardship of these legal disabilities under which they themselves lay at home," he wrote.[51]

Blackburne's assault on Secker upset Chandler and goaded him into action. The attacks against an American bishop, Chandler continued to believe, were grossly unfair and deserved a detailed response. His defense of Secker—and of a now quixotic campaign to bring bishops to America—was published in 1774 and ran 102 pages, plus a 31-page appendix that reprinted Secker's letter.

Chandler again pounded away at Whigs' insistence that episcopacy threatened civil liberties, and he stated in stronger terms than he had in his earlier tracts that the Church of England supported religious freedom. His earlier criticism of the archbishop was forgotten. Secker's mild disposition was ample evidence of the state church's good intentions toward dissenters, Chandler wrote. "His grace often advised the Society's Missionaries, in his Conversation with them before they came over, and in Letters afterwards, not to molest People of the different Denominations in the quiet enjoyment of their Principles," Chandler maintained. "And he was careful, in speaking of the proposed Episcopate, to shew that it ought not, and that it was never designed, to interfere with the Dissenters." Secker was no outlier, Chandler continued. American members of the Church of England would oppose any bishop with Laudian tendencies. American Anglicans, he said, "are as fond of their Liberties as other People, and would even join with the Dissenters in opposing the encroachments of episcopal Power, should there be any Occasion for it."[52]

But hanging over the latest debate was a lethal charge from the musty English past: Whigs' belief that Secker, Chandler, and other high church members were Jacobites wedded to both the Stuart claim to the throne and a church that suppressed dissent and backed divine-right monarchy. Indeed, Blackburne saw the whole scheme for American bishops as "one principal ingredient . . . to compleat the cure of jacobitism and toryism" and implement "a perfectly Laudean episcopacy."[53]

Chandler did admire conservative writers from that period, including the nonjurors. And he did defend orthodoxy in his various writings. But he was no "Jacobite." The term was an insult, akin to calling a twenty-first-century American a communist or a neo-Nazi, and Chandler knew he had to vigorously denounce any ties to this detested movement. The northern colonies in the 1770s, he indignantly declared, contained "not a single Jacobite among the episcopal Clergy, and not more than one in Ten Thousand among the Episcopal Laity."[54]

Blackburne had also accused Chandler and other "stanch Churchmen" of opposing the mild form of episcopacy sought by Secker. He claimed Chandler was particularly "zealous"—an accusation that opponents had long hurled at him. Chandler had no new defense to offer, but the attacks forced him to sound even more Whiggish than he had earlier in the debate. Timothy Tickle had tried to parry the allegation by repeatedly praising the reasonableness of Chandler's *Appeal to the Public*, and Chandler had asserted time and time again that his plan merely intended to provide better oversight of the American clergy. Still, he had to try to counter Blackburne, so Chandler again resorted to lessons of the past. Recent history, he maintained, had shown that the abuses of earlier centuries were over and that contemporary bishops understood "that Men should think and act for themselves in Matters of Religion." And "stanch Churchmen"—including himself, he added sarcastically—never opposed the bishops' embrace of religious liberty. "I am very certain that *the zealous Dr. Thomas Bradbury Chandler*," he wrote, using italics for emphasis, "has often, both publickly and privately, spoken of it with Applause, and boasted of it as an Honour to the Church of England."[55]

Chandler had been monitoring the debate in the London papers, and he seized on a column of May 6, 1769, written by a dissenter, who conceded that the Americans only objected to "Lords Bishops" and not to the bishops of limited powers that Chandler wanted. Nevertheless, for all the words and paper expended, Chandler could not rewrite history or undo the dark chapters in the English episcopal past. His defense of Secker proved to be his final published piece on the bishop's cause. The petition campaign, meanwhile, was over.[56]

The political climate by 1774 was hopeless. Samuel Johnson and Thomas Secker were dead, and further talk of American bishops was impossible from the ministry's perspective. It had enough headaches to deal with on the American front. Back in Elizabeth Town, Chandler's nemesis William Livingston had taken up residence in Liberty Hall, and the Sons of Liberty were becoming bolder and more active. Chandler's aggressive campaign for episcopacy had failed. He *had* succeeded in angering American dissenters and raising further fears about British intentions. He had also put a target on his back as the colonists' fight for their political rights came to a climax in 1775. The bishop's cause, in short, drove a bigger wedge between the high church missionaries and their radical foes. The distrust between the two parties grew, and Chandler's disdain for American radicals reached new heights.

CHAPTER 6

Loyalist
The Defense of British Authority

In February 1775, Parliament declared the obvious: the colonies were in a state of rebellion. For proof, it only needed to look at the events that had occurred four months earlier in two cities an ocean away. The First Continental Congress, which had begun meeting in Philadelphia in September 1774 to coordinate colonial strategy, approved a boycott of British imports and took other measures that portended the dissolution of empire. In Boston, the British garrison was under siege. After General Thomas Gage had seized gunpowder in neighboring Charlestown and cannon in Cambridge, four thousand militia from throughout New England descended on Boston and took up positions outside the city, leading Gage to fortify Boston Neck. Ratcheting up the pressure was the defiance of representatives from nineteen towns in Suffolk County, Massachusetts, who held a convention in early September. Denouncing "the attempts of a wicked Administration to enslave America," the convention approved a radical statement of American rights known as the Suffolk Resolves that called on the colonies to reject the Intolerable Acts and resist British attempts to curtail their rights. British officials, as did many colonists, including one Thomas Bradbury Chandler, saw the Suffolk Resolves as a treasonous call to take up arms against the king.[1]

Chandler was horrified and saddened by these dramatic developments, but he was not surprised. He had long believed that American radicals, led by Boston's rabble-rousers, were angling for independence. Seen as unthinkable in 1765, independence was inching closer to reality in the aftermath of the Boston tea party and an angry Parliament's attempts to punish the American rebels. The so-called Intolerable Acts—a series of four laws that closed Boston's port, revoked Massachusetts's charter, and curtailed town meetings—enraged a wide swath of the American public and greatly increased support for the revolutionary movement.

Chandler's options were few as radicalism gained ground in the 1773-75 period. Some loyalists such as Joseph Galloway served in the Continental Congress, the provincial assemblies or local committees in an attempt to moderate colonial demands and find a compromise. Chandler, though, had no interest in, or inclination for, serving in such bodies. Moreover, he was still smarting from his defeat in the bishop's campaign only a few years before. Chandler, nevertheless, believed the situation was so dire that he could not remain idle. The convening of the Congress in September, the formation of the Continental Association that month, the never-ending street protests—all of it alarmed this Anglican royalist. The tumults, as well as the sheer impertinence of the revolutionary movement, cried out for a response, and Chandler knew he had to act, and quickly. Thus he hurriedly wrote two lengthy political tracts in late 1774 and a third in early 1775. In these writings, Chandler poured out his contempt for rebellion and a movement that so boldly challenged British authority. Drawing on his vast knowledge of political and religious history, this exegete on government sought to educate Americans about the importance of authority, the glories of the British constitution, and the perils awaiting the colonists if they did not check American radicalism. The source of the colonies' troubles, Chandler explained, was not Parliament or King George III but New England radicalism. It was Boston's hotheads who were spawning two bastard ideologies, Chandler believed: republicanism and democracy.

Chandler's three powerful tracts thrust him into the front ranks of the loyalist opposition to independence and put him in the crosshairs of the Sons of Liberty, who were active in Elizabeth Town and New York City. Out of his coterie of northern Anglican ministers, Chandler was the first to publish a pamphlet attacking the revolutionary movement, although Charles Inglis had taken to the *New-York Gazette and Weekly Mercury* a few weeks earlier to warn colonists about the perils of rebellion. Inglis and Samuel Seabury followed Chandler with tracts of their own. The group's dynamics during these tense years had changed little from the bishop's campaign of the 1760s. Sharing common views and values, the three men again worked closely to defend king and empire.

1774: THE MARCH TOWARD REVOLUTION

The immediate cause of Chandler's anguish in September 1774 was the gathering of fifty-six delegates in Philadelphia for the First Continental Congress, which remained in session through October 26. At stately Carpenters' Hall, delegates from twelve colonies debated what to do about what they called the Intolerable Acts, which Parliament had passed months earlier to punish Boston in the wake of the Boston tea party. Mere days into their meeting, Paul Revere galloped into town to share a copy of the Suffolk Resolves with the delegates. On September 17, the Congress endorsed the resolves—a vote that John Adams called "one of the happiest Days of my Life.... This Day convinced me that America will support Boston or perish with her." Besides agreeing to petition the king, the Congress approved a boycott of British goods beginning in December known as the Continental Association, in which the colonies would no longer import British goods. Committees of inspection were formed in each colony to enforce the boycott. If Parliament failed to rescind the Intolerable Acts, the delegates agreed to implement a nonexportation agreement in September 1775.[2]

Chandler learned of these decisions in late October, only after the Congress had disbanded and its deliberations had become public knowledge. He had decided earlier, however, that he would not wait to see what the delegates would do. The crisis was too great for him to remain idle. In a preemptive strike against the Congress's work, Chandler published his first political tract on September 8, a mere three days after the delegates began meeting. In the dark about what was transpiring at Carpenters' Hall, Chandler composed a broad critique of the revolutionary movement.

By 1774, he well understood the American position, and heatedly disagreed with it. Leading thinkers, including John Dickinson, who was no radical but was a sharp critic of Parliament, argued that this legislative body did not have the power to tax the colonists because the House of Commons did not represent them. In his *Letters from a Pennsylvania Farmer*—the most widely read pamphlet in the colonies before the publication of *Common Sense* in 1776—Dickinson warned that if Parliament could "take money out of our pockets, without our consent ... our boasted liberty is but a sound and nothing else." Even more forceful was Thomas Jefferson's *A Summary View of the Rights of British Americans*, which denied that Parliament had *any* authority over the colonies. In questioning Parliament's right to suspend New York's legislature, Jefferson railed against the dangers of "one free and independent legislature" taking upon itself the power to suspend the authority of another. "Shall [the colonial] governments be dissolved, their property annihilated, and their people reduced to a state of nature, at the imperious breath of a body of men, whom they never saw, in whom they never confided . . . ?" Jefferson asked. "Can any one reason be assigned why 160,000 electors in the island of Great Britain should give law to four millions in the states of America, every individual of whom is equal to every individual of them . . . ?"[3]

Chandler's fifty-five-page tract, titled *The American Querist*, offered up his most powerful response to these beliefs. Consisting of one hundred questions, including one that specifically referenced Dickinson's *Pennsylvania Farmer*, the pamphlet methodically built a case for British authority and denounced the radical American view of an empire in which Parliament had limited authority over the colonies. For starters, Chandler rejected as preposterous the Jeffersonian argument that the colonial legislatures were equal to Parliament. Sovereignty, said this student of the nonjurors, cannot be divided. "The supreme legislative authority of every nation . . . [extends] to all the dominions of that nation." Chandler then attempted to show that the charters never granted independence to colonial legislatures. Quite the contrary. Chandler argued that the British Crown, and by extension Parliament, had authority over the colonists from the beginning. He asked his readers to consider this question: "Whether there be any proof or probability, that, when the first grants of land in America were made by the British crown to British subjects, it was intended by the former, or understood by the latter, that they were to be no longer subject to the supreme legislative authority of the British nation?"[4]

For Chandler, the answer was clear. In practical terms, "supreme legislative authority" meant Parliament had the right to levy taxes. Pennsylvania's charter, for instance, explicitly granted Parliament this right, according to Chandler, while Virginia's 1606 charter went even further: the king could raise taxes there without consulting Parliament and could use the money for the Crown's benefit.[5]

To this lover of government and monarchy, America of the early 1770s resembled England of the 1640s—it was a world turned upside down. Lower sorts were rioting, violence was growing, and good order was under assault. Mechanics, seamen, and artisans—the uncouth workers who were supposed to know, and to stay in, their place—were becoming increasingly active in the revolutionary movement. In the leading cities and ports throughout the colonies, these workers and seamen banded together and formed their own associations, such as the Mechanics Committee in New York City. Committee members marched through city streets, brawled with British soldiers, harassed customs officers and other British officials, and burned the writings of loyalists to the king. Opponents of the revolutionary movement faced tarring and feathering and worse. Tarring and feathering especially appalled Chandler and other loyalists. This centuries-old punishment involved stripping victims naked and pouring or brushing boiling black tar on their bodies, blistering their skin. The perpetrators then covered the victims with feathers and paraded them through town, with crowds gathering to jeer them. Living in a Presbyterian stronghold near New York City, Chandler observed this mayhem and felt personally threatened by it because of his notoriety as a prominent loyalist and as the leading advocate for an American episcopate. Chandler understood something else: elites, who were supposed to know better, were winking at the growing violence and, at times, even organizing riots and street protests.[6]

Sickened by the unruliness of American society and the assault on government, Chandler in *The American Querist* likened the revolutionary movement to an illness: "a dangerous swelling and inflammation" that arose from Whiggish radicalism and the protests that followed. Medical wisdom of the day said illness occurred when a body's "humours" got out of balance. In American society, Chandler explained, the same thing was occurring as democracy advanced and governmental authority broke down. The colonists' "imprudence and intemperance," as well as their "inflammatory publications and harangues," were throwing the body politic out of whack and leading to fevers that were ravaging the colonies and weakening government. Plain facts, Chandler told his readers, were the cure to these fevers and would save society from "notorious quacks and empirics, who have an interest in deceiving us." As he did during the bishop's campaign, Chandler attacked the hypocrisy of a movement that espoused liberty and freedom but attempted to muzzle its opponents through violence. Indeed, *The American Querist* opened by asking "whether Americans have not a right to speak their sentiments on subjects of government; and whether all attempts to check and discourage freedom of speech ... are not to be considered as unwarrantable usurpations, tending to introduce and establish a bondage of the worst kind?" But Chandler offered up a twist on this familiar argument: the radicals suppressed contrary opinions because they were "conscious of the weakness of [their] cause." They feared, in other words, loyalist arguments. These fears, he believed, were behind the burning of pamphlets and the physical intimidation of the king's most loyal supporters. Loyalist critiques were so potent that the radicals did not want the public to see them. Chandler would come to experience the rough treatment firsthand: the Sons of Liberty burned copies of *The American Querist* on the first day of its publication, and Chandler's later tracts met the same fate.[7]

Chandler also denounced as dangerous a democratic society where ordinary Americans would have a say in the running of their government. The Continental Congress, he complained, did not represent the collective wisdom of colonial society; it was a "government of unprincipled *mobs.*" "Ignorant men, bred to the lowest occupations," were guiding political affairs, he wrote. Overall, however, Chandler's tone was lawyerly and calm. He organized the one hundred questions carefully, building his case against radical arguments question by question. He did not assert—he asked, phrasing a question in such a way that the answer was obvious to any right-thinking American. All reasonable people, Chandler was convinced, would have to conclude that Parliament was supreme and had authority over the colonies. Chandler's approach gained a large audience, despite the Sons of Liberty's attempts to suppress the tract: *The American Querist* went through eleven editions and was published in London in 1775. Its impact on those colonists who backed Parliament or were neutral in the fight over American rights is unknown. But the pamphlet outraged American Whigs because of its attacks on the revolutionary movement, its defense of Parliament, and its denunciations of democracy. Chandler wanted to come across as reasonable, but the one-hundred-question format, along with his monarchical values and ridiculing of "Ignorant men" assuming leadership, angered Whiggish readers.[8]

In late October, about six weeks after publication of *The American Querist*, Chandler and the American public learned of the First Continental Congress's actions in which it approved the Suffolk Resolves and backed the New Englanders' calls for a Continental Association, including forming committees to enforce it. Chandler likened these developments to the lifting of a veil: all could now plainly see what he had long known—the radicals wanted to overthrow British authority and establish a republic.

With the plot to establish independence exposed, Chandler followed up *The American Querist* with a tract in late 1774 that warned the colonies were barreling toward disaster, and he urged Americans to act quickly to prevent this catastrophe. Called *A Friendly Address to All Reasonable Americans*, the tract again exuded reasonableness in an attempt to strengthen the loyalists' ranks and awaken Americans to the dangers Chandler said they faced.[9]

A Friendly Address to All Reasonable Americans questioned the central premises of the revolutionary movement and argued that American liberties would be safer in the empire than out. The English constitution "has always been the wonder of the world," Chandler said, "and under its protection and mild influence, the subjects of Great-Britain are the happiest People on earth." The colonists were blessed under this constitution, he continued, enjoying rights that oppressed people elsewhere envied. "Of all people under Heaven, the King's subjects in America, have hitherto had the least ground for complaint," he said.[10]

Chandler denied that Parliament had acted arbitrarily by passing the duty on tea. Contrary to what the radicals asserted, he said, this duty was no tax. After all, he pointed out, the colonists could avoid paying the duty simply by not drinking tea. And this small duty on a beverage hardly justified the violent response it spawned. "If this may be called a burden," he commented dryly, "so may the weight of an atom on the shoulders of a giant." Chandler praised South Carolina as a model of decorum that other colonies should emulate: the colonists there allowed the tea to land but boycotted its purchase. "Happy would it have been for the colonies, if this measure had been universally taken," he said. "In that case, we should still have enjoyed tranquility, uninterrupted by seditious alarms." In other places—Boston most notoriously—the colonists either destroyed the tea or sent it back. Both acts, Chandler said, were an insult to government. And it was this challenge to government that most angered Chandler, not the destruction of private property. Boston's behavior was criminal, and its punishment was proper and deserved, he argued: "the crime of the Bostonians . . . was an act of the highest insolence towards government."[11]

For the sake of argument, Chandler considered what Americans *should* do if their rights were invaded. Here, he laid out his pre-1688 conception of authority and his rejection of revolution. Rebellion was simply not an option, he counseled. Unhappy colonists could petition Parliament or the Crown, but nothing more. Americans would be wise to "shew their wisdom and prudence, to submit with patience to their present condition, rather than to provoke the power that oppresses them." But they were not patient; they were violent and insolent, Chandler lamented. The injured party, as a result, was not the people of Boston but the British government. "The most essential rights of government were audaciously invaded—the crime was notorious and unquestionable." Parliament had no choice but to punish the Bostonians. If it failed to act, Chandler said, this august body would see its power and authority evaporate. And such weakness was inconceivable if the doctrine of sovereignty were to have any meaning. "To use the words of the justly celebrated Dr. Blackstone, 'The bare idea of a state, without a power, somewhere vested, to alter every part of its laws, is the height of political absurdity.'"[12]

Chandler rejected the argument of Dickinson, Jefferson, and others that a law did not apply to those who did not have a say in its passage. In defending virtual representation, he noted that millions of Englishmen on the home islands "have no votes in elections, and are never consulted about the expediency of laws." Despite their lack of representation, people still must obey the government. "So long as a man resides with in any dominion, he is a subject of it, and is obliged to submit to its laws, as far as they concern him, whether he approves of them or not," he wrote. "There are many people in England, who are natives of the country, that do not consent to acts of Parliament—that are passed, unless by a bare *fiction* of the law; which can make a nominal consent, but not a real one. This is always the case of the Minority."[13]

The existence of colonial charters did not limit Parliament's authority, Chandler continued. From the earliest days of settlement, the colonists "well knew that the authority of Parliament was not to be suspended or withdrawn, in their favour; and they knew too, that they had no power of sending representatives to Parliament of their own choosing."[14]

Chandler also returned to a favorite theme from *The American Querist*: the revolutionary movement was out of control and posed grave dangers to government and authority. This time, he did not use a medical analogy about fevers. Instead, he turned to history to warn that the colonists' "own misconduct" was leading to their ruin. During the English Civil Wars of the 1640s, Chandler noted, Englishmen did not intend to start a revolution. But when critics of Charles I challenged the king, events spiraled out of control, and "seditious principles" steadily took hold among the public. "Men gave way to unfavourable suspicions concerning the King and his Ministers, and thus lost the reverence that is due to the regal authority," Chandler said. "They then began to take pleasure in blackening the King's character, and in giving an invidious turn to all his actions. From this they proceeded to caballing against him; and, at last, they took up arms deluded with the pretence of liberty, and property, and religious rights." And once they had taken up arms against the king, "they found it necessary to destroy him, for their own security. This soon brought on a general destruction of liberty and property, and the ruin of the nation, as well as of themselves. Such is the common progress, and the effect, of rebellions in general."[15]

Chandler believed that the colonies could still avoid disaster—if they ended their rebellious ways and pursued "moderate and wise measures." Such a course, he said, would entail making "a candid acknowledgment of our political errors and offences—a formal allowance of the rightful supremacy in general, of Great-Britain, over the American Colonies—a declaration of our aversion to a state of indepency [sic]." On the sticky subject of taxation, he urged the colonists to issue "a respectful remonstrance" and promise to pay. And instead of antagonizing Parliament with its belligerent demands for political rights, the Congress should propose "a reasonable plan for a general American constitution." Chandler did not say what such a constitution would be. But in *What Think Ye of the Congress Now?* he praised Joseph Galloway's 1774 Plan of Union as a thoughtful compromise, citing its "genuine spirit of candour and moderation on one side, and a due regard to the dignity and honour of Great-Britain on the other." (The First Continental Congress rejected the plan in 1774 as tepid and unworkable.) Galloway proposed keeping the colonies in the empire but creating an American parliament whose consent was required on taxation and trade. Chandler's main—and amorphous—requirement in *A Friendly Address* was that a constitution be "worthy of Great-Britain to give, and of the colonies to receive." Given the severity of the crisis and the colonists' anger toward Parliament, Chandler understood that a blanket submission on the Americans' part was not feasible. Predictably, though, Chandler viewed the colonists as being in a subordinate position. The two sides needed to agree on a constitutional settlement that would maintain parliamentary sovereignty and preserve American liberties.[16]

Chandler did believe a settlement was possible if reasonable Americans stood up and put the "obstinate, hot-headed Zealots" in their place. Members of the Church of England had an especially important role to play in ending the crisis, according to Chandler. Anglicans' longtime enemies were leading the charge for independence. History had amply shown that when Presbyterians and Congregationalists controlled society, they persecuted their religious rivals. "Their inveterate enmity to the Church of England, has polluted the annals of the British history," Chandler wrote. "Their intolerance in England, towards the members of the Church, when the sovereign power was usurped by them, is recorded in characters of Blood." Their ascension in the revolutionary movement left Church of England members with a fateful choice, Chandler said: renounce "your principles relating both to religion and government, or you can expect no quarter under the administration of such intemperate zealots." Chandler counseled American Anglicans to do their duty. After all, Church of England members have long been "the great obstacle in the way of those republican fanaticks," he said. "This Church has always been famed and respected for its loyalty, and its regard to order and government. Its annals have been never stained with the history of plots and conspiracies, treasons and rebellions."[17]

Chandler expected the Continental Association to produce a backlash in the colonies. Not only did the act create committees that would violate the liberties of those who rejected the nonimportation and nonexportation agreements, but the various boycotts would ruin the economy. He likened nonimportation to "cutting off an arm in order to get rid of a sore on a finger." Farmers—the backbone of the American economy—would especially suffer, Chandler warned. At bottom, the "rebellious Republicans" in the Congress would lead the colonies to ruin. When the fighting came, "a large majority of the Americans will heartily unite with the King's troops, in reducing America to order. Our violent republicans will then find themselves deserted by thousands and thousands in whom they now confide; and inexpressibly dreadful must be their disappointment."[18]

ATTACKS ON *A FRIENDLY ADDRESS*

A Friendly Address outraged members of the revolutionary movement, who saw it as the work of a "prostituted" high churchman seeking to scare Americans out of defending their rights. William Bradford, a Philadelphia printer, conceded in a letter to James Madison that the tract was "very artfully done, & I am afraid has had some bad effects on the lower Class of people." Its effectiveness led several Whigs to answer it, including a powerful response from Charles Lee, who came to the colonies in 1773 from England after serving in the British army. According to Bradford, readers suspected Chandler or Myles Cooper wrote it, and Lee had no doubt that the author was an "Ecclesiastick": "He has the want of candour and truth, the apparent spirit of persecution, the unforgiveness, the deadly hatred to Dissenters, and the zeal for arbitrary power, which has distinguished Churchmen in all ages." Lee did not waste time on constitutional niceties and dry arguments disputing parliamentary authority. Instead, he savaged Chandler's argument in one powerful paragraph, sarcastically noting that Chandler had concluded "the Parliament has a right to tax you without your consent; that the duty upon tea is no tax; that this duty is your only grievance; that the cause of Boston is their own concern; that it is not your cause; . . . that submission is to be paid to the higher powers, whatever character they be." Lee added, "Now I challenge the whole world to produce so many wicked sentiments, stupid principles, audaciously false assertions, and monstrous absurdities crowded together in so small a compass." Having quickly disposed of this hated ecclesiastic, the rest of Lee's essay explained why the Americans could win a military contest against the supposedly invincible British military.[19]

It was up to Philip Livingston, a New York City merchant and member of the powerful Livingston clan, to rebut Chandler's political and constitutional arguments. *A Friendly Address* must have grated on Livingston—he produced a thirty-page tract within a week of its publication. Livingston noted that Chandler's case rested on three main assertions: "That the duty on tea is no tax. The second, that if a tax, it is a small one, and Parliament hath a right to take from us a small matter without our consent. And the third, that a man may be rightfully bound by laws which he does not, and cannot asset to." Livingston, of course, denied that Parliament had the right to legislate for the colonies, but his main concern was to attack Chandler's premise that Americans were "bound by the laws of Heaven to obey its mandates" and that government was the protector of the citizenry's rights. During the constitutional debate that unfolded after the Stamp Act, American pamphleteers argued that rights were universal and inherent; a legislative body or law did not bestow them. As John Dickinson put it in 1766, "We claim [our rights] from a higher source—from the King of kings, and Lord of all the earth. They are not annexed to us by parchments and seals. They are created in us by the decrees of Providence. . . . They are born with us; exist with us; and cannot be taken from us by any human power without taking our lives."[20]

Livingston questioned Chandler's assertion that "if none of our legal rights have been invaded, no injury has been done us." What did Chandler mean by legal rights? Livingston asked. "Do you mean, my Reverend Sir, that any right (that of taxing ourselves for instance), if it be not confirmed by some statute law, is not a legal right, and therefore an invasion of such right, will neither justify resentment, nor authorise complaint?" Livingston also homed in on the paradox in one critical Chandler argument: Americans, in Livingston's paraphrase of a passage in *A Friendly Address*, "may be bound by laws we do not consent to, and yet possess all the rights of *English*-men." Natural rights, he wrote, were universal, extending to even the Frenchman or Turk; such rights were not something that the English constitution or Parliament bestowed. Like Dickinson and Jefferson, Livingston argued that the Crown could not "annihilate" American rights by withdrawing or amending colonial charters: "Those rights were conferred by the King of Kings, and no earthly Potentate can take them away."[21]

A *Friendly Address* also drew a scathing response from John Adams. In a short tract that he began writing in November 1774 but never finished or published, Adams rejected Chandler's premise that the people lacked the right to rebel or protest. The "Supream power of any Kingdom or State is the whole Body of the People," Adams wrote in a passage echoing John Locke, and the people reserve the right to judge for themselves whether a measure is just. Adams was especially bothered by Chandler's argument that subjects can only remonstrate to the supreme power "in a respectful Manner" against measures they consider oppressive. How would that work in practice? Adams wondered, for Chandler also said that the supreme power "can do no wrong" and was "perfectly wise, just and good." And that meant the supreme power would see *any* kind of remonstrance as disrespectful, Adams said.[22]

Chandler chose not to answer these attacks, likely because events were moving so fast in the closing days of 1774. The boycotts were in full swing, local committees were increasingly harassing loyalists, and royal authority throughout the colonies was collapsing. Chandler only needed to step out his front door to observe how powerful radicalism was becoming. In late 1774, the Elizabethtown Association authorized the burning of *A Friendly Address to All Reasonable Americans*, calling the pamphlet a threat to American liberties. Counties throughout New Jersey, meanwhile, had formed Committees of Correspondence during the summer months of 1774, and Essex County—home to Elizabeth Town—passed a series of resolutions protesting the Intolerable Acts and took the lead in organizing a New Jersey convention to coordinate the colony's response to London's crackdown. Besides rejecting Parliament's right to tax the colonies, the convention pledged to support Boston, backed the nonimportation and nonexportation agreements, and agreed to send representatives to the First Continental Congress. Adding insult to injury, Chandler's neighbor and rival William Livingston was appointed a delegate to the Congress.[23]

Faced with these growing threats, and encircled by radical Whigs in East Jersey challenging Crown and Parliament, Chandler in 1775 retreated to his study anew to denounce the revolutionary movement. The result was a pamphlet mocking the Continental Congress called *What Think Ye of the Congress Now?*, which he published anonymously. The Second Continental Congress was getting ready to meet in mid-May 1775, and Chandler again wanted to discredit it in the eyes of the American public. But loyalism's position had

What think ye of the CONGRESS *Now?*
OR, AN
ENQUIRY,
HOW FAR THE
AMERICANS
Are BOUND to ABIDE BY, and EXECUTE, the
DECISIONS of the late
CONTINENTAL CONGRESS.
WITH A PLAN,
By SAMUEL GALLOWAY, Esq;
FOR A
PROPOSED UNION
BETWEEN
GREAT-BRITAIN and the COLONIES.

To which is added, An
ALARM to the LEGISLATURE
OF THE
PROVINCE of NEW-YORK.
Occasioned by the present POLITICAL DISTURBANCES.
Addressed to the
REPRESENTATIVES in GENERAL ASSEMBLY convened.

"It is hoped and expected, that this Want of Confidence in the
Justice and Tenderness of the Mother Country, and this open
Resistance to its Authority, can only have found Place among
the lower and more ignorant of the People: The better and
wiser Part of the Colonies will know that Decency and Submission may prevail, not only to redress Grievances, but to
obtain Grace and Favour; while the Outrage of a public Violence can expect nothing but Severity and Chastisement."
General CONWAY.

NEW-YORK, Printed by J. RIVINGTON:
LONDON, Reprinted for RICHARDSON and
URQUHART, under the Royal Exchange. 1775.

FIG. 6 Title page of Chandler's *What Think Ye of the Congress Now?*, 1775, which was the third and final tract that he wrote denouncing the revolutionary movement. Shortly after its publication, he went into exile.

weakened since Chandler composed *The American Querist*, and he conceded some points that he had bitterly contested only a few months earlier as he tried to blunt the American Whigs' momentum. One admission was that "some" of the Parliament's actions were wrong and Americans "do not enjoy all the privileges of Englishmen." That admission led to a more startling one: "It is time that we were exempted, in a regular way, from parliamentary taxation, on some generous and equitable plan." *The American Querist*, by contrast, had defended parliamentary taxation and asserted that the colonial charters had carefully limited the authority of provincial legislatures.[24]

Chandler also softened—in a few places—his opinion of the congressional delegates, claiming with a straight face, "I never had any personal objections to any of them. Some of them are men for whom I have a peculiar regard, and who are generally esteemed for many excellent qualities." Chandler even stated that the Congress would have been considered legal if it had not overstepped its bounds—an extraordinary statement coming from a fervent monarchist who regularly derided the Congress as a mere committee and an illegal body at that, with no constitutional standing.[25]

But after offering up these concessions in the face of a strengthening revolutionary movement, Chandler proceeded to attack the Congress and to defend "the absolute authority" of Parliament. The crux of his case was that the delegates at the First Continental Congress had exceeded the scope of their instructions from their home colonies. They were sent to Philadelphia "to obtain for the Colonies an exemption from taxation by the British Parliament. In the pursuit of this great object, many of the Delegates are expressly directed by their respective constituents, to confine themselves to the use of such means and measures as are proper and lawful; . . . and some of them are very seasonably reminded, that they were to negotiate, not for an independent community, but for British America."[26]

Chandler argued that radical delegates outmaneuvered and tricked the moderates, whom he described as "honest and pacific." "The moderate party soon found, that they had been circumvented and ensnared; that they were allowed to have no influence in the debates," Chandler wrote. From there, he returned to a favorite theme: New England radicals were dragging the colonies into rebellion. "The people in New-England, if they have not actually levied war against the King, have manifestly discovered a disposition to levy war against him; and throughout the summer past they have been making such military preparations, as can have no other end than to enable them to fight the King's troops," Chandler said. Worse, the Congress approved a resolution praising New England's actions. The Suffolk Resolves were proof of New England's intentions, he continued. "Now if all this does not amount to an open revolt and rebellion, I have always mistaken the meaning of the word; and I shall be obliged to any gentleman, learned in the law or acquainted with history, if he will inform me, or the public, what rebellion is."[27]

For Chandler, the conclusion was unmistakable: the colonies were in rebellion, and rebellion, in his eyes, was simply unacceptable. To make his point, Chandler took a swipe at Charles Lee, who in his attack on *A Friendly Address* defended rebellion by saying that "at least ninety-nine Americans in a hundred" believed Charles I was an "execrable tyrant" and that only those blinded by "the Dæmon of Jacobitism" could fail to see Cromwell's actions as worthy. Chandler countered that Charles's execution was murder and Cromwell's actions constituted a rebellion. Rebellion by definition, Chandler said, was illegal. If Cromwell's "ravaging and laying waste his kingdoms—his dissolving the authority of the Lords and Commons,—and his total subversion of the constitution, did not amount to a rebellion; then the people of Suffolk [County] are not guilty of rebellion," Chandler said. And "all reputable writers, whether of our own or of foreign nations, and all our acts of Parliament, that mention it, call Cromwell's outrageous opposition to legal authority, a rebellion."[28]

Curiously, given that radicals wanted to weaken colonial councils, not strengthen them, Chandler believed that the Congress was angling to create powerful legislative upper chambers on the colony level that would rival Parliament's House of Lords. He based this belief on a congressional resolution that criticized colonial councils as "unconstitutional, dangerous, and destructive to the freedom of American Legislation." Two factors likely led Chandler to make this seemingly strange argument. One was that he and other loyalists worried that the Congress was establishing a national state with no checks and balances—no separate legislative chambers headed by an executive as existed under the British constitution. In addition, Chandler was offended that these men were striving to exercise the same authority as aristocrats did in Parliament's upper chamber.

"Here, Reader, if thou canst but read, you may see, that an American House of Lords is in agitation; in which the members must have the same rights, privileges, and honours, which the English constitution has given to the members of the House of Lords in the Mother Country," Chandler wrote. "They must be independent of the Crown, and independent of the representatives of the people."[29]

The second, closely related factor was Chandler's disdain for the social backgrounds of American Whigs who were assuming leadership positions in the revolutionary movement. Chandler used the resolution condemning colonial councils to poke fun anew at the pretentions of the revolutionary movement and its democratic impulse to place ordinary people in positions of authority: "The Committees of Correspondence will furnish us with Marquisses and the Committees of Observation, with Earls. The Viscounts may consist of Heroes that are famed for their exploits in tarring and feathering," he sneered. His larger point was to defend the colonial councils and the Crown's authority to appoint their members, for Chandler took the Congress's attack on the councils as an attack on monarchy. The revolutionaries, Chandler warned, wanted "to depress the power of the Crown, and to exalt the power of the people" in an effort to create an American republic.[30]

Chandler's personal pique surfaced in the tract, most likely a sign of the growing pressure he was feeling in the early months of 1775. He decried the burning of pamphlets by the Sons of Liberty and other revolutionaries in far harsher terms than he had in his two earlier tracts. In condemning the Sons, Chandler compared this revolutionary organization to the most hated religious group in Protestant culture, the Roman Catholic Church: "One of their ways of confuting pamphlets, like the old popish way of confuting hereticks, is by fire and faggot. This proceeds from the same bigotry, and is dictated by the same spirit, which commonly disgraced the dark ages preceding the Reformation." Chandler also still nursed wounds from his treatment at the hands of the *American Whig* during the bishop's campaign a decade earlier. Near the end of *What Think Ye of Congress Now?* Chandler resurrected the ghost of the *American Whig* in an effort to prove that the revolutionaries—specifically, Boston revolutionaries—had long been plotting to create a republican government independent of Great Britain. As proof, Chandler quoted an essay in which the *Whig* wrote of establishing a mighty American empire, built on the foundation of a regular American constitution. The circular letter of 1768 compiled by Boston's selectmen was further proof of the revolutionaries' intentions, Chandler continued. Indeed, he said, the Bostonians and the *Whig* even affixed a date: the revolution would commence in seven years, in 1775.[31]

> Thus we see the particular time for beginning this work was then already fixed and determined; and such predispositions were made, that the event was rendered indubitable, in the opinion of the

workmen. All these particulars were declared to the public, by the American Whig, on the 11th of April, 1768; and his prophecy was fully verified by the event. For we all know, that, before the revolution of seven years was completed, and exactly at the end of six years and five months, the first stone of the long projected building actually was laid by the people of Suffolk.[32]

The irony, of course, was that Chandler's fears of a plot mirrored that of the American radicals, who believed that the Crown and Parliament were out to enslave the colonies. The radicals saw the Stamp Act and other post-1763 British measures as a dangerous, calculated attempt by London to deprive the colonists of their liberties. Much of the blame, they believed, rested with the ministry, whose corruption and growing power were undermining the delicate balance of the British constitution. In addition, many believed that the Church of England, as an arm of the state, was aiding the effort and that Chandler's attempt to bring an Anglican bishop to America was part of the broader plot against American liberties. In the Whig view, history showed that power corrupts and causes governments to become more despotic.[33]

Chandler scoffed at these fears. The British constitution remained sound, and corruption was not eating away at the British government, he believed. Power does not corrupt; it preserves order, he said. Unlike his Whig countrymen, this student of 1688 and the nonjurors never saw a British plot to enslave America—he saw a plot to attack monarchy and launch a republican revolution. And Chandler wanted Americans to understand just how far back the plot against the king went and who, exactly, was behind it.

He also believed that recognizing the origins of the independence movement was essential to recognizing the current threat posed by the Continental Congress. Contemporaries (and, later, historians) may have seen the First Continental Congress as moderate in its composition and careful in its deliberations, but Chandler strongly disagreed. The delegates did not want to find a compromise with Parliament, he said; they wanted to complete their long-desired design of breaking away from London. The delegates have, in short, "altogether neglected the work they were sent upon . . . [and] rebellion and civil war are the necessary consequence of our being governed by the Congress."[34]

Chandler's tract concluded with a plea to "withdraw ourselves immediately from within the vortex of the Congress—that we may be at liberty to pursue the real good of our country, under the friendly direction of the law and sound policy." What he meant, of course, was that Americans had to reject both the Congress and rebellion. The provincial legislatures should regain the initiative by sending respectful addresses to the king and Parliament. "Candidly and generously confess, that a mistaken zeal for liberty has produced among us some tumultuous and disorderly proceedings, which are not to be justified," Chandler advised. "Beg that all these things may be buried in oblivion, and that there may be no repeating of past grievances. Profess, in your own names and in ours, loyalty and allegiance to the King in the strongest terms; and express our willingness to acknowledge the supremacy of Great-Britain in all cases excepting those of taxation. Give assurances that we dread the very thoughts of an absolute independency."[35]

Among loyalist writers, Chandler was the most forceful in rejecting protest and defending British authority. The Glorious Revolution and the debate surrounding it had taught him the dangers of rebellion, and the actions of American radicals only convinced him that history was repeating itself. By contrast, Anglican minister William Smith, a moderate who supported the defense of colonial rights but not independence or rioting, believed the decision whether to obey an unjust law was a matter of individual conscience, as was the decision whether to rebel. He rejected passive obedience in harsh terms. "The free-born soul revolts against it," he said in a sermon he delivered in June 1775. Smith praised English liberty, the growth of religious toleration, and colonists' struggles for their constitutional rights, which he described as "one of the grandest struggles, to which freemen can be called." Indeed, he considered "the cause of virtue and Freedom [to be] the CAUSE of God upon earth."[36]

But Smith's Whiggish notions were counterbalanced by conservative ones that resembled Chandler's. People were obligated to obey just authority, he told his audience: "by every method in your power, and in every possible case, support the Laws of your country." Like Chandler, Smith blanched at zealotry. "While you profess yourselves contending for Liberty, let it be with the temper and dignity of freemen, undaunted and firm, but without wrath or vengeance." And although Smith believed resistance to an unjust ruler was justified, he said it should be within the confines of the constitution.[37]

Chandler saw the post-1688 Church of England as a bastion of obedience and a check on liberalism; Smith praised it as an institution that supported liberty but not violence. The church, he said in his sermon, ignoring the nonjuring movement, supported the opponents of King James II in the Glorious Revolution and carefully defended the rights of Englishmen. "Did they not magnanimously set their foot upon the line of the constitution, and tell [his] Majesty to its face that 'they could not betray the public liberty,' and that the Monarch's only safety consisted 'in governing according to the laws'?" The church's behavior helped "kindle a flame that illuminated the land, and introduced that noble system of public and personal liberty, secured by the revolution." Since then, he said, the Church of England has been "jealous of the national rights, resolute for the protestant succession, favourable to the reformed religion, and desirous to maintain the faith of Toleration."[38]

Understanding that parliamentary actions—especially the Intolerable Acts—had alienated a large, and growing, number of Americans, many loyalist writers in 1774 and 1775 struggled to justify obedience to unpopular measures. No loyalist offered up a more conflicted view than Jonathan Boucher, an Anglican minister from Maryland. His 1774 *Letter from a Virginian* was so moderate and Whiggish that the Library of America, in a volume on revolutionary-era writings, questioned whether he wrote it, while a sermon he delivered in 1775 was positively Chandlerian in its calls for obedience. The answer to Boucher's wildly different views may well have had to do with his audience: Boucher wanted *A Letter from a Virginian* to persuade the broader public, and thus it took a Whiggish tone, while his sermon was aimed at a narrower audience—radical parishioners whom he wanted to confront.

In seeking to win over wavering Americans, *A Letter from a Virginian* did not mock the Continental Congress and the lower-class origins of the revolutionary movement's "beer-house gentry," as Chandler had described the Sons of Liberty in *What Think Ye of Congress Now?* "High Birth and Fortune . . . give no exclusive Title to Common Sense, Wisdom or Integrity," Boucher declared. "The lowest Orders of Men" have a right to examine the conduct of their governors, just as the gentry does. "The fundamental Principles of our Constitution are within the Reach of almost every Man's Capacity." But like William Smith and other loyalists, Boucher detested zealotry. Democracy was dangerous, he warned, because all men—rich, middling, or poor—"are govern'd more by their Temper than their Judgment." Men were easily misled; they were easy targets of "crafty designing Knaves, turbulent Demagogues, Quacks in Politics."[39]

Boucher saw the England of a century ago as a case in point. He denounced "the indiscreet Zeal and wild Passions of mad Enthusiasts" (Puritans and Presbyterians), as well as "slavish Bigots" (persecuting high church Anglicans). The criticisms of monarchy by the former enabled them "to throw a Veil over the horrors of Anarchy, and Rebellion" when war came, while the latter responded to regicide with a zeal "to sanctify the ridiculous and damnable Doctrines of Non-resistance and Passive-Obedience."[40]

Boucher warned his readers that American zealots were leading the colonies down the same dangerous path. He urged the delegates meeting in Philadelphia to rein in the extremists, and he appealed to their vanity, using language that must have made Chandler cringe. First, Boucher defended the existence of the Congress itself: "You, it is true, have not been summoned, or convened, by any formal constitutional Authority. . . . But you have been chosen as freely as the Circumstances of the Times would admit." Then he lavished praise on the delegates themselves: "We look up to you as the Oracles of our Country." He followed up this flattery by defending the right of commoners to participate in government: "All Orders of Men, who enjoy the Happiness of living under a free Government, may boldly assume the Character of Politicians; they inherit a right to it as much as the proudest Peer inherits a right to his Seat in Parliament."[41]

Boucher's argument became more conventional later in the tract. He questioned the effectiveness of the nonimportation and nonexportation agreements, defended Parliament's right to tax the colonies, and warned that independence would lead to civil war and disaster. Like Chandler, Boucher asserted that the colonies had thrived within the empire. "From the Infancy of our Colonies, to this very Hour, we have grown up and flourished under the Mildness, and Wisdom of her excellent Laws," Boucher declared. "Our Trade, our Possessions, our Persons have been constantly defended against the whole World, by the Fame of her Power, or by her Exertion of it."[42]

Boucher argued something far different in a 1775 sermon he gave at his church in St. Anne's Parish near Annapolis. The English-born minister, whose popularity suffered after he opposed cuts to Anglican ministers' salaries and appeared cool to the American cause, drew the ire of parish members who backed the revolutionary movement. When Boucher attempted to preach on Thursday, July 20, 1775—a day the Second Continental Congress had set aside for fasting and prayer—two hundred armed men drove him from his church. Unbowed, Boucher returned on Sunday, ready to deliver a sermon on a topic designed to enrage his radical foes—Christians must obey God and their earthly rulers.[43]

In delivering this provocative message at such a sensitive time during the revolutionary crisis, Boucher laid out a broad case for obedience that closely resembled Chandler's position. The duty to obey existed from the time of Jesus onward, Boucher said. "If the form of government under which the good providence of God has been pleased to place us be mild and free, it is our duty to enjoy it with gratitude and with thankfulness; and, in particular, to be careful not to abuse it by licentiousness," Boucher advised. But if the government was abusive, "still it is our duty not to disturb and destroy the peace of the community, by becoming refractory and rebellious subjects, and resisting the ordinances of God."[44]

The command to follow God meant individuals were not free to do as they pleased. Boucher defined liberty as "subserviency to law. 'Where there is no law,' says Mr. Locke, 'there is no freedom.'" When liberty was defined that way, the illegality of rebellion became clear, according to Boucher: "To pursue liberty, then, in a manner not warranted by law, whatever the pretence may be, is clearly to be hostile to liberty: and those persons who thus promise you liberty, are themselves the servants of corruption."[45]

Boucher also attacked the Lockean idea of government by compact as unworkable, because what men can make, men can undo. The inherent right to resist under Locke's compact would mean no government was safe, according to Boucher. Indeed, history showed that no society had ever formed a government in which people reserved the right to overthrow it. If one had, "it must have carried the seeds of its decay in its very constitution. For, as those men who make a government (certain that they have the power) can have no hesitation to vote that they also have the right to unmake it; ... [as a result,] it is morally impossible that there should be anything like permanency or stability in a government so formed."[46]

Like Chandler, Boucher drew his inspiration from Filmer and his patriarchal values: All individuals are natural subjects to someone in power over them, be it children in a family or subjects in a kingdom. Filmer further viewed government and monarchy as of divine origin. The creator wanted good government, and for that to happen Scripture decreed that, in Boucher's telling, "under the deputation and authority of God alone ... kings reign." For Boucher, the divine origins of monarchy meant princes received their commission from Heaven and they were "to be regarded and venerated as the vicegerent of God."[47]

Boucher's belief that government's authority was "absolute and irresistible" left him open to the charge that he countenanced unlimited obedience. He answered the accusation by carefully delineating between active and passive obedience, a delineation that echoed Archbishop John Whitgift's argument nearly two hundred years earlier:

If then, to resist government be to destroy it, every man who is a subject must necessarily owe to the government under which he lives an obedience either active or passive: active, where the duty enjoined may be performed without offending God; and passive, (that is to say, patiently to submit to the penalties annexed to disobedience,) where that which is commanded by man is forbidden by God. No government upon earth can rightfully compel any one of it's [sic] subjects to an active compliance with any thing that is, or that appears to his conscience to be, inconsistent with, or contradictory to, the known laws of God: because every man is under a prior and superior obligation to obey God in all things.[48]

Boucher agreed with Chandler that unhappy subjects have the right to remonstrate and petition, but not to protest or resist. To allow people to disobey a law they disagree with would mean the end of government, Boucher said. Obedience never made a man a bad subject, Boucher added, and society was better off when subjects patiently submitted to laws that they may not like. Parliament's imposition of a duty on tea was one example, Boucher said. Like Chandler, he portrayed it as an "insignificant" levy that two-thirds of the people of America will never have to pay. "Is it the part of an understanding people, of loyal subjects, or of good Christians, instantly to resist and rebel for a cause so trivial?" he asked. Even in a worst-case scenario where Parliament ignored remonstrances and petitions, good Christians must submit "to every ordinance of man, for the Lord's sake."[49]

Boucher's sermon was a grenade lobbed at his radical audience. Understanding how unpopular high churchmen and their values were among dissenters and American Whigs, two of Chandler's colleagues—Charles Inglis and Samuel Seabury—wanted to avoid antagonizing their readers. In their writings, both men adopted non-clergy personas and avoided the extremes of Chandler's and Boucher's position on authority. Inglis published a series of essays in the *New-York Gazette and Weekly Mercury* beginning in September 1774 in which he wrote as a patriotic "Freeholder" who reluctantly comes out of retirement to warn Americans about the dangers they faced from the revolutionary movement. Like *A Letter from a Virginian*, Inglis did not attack the Continental Congress. He instead emphasized that the colonies faced ruin if they rebelled against the king. Colonial grievances were not serious enough to justify the catastrophe that would result from a civil war,

Inglis argued. He, too, was dismissive of protests over the tea duty. To risk a bloody war over such a trivial thing, he wrote, would be "the highest Degree of Infatuation, Weakness and Want of Common Sense."[50]

Seabury, meanwhile, wrote as a farmer from Westchester County, New York. His *Letters of a Westchester Farmer* were well written and gained widespread attention. He had one significant advantage over Chandler, who had rushed *The American Querist* into print months earlier: He knew what the Congress had done when he wrote his first letter, titled *Free Thoughts on the Proceedings of the Congress at Philadelphia*. Seabury's tone was friendly and folksy: "I choose to address myself principally to You the *Farmers* of the Province of New-York, because I am most nearly connected with you, being one of your number." Chandler, too, had warned that independence would ruin the colonial economy, but Seabury couched his argument in language that a farmer would more easily understand. Prices for crops will drop, export markets will disappear, and farmers will end up bankrupt if the colonies leave the safety of the British empire, Seabury explained. In between such pithiness, Seabury worked in familiar loyalist allegations that hypocritical radicals would end up destroying American liberties. "Will you be instrumental in bringing the most abject slavery on yourselves?" Seabury asked New York farmers. "No, if I must be enslaved, let it by a King at least, and not by a parcel of upstart lawless Committee-men."[51]

Again writing as a plain countryman, Seabury addressed his second letter to "gentlemen merchants." This tract was more Chandlerian than his earlier one. It attacked New England delegates as extremists who were dragging the colonies into a war with Great Britain that the colonies could not win, denounced the Suffolk Resolves as treason, condemned the various associations as tyrannical, and dismissed the Continental Congress as illegal. And like Chandler and Boucher, Seabury argued that protests were both wrong and counterproductive. He ridiculed the idea that the colonists could challenge Parliament while swearing allegiance to the Crown. "To talk of subjection to the King of Great-Britain, while we disclaim submission to the Parliament of Great-Britain, is idle and ridiculous," Seabury wrote. "It is a distinction made by the American Republicans to serve their own rebellious purposes."[52]

Historians have long debated how much influence these loyalist writings had on the American public, with many arguing the tracts did little good and that the loyalists were on the defensive as the radicals pressed for war. But historians also agree that only about one-third of the colonists supported independence on the eve of the American Revolution. Chandler's prediction that military hostilities would not produce a swelling of support for the radical cause was astute: even after fighting broke out at Lexington, Concord, and Bunker Hill in 1775, most Americans remained unsure whether independence from Great Britain was a good idea.

For Chandler, that indecision offered a glimmer of hope in 1775 as he witnessed the madness swirling around him. As a student of history and an enemy of revolution, he could only warn Americans about the dangers they faced. His tracts, especially *The American Querist*, proved to be powerful pleas for order and sanity, and William Bradford feared "the lower Class of people" found them persuasive. His attacks on the revolutionary movement were savage and predictably enraged American radicals. Although he took the precaution of writing anonymously, Chandler's views were well known in both Elizabeth Town and the region, and his authorship was a poorly kept secret. Chandler, in short, was a marked man.

CHAPTER 7

Londoner
A Loyalist in Exile

In early May 1775, Thomas Bradbury Chandler fled to New York City, carrying only "some Articles of necessary Apparel." The decision to go into exile was not an easy one—it meant abandoning his family and his parish, and his departure drew criticism from at least one of his Anglican compatriots. But Chandler believed he had little choice. By late April, his friends were warning him that he was in great danger.[1]

Chandler's decision appeared prudent. His attacks on the revolutionary movement and the Continental Congress had made him one of the most detested "tories" in the middle colonies—and the opprobrium came on top of his notoriety as the leading advocate for an American episcopate. The cross-river trip to New York began a ten-year odyssey for Chandler that saw him become a London resident and American expatriate. This period was, in some ways, a quiet chapter in Chandler's eventful life. His health worsened during his time in a damp and sooty London, and he was seemingly a distant actor to the great drama of the American Revolution that was playing out across the Atlantic. But he was not idle. Chandler used his time at the seat of British power to resume his fight for an American episcopate, whose importance, he believed, was even more essential than before the colonial rebellion. At first blush, his new bishop's campaign seemed delusional, given the ongoing war and American hostility to the plan. But Chandler assumed British arms would prevail, and he was looking ahead to how London could restore its authority in the colonies when peace came. Chandler's thinking had changed little since 1765: he wanted the colonies' ties with Britain to rest on the firm union of church and state. A strong monarchy and an invigorated Church of England were essential to restoring order in the colonies, he believed. As he planned for the future, Chandler meanwhile pursued a second, more immediate cause: securing financial support for his fellow Church of England clergy in America as they struggled with persecution and poverty during the war.

Chandler missed his family terribly, but in some ways his London exile was a productive, even happy, time. He haunted bookshops and libraries, and he had the money and leisure to play tourist, soaking up British history and visiting seats of monarchical and political power. This time in England briefly reinforced Chandler's Anglophile sensibilities, especially his admiration for episcopacy and the Crown. But the shocking British military defeat at the hands of a ragtag rebel army and Parliament's decision to give up the fight infuriated Chandler. He saw surrender as a betrayal, and it likely contributed to his decision to return home in 1785 to a republic he loathed instead of removing to Canada and remaining in the British empire.

LAST DAYS IN AMERICA

As war neared in the mid-1770s, a vortex of events prompted Chandler to abandon Elizabeth Town. In December 1774, a large, enthusiastic crowd gathered at the Essex County courthouse to burn Chandler's *A Friendly Address to All Reasonable Americans*. The crowd did its work at the behest of the Elizabethtown Association, which denounced the tract as "infamous" and "containing many notorious falshoods" that would enable the British ministry to enslave the colonies. Then in April 1775, after a day of drinking, armed militia marched on Chandler's house. Their exact motives were unclear—Chandler's neighbor Elias Boudinot, a lawyer and leading revolutionary in New Jersey, speculated that someone with a personal grudge against Chandler egged the inebriated soldiers on. No matter. They certainly intended to rough up a person whom they considered an enemy to American liberties. Worried that such behavior would hurt the patriot cause, the Elizabeth committee intercepted the men before they could accost Chandler, according to Boudinot. It was a narrow escape, and it assuredly left Chandler shaken.[2]

Then came Lexington and Concord and the explosion of rage among the colonists that followed. On a cool night on April 18, 1775, some eight hundred British troops set out from Boston on a mission to seize ordnance and provisions in Concord, Massachusetts, and to capture two revolutionary firebrands, Samuel Adams and John Hancock. When the incursion was over the following day, eight Americans were dead and nearly three hundred British troops were killed or wounded.[3]

New York City learned of the bloodshed on April 22. One loyalist reported that "a mob of negroes, boys, sailors, and pickpockets" took to the city streets with drums beating to urge colonists to arm themselves to defend American liberties. On April 24, about one-third of the city's population—eight thousand in all—gathered outside City Hall to denounce British actions. The Sons of Liberty, meanwhile, stole British military provisions stored aboard two docked ships that were intended for the troops in Boston. They also looted the City Hall arsenal of one thousand muskets and bayonets, as well as ammunition. Militia companies formed, and a "Committee of Sixty" demanded that the populace subscribe to a General Association or else face retribution.[4]

Across the Hudson River, a dispatch rider reached Elizabeth Town on April 23, a Sunday, with a message from Boston addressed to "all friends of American liberty" that British troops "without any provocation" attacked and killed American militia at Lexington. In Chandler's neighborhood, "the late melancholy news from Boston" was causing "strange commotions among the people," according to New Jersey Chief Justice Frederick Smyth. For the king's supporters, violence was becoming all too common, and Chandler remained a prominent target of the revolutionaries. Thus, he made the difficult decision to leave his growing family—his wife, Jane, was forty-two years old and his children ranged in age from seven months old to twenty-four years old—and cross into New York from New Jersey.[5]

In New York City, Chandler could rely on a loyalist network for help, as well as a British military presence for protection. But upon his arrival in a New York seething with anger toward the British, Chandler realized he had stumbled into an even more dangerous situation than he had left behind. His diary, whose first entry was dated May 15, 1775, described a city that was in "utmost Confusion, and the Friends of Government under the severest Persecution." Chandler believed it was too dangerous to take a room where he normally stayed in the city, so he headed to the house on Greenwich Street of longtime New York Attorney General John Tabor Kempe, who was a vestryman at Trinity Church. Chandler believed Kempe's house was "a Place unsuspected, and less liable to Insults." This was another questionable decision; Kempe was a prominent British official and Anglican whose loyalties would be suspect to the roving bands of revolutionaries. (Kempe, indeed, remained loyal to the king during the war and fled to England in 1783 after the British evacuated New York City.)[6]

Within days of his arrival, Chandler's presence was known to the Sons and other revolutionaries, and he said he received intelligence that they were "determined to pay me a Visit." His friends were now counseling him to go into exile. Surrounded by unruly mobs and forced to keep "close at Mr. Kempe's," Chandler agreed. On the evening of May 16, he secured passage aboard the *Exeter*, an imposing British ship of the line that had a crew of five hundred and carried sixty-four cannons.[7]

But the *Exeter* would not sail for Bristol, England, until later in May, and Chandler could not safely remain at Kempe's house in the interim. Rescue came in the form of a British naval officer named Captain James Montagu, the son of an admiral, who commanded the *Kingfisher*, a sleek fourteen-gun Swan Class sloop with a crew of 125 men. Montagu invited Chandler to take refuge aboard his ship. Chandler gratefully accepted, believing the *Kingfisher* to be "the only Place of Safety near New-York." On May 17, with assistance from loyalist John Wetherhead, a British native and New York City merchant, Chandler left Kempe's for the *Kingfisher*.[8]

Joining Chandler on the *Kingfisher* were two colleagues whom he knew well: Myles Cooper, president of King's College, and James Rivington, the printer of numerous loyalist tracts, including Chandler's. Derided "as an incendiary employed by a wicked Ministry to disunite and divide us," Rivington was considered a traitor to the American cause despite his protestations that he printed loyalist tracts merely out of a commitment to free speech. Cooper was equally unpopular because of his writings attacking the revolutionaries and his leadership of a college seen as a bastion of Anglicanism. After news of Lexington and Concord broke, someone circulated a handbill on April 25 blaming Cooper, Rivington, and three others for the British attack on Americans in Massachusetts. The handbill told the five loyalists to "Fly for your lives or anticipate your doom by becoming your own executioners." For the moment, Cooper and Rivington refused to leave. But on May 10, a drunken mob of several hundred planned to seize the pair. The crowd approached Cooper's residence, with murmurs that they were ready to tar and feather him. With help from an unexpected source—Alexander Hamilton, who was a student at King's College—Cooper managed to escape. The Sons of Liberty, meanwhile, attacked Rivington's house and destroyed his press; a second mob later burned the house down. Both Cooper and Rivington boarded the *Kingfisher* that day, to be joined several days later by Chandler.[9]

In April and May, Chandler's other colleagues were under siege as well. All were reviled and faced arrest or worse. As Chandler's good friend Jonathan

Boucher put it years later, the burgeoning independence movement struck the Anglican clergy with the force of a storm. The crisis, he wrote, was "a torrent [that] swept away all cool and sober thought." In a letter to William Smith dated May 4, Boucher said he was afraid of being "maul'd by Committees." He was further alarmed by a rumor "confidently Circulated here, that Chandler and Cooper are both proscribed. I hope in God that this too is one of the Stories I have now learn'd to call a *Putamite*." The rumors, of course, would prove to be true.[10]

As spring turned to summer in 1775, Boucher was increasingly afraid to leave his house. By June, revolutionaries were pressuring him to sign Maryland's Articles of Association, which he would not do because it advocated taking up arms against the king. He refused to sign, explaining that "I should have been most base, and of course most miserable, had I done otherwise." The decision sealed his fate, and Boucher planned to join Chandler in exile in London. In August, Boucher traveled to Annapolis and made the arrangements.[11]

Most of Chandler's other colleagues stayed, including Samuel Seabury and Charles Inglis.[12] On May 30, Inglis reported to the Society for the Propagation of the Gospel that "we are here in a very alarming Situation. Doct. Cooper & Doct. Chandler have been obliged to quit this Country and sailed for England last week. I have been obliged to retire a few days from the threatened Vengeance of the New England people, who lately broke into this Province. But I hope I shall be able to keep my station." There Inglis remained until January 1784, when he went to London following the British evacuation of New York City a few months earlier.[13]

William Smith remained as well—and he criticized Chandler for abandoning his congregation. "If our Clergy were generally to quit their people at this time I saw we should not have the appearance of a Church or people left," he wrote after learning of Chandler's departure. But Smith later changed his mind when conditions deteriorated. In August 1776, with the British army marching toward Philadelphia, Pennsylvania's Supreme Executive Council ordered the arrest of Smith and forty others, charging that they "have in their general conduct and conversation evidenced a disposition inimical to the cause of America." His arrest was the first of a series of setbacks that ended in 1779, when Smith fled with his family to Chestertown, Maryland, following the British withdrawal from Philadelphia and the loss of his provostship at the College of Philadelphia. He remained in Chestertown until the end of the war.[14]

Thus, out of his circle of friends and acquaintances, Chandler was the first to go into exile. He also was one of the first loyalists to choose London. In mid-1775, the exiles typically headed to Boston, because of the large British military presence there. Boston, however, was surrounded by a newly formed Continental Army and life took on the air of a besieged garrison town. Food supplies were low. As conditions deteriorated, residents and loyalist refugees alike began to leave. By mid-July, two-thirds of Boston's population had left, according to one contemporary estimate. With conditions in Boston poor, many of this vanguard of loyalist exiles went to Halifax, Canada. But conditions were little better in Halifax than they were in Boston—in some ways, they were worse. The weather was forbidding, with exiles complaining of the "foggy chilling air," and living conditions in this remote northern British outpost were primitive.[15]

London, the giant metropolis and civilized seat of the British empire, looked increasingly enticing to those Americans who sided with the king. London certainly was the most attractive option to Chandler. An exile in hated Boston—even a temporary one—was unthinkable, and he did not consider Halifax an option at this time. In addition, Chandler knew the attractions of London firsthand, as he had visited the city in 1751 when he was ordained.[16]

THE LONDON YEARS

On May 19, with Cooper, Rivington, and Chandler safely aboard, the *Kingfisher* set sail for Sandy Hook, New Jersey, across the bay from New York. There, the schooner met up with the *Exeter*, and Chandler and Cooper transferred their meager belongings to the British naval ship. Rivington sailed later for England, where he remained until 1777 when he returned to New York with the city securely in British hands. Chandler and Cooper were greeted kindly by two other passengers. Then the waiting for "a proper Wind" began, Chandler noted in his diary.[17]

On May 25, the *Exeter* raised anchor, accompanied by more than twenty vessels that were headed for various ports across Europe. By evening, the New Jersey shoreline was a distant speck: Chandler estimated the *Exeter* had covered six leagues already. What Chandler felt as the ship of the line carried him farther from his family and former life is unknown. An emotional man whose correspondence and political writings could be volcanic, Chandler did not describe his feelings as the *Exeter* set sail. He brought a reporter's eye to his diary, recounting what he was seeing, typically in straightforward prose. The cold Atlantic air grabbed Chandler's attention; the weather during these first few weeks at sea was miserable—rainy or foggy, Chandler said, and when the *Exeter* arrived at what Chandler suspected was the Grand Banks off Newfoundland, the ship encountered "a large Island of Ice, by which Time we experienced the Weather to be almost intolerably cold." For the passengers, diversions were few. "We attempted to fish, but the Sea ran too high," Chandler reported at one point. The weather remained "almost intolerably cold" and the winds strong as the *Exeter* navigated the Atlantic.[18]

Two weeks later, Chandler and his fellow passengers were "hoping to find ourselves off the Coasts of Ireland, but were disappointed, owing chiefly ... to the bad Steerage of the Ship." Six days later, Chandler could report positive news: "At 4 in the Morning we had a Sight of Lundy at a great Distance right ahead." Lundy was the largest island in the Bristol Channel, about twelve miles off Devon in southwestern England. The nearly six-week crossing was almost over. The final days aboard were ones of anticipation and wonder. Chandler was thrilled to spot "a large Tortoise of the Logerhead kind," a sight he described as "unexampled in the Bristol Channel." The final night aboard the *Exeter* involved one final indignity—the weather was blustery, according to Chandler. But the winds were favorable and the ship anchored in Kingroad. At last, Chandler had arrived in the British Isles, the place Shakespeare famously described as "this royal throne of kings, this sceptered isle." After nearly two months at sea, Chandler and Cooper did not linger aboard the *Exeter*. They headed northeast by water on the Bristol Channel to Bristol, a thriving maritime port on England's southwestern coast. Bristol was a major center in the triangular African slave trade, and its large fishing fleets roamed the Grand Banks in search of cod.[19]

Safely in Bristol, Chandler and Cooper enjoyed a breakfast at the White Hart Inn, a popular stopping point for travelers. Chandler then attended services at the gothic-towered St. Stephen's Church, whose history dated to 1248. Chandler looked up an old friend, Josiah Tucker (1712–1799), dean of Gloucester, but he was out of town. How the two became friends is unclear, but their relationship says much about Chandler the man and disciple of Samuel Johnson. As dean of Gloucester since 1758, the Oxford-educated Tucker became an influential economic thinker and earned a reputation as a liberal clergyman and social reformer. He first wrote a history of Methodism that was published in 1742. Tucker, who came to know the Bristol maritime economy intimately as dean, then wrote widely on trade, including works that influenced Adam Smith. Tucker and Chandler would have had much to discuss had they met up. Tucker believed the British economy would be better off if the American colonies gained independence—an argument Chandler assuredly rejected. But Tucker also dismissed American claims as absurd—a stance Chandler assuredly welcomed.[20]

After so much time at sea, Chandler and Cooper decided to linger a few days in Bristol before embarking on the approximately 118-mile overland journey to London. The area contained many delights for an American tourist. Chandler first visited a glass house—a marvel in an age when glass remained an expensive commodity—and the majestic St. Mary Redcliffe cathedral, a medieval church that Chandler erroneously believed was built by a private person and finished in 1474. (Merchants built it over several centuries.) His taste in architecture was excellent, however. Two centuries earlier, Queen Elizabeth had praised Redcliffe as the "fairest, goodliest, and most famous parish church in England."[21]

A day later, Chandler, "with an agreeable Company, in three carriages," visited the "charming" seat of Edward Southwell, a member of Parliament. "Charming" was quite the understatement. Southwell's estate, known as King's Weston, was a massive, and magnificent, English baroque mansion completed in 1719. Chandler was dutifully impressed with King's Weston's opulence, but the country parson whose salary was fifty pounds a year was in awe of Southwell's wealth. Chandler estimated this English gentleman earned £11,000 per annum, an unfathomably large sum for the times.[22]

Cooper and Chandler, after visiting the nearby village of Bath and taking in the Roman-era sites there, finally left Bristol on July 6. They traveled on a new type of conveyance known as a diligence—a large, four-wheeled carriage invented in France that held up to sixteen people and was divided into two or three enclosed compartments. The pace was fast for the times and likely bone-rattling, yet pleasant. From his perch, Chandler admired the blur of passing towns, including Marlborough and Reading. By evening, he and Cooper were in London. Weary and dusty after a long day on the road, they retired to their lodgings on Margaret Street in Cavendish Square, in London's West End near what today is the shopping district of Oxford Circus.[23]

The following day, Chandler headed into the city, where he could meet with his loyalist compatriots from New Jersey and New York. Their gathering place was known as the New York coffeehouse, because it was the preferred meeting spot for exiles from the middle colonies. The ranks of American loyalists in the United Kingdom and London grew steadily in 1775 as the crisis across the Atlantic worsened. According to the research of historian Mary Beth

Norton, 122 heads of families arrived in the British Isles in 1775, followed by another 139 in 1776—some one thousand people in all. Those figures included a small contingent from New Jersey—five heads of families from New Jersey in 1775 and two in 1776. Over the course of the revolutionary crisis, thirteen thousand loyalists would migrate to Great Britain. In London, these political refugees primarily saw themselves as provincials from the North or the South. Southern loyalists, as a result, convened at the Carolina coffeehouse where they could mingle with their fellow Southerners, while the New Englanders had a coffeehouse of their own. The New York coffeehouse served a practical function as well: Chandler had his mail sent there, and on his first full day in London, he eagerly picked up a packet containing "several Letters from my Friends."[24]

Chandler was now a resident of a city at war. In May, American troops had captured Fort Ticonderoga in New York, and in June British and American forces had fought a bloody battle at Bunker Hill near Boston. After receiving news of Bunker Hill on July 25, in which the British suffered 228 killed and 826 wounded—40 percent of their troops in the battle—London knew it was in for a fight. Prime Minister Lord North warned the king "that the War is now grown to such a height, that it must be treated as a foreign war." George agreed, and the king urged Parliament to act.[25]

With the war underway, Chandler believed he possessed important insights into the rebellion, and he pressed to meet with British officials. On July 8, he had breakfast with a privy counselor and future secretary of war named Charles Jenkinson (1729–1808), 1st Earl of Liverpool. He then went to Lambeth Palace on the Thames to meet with Archbishop of Canterbury Frederick Cornwallis. Chandler did not record what they discussed, but he likely gave Jenkinson and Cornwallis his take on the American situation.[26]

In August, Chandler reported dining with the archbishop and (for American Whigs) the detested Charles Townsend, whom Chandler described as one of the Lords of the Treasury. "Was treated with the most cordial Kindness, was shewn by his Grace all his Gardens, and by his Lady all the Rooms belonging to the Palace."[27]

Chandler likely used these meetings to glean as much information as he could about British war policy, which he then passed on to loyalists in America. He also developed his own peace plan, which he did not describe. He succeeded in gaining an audience with Lord Germaine on December 14, 1775, after the latter was appointed to the superintendence of the American department. Chandler congratulated Germaine on his new job and said he hoped the superintendent would be able to restore "Peace and Tranquility to that unhappy country." With a touch of self-importance, Chandler noted in his diary that he was appointed "spokesman" by the American gentlemen in London.[28]

Chandler in late 1775 and early 1776 felt reconciliation between Britain and its American colonies was still possible, was trying to make that happen, and strongly believed that episcopacy could play a role in cementing America's ties to the mother country. During his London exile, as a result, Chandler resumed his quixotic attempt to bring a bishop to America. For him, neither the war nor overwhelming opposition in the United States to an American episcopate posed an obstacle. Chandler was looking ahead to the day when peace returned and the colonies were back in the empire. Like most people in London, he expected the war to be short and the British to win. After the rebels were vanquished, Chandler wanted a strong state church in place to help reassert royal authority in the colonies.

In early 1776, Chandler discussed the bishop's cause with Archbishop of York Robert Hay and Bishop of London Richard Terrick, and Chandler said he received a sympathetic hearing. In his telling, Hay and Terrick assured him that an American episcopate still had substantial support in the government. Indeed, the Earl of Dartmouth agreed with Chandler's reasoning, stating a few months earlier that the outbreak of fighting increased the need for an American bishop because of the role the office would play in reestablishing British authority. Other officials believed that when peace came, the government would need to model the American Anglican church as closely as possible on the one in Britain. The Archbishop of York, William Markham, who succeeded Hay in 1776, attributed the rebellion to the machinations of "fanatics and sectaries" who ran amuck because of the government's failure to support the established church. But installing a bishop in America hinged on Britain's ability to quell the rebellion, and the political situation only worsened in the opening months of 1776 as the colonists inched toward declaring independence, thanks partly to the efforts of a former corset maker and schoolteacher newly arrived in the colonies from England named Thomas Paine.[29]

Paine's *Common Sense* offered up a simple but powerful argument for independence, and it became an instant sensation when it was published on January 9, 1776, going through twenty-five editions within twelve months. Chandler did not mention *Common Sense* in his diary, nor did he write any tracts denouncing it, but the tract lampooned Chandler's high church values and made his episcopal campaign even more quixotic than it was a few months earlier.

Paine wrote *Common Sense* with Protestant dissenters in mind, laying out a vision of a republican future in which the people, and not the king, would rule. This English radical with a Jeffersonian faith in the people attacked the bedrock Chandlerian tenet that monarchy was superior to republicanism. In making such a bold claim, Paine ridiculed the belief that individuals lucky enough to be born into a dynastic family were "exalted above the rest." Paine was especially contemptuous of hereditary succession, calling it an "insult and imposition on posterity": an accident of birth was no guarantee a ruler would possess the wisdom and talent to lead, he said.[30]

In Paine's telling, history amply demonstrated the folly of monarchy. "England since the conquest [in 1066] hath known some few good monarchs, but groaned beneath a much larger number of bad ones," Paine observed, summing up the parade of monarchs as "the *foolish*, the *wicked*, and the *improper*." Paine also disputed the virtually universal belief in 1776 that England's constitution was superior to other forms of government. A mixed government consisting of a bicameral parliament with the Crown at its head was not a strength but a weakness, he said, because of the constitution's complexity.[31]

Paine attributed the English constitution's weaknesses to the remains of two ancient tyrannies: monarchical and aristocratic. "The two first, by being hereditary, are independent of the People; wherefore in a *constitutional sense* they contribute nothing towards the freedom of the State." The only solution, Paine concluded, was to blow the whole thing up and replace the constitution with a republican government featuring annual elections and headed by "a President only." To those Americans who wanted to retain monarchy, Paine responded that in his new republic "*the law is king*. For as in absolute governments the King is law, so in free countries the law *ought* to be King; and there ought to be no other."[32]

In Paine's republic, there would be no union of church and state in which the divine authority of the king was sanctified by the church. Indeed, there would be no king at all. Thus, *Common Sense* threatened Chandler's campaign for a bishop. It helped convince wavering Americans that independence was not only possible but desirable—independence would allow Americans to start anew by ending monarchy and establishing republican governments. That, of course, is precisely what happened. The thirteen colonies began creating republican state governments in spring 1776, and the Continental Congress approved a declaration of independence in July.

Chandler and other loyalists opposed these developments. They defended monarchy, attacked republicanism, and dismissed *Common Sense* as a poorly written tract by an uneducated Englishman that would not stand the test of time. The loyalists, of course, wanted the colonies to remain in the empire, to be ruled under the Crown. If British arms prevailed, London would resume its control over the American continent, and a bishop, according to Chandler, would help ensure London's authority. Defeat would mean Paine's republic would prevail and no king would rule.

With the stakes so high, Chandler monitored military developments closely from London. In the early years of the American Revolution, he retained his confidence in the British military. Things certainly looked promising after General William Howe captured New York City, routed George Washington's army, and swept through New Jersey in late 1776. In March 1777, some six months before the humiliating British defeat at Saratoga, Chandler implored Samuel Seabury to keep his faith in the king's troops: "For God's Sake, keep up your Spirits a little longer . . . every Thing will end well at last. The next campaign will crush the Rebellion, in all Probability. Another large Army is now going over from hence."[33]

Chandler also had a great deal of confidence in John Burgoyne, believing the general's Canadian-based army possessed enough men and arms to successfully invade New York State. Burgoyne's surrender at Saratoga in October 1777 thus came as a great shock. Chandler got word of the disaster sometime in November or December, and "we were all struck into Confusion by an Arrival from Quebec, with an Account . . . of Gen. Burgoyne's having been obliged to surrender his Army to the Rebel Forces. Although we were apprehensive of the great Difficulties and Hardships our galiant General had to overcome we were not prepared for the News of such a compleat overthrow."[34]

The setback left Chandler apprehensive, but his optimism was mostly unshaken. Even the Americans' alliance with hated Catholic France in early 1778 did not greatly worry him. "As to a war with France, it is generally expected, and we are not badly prepared for it," Chandler wrote in a June 1778 letter to Seabury. He also categorically rejected any talk "of nominal or *real* Independency" for the rebels. Most right-thinking people in Britain believed the army could still dispatch the Americans, and Chandler agreed.[35]

Confident of British victory, Chandler pressed on with his episcopal campaign. In a meeting with John Moore, the Bishop of Bangor, on January 13, 1777, Chandler and Boucher urged the SPG to form a committee that would "prepare an Account of the Attempts that have been formerly made by that Body to obtain an American Episcopate, and of the Reasons of the Failure." In May, the Society discussed Chandler's proposal. He shared a letter from

Inglis, dated April 2, 1777, noting that the New York clergy had authorized Chandler, Cooper, and John Vardill, who was a professor of moral philosophy at King's College before going into exile, to act on their behalf. The Society agreed to appoint a thirteen-member committee consisting of six bishops and seven SPG members. Nothing, however, came of the committee for an obvious reason: an American episcopate was simply impossible while the Americans and British were at war. Chandler apparently understood this. In his diary, he did not discuss an American episcopate again, nor did he mention the issue in his extant correspondence with his American colleagues until after the war. In 1780, Chandler did pay to have fifty more copies of his *Appeal to the Public* printed, evidence that Chandler circulated his tract in an effort to garner support for an American episcopate.[36]

But the political situation in 1780 was worse than it was in 1776. The British military effort was faltering, and London was scaling back its ambitions for the Church of England in the colonies. The Cabinet and the king in 1780 approved a plan by William Knox, a former colonial agent in London for Georgia and East Florida, titled "Considerations on the Great Question: What is fit to be done with America?" The plan called for forming a new colony in present-day Maine in which the Church of England would be established. Knox, however, wavered on the question of an American episcopate, writing that his plan "supposes the Appointment of Bishops." Chandler did not comment on Knox's idea, but he would likely have opposed it because he wanted a bishop for *all* the former northern colonies, and nothing came of the plan anyway. The Crown never presented it to Parliament due to opposition from Attorney General Alexander Wedderburn.[37]

CHANDLER'S CAMPAIGN TO HELP AMERICAN CLERGY

As he campaigned for a bishop, Chandler pursued a second cause: advocating on behalf of destitute American clergy who, in Chandler's words, were "suffering for their Loyalty" to the Crown. His motives were several. Compassion and the needs of the church were foremost in his attempt to get money for Anglican ministers. Chandler was genuinely pained to learn through correspondence of the trials they were facing, and he reacted with anger at each story of persecution he heard. When Samuel Seabury described how his property had been plundered, Chandler commiserated. "Your Situation not withstanding is truly deplorable, and I shall never be easy till I see you distinguished and provided for in such a way, that your mind may be freed from private Anxieties," he wrote in 1777. "I will do all in my Power towards obtaining for you a present Support."[38]

Yet he also was acting partly out of guilt: Chandler had abandoned America for the safety of London. His fellow ministers stayed, to face the wrath of the American radicals. In addition, aiding the American clergy was a way for Chandler to deal with the deep psychic pain of having left his family, as a 1777 letter to Samuel Seabury made plain: "It is the greatest Alleviation of my uneasiness at this cruel Absence from my Family, that it affords me an Opportunity of doing Something to mitigate the Difficulties of my Brethren and Sisters, and perhaps of promoting the general Interest of the American Church."[39]

On December 7, 1775, Chandler, accompanied by Myles Cooper, met with the archbishop, the Bishop of London, and others "about a proper Method of assisting the American clergy in their present Distresses." The bishops agreed to remit the Americans' salaries as missionaries. They also agreed to undertake a subscription on the clergy's behalf, based on a plan that Chandler delivered to the archbishop on December 13, 1775. By April 1776, the Society had raised some £2,000, and it left it up to Chandler to determine how to distribute the funds.[40]

On June 10, 1776, Chandler wrote Charles Inglis with directions for how the clergy of Connecticut, New York, and New Jersey could draw on the subscription fund. Inglis said he received a list from Chandler of those missionaries who were to receive help, the sums they were to receive, and instructions for Inglis "desiring that I would give them Notice, & inform them how to draw for the Money." But distributing the money during a war was no easy task. Inglis went on to say that, with a few exceptions, "I have not yet been able to give Intelligence of this to any." Chandler also let Inglis know that the Society awarded a large sum to the clergy in Massachusetts and New Hampshire, "but I imagine General Howe left Boston before the money could get there ... [and I know not what] is become of it."[41]

Despite these obstacles, Chandler persevered and continued to seek additional money. On March 8, 1777, he visited the archbishop to ask him for sixty pounds for the clergy. Throughout the war, Chandler acted as an advocate on his colleagues' behalf. This involved presenting memorials on behalf of loyalist clergy and publicizing their plight. Chandler published extracts of Seabury's letters in the *Morning Chronicle* and apprised church leaders of the persecution the American clergy faced during his many meetings with them. Chandler, for instance, developed a close working relationship with the Bishop of Oxford and used this relationship to remind him about Seabury's ordeal, Chandler told Seabury in a May 1777 letter: "I have taken much more Pains to get your true Character known by People here." A year earlier, Chandler successfully lobbied to procure a military chaplaincy for Seabury, informing him "I have over and over insisted upon [the position] as a reward far inadequate to your merit."[42]

While trying to help his American brethren, Chandler puzzled over some of the dilemmas posed by the rebellion. What should the American clergy do about the liturgy and the requirement that church members pray to the king? It was not a rhetorical question. When the colonies declared independence, most Anglican clerics rightly feared being charged with treason by American authorities if they used the Anglican liturgy. In 1776, Inglis aptly described the terrible dilemma the clergy faced. Failure to pray for the king according to the liturgy would violate their duty and oath, but "yet to use the Prayers for the King & Royal Family would have drawn inevitable Destruction on them," he wrote. "The only Course which they could pursue to avoid both evils, was to suspend the public Exercise of their Function, & to shut up their Churches." After 1776, most did that. Chandler believed the Anglican parishes, north and south, needed to maintain a united front. In 1779, he wrote, "I hope they will act with the strictest Harmony and *Uniformity*, and either *all* proceed, or *all* keep back. It is taken for granted that it is no Question among them, whether they may pray *for the Congress* &c., as well as omit praying for the King. The former would actually be joining in the Rebellion; whereas the latter, all Circumstances considered, is no more than forbearing to exercise an agreeable Part of their office, in compliance with urgent Necessity."[43]

Chandler's duties included handling the financial accounts of various Anglican colleagues. One example was the Reverend George Panton of New Jersey, who was ordained in 1770, fled to New York City in 1776, and became a British military chaplain in 1778. On December 4, 1778, and June 14, 1779, Chandler paid two of Panton's bills totaling fourteen pounds, and Panton forwarded twenty-two pounds to Chandler for other expenses. Some large sums were involved. In 1779, the Society passed along £105 to Chandler on Panton's behalf. Chandler used this and other money to pay more of Panton's bills, including ten pounds the latter owed to "G.P." on June 27, 1780, and £587 to "Harley" on December 18, 1780.[44]

Chandler's financial work on behalf of Panton and others included investing in the stock market. Chandler recorded in his diary on July 17, 1781, "Left this day with Mr. Phyn Mr. Panton's 2 Receipts from the bank, one for 1,050 pounds, and the other for 300 pounds stock." Chandler later wrote he was hopeful the stock would generate six pounds in interest. When Chandler left London in 1785, he recorded that he "transferred at the Bank £1,980 . . . it being his property, heretofore held in my own name." And on October 19, 1781, Chandler said he "Purchased for Rev. [Jeremiah] Leaming [of Norwalk, Connecticut] . . . 265 pounds at £56 1/8, producing the interest of £7:19:0; it cost with brokerage £149:1:3."[45]

Chandler's own finances during his exile were relatively sound. He still received his annual salary of fifty pounds as an SPG missionary despite having left Elizabeth Town. And as a reward for his "Merit and Services" to the king, Chandler in April 1775 was awarded a generous £200 a year pension from the British government—twice as high as the typical pension for an American loyalist and further evidence of his importance to loyalist ranks. The government awarded the pension before he had even arrived in London. Nevertheless, the wheels of bureaucracy turned slowly, and money was tight his first year and a half in London until he actually began receiving his pension in July 1776. In February 1776, Chandler borrowed twenty pounds from Francis Blackburne, the liberal Anglican writer whom Chandler had tangled with a few years earlier during the bishop's campaign. In August, Chandler repaid the money, as well as an additional fifty pounds he had borrowed from Blackburne. Chandler did not receive his first pension payment until July 15, when he reported to the Treasury to collect the £200 in full. After that, Chandler received the money quarterly, in October, January, April, and July.[46]

London was expensive, and many of his fellow loyalist exiles moved constantly to find cheaper lodgings or to take on paying work. Chandler never had to do that. During his ten years in the city, he rented a room at a London house—he did not say where—owned by a married couple named Myers. He likely found his lodgings through the church; according to Chandler, the husband was a constable of the parish where he lived. Chandler's rent was nearly forty pounds a year—80 percent of his ministerial salary—and these lodgings would have been unaffordable without the £200 pension. His income was large enough that he could help his family and others financially. One borrower was a surprising one—his landlord. In 1784, Chandler lent the Myers £10:10:0.[47]

During his exile, Chandler sent his wife nearly £300 in cash or to her account, the highest amount being seventy-one pounds in 1782. He also repeatedly helped his son William, who had turned twenty in 1776. In 1779, Chandler

FIG. 7 British School, *Saint James's Palace with a View of Pall Mall*, eighteenth century. Chandler dined at St. James's Palace (right), a marvel of Tudor architecture that was built by Henry VIII in the 1530s. National Trust Collections. Photo © National Trust Images.

bought him a flute, a small sword, and a hat, and covered his traveling expenses when William visited England that year. A year earlier, he had sent William ten pounds in cash and eighteen pounds in 1780. In all, Chandler spent £76:19:7 on William in 1779. He also lent William several pounds in 1784 when the latter arrived from Nova Scotia and paid a number of his bills totaling £51:6:6. Chandler did not ignore his own needs. He bought a wig and clothes, as well as a mahogany case containing forty-eight knives and forks with silver handles, and later added "a compleat set of Tea china, blue and gilt."[48]

All in all, Chandler enjoyed a relatively comfortable lifestyle, with much time to explore London's treasures. One of his first stops after arriving in London was the British Museum, where he admired the Magna Charta. He also dined at St. James Palace, a marvel of Tudor architecture featuring gothic towers that was built by Henry VIII in the 1530s. When Chandler visited, the palace was the monarch's principal London residence. Chandler shared a table with the king's chaplains, where they exchanged small talk about some of the wonders of life in this metropolis of nearly one million people. During the meal, Chandler recorded, "it was there asserted, and universally admitted, that no less than 2,000 Stage-Coaches set out from London every Monday, and that the Number of Horses belonging to the City is 70,000; and that there is a Clock in the Palace, which requires winding up but once a Year."⁴⁹

Chandler the scholar and bibliophile found London's intellectual atmosphere especially stimulating. One of his first stops after leaving the colonies was Oxford. He wandered the city's streets, visited the study of philosopher Roger Bacon (ca. 1219–1292), and explored Oxford's colleges, making stops at the Observatory and "the grand Library" of Christ's Church. Chandler got to mingle with Oxford's dons, attending one sumptuous party that took place on a "grand Barge, and [we] were attended by another, containing Servants, Provisions, Liquors, &c. for the Company." He, of course, haunted libraries and art galleries, perusing the books and examining the collections of the statues from antiquity. He routinely bought books and pamphlets for himself and for others. Some purchases he mailed right away; others he held onto. His shopping spree was so large that he needed twenty-two boxes to hold all the books when he departed London in 1785.⁵⁰

In November 1775, Chandler took in a play at the famed Drury Lane Theatre, where he saw London's leading actor, David Garrick, play Benedict in Shakespeare's *Much Ado About Nothing*. Attending a play at Drury Lane was something of a wicked thing for a man of the cloth to do. Sir John Hawkins described the theater and the surrounding neighborhood as "the very hotbeds of vice; how else comes it to pass that no sooner is a playhouse opened in any part of the kingdom, then it becomes surrounded by an halo of brothels?" Crowds at the Drury Lane Theatre could be raucous. Seating was not reserved, and "the audience arrived early, milled around outside until the door was thrown open, and then stampeded in to grab places," according to a historian of the theater. Chandler apparently never returned.⁵¹

He also experienced another aspect of London's seamier side. During his first months in the city, his pocket was picked three times. The first time, the thief made off with a handkerchief, even though "it was closely buttoned"; the same thing happened again only five days later, despite Chandler's vigilance. The Lord's house proved to be no sanctuary, either. In March of 1776, a pickpocket divested him of his watch as he stood among the crowd at the church door. Chandler was so upset at this loss that he paid three shillings for an advertisement offering a reward of two guineas for its return. Not that he was under any illusions about the watch's return. He suspected "a Gang of Villains" was responsible for the theft, for "another Gentleman at the same Time and Place lost his Watch, while he was standing with the Plate to collect the charitable Contributions of the People."

Chandler performed a few baptisms and preached once, shortly after his arrival in 1775, but he took no outside paying jobs. Jonathan Boucher, by contrast, was perpetually scrambling to augment his income after his arrival in England on October 20, 1775. One key difference was that Boucher brought his wife to England while Chandler's stayed behind in the parish house. A second was that Boucher's pension was only £100—half of what Chandler received. With money tight, Boucher first took work as a writer, then as a curate in Paddington. In 1779 he became the Society's undersecretary, a position that paid £100 a year.[52]

In his diary, Chandler never evinced any of the bitterness that Boucher and some other loyalist exiles did. Like Chandler, Boucher made the social rounds. But unlike Chandler, he found his meetings with the Bishop of London and the Archbishop of Canterbury a waste of time. Boucher groused that the church hierarchy believed it was doing "wonders when they give you a dinner." Boucher and some other Americans felt like second-class citizens in London, that the British looked down on the colonists as bumpkins. Chandler did not see things that way. He praised the graciousness of his British hosts and found his meetings generally productive. He believed he enjoyed some sway, telling Seabury in 1777 "though I cannot pretend to have any very inconsiderable Influence, yet I must have been very indolent since my being in this Country if I have not acquired *some* Influence; and whatever it is, you may rely upon it being devoted to your Service."[53]

Chandler also made sure he cultivated his ties with leading loyalists. Two prominent examples were the former Massachusetts governor Thomas Hutchinson and Francis Bernard, who also had been a governor of that colony as well as of New Jersey. Hutchinson was a leader of the loyalist community, and he frequently invited Chandler to dine with him. On one occasion, Hutchinson and Bernard called on Chandler, presumably at his lodging. Invariably, these get-togethers with Hutchinson and Bernard brought Chandler into close contact with British officialdom. One September day in 1775, Chandler traveled with Hutchinson in the latter's coach to Fulham Palace, the magnificent home of the Bishop of London. About a week later, the pair dined with Robert Auchmuty, judge of the admiralty; John Robinson, a member of the American Board of Commissioners of the Customs; the poet Joseph Green; "and several other Gentlemen, who have lately fled Boston," Chandler reported. As that passage indicates, these sessions were not always about politics and the war. Besides meeting a poet, Hutchinson introduced Chandler to the author and merchant Israel Mauduit

(1708–1787), who had written an influential book opposing British military involvement in Germany.⁵⁴

Chandler's emotions during his ten-year exile ran the gamut. He missed his family terribly and was bitter at the rebels (as he now always called them) for forcing him to flee Elizabeth Town. He especially missed his beloved Polly, the youngest daughter who was a mere seven months old in 1775 when he hurriedly departed from Elizabeth Town. In a poignant letter Chandler wrote in early 1779, he lamented that "she was but a Green Gosling when I left her; and my Absence has been so long that, on the first Sight, I should probably not know her." For this great personal loss, he sarcastically gave "thanks to those dear creatures, the American Rebels, and *our* americanized Generals! But this is too tender a Subject [to discuss]."⁵⁵

As the war dragged on, Chandler remained in close touch with his colleagues across the Atlantic. He wrote regularly to Charles Inglis and Samuel Seabury, as well as his family, keeping them abreast of developments in England and forwarding pamphlets and other items of interest. The correspondence was so heavy, in fact, that Chandler complained of the burden. When Seabury scolded him for not writing more and sooner, Chandler responded defensively: "The truth is, I have a number of *constant* correspondents, and so many occasional ones, that I have been obliged to make it a rule to write no letters but *in answer* to theirs . . . ; for by the time I have got through this task, I am so tired and surfeited of writing, that I have but little inclination to strike out as a *volunteer*."⁵⁶

Chandler's moods shifted, depending on political and military developments. Battlefield victories raised his spirits, as did changes in administration. Greater resolve, and more money, would turn the tide for the Redcoats, he continually believed. Yet the trend was ominous, and Chandler knew it. When talk arose in London of pursuing peace with the rebels, he advised his British friends to fight on.

December 1780 was one such time late in the war when his mood was hopeful. In a letter to Samuel Seabury, he reported, "One of the best Things I can inform You of is, that we have got a good Parliament, with a respectable, secure Majority in Favor of Administration, and resolved to support the King in pursuing the most vigorous Measures for bringing the War to an honorable and proper Termination. All the supplies called for have been granted without a Division."⁵⁷

But then came Cornwallis's surrender at Yorktown on October 19, 1781, dashing the last, best chance of a British military victory, and in March 1782,

Parliament empowered the king to negotiate peace with the Americans. Chandler, nevertheless, was not yet ready to concede defeat. "The death of Lord Rockingham, about a month ago [in July], has produced another change, which I hope will be advantageous.... Lord Shelburn, a warm and avowed enemy to the independence of the Colonies, is the Minister being at the head of the Treasury.... It is thought that the Administration will soon undergo a second refinement, without which the strength of the nation cannot be properly exerted. In the meanwhile, I am well assured that it is the fixed purpose of Lord Shelburn not to lose the colonies.... The negotiations for peace are, for the present, at an end; and nothing remains but to fight it out."[58]

Chandler was badly misinformed. On November 30, 1782, the two sides signed a preliminary peace treaty in Paris, and on February 4, 1783, Britain declared an end to hostilities. The rebels had won. Chandler's mood quickly turned bitter—he was livid about the British capitulation to the Americans, and he complained that Shelburne had "plunged the Nation into irretrievable ruin and everlasting infamy. We have been at a loss to account for such monstrous conduct." Feeling badly betrayed, Chandler pinned his last hopes on Parliament. He was, of course, to again be disappointed—Parliament approved the peace terms. Chandler, who had long defended the Crown, the constitution, and the empire, turned his fury on the entire British nation. "When the terms of the Peace were known, we were in hopes that the Parliament would have so much wisdom and Spirit as to set it aside, and to renew the war with proper vigour," he wrote in March. "But it is over with England, her Stamina have failed; her Constitution is ruined; and her Disposition must follow."[59]

His complaint that Britain's constitution was ruined was telling. A decade in exile had only strengthened Chandler's belief that the health of the political nation rested on the union of church and state. A strong monarchy and an invigorated Church of England were essential—it was why he wanted an American bishop so badly. The loss of the colonies was thus devastating, and Chandler had no confidence in the survival of a new American nation populated by dissenters, in which church and state would be separate and democracy would prevail.

THE END OF HIS EXILE

With the war lost and the British preparing to evacuate New York City in 1783, Chandler would soon have a new friend in London: Charles Inglis. On November 1, 1783, Inglis resigned as rector of Trinity Church and arrived in London in January 1784. He was part of a massive exodus that saw more than 28,000 loyalists flee the city after the signing of the peace treaty. Inglis concluded that staying in New York was not tenable. He was not only a loyal supporter of King George but a harsh critic of the revolutionary regime. In 1779, Inglis had attacked the Continental Congress and the independence movement anew in a series of powerful essays published in New York and London as *Letters of Papinian* that outraged the revolutionaries. Inglis derided the American public as dupes of a dishonest and conniving leadership, called the Revolution a failure, and lambasted the Congress as hypocritical tyrants.[60]

Inglis did not stay in London long, however, and Chandler himself was becoming increasingly restless. He was, as yet, unsure what to do or where to go. "I am extremely impatient to hear in what manner the concessions of this country affect the minds of people in America, both of the Loyalists and of the now legalized, sanctified rebels," he inquired in a letter home on March 15, 1783. In the run-up to war, Chandler had repeatedly predicted that the Americans would never be able to get along with each other; in this letter he was still worrying about the prospects of civil war. "I want much to know, whether the country is likely to become peaceable; or whether there is not a greater probability of a contest, previous to it, between the Republicans and Anti-Republicans, which must again bring on a deluge of blood."[61]

In this early stage of peace, Chandler hoped the victorious Americans would be magnanimous to the loyalists and that the king's supporters could safely reside among the former rebels in the newly independent thirteen states. If that were not possible, Chandler believed that the loyalists would have to "remove into some part of what are now British dominions." Chandler himself had several options. In 1777, Chandler, Myles Cooper, and John Vardill had petitioned the king for one hundred thousand acres "on the Waters of the Ohio" in Canada, where they pledged "to introduce peaceable, industrious and orderly Settlers." Nothing came of this scheme, but it was indicative of Chandler's thinking. Only two years into the war, at a time when he was confident the British would win, Chandler saw relocating to Canada as a strong possibility. Nearly a decade later, it remained a serious option. "In what part of the world I shall fix myself is at present impossible to [say]," he told Seabury in 1783. "Canada appears, at this instance, to be most eligible." A cryptic entry in his diary indicated he wanted his family to move there as well, for he reported in August 1784, "I directed Mrs. C. to accommodate herself for the winter at Eliz. Town, as it is too late for her to think of removing to Nova Scotia this season."[62]

The British outpost drew more than twenty thousand loyalists from New York City alone in the days following the signing of the 1783 peace treaty. Many exiles in Britain also decided to go to Nova Scotia, believing they could not safely return to the United States—passions were running too high. They had good reason to be fearful. A number of loyalists were refused readmittance to Massachusetts, for example, while a party of armed men confronted a returning New Jersey loyalist and forced him to leave the state. Article 5 of the Paris treaty had obligated the Continental Congress to "earnestly recommend" to the states that they protect loyalist rights and estates, while article 6 pledged that no loyalist shall "suffer any future Loss or Damage, either in his Person, Liberty, or Property." But the states and local communities routinely ignored these provisions.[63]

Chandler gave no indication in 1783 and 1784 whether he was considering returning to New Jersey. Certainly he had reason to wonder what kind of reception he would receive if he moved back to Elizabeth Town; after all, the local militia had tried to storm his house and large crowds had burned his pamphlets. In addition, after nearly a decade of brutal civil war and repeated British invasions, many residents of New Jersey were not ready to welcome back their loyalist neighbors. The state legislature received numerous petitions in the early 1780s from residents who opposed the return of loyalist exiles to New Jersey. One petition from Monmouth County warned that loyalists would become "a pest and disturbers" of the peace; another petition condemned loyalists as "traitors, robbers, and murderers."[64]

But in another sense, Chandler's wishes did not matter at this point. Church responsibilities kept him anchored in London, and he was weighed down by severe personal issues. For more than two decades, Chandler suffered from a cancerous nose, which was worsening in the 1780s and becoming increasingly painful. The pain became so bad that he retreated one summer to the Isle of Wight, where he subsisted on goat's milk "in the hope that he might thereby be benefited; but neither that nor any other expedient that medical skill could suggest had any favourable effect," according to a nineteenth-century historian who interviewed Chandler's daughter. On top of poor health, Chandler suffered a parent's worst nightmare. Two of his children died within months of each other in 1784—a "beloved" daughter and his only son, William. William, who was born on May 7, 1756, graduated from King's College in 1774 and served as a captain in the New Jersey Volunteers, a loyalist battalion. William had visited his father several times during the war—Chandler would rent a room for his son for two guineas a week at the Myers—and they corresponded frequently. William was visiting his father when he became ill. Chandler took the loss stoically, if his diary is any indication. He noted that William, in his twenty-ninth year, died at 2:10 p.m. on October 22 after a seven-day illness. "God's will be done!" he exclaimed. Chandler's next entry came one week later, when he recorded the mundane news that "[I] took in 39 Sacks of Coal." Earlier, he had bought five mourning rings and shipped them to New York.[65]

The main reason Chandler remained in London was the church. With the war lost, Whitehall belatedly agreed that episcopacy could help keep a colony loyal to the Crown. This admission was a vindication for Chandler and others who had for years argued the importance of episcopacy to maintaining royal authority. In Canada, the Crown would not repeat the mistakes it had made in the thirteen colonies to the south. Nova Scotia, where the loyalist community was forming, would get a bishop, and Chandler was the leading candidate. Indeed, in a letter Seabury wrote in September 1783, he reported, "Dr. Chandler's appointment to Nova Scotia will, I believe, succeed. And possibly he may go there this autumn, or at least, early in the spring."[66]

But, in a cruel irony, this development came too late. The thirteen colonies were lost and Chandler's health was so poor that he did not think he could fulfill the demanding position of bishop. He also was too sick to take a leading role in securing an American episcopate. Instead, leadership fell to Inglis and Seabury. In March 1783, they and sixteen other clergy petitioned General Guy Carleton for the appointment of an ecclesiastical bishop, emphasizing that "the fixing of a Bishop in Nova Scotia ... will strengthen the attachment, and confirm the loyalty of the Inhabitants." A second petition on March 26 recommended Chandler be named the bishop. Carleton agreed on the need to establish an episcopate, but Lord North questioned whether the laity would support an American bishop. North, though, did agree that Chandler was the strongest choice for a bishop because of his "Character, Merit, and Loyalty." In December 1783, Lord North informed Carleton that "a Resolution has been taken to establish an Episcopate in Nova Scotia." It took several more years of bureaucratic maneuvering, but in August 1787, Inglis was consecrated as Bishop of Nova Scotia.[67]

As the bishop's campaign wound down in the mid-1780s, an ailing Thomas Bradbury Chandler wanted to go home to Elizabeth Town to his family. He no longer was considering exile in Canada. But the drawn-out maneuvering over the American episcopate delayed his departure: to leave London for America, he needed the permission of John Moore, who had become

Archbishop of Canterbury in 1783, and His Grace was reluctant to give it until the Nova Scotia question was settled. Chandler waited two long years before he finally took matters into his own hands. On April 19, 1785, he "engaged a passage in the *Mentor*." On April 21, according to his diary, he met with Moore and "obtained the Archbishop's consent to cross the Atlantic on a visit to my family." A letter to his friend Samuel Seabury explained what happened during a whirlwind three days. "The *Mentor* was the last Ship of the season that was bound to New-York; in the full maturity of deliberation I resolved to take my passage in her," Chandler recalled. "As soon as this resolution was formed, and before it was known to any one but Mr. Boucher, I waited on the Archbishop to inform [him] of it, and to resign my professions to the Nova-Scotia Episcopate. On talking the matter over, his Grace approved of the voyage."[68]

But the archbishop was not yet ready to release Chandler from "the above-mentioned claim" to the bishopric. The best compromise that Chandler could get was that he would relocate to Elizabeth Town and there "hold myself in readiness to obey his Summon when he should be able to make it."[69]

With the all-important meeting behind him, Chandler stepped up his preparations to depart. On April 29, he made a down payment of twenty-five pounds for passage on the *Mentor*. Then he began packing. Into an "old large black trunk" went his clothes for the sea voyage and his ointments; into a "little flat hair trunk" went his breeches and under stockings. On May 16, Chandler bade farewell to London and went to Gravesend, a river town about twenty-five miles from London, where the *Mentor* was docked. The next day, the ship set sail.[70]

Reviled when he left ten years earlier, forced to flee a radical faction that wanted to string him up on the nearest Liberty Pole, Chandler arrived in Elizabeth Town after a voyage of fifty-five days to a far different scene. Elizabeth Town's Presbyterians must have still looked askance at their old high church nemesis, but Chandler was relieved to find a sympathetic, even adoring, crowd awaiting him. Indeed, he reported that the throng greeting him was so great, "I have not been able to command half an hour time together—such is the amazing crowd of visitors from all quarters . . . old and young, black and white, male and female, whig and tory, Churchman and Dissenters, not only from this but from all the neighboring towns, to congratulate me on my return to this country! When I tell you that I have not yet been able to open one of my 22 boxes of books, you will form some opinion of my want of time."

His health, however, remained poor. Inglis noted in an October 1785 journal entry that his good friend had not improved. Nevertheless, Chandler was still in line to become Bishop of Nova Scotia, and he was regularly corresponding with his colleagues about the position. Chandler supported Seabury's decision to go to Scotland to get consecrated as Connecticut's bishop—a consecration that the Archbishop of Canterbury did not support. In mid-October, Inglis hand-delivered a letter from Chandler to Moore backing Seabury's decision. At their meeting, Inglis and the archbishop discussed Chandler. "[Moore] expressed a doubt whether Chandler would be able to discharge the duties of bishop on account of his disorder," Inglis reported. "But I hinted to him that the Doctor himself had promised to write soon to his Grace, and would probably speak more fully on that subject."[71]

Chandler in early 1786 hoped his health would recover enough to allow him to become bishop. The archbishop, however, was skeptical, and he moved ahead with plans to find a replacement. His first choice was Jonathan Boucher, but Boucher turned down the offer because Chandler had not yet relinquished his claim to the position. In May 1786, a meeting of bishops agreed that Chandler was too sick to go to Nova Scotia, and they were now recommending Inglis for the post. Like Boucher, Inglis did not want to accept because of Chandler. "I told his Grace that Dr. Chandler was my very worthy friend—that I would sooner suffer one of my limbs to be chopped off than betray the confidence reposed in me by a friend, or interfere with his views." The bishops, however, had informed Chandler of their decision, and in June Chandler wrote Inglis to let his friend know that "he totally relinquished all claim to the Episcopate of Nova Scotia, and wished me to be appointed." Chandler went further by writing a strong recommendation to the archbishop backing Inglis for the position.[72]

And so it was done. Inglis became Bishop of Nova Scotia, and the bishop's campaign was over.

EPILOGUE

A ROYALIST IN A REVOLUTIONARY WORLD

In 1787, Thomas Bradbury Chandler's life was nearing its end. Too sick to preach or to assume a bishopric, he spent his final days in the parish house along the banks of Elizabeth Creek, tending to his garden and the needs of his wife and children.[1] His pen was silent, and he never publicly commented on the political storms that were roiling the young United States after the Revolution. For that reason, we do not know what Chandler thought of the tumultuous 1780s and the republican governments that were taking shape. But we can well imagine what he was thinking. He assuredly disliked both the Articles of Confederation and the republican state governments, including New Jersey's, that had arisen during the war. And he assuredly disapproved of—and most likely was unsurprised by—the democratic chaos engulfing American society in the years after the Revolution.

Chandler likely felt a measure of vindication as his longtime radical foes denounced the chaos and campaigned for a federal constitution that would create a powerful executive and place a check on an unruly populace. Ironies abounded regarding this turn of events. Chandler's old neighbor and nemesis William Livingston, after a maddening experience as wartime governor of New Jersey, emerged from the American Revolution with the Chandlerian view that the people had too much power. The state constitution of 1776 had gutted the gubernatorial office and created a powerful legislature that controlled the new state government. The governor lacked a veto, patronage, and control of the purse strings. Without these crucial powers, Livingston had to resort to extraordinary measures to wield authority during the war, using the Council of Safety and other revolutionary bodies to bypass the legislature. Livingston also believed that the national government suffered from the same constitutional defects as the states. Thus, in a great irony, this foe of an American episcopate and the British monarchy sided with former royalists in the mid-1780s and backed the movement to create a strong federal government and curtail the power of the people. As the most recent biographer of Livingston concluded, the governor came to believe that the American experiment "needed a stronger executive to persevere. The individual could not be trusted."[2]

Livingston's views were widely shared among the elite of all political leanings, including James Madison. In state after state, constitutional architects in the mid-1770s had made the legislature supreme at the expense of the executive. The people through their unicameral assemblies were dominating politics and implementing policies, such as issuing more paper money to help debtors, that threatened ruin for merchants and others. For many revolutionary elites, these constitutional architects had replaced one tyranny (the tyranny of the king) with another (the tyranny of the people). The state constitutions lacked proper checks and balances, they agreed. In addition, the 1780s saw Shays' Rebellion and other disorders threaten both elites' control and governmental authority. The decade, as a result, witnessed a "republican frenzy" and a "rage of excessive democracy" in the words of two contemporary critics. Throughout the states, powerful assemblies dominated by democratic interests were interfering with "the security of private rights, and the steady dispensation of Justice," Madison wrote.[3]

Thus, Chandler's warnings about the dangers of democracy and individualism had come to pass. He had long lectured on the need for a powerful central government in which the people would owe it proper deference. His political tracts warned that rebellions produced violence and tended to spiral out of control. As Chandler predicted, Americans intoxicated with the heady promises of the Declaration of Independence and the American Revolution were seeking more rights for themselves and defying the government when it suited their purposes. Authority was breaking down. In response to the tumults, former revolutionary leaders sought to reassert control by creating a strong federal government that would weaken local control and curb democratic forces. The result was the 1787 constitution, which created a powerful presidency that former royalists admired, as well as an upper chamber of elites designed to counterbalance the exuberance of the people's lower house. The new federal government was armed with the power to tax and safeguard the national interest. For all these reasons, opponents of the 1787 constitution, known to history as Anti-Federalists, denounced the antidemocratic tendencies of the new federal government and its proponents.[4]

Fears that the constitution would lead to an aristocracy were overblown. Democracy and individualism did expand in a United States that came to straddle a continent. The new republic also enshrined religious freedom and barred the establishment of a state church. All these developments repudiated a Chandlerian world resting on the union of church and state. But the expansion of democracy and individualism came only over time. Ratification of the constitution did not immediately settle what kind of society the United States would become. The 1790s, as a result, witnessed a fierce duel between aristocratic-leaning Federalists and Jeffersonian democrats over the direction of the government and economy, as well as debate over the implications of the French Revolution—an epochal event that horrified the former and thrilled the latter.[5]

Chandler did not live to see these changes unfold. On June 17, 1790, he died at age sixty-four after a years-long illness had, in his own telling, left him "much reduced in body." The timing was fitting in the sense that Chandler departed the scene when a new type of conservatism was emerging, a conservatism that rejected the traditional British values he cherished. Post-1790 conservatives in the United States embraced individualism and came to see government as an enemy of liberty, not a protector of it. History had a role in this important development. Born fifty years before the United States declared independence, Chandler was shaped by a worldview that looked primarily to the British past for inspiration. Until his final days, he admired Great Britain, revered its constitution and monarchy, and derived many of his principles from British history, especially the Glorious Revolution. To understand monarchy, episcopacy, and obedience, he looked to the debates surrounding the nonjurors and the Bangorian controversy, as well as the Puritan challenge to episcopacy and the Church of England in the sixteenth century.[6]

Americans born after 1775, by contrast, came of age in an independent nation, divorced from the British empire, and the historical memory that shaped them was not the Glorious Revolution but the American Revolution. Their historical memory was classical republicanism, not monarchy or the religious strife of the seventeenth century.[7] Thus, in the 1790s, the conservative movement began heading in directions that Chandler would have opposed—most importantly in its embrace of individualism and personal liberty. A product of the Enlightenment and an outgrowth of classical liberalism, "modern conservatism arose as a defence of the individual against potential oppressors, and an endorsement of popular sovereignty," wrote British philosopher Roger Scruton in a 2017 book on conservatism. "The first and most far-reaching idea was that the legitimacy of a government depends on the consent of those who are subject to it. Authority is conferred on the government by the people."[8]

Conservatism came to mean "a commitment to individual liberty, tempered by the conviction that true freedom entails more than simply an absence of restraint; a belief in limited government, fiscal responsibility, and the rule of law; veneration for our cultural inheritance combined with a sense of stewardship for Creation," wrote historian Andrew J. Bacevich.[9]

Modern conservatives dismiss Chandler's worldview as premodern and reject its "blood-and-throne" elements. Their heroes are not Thomas Bradbury Chandler or Samuel Seabury but British statesman Edmund Burke and the drafters of the 1787 constitution. They praise classical republicanism—a concept loathed by Chandler, Seabury, Jonathan Boucher, Charles Inglis, and other "Friends of Government." In 1775, democracy and republicanism were dirty words to high church traditionalists and many other Americans. Not so to conservatives after 1790.[10]

Chandler, of course, did look backwards, to English history, but it would be simplistic to dismiss him as hopelessly old-fashioned. In education, he embraced the forward-looking values of the Enlightenment that he, Samuel Johnson, and others called the New Learning. It was Yale and Puritanism that Chandler found backward. He prized rigorous thinking and insisted on carefully examining both sides of an issue. Chandler may have rejected Locke's premises on governing and democracy, but he owned four of Locke's books. Chandler also accepted religious toleration, albeit grudgingly and with limits, and the 1688 political settlement that solidified parliamentary supremacy in the British constitution.

For Chandler, history was a tool that enabled him to understand the central issue that animated his life: how to ensure obedience and strengthen government. Examining this core question meant Chandler's intellectual peregrinations went well beyond Locke, Blackstone, and other mainstays among colonial intellectuals. In his *Writing the Rebellion*, historian Philip Gould maintained that Chandler, Jonathan Boucher, and certain other loyalist writers ascribed to a cyclical version of history: as rebellions spiraled out of control, civilization was lost and barbarity followed. Chandler did believe that rebellions led to unintended consequences, but his view of history was not cyclical. History, for him, was a guide and a teacher. He studied it so he could understand the importance of monarchy, episcopacy, and obedience. History enabled him to identify the conundrum of democracy and of the Lockean belief that government rested on the will of the people: When people enjoyed the liberty to do as they please, how can government maintain order?[11]

It was a timeless question. Like earlier generations, Americans in the 1790s struggled to answer it. In Chandlerian echoes, the Federalist Party responded that the better sort needed to lead and that the United States had to maintain social hierarchy and class deference if the young nation was to fully realize its potential. Federalists still admired Great Britain and its mixed constitution preserving the aristocracy's authority, and they rejected the radicalism of revolutionary France. John Adams had attacked one of Chandler's tracts for its antidemocratic arguments, but he nevertheless questioned how a government could command the respect of its subjects when no monarch or aristocracy was present. As vice president in the first administration under the 1787 federal constitution, Adams believed George Washington should be addressed as "His Elective Majesty" or "His Highness." Thomas Jefferson's Democratic-Republican Party rejected such aristocratic pretensions. It believed that the United States could best preserve good order by giving everyone a stake in government. It further believed that good government meant limited government, one that rested on the consent of the yeomanry and its commonsense values of hard work and commitment to agrarian democracy. Democratic-Republicans supported the French Revolution and its promise of equality and liberty.[12]

Outside the United States, the French Revolution was providing additional fodder to those elites who worried that democracy was ripping apart the bands of society. Edmund Burke feared violent revolution because it led to anarchy and undercut order. People were entitled to rights, he believed, but rights carried responsibilities and a corresponding duty to act morally. He saw the French Revolution and its violent excesses as democracy running amuck; the revolutionaries were putting liberty over the duties of the subject.[13]

Burke rejected extreme individualism because it endangered liberty. In his view, "men have no rights to [do] what they please: their natural rights are only what may be directly deduced from their human nature," historian Russell Kirk noted. Individuals might enjoy freedom in a state of nature, Burke said, but they cannot disregard their obligations to society. Burke's principles became a tenet of modern conservatism: freedom must be exercised responsibly. "Human beings come into this world burdened by obligations and subject to institutions and traditions that contain within them a precious inheritance of wisdom," Scruton observed, "without which the exercise of freedom is as likely to destroy human rights and entitlements as to enhance them."[14]

Burke's principles rested on Christian foundations: humankind and the state are creations of God's beneficence. "And what is our purpose in this world? Not to indulge our appetites, but to render obedience to divine ordinance," he wrote. And religion had an important role to play by inculcating reverence in leaders and an appreciation for law and order.[15] Chandler could not have put it any better. He loved the Church of England because it instilled in its members a reverence for monarchy and authority. Obedience was what mattered.

APPENDIX

THE LIBRARY OF THOMAS BRADBURY CHANDLER

Despite earning a meager fifty pounds a year in salary, Thomas Bradbury Chandler managed to accumulate one of the most impressive private libraries in early America. At his death in 1790, Chandler owned 1,527 books, plus 96 pamphlets and tracts. By comparison, the typical library of a colonial-era parson was about 150 volumes, and Chandler's holdings surpassed those of his close Anglican colleagues. The Reverend Charles Inglis's "Catalogue of My Books" listed 256 books and tracts. Elsewhere, Patrick Henry—the fiery patriot orator of "give me liberty or give me death" fame—owned 200 books; wealthy Virginian planter Robert Carter III owned about 1,000; and Thomas Jefferson—likely the greatest bibliophile in early America—possessed 2,640 books in 1783.[1]

For the elite, books were as precious and valuable as gold because of their rarity, cost, and importance. Books were a portal to another world that was beyond the reach of ordinary people, who at best owned a Bible and one or two other titles. As historian Rhys Isaac has noted, "Those fitted for book learning were assumed to be of a superior nature to those who did the material work that sustained civilization." It was with reverence that educated individuals of limited financial means entered a private library. When Presbyterian clergyman Philip Vickers Fithian had the chance to peruse the shelves at Robert Carter's library at Nomini Hall, he seized it as an opportunity to pick the brains of "mighty-Men." Benjamin Franklin had a similarly happy experience when he was a teenager trying to make his way in the world. He arrived in New York City carrying a stack of books—not the usual accoutrements of a runaway teen. Governor William Burnet learned of this unusual visitor and asked to meet with him. Franklin accepted, and the governor showed the youth his library, which, Franklin reported with admiration, "was a very large one, and we had a good deal of conversation about books."[2]

It took Chandler many years and much diligence to accumulate his treasure trove of books and pamphlets. American booksellers were few in number in the eighteenth century, and purchasing volumes overseas took time, money, and connections. Ships needed at least three months to deliver their cargo, and they were at the mercy of the weather and of privateers in time of war.

When he was conducting research for a pamphlet or tract, Chandler often borrowed books from his mentor, Samuel Johnson, as well as from colleagues such as Charles Inglis. He also took advantage of the library at King's College after that institution was founded in 1754. (Its first president was Johnson.)[3]

But London was Chandler's most important source of books. In the pre-revolutionary years, he worked with a London bookseller, who would ship books to Chandler by the boxful. The arrival of a book shipment was a joyous occasion for Chandler. In 1767, for instance, he recorded that "a new scene of temptation has opened upon me within two days, which without the most resolute opposition will interfere with the work I have in hand, and cause me to swerve from my duty, viz. a box of books from my London bookseller." Among the elite, Chandler's experience was not unusual. The colonies were an important market for British booksellers: From 1700 to 1780, 45 percent of English book exports by volume went to the American mainland and the West Indies; by 1770, England was exporting more books to America than to Europe.[4]

Chandler relied on friends and colleagues for an entrée into the London book market. Familial connections were often important to private collectors and American booksellers as they tried to learn which books were available and from whom. In 1771, for instance, Chandler asked Samuel Johnson's son who was in England "to find out and recommend to me a proper book-seller; for I have always been concerned with improper ones." Chandler had been trying to establish a relationship with John Rivington and was having little luck. Rivington, Chandler reported with disappointment, "has never sent me anything, not so much as a letter," despite the fact that Rivington had published Chandler's pamphlets on the bishop's cause in England.[5]

When Chandler traveled to London in 1751 for ordination, he was introduced to the London book market. He became intimately acquainted with it during his decade in exile that began in 1775, for Chandler could now buy directly from London's booksellers. He had plenty of time on his hands and cash in his pocket—he was receiving a pension of £200 a year from the British government, plus his annual salary of £50. Chandler also bought books on behalf of colleagues and shipped them to America for them. But his joy was buying books for himself. When he returned to Elizabeth Town in 1785, Chandler needed twenty-two boxes for the books he had accumulated during his ten-year London stay.[6]

Chandler read widely, although he retained a distaste for science and philosophy. He enjoyed music, poetry, history—especially English history—and biographies of everyone from Mary Queen of Scots to a female polymath named Anna Maria van Schurman. A bit of the whimsical could be found on his shelves. He owned a book on the *Art of Cookery*, and a tome on the medicinal effects of music, singing, and dancing on the human body. And nestled between a book on the Church of England and one on the creation story was the plainly titled but deliciously suggestive *Reflections upon Ridicule; or what it is that makes a man ridiculous, and the means to avoid it*, which was first published in 1717 and popular enough to have gone through at least six editions. Chandler also owned the page-turning *The Fourth Volume of Letters Writ by a Turkish Spy, who liv'd five and forty years undiscover'd at Paris*. Then there was Chandler's fascination with the stage; among the fifteen or so books on drama was a 1740 memoir titled *An Apology for the Life of Mr. Colley Cibber*, who was an actor, playwright, and poet.

Chandler was not much one for novels, however, and the few that this Anglican minister possessed were often heavy on sermonizing. Tobias Smollett's *The Adventures of Ferdinand Count Fathom*, for example, was a picaresque tale published in 1753 that recounts, in the author's words, a "Shrewd villain of monstrous inhumanity" who wanders through Europe, swindling all whom he encounters. Commenting on this drab tale, Sir Walter Scott charitably described *The Adventures of Ferdinand Count Fathom* as a treatise on human depravity.[7]

But what really interested Chandler was plumbing the past for insights into the contemporary causes that animated him. The core of his library was on religious history. Chandler wanted to understand the state church's place in society and what rights, if any, dissenters possessed. Thus, he had a substantial collection of books on dissenters' rights (to refute them, that is) and the church constitution. Judging by the number of their books he owned, Chandler's two favorite authors were Gilbert Burnet and Benjamin Hoadly—although Chandler disagreed mightily with their views.

The following is a sampling of Chandler's library, chosen to reflect the diversity of his interests while listing the key works most important to his intellectual causes: 290 titles out of 1,527 listed in the *Catalogue of Books, for Sale by Mrs. Chandler, in Elizabeth-Town, New-Jersey; Being the Library of the late Rev. Dr. Chandler, deceased* (Elizabeth-Town, NJ: Shepard Kollock, 1790). The works here are listed exactly as they were in the catalog, and in the same order (the cataloger did not follow strict alphabetical order). Some entries give the size of the book (e.g., folio, quarto), and most include the price in pounds, shillings, and pence. I have added subject headers and provided the author, title, year published, and additional information about the work when known. Brief biographical information on authors with multiple listings (whose names appear in boldface) follows the catalog. All 1,527 titles, with similar information, can be found in the online version of the appendix at http://scottrohrer.net/.

SELECTED WORKS IN CHANDLER'S LIBRARY

Account of the Conspiracy in 1683	0 1 6	HISTORY
Abridgment of Hooker	0 3 0	RELIGION A collection of works by the famed Anglican theologian Richard Hooker (1554–1600).
Apologia Eclesiae Anglicanae	0 1 6	RELIGION John Jewel, *Apologia Ecclesiae Anglicanae*, 1606. Jewel (1522–1571) was Bishop of Salisbury.
Answer to the Dissenter's Pleas	0 2 0	RELIGION Thomas Bennet, *An Answer to the Dissenter's Pleas for Separation; or An Abridgment of the London Cases* [...], 1711.
Amyntor (by Toland)	0 2 0	RELIGION John Toland, *Amyntor, or a Defense of Milton's Life* [...], 1698. Toland (1670–1722), a rationalist philosopher and freethinker, argued that nothing contrary to reason can be part of Christianity.
Answer to the Committee (by Bp. Bangor)	0 2 6	RELIGION Benjamin **Hoadly**, *An Answer to the Representation Drawn Up by the Committee of the Lower House of Convocation concerning several dangerous positions and doctrines contained in the bishop of Bangor's Preservative and Sermons, by Benjamin, Lord Bishop of Bangor* [...], 1718. This book involved a debate over church government.
Atterbury's Sermons, 2d vol. gift	0 5 0	RELIGION Francis **Atterbury**, *Fourteen Sermons Preach'd on Several Occasions* [...], 1708; a collection of sermons on "several subjects" was also published in 1723.
Account of the Societies for the propagation of the Gospel	0 5 0	RELIGION
Atterbury answers Wake	0 3 6	RELIGION Francis **Atterbury**, *The Rights, Powers and Privileges of an English Convocation, Stated and Vindicated in Answer to a Late Book of Dr. Wake's, Entitled the Authority of Christian Princes Over Their Ecclesiastical Synods Asserted*, 1697.
Amesh Medalla Theologiae	0 1 6	RELIGION William Ames, *Amish Medulla Theologiae*, 1627. Ames (1576–1633) wrote a systematic exposition of Calvinist principles.

APPENDIX 189

Atterbury against Wake 50	0 3 0	RELIGION
Anderson on Religion and Loyalty	0 2 0	RELIGION Henry Anderson, *Religion and Loyalty maintained against all modern opposers in a treatise on the 29th of May 1681, being trinity-Sunday and anniversary day of His Majesties happy birth*, 1684. This was a published sermon and was dedicated to Charles II, defender of the faith.
Bramhall's (Arch Bishop) Works. Fol.	0 10 0	RELIGION *The Works of John Bramhall.* Bramhall (1594–1663), Archbishop of Armagh and an Anglican apologist, doggedly defended the Church of England against Puritans and Catholics.
Beveridge on the 39 Articles. Fol.	0 6 0	RELIGION William Beveridge, *The Thirty-Nine Articles of the Church of England, with an exposition on the first thirty articles; founded upon principles of reason* [...], 1716. Beveridge (1637–1708) was Bishop of St. Asaph.
Bacon's Government of England Fol.	0 10 0	HISTORY Nathaniel Bacon, *An Historical and Political Discourse of the Laws and Government of England* [...], 1682; the coauthor was John Seldon. The book covered "first times" to the end of Elizabeth's reign and sought to vindicate the ancient ways of Parliaments in England.
Bilson on Christian Subjection, 4to	0 6 0	RELIGION Thomas Bilson, *The True Difference Betweene Christian Subjection and Unchristian Rebellion* [...], 1585.
Burnet's Collection of 18 papers, &c., 4to	0 4 0	RELIGION/HISTORY Gilbert **Burnet**, *Collection of Papers Relating to the Affairs of Church and State in the Reign of James II*, 1689.
Boyer's History of Queen Ann. Fol.	0 12 0	HISTORY Abel Boyer, *The History of the Life and Reign of Queen Anne*, 1722.
Beauty and Virtue	0 4 0	PHILOSOPHY Francis **Hutcheson**, *An Inquiry Into the Original of Our Ideas of Beauty and Virtue*, 1726. Went through several editions.
Bates and Skinner on the Troubles in England	0 3 0	HISTORY George Bates and Thomas Skinner, *A Short Historical Account of the Late Troubles in England*, 1685. Bates was a physician to Charles I and II; Skinner was a medical doctor as well. This book was about the English Civil Wars.
Bonnel's Life, No. 2145	0 1 6	BIOGRAPHY/RELIGION William Hamilton, *The Life and Character of James Bonnel, Esq; Late Accompant General of Ireland*, 1703. This book dealt with King James II's defeat in Ireland. Bonnel was born 1653 in Geneva; he went to Ireland in 1684 as "accountant general" and was a Protestant who stood up to James.

Birch's Life of Tillotson	0 5 0	RELIGION/BIOGRAPHY Thomas Birch, *The Life of the Most Reverend Dr. John Tillotson: Lord Archbishop of Canterbury*, 1753. Tillotson was archbishop from 1691 to 1694.
Bedford on the Stage	0 3 0	RELIGION Arthur Bedford, *The Evil and Danger of Stage-Plays: Shewing Their Natural Tendency to Destroy Religion, and Introduce a General Corruption of Manners* [...], 1706. Bedford was rector of Newton St Loe in Somerset.
Bernard de Mensuriset Ponderibus Antiquis	0 2 6	SCIENCE Edward Bernard, *De Mensuris et Ponderibus antiquis Libri tres*, 1688. He was a British astronomer who wrote the most authoritative treatise on ancient measurement.
Burnet's (Bishop) Charges	0 3 0	RELIGION Gilbert **Burnet**, *A Charge Given at the Triennial Visitation of the Diocese of Salisbury in October 1704*.
Burnet on the Catechism	0 3 0	RELIGION Gilbert **Burnet**, *An Exposition on the Church Catechism, for the use of the diocese of Sarum* [...], 1710.
Blennerhassett against the Deists	0 2 6	RELIGION William Blennerhassett, *The Universal and Eternal System: Also, the Principal Points of the Deists, Against Christianity, Stated and Answered*, 1752.
Boyce on Episcopacy	0 3 0	RELIGION Joseph **Boyse**, *Episcopacy, A Clear Account of the Antient Episcopacy, proving it to have been Parochial, and therefore inconsistent with the present model of Diocesan Episcopacy*, 1712. Boyse (1660–1728), an English Presbyterian in Ireland, argued for Presbyterian dissent.
Burnet's Answer to Law	0 2 0	RELIGION Gilbert **Burnet**, *An Answer to Mr. Law's Letter to the Lord Bishop of Bangor* [...], 1717.
Bangor's (Bishop) Appeal to the Christian Laity	0 2 6	RELIGION William Hendley, *An Appeal to the Consciences and Common Sense of the Christian Laity, whether the Bishop of Bangor in his preservative, &c., Hath not Given up the Rights of the Church, and the powers of the Christian Priesthood*, 1717.
Brady's fourteen Sermons	0 4 0	RELIGION Nicholas Brady, *Fourteen Sermons, Preached on Several Occasions* [...], 1704. Brady (1559–1620), an Irish-born Anglican divine and poet, was a strong supporter of the Glorious Revolution.
Burnet's Vindication in Answer to Hickes	0 1 6	RELIGION 1696; this book was Gilbert **Burnet**'s answer to George **Hickes** in the Bangorian controversy.
Book of Common Prayer, by Clarke	0 2 6	RELIGION Samuel **Clarke**, *The Book of Common Prayer Reformed According to the Plan of the Late Samuel Clarke* [...], 1774.

Byng's Expedition to Sicily	0 2 0	HISTORY Thomas Corbet, *An Account of the Expedition of the British Fleet to Sicily, in the Years 1718, 1719, and 1720, Under the Command of Sir George Byng* [...], 1739.
Bedford on Newton's Chronology	0 3 0	RELIGION/HISTORY Arthur Bedford, *Animadversions Upon Sir Isaac Newton's Book, Intitled The Chronology of Ancient Kingdom's Amended* [...], 1728. Bedford was rector of Newton St. Loe in Somerset. This book deals with religious history and attacks Newton.
Bangorian Tracts 2797	0 5 0	RELIGION Published 1717; a collection of fifty-four tracts on the Bangorian controversy.
Bangor's (Bp.) Rights of Subjects	0 3 0	RELIGION Benjamin **Hoadly**, *The Common Rights of Subjects Defended and the Nature of the Sacramental Test Considered, in Answer to the Dean of Chichester's (Dr. Thomas Sherlock's) "Vindication of the Corporation and Test Acts,"* 1719.
Burnet on the Rights of Princes	0 2 6	RELIGION Gilbert **Burnet**, *The History of the Rights of Princes in the Disposing of Ecclesiastical Benefices and Church Lands* [...], 1682.
Biographia Britannica 2d vol. Fol.	no price listed	REFERENCE *Biographia Britannica: Or the Lives of the Most Eminent Persons who Have Flourished in Great Britain and Ireland, from the earliest ages, down to present times* [...]. This work went through many editions, one of which appeared in 1766.
British Essays, by Boswell	0 2 6	HISTORY James Boswell, *British Essays in Favour of the Brave Corsicans: By Several Hands, Collected and Published by James Boswell*, 1769. Boswell (1740–1795) was the famous biographer and diarist.
Browne's Effects of Music, Singing & Dancing	0 2 6	SCIENCE Richard Browne, *Medicina Musica*, 1729. This book was on the medicinal effects of music, singing, and dancing on the human body.
Balcarras's (Lord) Account of Scotland	0 2 0	HISTORY *The Earl of Balcarras's Account of the Affairs of Scotland, Relating to the Revolution in 1688, as Sent to King James II*, 1754.
Brett's Answer to Hoadley	0 2 6	RELIGION Thomas Brett, *Answer to (Hoadly's) "Plain Account of the Sacrament,"* 1735.
Bennet's 39 Articles	0 2 6	RELIGION Thomas Bennet, *An Essay on the Thirty Nine Articles of Religion, Agreed on and Revised in 1562, 1571* [...], 1715.

Bull's Life (by Nelson)	0 4 0	RELIGION/BIOGRAPHY Robert Nelson, *The Life of Dr. George Bull, Late Lord Bishop of St. David's. With the History of those Controversies in Which He Was Engaged* [...], 1714.
Craig on the Succession. Fol.	0 5 0	RELIGION/HISTORY Sir Thomas Craig, *The Right of Succession to the Kingdom of England, in Two Books; Against the Sophisms of Parsons, the Jesuits, Who Assumed the Counterfeit Name of Doleman* [...], 1703; this is a late edition dealing with issues from the Tudor period.
Cranmer's Answer to Bishop Gardner. Fol.	0 7 0	RELIGION Thomas Cranmer, *Answer unto a Crafty and Sophistical Cavillation devised by Stephen Gardiner*, 1531. Cranmer (1489–1556) was Archbishop of Canterbury under Henry VIII and Edward VI.
Cumberland on the Laws of Nature. 4to.	0 8 0	RELIGION/PHILOSOPHY Richard Cumberland, *A Treatise on the Laws of Nature* [...], 1727. The book's purpose was to enforce the obligation of the dictates of reason and the necessity of revelation and the practice of virtue and religion. Cumberland (1632–1718) was a philosopher and Bishop of Peterborough; he also was a Williamite and Whig. His *De Legibus Naturae* argued for limits on royal power.
Collin's Scheme of Literal Prophecy	0 3 0	RELIGION Anthony Collins, *The Scheme of Literal Prophecy Considered; In a View of the Controversy Occasioned by a late book intitled A Discourse of the Grounds and Reasons of the Christian Religion* [...], 1726. Collins (1676–1729) was an English deist, freethinker, and friend of John **Locke**. His foes were bishops and Samuel **Clarke**.
Chillingsworth's Life (by Maizeux)	0 4 0	RELIGION/BIOGRAPHY Peter des Maizeux, *The Life of William Chillingworth*, 1719. Chillingworth (1602–1644) was the godson of Archbishop William Laud. He supported Charles I in the Civil Wars but was a reluctant Anglican who argued for rationalism. He believed in the right of individuals to interpret the Bible.
Calamy Against Hoadley, or a Defence of Non-Conformity, 3 vols.	0 9 0	RELIGION Edmund **Calamy**, *A Defence of Moderate Non-Conformity in Answer to the Reflections of Mr. Olyffe and Mr. Hoadly* [...]; *Part I and II*, 1703. This book was in answer to Benjamin **Hoadly**, *A Defence of the Reasonableness of Conformity*, 1703.
Character of a Primitive Bishop	0 2 0	RELIGION John Pitts, *The Character of a Primitive Bishop, in a Letter to a Non-Juror: Wherein is Contain'd I. A Vindication of the Present Church of England* [...], 1709.

Church of England Defended (by Trap)	0 3 0	RELIGION Joseph Trapp, *The Church of England Defended against the Church of Rome, in Answer to a Late Sophistical and Insolent Popish Book*, 1727. Trapp (1679–1747) was an English divine, poet, and high church pamphleteer.
Conduct of Dissenters, &c.	0 4 0	RELIGION *The Conduct of the Dissenters Considered. In a Letter to the Bishop of Bangor (Benjamin Hoadly)*, 1719.
Church of England's Wish, No. 1 & 2	each at 0 2 0	RELIGION John Gilbert, *The Church of England's Wish for the Restoring of Primitive Discipline*, 1703.
Collier's Reasons, &c., refusing to Preach	0 1 0	RELIGION Jeremy Collier (1650–1726) was a nonjuror bishop and theologian.
Chishull's Charge of Heresy against Dodwell	0 2 0	RELIGION Edmund Chishull, *A Charge of Heresy, Maintained Against Mr. Dodwell's Late Epistolary Discourse*, 1706. Chishull (1671–1733) was an Oxford graduate and theologian; he engaged with Henry **Dodwell** over mortalism.
Constitution of the Primitive Church	0 3 0	RELIGION Peter King (1st Baron), *An Enquiry Into the Constitution, Discipline, Unity and Worship of the Primitive Church, that flourished within the first three hundred years after Christ*, 1719.
Cudworth on Immutable Morality	0 2 0	RELIGION Ralph Cudworth, *A Treatise Concerning Eternal and Immutable Morality*, 1731. Cudworth (1617–1688) was master of Christ's College, a philosopher, and a Cambridge Platonist—he advocated religious toleration and charity.
Case Stated between the Church of Rome and Church of England (by Leslie)	0 3 0	RELIGION Charles **Leslie**, *The Case Stated between the Church of Rome and Church of England*, 1714. This book was well known for taking on Catholicism.
Call to the Unconverted (by Baxter)	0 1 6	RELIGION Richard Baxter, *A Call to the Unconverted, to Turn and Live: And Accept of Mercy*. Baxter (1615–1691) was a Puritan leader.
Companion for the Persecuted (by Kettlewell)	0 1 0	RELIGION John Kettlewell, *A Companion for the Persecuted: Or an Office for Those Who Suffer for Righteousness [. . .]*, 1693. Kettlewell (1653–1695) was a nonjuror.
Crown and Church	0 4 0	RELIGION George **Rye**, *The Supremacy of the Crown, and the Power of the Church, Asserted and Adjusted. A Sermon Preached Before the University of Oxford, at St. Mary's, on Sunday, Jan. 17, 1713/14 [. . .]*.

Calamy's Sermons	0 3 0	RELIGION Benjamin Calamy, *Sermons Preached upon Several Occasions*, 1726. Calamy (1642–1686), the second son of Edward **Calamy**, was a vicar and one of his majesty's chaplains in ordinary.
Case of Ireland (by Mollyneux)	0 3 0	POLITICAL SCIENCE William Mollyneux, *The Case of Ireland Being Bound by Acts of Parliament in England Stated*, 1698. Mollyneux (1656–1698), from Dublin, was a natural philosopher who wrote on politics. There were at least four volumes of this book; it is unclear which volume Chandler owned.
Clarke's Answer to Wells, &c.	0 3 0	RELIGION Samuel **Clarke**, *A Letter to the Reverend Dr. Wells, Rector of Cotesbach in Leicestershire, in Answer to His Remarks, &c.*, 1714.
Chandler, White and Stewart on Subscription	0 4 6	RELIGION Samuel Chandler's *Case of Subscription to Explanatory Articles of Faith as Qualification for Admission into the Christian Ministry, Calmly and Impartially Reviewed. In Answer to [. . .] The Rev. Mr. John White's Appendix to his Third Letter to a Dissenting Gentleman*, 1748.
Clarissa Harlowe, 8 vols.	1 16 0	NOVEL Samuel Richardson, *Clarissa Harlowe: Or the History of a Young Lady*, 1747. Richardson (1689–1761) wrote epistolary novels; this novel is considered his finest.
Caldewood's Altare Damascenum. 4 to	0 6 0	RELIGION David Calderwood, *Altare Damascenum*, 1623. Calderwood (1575–1650), a Scottish Presbyterian minister and historian of the Scottish church, opposed James I and his attempt to introduce episcopal government in Scotland. He wrote this book, which was an attack on episcopacy, while in exile in Holland.
Carrol against Locke	0 3 0	RELIGION William Carroll, *A Dissertation Upon the Tenth Chapter of the IVth Book of Mr. Locke's Essay Concerning Human Understanding*, 1706. In this book, Carroll (–1711), an Anglican theologian, accused John **Locke** of atheism.
Clarendon's Survey of the Leviathan	0 2 0	GENERAL Edward Hyde, 1st Earl of Clarendon, *A Brief View and Survey of the Dangerous and Pernicious Errors to Church and State in Mr. Hobbes's Book, Entitled Leviathan*, 1676. Hyde (1609–1674) was a historian and statesman.
Cases of Conscience (by Barlow)	0 1 6	RELIGION Thomas Barlow, *Several Miscellaneous and Weighty Cases of Conscience, Learnedly and Judiciously Resolved by the Right Reverend Father in God, Dr. Thomas Barlow, Late Lord-Bishop of Lincoln*, 1692. This book was about the toleration of Protestants, Jews, and others.

Case of Vicarages (by Kennett)	0 3 0	RELIGION White Kennett, *The Case of Impropriations and of the Augmentation of Vicarages and Other Insufficient Cures, Stated by History and Law, from the First Usurpation of the Popes and Monks to Her Majesty's Royal Bounty Lately extended to the poorer clergy of the Church of England*, 1704. Kennett (1660–1728) was Bishop of Peterborough.
Count Fathom, 2 vols.	0 8 0	NOVEL Tobias Smollett, *The Adventures of Ferdinand Count Fathom*, 1753. Smollett (1721–1771) was a Scottish writer best known for his picaresque novels.
Connoisseur, 3 vols. Incompleat	0 8 0	GENERAL Bonnell Thornton and George Colman, *The Connoisseur, by Mr. Town, Critic and Censor-General*, 1767. This series had more than twenty-one volumes and featured chapters on such things as the Survey of the Town; Virtue; the Ocean of Ink; and an Account of a New Order of Females called Demi-Reps.
Cato's Letters, 4th vol.	0 2 0	POLITICAL HISTORY This collection of 144 essays by famed radical Whigs John Trenchard and Thomas Gordon was published between 1720 and 1723.
Compleat Gamester	0 2 6	GENERAL/LEISURE Charles Cotton, *Compleat Gamester: Or full and easy instructions for playing at above Twenty several GAMES upon the Cards* [...], 1725.
Dodwell's Reply to Baxter	0 1 6	RELIGION Henry **Dodwell**, *A Reply to Mr. Baxter's Pretended Confutation of a Book Entituled, Separation of Churches from Episcopal Government, &c., Proved Schismatical. To which are added, Three letters written to him in the year 1673* [...], 1681. Dodwell was responding to Richard Baxter, the Puritan leader, who attacked Dodwell's *Separation of Churches from Episcopal Government, as Practiced by the present Non-Conformists, Proved Schismatical* [...], 1679.
Divine Feudal Laws (by Puffendorf)	0 3 0	RELIGION Samuel von Pufendorf, *The Divine Feudal Law: Or Covenants, Represented, Together with means for the uniting of Protestants* [...], 1685. Pufendorf (1632–1694) was a German jurist, political philosopher, and economist.
De Laune and others. 4to. 1945	0 8 0	RELIGION Thomas **De Laune**, *Plea for the Non-conformists, giving the true state of the dissenters' case* [...], 1683. This was a key work that dissenters often cited.
Dawson's Short and Safe Expedient	0 3 0	RELIGION Benjamin Dawson, *A Short and Safe Expedient for Terminating the Debates about Subscriptions, occasioned by a celebrated performance entitled The Confessional* [...], 1769. Dawson, rector of Burgh in Suffolk, was described on the title page as a "Friend to Religious and Civil Liberty."

Debate between the Houses of Lords and Commons	0 1 0	POLITICAL HISTORY *The Debate at Large, Between the House of Lords and the House of Commons* [...] *Anno 1688*, published in 1695.
Dignity of the Clergy	0 2 6	RELIGION John Groome, *The Dignity and Honour of the Clergy, Represented in an Historical Collection: Shewing How Useful and Serviceable the Clergy Have Been to this Nation by Their Universal Acts of Charity* [...], 1710. Groome (ca. 1678–1760) was vicar of Chidderditch in Essex; he felt the clergy were unfairly attacked.
Defence of Pluralities, No. 1 & 2	each at 0 2 0	RELIGION Henry Wharton, *A Defence of Pluralities, or Holding Two Benefices with Cure of Souls: As now Practiced in the Church of England*, 1692.
Deist's Manual	0 2 0	RELIGION Charles Gildon, *The Deist's Manual: Or a Rational Enquiry into the Christian Religion. With some consideration into Mr. Hobbes, Spinosa, the Oracles of Reason, Second Thoughts, &c.* [...], 1705.
Dickinson's (Jona.) Christian Faith	0 2 0	RELIGION Jonathan Dickinson, *The True Scripture Doctrine Concerning Some Important Points of Christian Faith*, 1741. Dickinson (1688–1747) was an influential Presbyterian leader who helped found the College of New Jersey (later Princeton University) and served as its first president.
Dawson on Loyalty and Obedience	0 2 0	RELIGION Thomas Dawson, *A Treatise of Loyalty and Obedience: Wherein the Regal Supremacy is Asserted; and the Justice of the Late Revolution is Shewn to be Consistent with the Doctrines of the Church* [...], 1710.
Duty of Inferiors	0 2 0	RELIGION
Delarrey on Charles I, 1st vol.	0 2 6	HISTORY Isaac de Larrey, *The History of the Reign of King Charles the I. Containing a more Particular and Impartial Account of the Rebellion and Civil Wars* [...], 1716. De Larrey (1638 or '39–1719) was a historian who fled France after the Edict of Nantes in 1685 and became the historiographer to the king of Prussia.
Discourse in Vindication of Bramhall	0 1 0	RELIGION Samuel **Parker**, *A Discourse in Vindication of Bishop Bramhall and the Clergy of the Church of England, from the Fanatick Charge of Popery: Together with Some Reflections upon the Present State of Affairs. Shewing that There are No Grounds for any Present Fears or Jealousies of It, but only from the Non-conformists*, 1673. Bramhall (1594–1663) was Archbishop of Armagh and an Anglican apologist

Danby's Letters	0 1 6	GENERAL/ HISTORY
The earl of Danby was Thomas Osbourne (1632–1712), a leading politician in the reigns of Charles II and William III who played an important role in the Glorious Revolution.
Dissenter's Reason and Answer to ditto	0 5 0	RELIGION
Dodwell's farther Prospect of the Case in View	0 1 0	RELIGION
Henry **Dodwell**, *A Further Prospect of the Case in View, in Answer to Some New Objections Not There Considered*, 1707.
Delaune's Plea for Non-Conformists	0 1 6	RELIGION
Thomas **De Laune**, *A Plea for the Non-Conformists, Showing the True State of Their Case* [...], 1684. De Laune (–1685) was a nonconformist writer.
Dodwell Case in View	0 1 0	RELIGION
A Presbyter of the Church of England, Mr. Dodwell's Case in View Thoroughly Consider'd. Or the Case of Lay-Deprivations and Independency of the Church (in Spirituals) Set in a True Light [...], 1705; this was written in answer to Henry **Dodwell**.
Defence of the Rights of the Christian Church	0 3 0	RELIGION
Matthew Tindal, *A Defence of the Rights of the Christian Church, Against A Late Visitation Sermon, Intitled the Rights of the Clergy in the Christian Church Asserted* [...], 1707. Tindal (1657–1733) was an English deist and fellow at All Souls' College, Oxford.
Davenant on Public Revenues	0 1 0	ECONOMICS
Charles Davenant, *The Political and Commercial Works of that celebrated writer, Charles Davenant, LL. D., Relating to the Trade and Revenue of England, the Plantation Trade* [...], 1771. Davenant (1656–1714) was an English economist.
Defence of Ecclesiastical Polity	0 2 0	RELIGION
William Covel, *A Just and Temperate Defence of the Five Books of Ecclesiastical Polity Written by Richard Hooker*, 1603.
Edward VI. Review of the Liturgy. 4to.	0 3 0	RELIGION
Edward VI (1537–1553) was Henry VIII's eldest son and, during his short reign, a Protestant reformer.
Ellis Retractations and Repentings. 4to.	0 2 0	RELIGION
John Ellis, *S. Austin Imitated, or Retractions and Repentings in Reference unto the Late Civil and Ecclesiastical Changes in This Nation*, 1662. Ellis (1606–1681) was a minister and theologian who sided with Parliament in the Civil Wars.
Eachard on the Revolution	0 2 6	HISTORY
Laurence Eachard, *The History of the Revolution and the Establishment of England, in the Year, 1688*, 1725. Eachard (1670–1730) was a British historian.

Euclid's Elements (by de Chales)	0 3 0	MATHEMATICS Claude Millet François de Chales, *The Elements of Euclid, explained and demonstrated in a new but easy method* [...], 1645. Chales (1621–1678) was a French mathematician; Euclid was the famed Greek mathematician considered the father of geometry.
Examination of Burnet's own Times, 2 vols.	0 6 0	RELIGION Thomas Salmon, *An Impartial Examination of Bishop Burnet's History of his Own Times* [...], 1724.
Episcopacy, by Divine Right, asserted in 1640	0 1 6	RELIGION Bishop Joseph Hall, *Episcopacy, by Divine Right, asserted*, 1640. Archbishop William Laud directed Hall (1574–1656) to write this work and then changed much of it.
Examination of Sherlock	0 4 0	RELIGION James Parkinson, *An Examination of Dr. Sherlock's Book Entituled the Case of Allegiance due to Sovereign Powers Stated and Resolved* [...], 1691. Thomas Sherlock (1678–1761) was Bishop of London.
L'Estrange's brief History of the Times	0 2 0	POLITICS Roger **L'Estrange**, *A Brief History of the Times*, 1687. This book deals with the murder of E. B. Godfrey (1621–1678), whose mysterious killing was blamed on Catholic plotters.
European Settlements in America, 2nd vol.	0 2 0	HISTORY
Excellency of the Church of England	0 3 0	RELIGION Henry Stebbing, *The Excellency of the Constitution of the Church of England Consider'd, as to the Frequency of its Worship: A Sermon* [...], 1732.
Falkner's two Discourses. 4to.	0 2 6	RELIGION William Falkner, *Two Treatises: The First Concerning Reproaching and Censure. The Second an Answer to Mr. Serjeant's Sure-footing* [...], 1684. Falkner (d. 1682) was a staunch defender of the Church of England.
Fire of the Altar	0 2 0	RELIGION Anthony Horneck, *The Fire of the Altar, or Certain Directions How to Raise the Soul into Holy Flames, Before, At, and After Receiving the Blessed Sacrament of the Lord's Supper* [...], 1724. Horneck (1641–1697) was a German theologian and influential evangelical figure who came to England.
Folly of Infidelity (by Philaletes)	0 2 6	RELIGION Thomas Curteis, *A Dissertation on the Unreasonableness, Folly, and Danger of Infidelity, occasioned by a late virulent book intitled, A Discourse of the Grounds and Reasons of the Christian Religion. By Theotimus Philalethes*, 1725.
Filmer on the Power of Kings	0 1 6	POLITICAL SCIENCE Robert **Filmer**, *Patriarcha: or the Natural Power of Kings. By the Learned Sir Robert Filmer Baronet*, 1680. This was Filmer's best-known work and an important influence on Chandler.

Filmer's Observations	0 2 0	POLITICAL SCIENCE Robert **Filmer**, *Observations Concerning the Original [...] Forms of Government*, 1696; or it possibly was Filmer, *Observations Upon Aristotle's Politiques, Touching Forms of Government, Together with Directions for Obedience to Government in Dangerous and Doubtfull Times*, 1652.
Filmers' Works	0 2 0	HISTORY Works of Robert **Filmer**.
Fowler on Christian Liberty	0 1 6	RELIGION Edward Fowler, *Libertas Evangelica: Or, a Discourse of Christian Liberty, being a farther pursuance of the argument of the Design of Christianity*, 1680. Fowler (1632–1714) was rector of Alhallows Breadstreet, London, who in 1691 became Bishop of Gloucester. He was a critic of Hobbes.
Faith and Duties (by Burnet)	0 3 0	RELIGION Thomas Burnet, *The Faith and Duties of Christians. A Treatise in Eight Chapters* [...], 1728. Burnet (ca. 1635–1715) was rector of Charterhouse in 1685 and in 1688 became chaplain in ordinary to King William but was stripped of the title in 1692.
Gun-Powder Plot	0 1 0	POLITICAL HISTORY
Grotius de Imperio Summarum Potestatum	0 3 0	LAW Hugo Grotius, *De Imperio Summarum Potestatum circa sacra desumptae*, 1668. Grotius (1583–1645) was a Dutch jurist who laid the foundation for international law, based on natural law.
God and the King	0 2 0	RELIGION Richard Mocket, *God and the King: Or a dialogue shewing that our sovereign lord the King, being immediate under God within his dominions, doth rightly claim whatsoever is required by the oath of allegiance; as also the duty and allegiance of the Subject* [...], 1725. Mocket (1577–1618) was warden of All Souls's College—a churchman and academic.
Grand Essay	0 2 0	RELIGION/PHILOSOPHY William Coward, *The Grand Essay: Or a Vindication of Reason, and Religion, Against Impostures of Philosophy* [...], 1704. Coward (1657–1725) was a physician, writer, and poet whose views Parliament denounced as blasphemous.
Gibson's History of the Affairs of Europe	0 2 6	HISTORY William Gibson, *A History of the Affairs of Europe, from the peace of Utrecht to the conclusion of the quadruple alliance. With a treatise of the religious and civil interests of Europe*, 1725.
Grove's Philosophy, 1st vol.	0 4 0	RELIGION Henry Grove, *A System of Moral Philosophy: Of the Importance and Certainty* [...] *and of the Nature of Happiness* [...], *by the late Reverend and Learned Mr. Henry Grove of Taunton*, 1749. Grove (1684–1738) was a nonconformist minister.

Great Britain's True System	0 5 0	ECONOMICS Malachy Postlethwayt, *Great-Britain's True System: Wherein is Clearly Shewn, I. That an Increase of the Public Debts and Taxes Must, in a Few Years, Prove the Ruin of the Monied, the Trading, and the Landed Interest* [...], 1757. Postlethwayt (1707–1767) was a commercial financial expert.
Gibson's Codex, 2 vols. Fol.	1 4 0	RELIGION Edmund Gibson, *Codex Juris Ecclesiastici Anglicani: Or, the Statutes. Constitutions, Canons, Rubricks and Articles, of the Church of England*, 1713.
Hobbes' Leviathan.	0 3 0	POLITICAL PHILOSOPHY Thomas Hobbes, *Leviathan; Or, the Matter, Form, and Power of a Common-Wealth, Ecclesiastical and Civil*, 1651. Hobbes (1588–1679) was a famed English philosopher with wide-ranging interests, including science and mathematics. In *Leviathan*, his most famous work, he outlined social contract theory.
Historical Acct. of Comprehension & Toleration	0 2 6	RELIGION William Baron (1636–1714), *An Historical Account of Comprehension, and Toleration. From a general Retrospect on the Several Reformations at first, with the pernicious Principles and Practices of that which the dissenters among us have followed* [...], *by the author of the Dutch way of toleration*, 1705.
History of the Last Parliament	0 1 6	HISTORY Jonathan Swift, *The History of the Last Session of Parliament, and of the Peace of Utrecht. Written at Windsor in the Year,* 1713. Swift (1667–1745) was the famed satirist, essayist, and cleric.
Hoadley's Tracts	0 3 0	RELIGION Benjamin **Hoadly**, *Several Tracts Formerly Published, Now Collected* [...] *To Which Are Added Six Sermons, Never Before Publish'd*, 1715.
Hicks's Devotions, No. 1 & 2	each at 0 3 0	RELIGION George **Hickes**, *A Book of Devotions*, 1705.
Hoadley's 26 Sermons, Elegantly bound	0 8 0	RELIGION A collection of sermons by Benjamin **Hoadly**.
Hoadley's Terms of Acceptance	0 3 0	RELIGION Benjamin **Hoadly**, *Several Discourses Concerning the Terms of Acceptance with God* [...], 1711.
Hoadley's ditto	0 3 0	RELIGION
Hoadley on the Sacrament, No. 1 & 2	at 3ƒ 0 6 0	RELIGION Benjamin **Hoadly**, *A Plain Account of the Nature and End of the Sacrament of the Lord's Supper* [...], 1735.
Hoadley's ditto 1694 & 160	at 3 ƒ 0 6 0	RELIGION Benjamin **Hoadly**, *Several Tracts formerly published, now collected into one volume* [...], 1715.

Hicks' Apologetical Vindication, No. 1 & 2	each at 0 2 0	RELIGION George **Hickes**, *An Apologetical Vindication of the Church of England: In answer to her adversaries who reproach her with the English heresies and schisms* [...], 1706.
Hoadley's Original of Government, No. 1 & 2	0 3 0	POLITICAL HISTORY Benjamin **Hoadly**, *Original and Institution of Civil Government Discuss'd. Viz. I. An examination of the patriarchal scheme of government. II. A defense of Mr. Hooker's judgment* [...], 1710.
Hoadley's Measures of Succession	0 1 6	RELIGION Benjamin **Hoadly**, *The Measures of Submission to the Civil Magistrate Consider'd: In a defense of the doctrine deliver'd in a sermon preach'd before [...] the lord-mayor of London* [...], 1705.
Hoadley's Preservative	0 2 0	RELIGION Benjamin **Hoadly**, *A Preservative Against the Principles and Practices of the Non-jurors Both in Church and State, or an appeal to the consciences and common sense of the Christian laity* [...], 1716.
Hicks' Constitution of the Church	0 3 0	RELIGION George **Hickes**, *The Constitution of the Catholick Church, and the Nature and Consequences of Schism* [...], 1716.
Hoadley's on Conformity	0 4 0	RELIGION Benjamin **Hoadly**, *Reasonableness of Conformity to the Church of England, represented to the dissenting ministers; in answer to the Tenth Chapter of Mr. Calamy's Abridgment of Mr. Baxter's History of His Life and Times* [...], 1703.
Hucheson's Philosophia Moralis	0 3 0	PHILOSOPHY Francis **Hutcheson**, *Philosophia Moralis Institutio Compendiaria*, 1742.
History of Parliament	0 3 0	POLITICAL HISTORY
Hoadley's Measures of Submission, No. 1 & 2	0 1 6	RELIGION Benjamin **Hoadly**, *Measures of Submission to the Civil Magistrate Considered. In a Defense of the Doctrine Deliver'd in a Sermon Preach'd before [...] the Lord-Mayor [...] of London* [...], 1705.
Hale's (Bp.) Cases of Conscience	0 2 0	RELIGION
Hale on the Power of Parliaments	0 2 6	POLITICAL HISTORY/LAW Matthew **Hale**, *The Original Institution, Power, and Jurisdiction of Parliaments. In Two Parts* [...], 1707. Hale (1609–1676) was a noted jurist and barrister.
History of Addresses, 2 vols.	0 4 0	RELIGIOUS HISTORY John **Oldmixon**, *History of Addresses*, 1709, vol. 1; *The History of Addresses. With Remarks Serious and Comical. In Which a particular Regard is had to all such as have been presented since the impeachment of Dr. Sacheverell*, 1711, vol. 2. Daniel Defoe was coauthor.

Hutchinson's Defence of the Ancient Historians	0 4 0	HISTORY Francis Hutchinson, *A Defence of the Ancient Historians: With a particular application of it to the history of Ireland and Great-Britain, and other Northern nations* [...], 1734. Hutchinson (1660–1739) was Bishop of Down and Connor; he wrote extensively on social and economic issues.
History of the Late Minority	0 2 0	POLITICAL HISTORY John Almon, *The History of the Late Minority. Exhibiting the Conduct, Principles, and Views, of That Party, During the Years 1762, 1763, 1764, and 1765. The Third Impression*, 1766. Almon (1737–1805), an English political writer and journalist, fought for the right to publish parliamentary debates.
Higden's View of the English Constitution	0 2 0	POLITICAL SCIENCE William Higden, *A View of the English Constitution, with respect to the sovereign authority of the prince, and the allegiance of the subject. In vindication of the lawfulness of taking oaths, to her majesty, by law required*, 1709. Higden (1662 or '63–1715) was an English writer.
Hunt's Arguments, 2035		This possibly was a work by Thomas Hunt, a polemicist in the late seventeenth century who attacked Whigs and dissenters.
Harmer against Burnet	0 2 6	RELIGION Anthony Harmer, *A Specimen of some Errors and Defects in the History of the Reformation of the Church of England written by Gilbert Burnet, D. D.*, [...], 1693. In the *History of the Reformation*, Burnet argued for a stronger Parliament that would have more say about the royal succession and clerical appointments.
Hume's Hist. of England, 5th. vol.	0 4 0	HISTORY David Hume, *The History of Great-Britain, Containing the Reigns of James I and Charles I*, 1754. Hume (1711–1776) was the famed philosopher, historian, and essayist.
History of King William, 3 vols.	0 10 0	BIOGRAPHY
Johnson's Works. Fol.	0 7 0	GENERAL Samuel Johnson, *Works of Samuel Johnson* [...]; the famed poet, essayist, and biographer.
Independent Reflector	0 4 0	PERIODICAL The weekly journal by William Livingston, John Morin Scott, and William Smith; it first appeared on November 30, 1752.
James IId's Life	0 3 6	BIOGRAPHY
Jameson on the Hierarchy	0 3 0	RELIGION William **Jameson**, *Nazianzeni querala et votum justum: The fundamentals of the Hierarchy examin'd and disprov'd: wherein the choicest arguments and defences of* [...] *A.M.* [...] *the author of an enquiry into the new opinions (chiefly) propagated by the Presbyterians in Scotland* [...], 1697.

APPENDIX 203

Jameson on Episcopacy	0 3 0	RELIGION William **Jameson**, *The Sum of the Episcopacy Controversy, as it is pleaded from the holy scriptures: Wherein the scripture-arguments for presbytery are vindicated; those for prelacy confuted* [...], 1713.
Interest of Princes and States (by Bethel)	0 1 6	POLITICAL SCIENCE Slingsby Bethel, *The Interest of Princes and States of Europe*, 1681. Bethel (1617–1697) was a member of Parliament with Republican sympathies during the Civil Wars.
Institution of a Christian Man. 4to.	1 4 0	RELIGION *The Godly and Pious Institution of a Christian Man, containing an exposition of the Creed* [...], 1537. This was known as the Bishops Book because the bishops compiled it at the behest of Archbishop Thomas Cranmer (1489–1556).
Kingston's History of Conspiracies	0 3 0	POLITICAL HISTORY Richard Kingston, *A True History of the Several Designs and Conspiracies, against his Majesties sacred person and government, as they were carry'd out from 1688 till 1697* [...], 1698.
King's Supremacy Asserted	0 1 6	POLITICAL HISTORY Robert **Sheringham**, *The King's Supremacy Asserted, or a Remonstrance of the King's Right Against the Pretended Parliament*, 1660.
London Magazine, 15 vols.	3 15 0	PERIODICAL This periodical was established in 1732.
Locke's Works. Fol. 3 vols.	2 10 0	POLITICAL PHILOSOPHY This three-volume collection of **Locke**'s works was likely a 1722 edition.
— Of Human Understanding. Fol.	0 5 0	POLITICAL PHILOSOPHY This likely was **Locke**, *The Limits of Human Understanding*.
— Reasonableness of Christianity	0 2 0	RELIGION **Locke**, *The Reasonableness of Christianity, as Delivered in the Scriptures*, 1695.
— and Stillingfleet on the Trinity, 3 vols.	0 6 0	RELIGION
— on Human Understanding, 2 vols.	0 7 0	POLITICAL PHILOSOPHY **Locke**, *An Essay Concerning Human Understanding*, 1689.
Laud against Fisher. Fol.	0 4 0	RELIGION
Laud's (Abp.) Life. Fol. (by Heylin)	0 6 0	RELIGIOUS BIOGRAPHY By Peter Heylin. William Laud (1573–1645) became Archbishop of Canterbury in 1633 and was executed in 1645.
L'Estrange's Erasmus	0 1 0	RELIGION Roger **L'Estrange**, *Twenty Select Colloquies out of Erasmus Roterodamus*, 1680. In this work, L'Estrange, who opposed the emerging religious and political toleration, placed Erasmus in a middle position between the dangerous extremes of Puritanism and popery.

Laws of Massachusetts Bay. Fol.	0 8 0	LAW
Leland's Answer to Tindal, 2 vols.	0 8 0	RELIGION *An Answer to a Late Book intituled Christianity as old as the creation*, 1733. Matthew Tindal (1657–1733) was an English deist and fellow at All Souls' College, Oxford; John Leland was a dissenting minister in Dublin.
Lowth on Church Power	0 2 0	RELIGION Simon Lowth, *Of the Subject of Church-Power, In Whom It Resides, Its Force, Its Extent, and Execution, that it opposes not civil government in any one instance of it*, 1685. Lowth (1636–1720) was a nonjuring clergyman and a controversialist on the bishops. He defended episcopal succession against any right of disposition by a civil magistrate.
Law's Answer to Hoadley on the Sacraments, No. 1 and 2.	0 3 0	RELIGION William **Law**, *A Demonstration of the Gross and Fundamental Errors of a Late Book: Called A Plain Account of the Nature and End of the Sacrament of the Lord's Supper*, 1737. **Hoadly** published *A Plain Account of the Nature and End of the Sacrament of the Lord's Supper* in 1735. Law answered with *A Demonstration of the Gross and Fundamental Errors* [...].
Lives of the Archbishops	0 3 0	RELIGION
Law on Christian Perfection	0 7 0	RELIGION William **Law**, *A Practical Treatise upon Christian Perfection*, 1726. This work deeply influenced the Wesleys and George Whitefield.
Lindsay's Apology	0 4 0	RELIGION *The Apology of Theophilus Lindsey, A.M., on resigning the vicarage of Catterick, Yorkshire*, 1774. Lindsey (1723–1808) resigned because he objected to Church of England subscription articles. He later founded the first Unitarian congregation in Britain.
Law's Appeal	0 3 0	RELIGION William **Law**, *An Appeal to All that Doubt, or Disbelieve the Truths of the Gospel, whether they be Deists, Arians, Socinians, or nominal Christians* [...], 1756.
Leland de Scriptoribus Britannicis, 2 vols.	0 6 0	RELIGION John Leland, *Commentarii de Scriptoribus Britannicis auctore Joanne Lelando*, 1709.
Law's Three Letters to Hoadley, with Burnet's Answer	0 3 0	RELIGION William **Law**, *Three Letters to the Bishop of Bangor*, 1717. This book was part of the Bangorian controversy.
Letter to Protestant Dissenters	0 3 0	RELIGION *A Letter to the Protestant Dissenters, relating to the too great Neglect of Family-Worship, and decay of practical religion amongst us. By the Direction of some London ministers*, 1720.

Laws of Maryland in 1727. Fol.	0 3 0	LAW
Mayhew's [Sermons]	0 4 0	RELIGION Jonathan Mayhew, *Seven Sermons upon the Following Subjects* [...], 1749. Mayhew (1720–1766) was the well-known Congregational minister of Boston and radical Whig who defended American rights. Topics in this work included the difference between truth and falsehood; the right and duty of private judgment; and the love of God.
Memoirs of Lord Dundee, and the Massacre of Glenco	0 1 0	HISTORY/BIOGRAPHY John Graham, *Memoirs of the Lord Viscount Dundee, the Highland-Clans, and the Massacre of Glenco* [...], 1711. This massacre occurred in 1692 in the Scottish Highlands, in Glen Coe. Scottish history was a particular interest of Chandler's.
Morley's Treatises. 4to.	0 2 6	RELIGION George Morley, *Several Treatises, Written upon Several Occasions*, 1683. Morley (1597–1684) was, interestingly, a defender of Charles II and a foe of Catholicism. He served as Bishop of Worcester and then of Winchester.
Maria A'Schurman	0 2 6	BIOGRAPHY Anna Maria van Schurman (1607–1678) was a polymath who exchanged letters with philosopher Descartes, religious reform thinker Jean de Labadie, and others. She was at the center of a network of intellectual women.
Marshall's Defence of the Constitution	0 2 0	RELIGION Nathaniel Marshall, *A Defence of Our Constitution in Church and State; or an Answer to the Late Charge of Non-Jurors accusing us of heresy and schism; perjury and treason* [...], 1717.
Manley's (Sir Rog.) History of Rebellions	0 2 6	HISTORY Sir Roger Manley, *The History of the Rebellions in England, Scotland, and Ireland* [...] *from the year 1640 to the beheading of the Duke of Monmouth in 1685. In three parts*, 1691. Manley (ca. 1626–ca. 1688) was a historian, royalist, and late governor of Land Guard-Fort.
Mentzer's Vindication of Lutheranism	0 3 0	RELIGION Balthasar Mentzer, *A Vindication of the Lutheran Religion from the Charge of Popery: In several letters to a friend. Wherein the Lutheran principles are fully explained and confirm'd* [...], 1720. Mentzer (1565–1627) was the pastor of the Augustan Church in London.
Macpherson's Original Papers, 2 vols. 4to.	3 0 0	HISTORY James Macpherson, *Original Papers; Containing the Secret History of Great Britain, from the Restoration, to the accession of the House of Hannover. To which are prefixed extracts from the* LIFE *of James II* [...], vol. 1, 2nd ed., 1776.

Milton's Iconoclastes	0 2 6	**POLITICAL HISTORY** John Milton, *Eikonoklastes, In Answer to a Book Intitl'd Eikon Basilike* [...], 1649. Milton (1608–1674) was a poet and intellectual who served under Oliver Cromwell. This is one of his most famous works; it defended the execution of Charles I and argued that the king must follow the rule of law.
Memoirs of Scotland	0 3 0	**POLITICAL HISTORY** David Moysie, *Memoirs of the Affairs of Scotland; Containing an impartial Account of the most remarkable Transactions in that Kingdom, from K. James VI. His taking up the Government in 1577, till his accession to the Crown of England in 1603* [...], 1755.
Memoirs of the Life of Tenison	0 3 0	**RELIGIOUS BIOGRAPHY** *Memoirs of the Life and Times of the most reverend father in God, Dr. Thomas Tenison, late archbishop of Canterbury* [...], 1716. Tenison (1636–1715) was a strong supporter of the Glorious Revolution.
Miller's Gardeners Dictionary. Fol.	0 16 0	**REFERENCE** Philip Miller, *The Gardeners Dictionary: Containing the Methods of Cultivating and Improving the Kitchen, Fruit and Flower Garden* [...], 1735; in two vols.
Monthly Review, 10th vol.	0 3 6	**PERIODICAL**
Moyle's Works. 2 vols.	0 6 0	**POLITICAL PHILOSOPHY** Walter Moyle, *The Whole Works of Walter Moyle, Esq., that were published by himself* [...], 1727. Moyle (1672–1721) was an English writer who advocated classical republicanism.
Newton Optices. 4to.	0 4 0	**SCIENCE** *Isaaci Newtoni Optices Libris Tres: Accedunt Ejusdem Lectiones Opticae*, 1670s. This book, by famed scientist Isaac Newton (1642–1727), is about the lessons of optics and light and color.
— Principia Mathematica. 4to.	0 6 0	**MATHEMATICS** Isaac Newton, *The Mathematical Principles of Natural Philosophy* [...], 1729.
Norris's Treatises on Curious Subjects	0 2 6	**RELIGION** John **Norris**, *Treatises upon Several Curious Subjects* [...], 1730.
— On Reason and Faith	0 2 6	**RELIGION** John **Norris**, *An Account of Reason and Faith: In Relation to the Mysteries of Christianity* [...], 1724. A very popular work that went through fourteen editions.
Notion of Schism. by W.C.	0 1 0	**RELIGION** Robert Conold, *The Notion of Schism Stated according to the antients, and considered with reference to the non-conformists: and the pleas for schismaticks examined* [...], 1677. (The initial W. in the catalog entry was apparently an error.)

Nye's Answer to Toland on the Canon of Scripture	0 3 6	RELIGION Stephen Nye, *An Historical Account and Defence of the Canon of the New Testament. In Answer to Toland's. Amyntor* [...], 1700; John Toland, *Amyntor: Or a Defence of Milton's Life. Containing I. A general apology for all Writings of that kind. II. A Catalogue of Books attributed in the Primitive Times to Jesus Christ* [...], 1699. Toland (1670–1722) was a rationalist philosopher and freethinker; Nye (1648–1719) was a theologian known for his Unitarian views.
Nugent's Origin of Human Knowledge	0 3 0	POLITICAL PHILOSOPHY Thomas Nugent, *An Essay on the Origin of Human Knowledge. Being a Supplement to Mr. Locke's Essay on the Human Understanding. Translated from the French* [...] *by Mr. Nugent* [...], 1756. The original author, Étienne Bonnot de Condillac (1714–1780), was a French philosopher and epistemologist who wrote on philosophy and philosophy of the mind, and was a disciple of **Locke**.
Ollyffe against Calamy	0 2 6	RELIGION John Ollyffe, *A Defence of Ministerial Conformity to the Church of England, in Answer to the Misrepresentations of the terms thereof by Mr. Calamy* [...] *in his abridgment of the history of Mr. Baxter's life and times*, 1702. Ollyffe (1647–1717) was an Anglican clergyman and writer.
Olyffe and others on Conformity	0 2 6	RELIGION Calamy's work set off a spirited debate on conformity.
Owen on Presbyterian Ordination	0 3 0	RELIGION John Owen (1616–1683) was a leading a nonconformist and Presbyterian who became a Congregationalist. He served as pastor of Coggeshall in Essex. This was not one of his major works.
Ollyffe against Treason	0 6 0	POLITICAL George Olyffe, *The Madness of Treason and Disaffection against the Present Government*, 1724. He was minister of Wendover and Great Kimbrel in Bucks.
Olyffe's Second Defence	0 1 6	RELIGION John Olyffe, *A Second Defence, in Answer to Mr. Calamy's objections against the first*, 1705.
Pamphlets 22, containing Attwood's Scotch Patriot Unmasked, &c.	0 6 0	HISTORY William Atwood, *The Scotch Patriot Unmask'd in Animadversions upon a Seditious Pamphlet Entitled, The Reducing Scotland by Arms, and Annexing It to England as a Province* [...], 1705.
Primer of Henry VIII	0 12 0	RELIGION Richard Grafton, *Primer of Henry the VIII*, 1545. Primers are private prayer books. The Grafton version was authorized by Henry; it contained a royal preface and a calendar of saints' days.

Pierce's Vindication of the Dissenters	0 4 0	RELIGION James Pierce, *A Vindication of the Dissenters: In answer to Dr. William Nichols's Defence of the Doctrine and discipline of the Church of England* [...], 1717.
Potter on Church Government	0 3 0	RELIGION John Potter, *A Discourse of Church Government: wherein the rights of the church and the supremacy of Christian princes are vindicated and adjusted*, 1707. Potter (1674–1747) was Archbishop of Canterbury. This was an important book for Chandler and his mentor, Samuel Johnson.
Proceedings in Parliament against Atterbury	0 3 0	POLITICAL/RELIGIOUS HISTORY Henry Anderson, *Proceedings in Parliament against Dr. F. Atterbury, Bishop of Rochester; John Plunket* [...], *Upon Bills of Pain and Penalties for a Treasonable Conspiracy*, 1744. Plunket was a coconspirator. A parliamentary committee was appointed to investigate January 1723.
Parker on Religion and Loyalty	0 2 0	RELIGION Samuel **Parker**, *Religion and Loyalty: Or a Demonstration of the Power of the Christian Church* [...] *from the Beginning of Christianity to the End of the Reign of Julian*, 1684.
Prideaux's Ecclesiastical Tracts	0 3 6	RELIGION Humphrey Prideaux, *Ecclesiastical Tracts: I. Validity of the orders of the Church of England. II. The Justice of the Present Established Law ... III. Award of Charles I, shewing that personal tithes are still due by the law of the land* [...], 1710. Prideaux (1648–1724) was dean of Norwich, a Whig, and a low churchman.
Psalter in Arabic	0 2 6	RELIGION
Passeran's 12 Discourses on Religion & Government	0 2 6	RELIGION/POLITICAL SCIENCE Albert Count de Passeran, *Twelve Discourses concerning Religion and Government, Inscribed to all Lovers of Truth and Liberty* [...], 1734.
Pierce's Tracts	0 3 0	RELIGION James Peirce, *A Vindication of the Dissenters: In Answer to Dr. William Nichols's Defence of the Doctrine and Discipline of the Church of England* [...], 1717.
Parker's Answer to Rehearsal	0 2 0	RELIGION Samuel **Parker**, *A Reproof to the Rehearsal Transposed, in a Discourse to its Author*, 1673. This involved a debate with Andrew Marvell (1621–1678), a well-known poet and political satirist, who served in Parliament during the Cromwell reign (although he first opposed Cromwell). Marvell attacked Parker's various tracts against dissenters, including his major work *Discourse of Ecclesiastical Politie* (1670), which advocated state regulation of religious affairs.
Practice of Ecclesiastical Courts	0 1 0	RELIGION Henry Consett, *The Practice of the Spiritual or Ecclesiastical Courts: Wherein is contained their original stile and causes usually tryed in them* [...], 1700.

Political State of Great Britain in 1711–12–14	0 6 0	HISTORY
Religion of a Church of England Woman	0 3 0	RELIGION
Right of Succession of the Crown of England. Fol.	0 5 0	POLITICAL HISTORY George Harbin, *The Hereditary Right of the Crown of England Asserted; the History of the Succession since the Conquest clear'd; and the English Constitution vindicated from the misrepresentations of Dr. Higden's View and Defence* [. . .], 1713.
Reply to Whitgift by Cartwright	0 2 0	RELIGION Thomas Cartwright, *A Replye to an Answere made of M. Doctor Whitgifte againste the Admonition to the Parliament*, 1573. This involved the legendary duel between Cartwright (1535–1603), who was a leading Puritan and bitter foe of episcopacy, and John Whitgift (1530–1604), the Archbishop of Canterbury under Queen Elizabeth who tried to stamp out dissent.
Royal Martyr, by Boswell, 2 vols.	0 5 0	GENERAL John Boswell, *The Case of the Royal Martyr Considered with Candor; or an answer to some libels lately published in prejudice to the memory of that unfortunate prince; particularly to I. A Letter to a clergyman, relating to his sermon on the 30th of January* [. . .], 1758.
Rebellion in 1715	0 3 0	HISTORY Robert Patten, *The History of the Rebellion in the Year 1715: With Original Papers and the Characters of the Principal Noblemen* [. . .], 1745. This book was about the attempt by the "Old Pretender," James Francis Edward Stuart, to regain the British throne.
Rye against the Non-jurors	0 6 0	RELIGION George **Rye**, *A Treatise against the Nonconforming Nonjurors in Answer to the Objections which Mr. Dodwell, Dr. Hickes and Others Have Brought Against the Church of England*, 1719.
Redeemer and Sanctifier, by Watts	0 3 0	RELIGION Isaac Watts, *The Redeemer and Sanctifier: Or the Sacrifice of Christ and the Operations of the Spirit Vindicated* [. . .], 1736. Watts (1674–1748) was the famed Anglican hymnist and theologian. His works were a staple at Puritan-dominated Yale, where Chandler attended college.
Reflections on Ridicule	0 2 0	GENERAL Jean Baptiste Morvan de Bellegarde, *Reflections upon Ridicule; or what it is that makes a man ridiculous, and the means to avoid it. Wherein are represented the different manners and characters of persons of the present age*, 1717.
Rohault's System of Natural Philosophy, 2 vols.	0 8 0	SCIENCE Jacques Rohault, *Rohault's System of Natural Philosophy, Illustrated with Dr. Samuel Clarke's notes taken mostly out of Sir Isaac Newton's philosophy* [. . .], 1728.

Roe on Enthusiasm	0 6 0	RELIGION Samuel Roe, *Enthusiasm Detected, Defeated. With previous considerations concerning regeneration, the omnipresence of God, and divine grace* [...], 1768.
Ridley's Review of the Life of Cardinal Pole	0 6 0	RELIGION/BIOGRAPHY Glocester Ridley, *A Review of Mr. Philips's History of the Life of Reginald Pole*, 1765. Ridley (1702–1774) was an English writer.
Revolutions of Morocco	0 2 6	HISTORY John Braithwaite, *The History of the Revolutions in the Empire of Morocco, upon the death of the late emperor Muley Ishmael* [...], 1729.
Stillingfleet's Grounds of the Protestant Religion. 4to.	0 10 0	RELIGION Edward Stillingfleet, *A Rational Account of the Grounds of the Protestant Religion: Being a Vindication of the Lord Archbishop of Canterbury's Relation of a Conference* [...], 1665. Stillingfleet (1635–1695) was dean of St. Paul's and a chaplain in ordinary to the king, and was an influential defender of Anglicanism.
Sheringham on the King's Supremacy	0 1 6	POLITICAL SCIENCE Robert **Sheringham**, *The King's Supremacy Asserted, or a Remonstrance of the King's Right Against the Pretended Parliament*, 1660 and 1682.
Sanderson's Preservative against Schism, 3 vols.	0 12 0	RELIGION Robert Sanderson, *A Preservative Against Schism and Rebellion: In the most trying times* [...], 1722. Sanderson (1587–1663) was Bishop of Lincoln.
Smith on the Modern Pleas for Schism	0 5 0	RELIGION Joseph Smith, *Modern Pleas for Schism and Infidelity* [...], 1715. Smith (1670–1756) was a churchman and provost of Queen's College, Oxford.
Sermons on the Rebellion in 1745. 4to.	0 5 0	RELIGION This likely was a collection of fast-day sermons on the rebellion of 1745 when a Stuart tried to regain the throne.
Sancroft's Sermons	0 2 0	RELIGION William Sancroft, *Sermons Preached by the Most Reverend Father in God William Sancroft, late lord arch-bishop of Canterbury* [...], 1703. Sancroft (1617–1693) was one of the seven bishops imprisoned in 1688 for seditious libel against James II.
Spirit of Patriotism at the Accession of George I.	0 1 6	GENERAL Henry St. John Bolingbroke, *Letters on the Spirit of Patriotism: On the Idea of a Patriot King: And on the state of parties, at the accession of King George the First* [...], 1749. Bolinbroke (1678–1751) was a Tory leader and government official who supported the Jacobite rebellion of 1715.

Sherlock against Hoadley	0 5 0	RELIGION Bishop of London Thomas Sherlock, who in 1718 was dean of Chicester, and Bishop of Bangor Benjamin **Hoadly** wrote several tracts in opposition to each other during the Bangorian controversy. One possibility was Sherlock, *The Condition and Example of Our Blessed Saviour Vindicated: In Answer to the Bishop of Bangor's Charge of Calumny Against the Dean of Chicester*, 1718. Another possibility was **Hoadly**, *An Answer to a Calumny Cast Upon the Bishop of Bangor, by the Reverend Dr. Sherlock [...] Refutation of Bishop Sherlock's Arguments Against the Repeal of the Test and Corporation Acts*, 1718.
Sykes' Letters to Sherlock	0 3 0	RELIGION Arthur Ashley Sykes wrote a series of letters in 1717; one was *A Second Letter to the Reverend Dr. Sherlock, Being a Reply to his Answer, &c.* [...], 1717. Sykes (1684–1756) was a **Hoadly** ally who opposed the nonjurors.
Savage's Powers of a Sovereign	0 1 6	POLITICAL SCIENCE/GENERAL Gerard Noodt, *The Power of the Sovereign, and the Right of Liberty of Conscience: In Two Discourses* ..., 1708. John Savage (1673–1747) was the translator; Noodt (1647–1725) was a Dutch jurist.
Sparrow's Collection of Canons, &c. 4to.	0 6 0	RELIGION Anthony Sparrow, *A Collection of Articles, Inquisitions, Canons, Orders, Ordinances, & Constitutions Ecclesiastical, with other publick records of the Church of England* [...], 1684. This work covers Edward VI and Elizabeth and their efforts to promote unity during the Tudor period.
Squire's Answer to the Independent Whig	0 1 6	RELIGION Francis Squire, *An Answer to Some Late Papers, Entitled The Independent Whig; so far as they relate to the Church of England, as law established* [...], 1723. Squire was rector of Exford and vicar of Cutcombe and Luxborow, Somerset.
Select Tracts of Dissenters	0 3 6	RELIGION
— Sherlock. Resistance	0 3 0	RELIGION/POLITICAL PHILOSOPHY William Sherlock, *The Case of the Allegiance due to Sovereign Powers, Further Consider'd and Defended: with a more particular respect to the doctrine of non-resistance and passive-obedience. Together with a reasonable perswasive to our new dissenters*, 1691. Sherlock (1641–1707) was dean of St. Paul's and the father of Thomas Sherlock.
State of Parties in Great-Britain in 1712	0 2 6	RELIGION/POLITICAL HISTORY *The Present State of Parties in Great-Britain, particularly an enquiry into the state of dissenters in England, and the Presbyterians in Scotland; their religious and political interest consider'd, as it respects their circumstances before and since the late acts against occasional conformity in England* [...], 1712.

212 APPENDIX

Swift's Miscellanies.	0 3 0	GENERAL Jonathan Swift, *The Works of Jonathan Swift, Dean of St. Patrick's Dublin. Consisting of Miscellanies in Prose* [...], 1765.
Strype's Life of Smith	0 3 0	BIOGRAPHY John Strype, *The Life of the Learned Sir Thomas Smith, Kt., doctor of the civil law: principal secretary of state to King Edward the Sixth, and Queen Elizabeth* [...], 1698.
Secker's Sermons	0 8 0	RELIGION Thomas Secker; seven volumes of his *Sermons on Several Subjects* were published in 1771, and *Nine Sermons Preached in the Parish of St. James, Westminister*, was published in 1758. This work was likely part of Chandler's research for his 1774 tract defending Secker and the campaign for an American episcopate.
State of Britain, No. 50. in 1711 & in 1783	at 4ƒ 0 8 0	GENERAL
Synge's 8 Sermons	0 3 0	RELIGION Richard Synge, *Loyalty to His Majesty, King George, Recommended in Eight Sermons. Upon the following subjects* [...], 1720. Synge was chaplain at Somerset House. Subjects included a thanksgiving sermon on the quashing of the late rebellion; the happy accession of George; advice to malcontents; the advantages of good government; and the blessings of "happy revolution."
Special Verdict against the Protestant Reconciler	0 2 0	RELIGION Laurence Womack, *Suffragium Protestantium: Wherein our governours are justified in their impositions and proceedings against dissenters. Meisner also and the verdict rescued from the cavils and seditious sophistry of the Protestant Reconciler* [...], 1683. Womack (1612–1686) was Archdeacon of Suffolk who later became a bishop. He also wrote a tract defending bishops' right to sit in Parliament and others attacking Calvinism and the Synod of Dort.
Strength & Weakness of Human Reason	0 3 0	RELIGION Isaac Watts, *The Strength and Weakness of Human Reason: Or the important question about the sufficiency of reason to conduct mankind to religion and future happiness, argued between an inquiring deist and a Christian divine* [...], 1731.
Short Method with Deists	0 1 6	RELIGION Charles **Leslie**, *A Short and Easie Method with the Deists. Wherein the certainty of the Christian religion is demonstrated by infallible proof from the four rules* [...], 1699.
Stillingfleet and Burnet's Conference	0 2 0	RELIGION Edward Stillingfleet, *A Relation of a Conference Held about Religion* [...] *with some gentlemen of the Church of Rome, at London*, 1676.

Survey of the West Indies	0 3 0	TRAVEL Thomas Gage, *A New Survey of the West-Indies: Or, the English American his travel by sea and land: Containing a journal of three thousand and three hundred miles within the main land of America* [...], 1677.
Sprat's History of the Royal Society	0 4 0	GENERAL Thomas Sprat, *The History of the Royal-Society of London, for the Improving of Natural Knowledge*, 1677.
Tyrrel of English Government. Fol.	0 8 0	HISTORY James Tyrrell, *General History of England: Both Ecclesiastical and Civil; From the Earliest Accounts of Time, to the Reign of His Present Majesty, King William III*, 1696. Tyrrell (1642–1718) was a Whig philosopher, author, and historian. He supported Locke and defended the liberty of the people.
Trial of the Seven Bishops	0 4 0	RELIGION William Sancroft, *The Proceedings and Tryal in the Case of the Most Reverend Father in God* [...] [the title then lists each bishop], 1688. Sancroft (1617–1693) was Archbishop of Canterbury and one of the seven tried.
Turner against Whiston	0 3 0	RELIGION Robert Turner, *A Discourse of the Pretended Apostolic Constitutions: Wherein all principal evidence* [...] *brought by Mr. (William) Whiston in his essay on those books, to prove them genuine, is examined and confuted*, 1715. Turner was vicar of St. Peter's, Colchester. Whiston (1667–1752) quit the Church of England and became a Baptist because of a dispute over the Anglican creed; he also rejected the Nicene Creed.
Tillotson's Life	0 2 6	RELIGIOUS BIOGRAPHY *The Life of the Most Reverend Father in God John Tillotson, arch-bishop of Canterbury* [...], 1717; a second version was Thomas Birch, *The Life of the Most Reverend Dr. John Tillotson, lord archbishop of* [...], 1752.
True Loyalist	0 2 6	MUSIC *The True Loyalist: Or, Chevalier's Favourite: Being a Collection of Elegant Songs, Never Before Printed. Also Several other Loyal Compositions. Wrote by Eminent Hands*, 1779. These were a collection of Jacobite song texts.
Templer Versus Hobbes	0 2 6	RELIGION/PHILOSOPHY John Templer, *Idea Theologiae Levianthanis*, 1673. Templer (–1693) was an Anglican clergyman who attacked Hobbes's famous book.
Temple (Sir John) on the Irish Rebellion	0 3 0	HISTORY Sir John Temple, *The Irish Rebellion: Or, an history of the beginnings and first progress of the general rebellion, raised within the kingdom of Ireland, upon the three and twentieth day of October, 1641* [...], 1746.

214 APPENDIX

Treason Unmasked	0 1 6	POLITICAL HISTORY *Treason Unmask'd: Or the Queen's title, the revolution, and the Hanover succession vindicated. Against the treasonable positions, of a book lately publish'd, intitled, The Hereditary Right of the Crown of England Asserted* [...], 1713.
Taylor's Rule of Conscience, 2 vol.	0 5 0	RELIGION Jeremy Taylor, *Ductor Dubitantium, Or The Rule of Conscience in all her generall measures; serving as a great instrument for the determination of cases of conscience* [...], 1660.
Vindication of the Church of England's Ordination	0 1 6	RELIGION Gilbert **Burnet**, *A Vindication of the Ordinations of the Church of England, in which it is demonstrated that all the essentials of ordination, according to the practice of the primitive and Greek churches, is still retained in our church* [...], 1677.
Vindication of the Last Parliament	0 2 0	POLITICAL HISTORY *A Vindication of the Last Parliament. In four dialogues between Sir Simon and Sir Peter*, 1711.
Wake's State of the Church. Fol.	0 10 0	RELIGION William **Wake**, *The State of the Church and Clergy of England, in their councils, convocations, synods, conventions, and other public assemblies; historically deduced from the conversion of the Saxons, to the present times* [...], 1703.
Walker's Suffering of the Clergy. Fol.	0 10 0	RELIGION John Walker, *An Attempt Towards Recovering an Account of the Numbers and Sufferings of the Clergy of the Church of England* [...] *who were sequester'd, harass'd, &c., in the late times of the Grand Rebellion* [...], 1714. Walker (1674–1747) was a clergyman and historian who wrote on the Civil War and interregnum. This book was about those clergy who were deprived during the war.
Whitgift's Defence of the Ecclesiastical Regiment	0 3 0	RELIGION John Whitgift, *A Defence of the Ecclesiastical Regiment in Englande defaced by T.C. (Thomas Cartwright) in his Replie against D. Whitgift* [...], 1574.
Watson's Summary View. Fol.	0 4 0	RELIGION Thomas Watson, *A Summary View of the Articles Exhibited Against the Late Bishop of St. David's, and of the Proofs Made Thereon* [...], 1701. Watson (1637–1717) was a deprived bishop of St. David's.
Wilson's History of James I. Fol.	0 3 6	HISTORY
Wake's Sermons, 3 vols.	0 15 0	RELIGION William **Wake**, *Sermons and Discourses on Several Occasions*, 1716.
Warwick's Memoirs	0 3 0	HISTORY Philip Warwick, *The Memoirs of the Reign of King Charles the First* [...]. Warwick (1609–1683) was a writer and politician.

Warne on Unity	0 3 0	RELIGION Jonathan Warne, *An Attempt to Promote True Love and Unity Between the Church of England and the Dissenters who are Calvinists, of the Baptist, Independent, and Presbyterian Perswasions; by setting down the Thirty-Nine Articles* [...], 1741.
Worcester's (Bp.) Answer to Locke, No. 1 & 2	0 1 6	RELIGION Edward Stillingfleet, *The Bishop of Worcester's Answer to Mr. Locke's Letter, concerning some passages relating to his essay of Human Understanding* [...], 1697.
Wake's Appeal on the Supremacy	0 3 0	RELIGION William **Wake**, *An Appeal to All the True Members of the Church of England, in behalf of the king's supremacy*, 1698.
Warren's Answer to Hoadley	0 3 0	RELIGION Richard Warren, *An Answer to a Book Intituled "A Plain Account of the Nature and End of the Sacrament"* [...], 1736.
Warren on Obedience to Bishops	0 1 6	RELIGION Robert Warren, *A Seasonable Exhortation to the Duty of Obedience to the Bishops of Our Established Church, More Particularly as to Confirmation: Occasion'd by the Right Reverend the Lord Bishop's primary and general confirmation*, 1723.
Wells and Nelson against Clarke	0 3 0	RELIGION Edward Wells, *A Second Letter to the Reverend Dr. (Samuel) Clarke, rector of St. James, Westminster: Being an Answer to the close of his reply to Mr. (Robert) Nelson; Together with part of two letters from Mr. Nelson wherein notice is taken of Dr. Clarke's most foul quotations* [...], 1715. Wells was rector of Cotesbach in Leicestershire. This debate involved the Trinitarian controversy.
Walton's Lives of Donne, &c.	0 4 0	BIOGRAPHY Izaak Walton, *The Lives of Dr. John Donne, Sir Henry Wotton, Richard Hooker, and George Herbert* [...], 1675. Donne, Wotton, and Herbert were poets; Wotton also was a diplomat and author. Richard Hooker (1554–1600) was a famous Anglican theologian.
Weekly Miscellany, 2 vols.	0 8 0	PERIODICAL
Whiston's Memoirs of his own Life	0 6 0	RELIGIOUS BIOGRAPHY William Whiston, *The Memoir of the Life and Writings of Mr. William Whiston. Containing memoirs of several of his friends also* [...], 1749.
Winstanley's Christian Calling	0 4 0	RELIGION J. Winstanley, *The Christian Calling in Four Parts: I. Of our duty in general. II. Of our duty to God. III. Of our duty to man. IV. Of our duty to ourselves* [...], 1754; he was rector of Llanwenarth.
Watt's Art of Reading and Writing English	0 1 0	LANGUAGE Isaac Watt, *The Art of Reading and Writing English: Or the chief principles and rules of pronouncing our mother tongue, both in prose and verse* [...], 1722.

Whitby's Answer to Dodwell	0 2 0	RELIGION
		Daniel Whitby, *Reflections on Henry Dodwell's Epistolary Discourse; with an answer to some passages on Dr. Whitby's paraphrase and annotations on the New Testament* [...], 1707.

KEY AUTHOR BIOGRAPHIES

Francis Atterbury (1663–1732), a Jacobite bishop and high church Tory, was accused of plotting to return the Stuarts to the throne in a conspiracy that began in 1720 and collapsed in 1722.

Gilbert Burnet (1643–1715) was one of Chandler's favorite authors because of his insights into episcopacy: Burnet was Bishop of Salisbury and a Scottish philosopher and historian.

Edmund Calamy (1671–1732) was an eminent nonconformist minister.

Samuel Clarke (1675–1729), an English philosopher and influential Anglican clergyman, was a latitudinarian.

Thomas De Laune, who died in 1685, was a nonconformist writer.

Henry Dodwell (1641–1711) was an Irish scholar and theologian who defended the deprived nonjuror bishops.

Robert Filmer (1588–1653) was the controversial royalist who defended the divine right of kings.

George Hickes (1642–1715) was an important nonjuror and opponent of Benjamin Hoadly's.

Benjamin Hoadly (1676–1761) was an authority on ecclesiastical government and a favorite Whig author because of his defense of the individual. Hoadly was Bishop of Bangor; his views questioning the church's institutional powers ignited the Bangorian controversy.

Francis Hutcheson (1694–1746) was arguably the leading Enlightenment figure in Scotland.

William Jameson (1689–1720) was a Presbyterian controversialist and a lecturer on history at Glasgow University.

William Law (1686–1761) was a second-generation nonjuror. His mystical and theological writing influenced the evangelical movement of the day.

Charles Leslie (1650–1722) was Irish and a strong supporter of the Stuarts. He took up the nonjuring cause after he was deprived by William and Mary.

Roger L'Estrange (1616–1704) opposed dissenters and Whigs and defended royalist claims.

John Locke (1632–1704) was the famed English political philosopher who influenced generations of American colonists.

John Norris (1657–1711), rector of Bemerton, was an important philosopher who defended human freedom and criticized Locke.

Samuel Parker (1640–1688) was Bishop of Oxford and a fierce foe of dissenters with strong Erastian views. James II saw him as a moderate in his view toward Catholics. Parker defended John Milton and helped get him out of prison.

George Rye was a foe of the nonjurors.

Robert Sheringham (1602–1678) was a royalist who was a fellow at Gunvill and Caius College, Cambridge.

William Wake (1657–1737), dean of Exeter and chaplain in ordinary to her majesty, became Archbishop of Canterbury in 1716.

NOTES

A NOTE ON SOURCES

Quotations from primary sources retain the original spellings and punctuation. In the notes, short titles have generally been used; the full entries can be found in the bibliography. Works and individuals frequently cited have been identified by the following abbreviations:

Chandler Family	Chandler, *Chandler Family*
Memorandums	Thomas Bradbury Chandler, "Memorandums, 1775–1786," Christoph Keller Jr. Library, General Theological Seminary of the Episcopal Church
Seabury Collection	Bishop Seabury Collection. Christoph Keller Jr. Library, General Theological Seminary
SJ	Samuel Johnson
SJ Writings	Schneider and Schneider, *Samuel Johnson, President of King's College*
SPG	Society for the Propagation of the Gospel in Foreign Parts
TBC	Thomas Bradbury Chandler

INTRODUCTION

1. Scotland, *George Whitefield*, 147.
2. TBC to SJ, Aug. 20, 1764, in *SJ Writings*, 1:344.
3. See, for example, Livingston, *Other Side of the Question*, 17; and Lee, "Strictures on a Pamphlet," 385.
4. TBC, *Life of Samuel Johnson*, 63–66; TBC to SJ, Aug. 20, 1764, in *SJ Writings*, 1:344.
5. TBC to SPG, July 8, 1764, SPG, image 205, vol. 24; TBC to SPG, July 5, 1762, SPG, image 197, vol. 24; and TBC to SJ, Aug. 20, 1764, in *SJ Writings*, 1:344.
6. A number of historians have examined Chandler and the bishop's cause. The most recent treatments of the latter are Engel, "Revisiting the Bishop's Controversy"; and Walker, "Church Militant." See also Doll, *Revolution, Religion, and National Identity*; Bell, *War of Religion*; Rhoden, *Revolutionary Anglicanism*; Bridenbaugh, *Mitre and Sceptre*; Cross, *Anglican Episcopate*; and Elliott, *Anglican Church Policy*. In addition to Mills, "Internal Anglican Controversy over an American Episcopate," see his historiographical review of the literature in "Colonial Anglican Episcopate," which is dated but remains useful. Fuller treatments of Chandler include my vignettes of him in *Jacob Green's Revolution*; Rohrer, "'Under the Claw of an Inraged Lion'"; McCulloch, "Thomas Bradbury Chandler"; Dexter, "Thomas Bradbury Chandler"; Hoyt, *Sketch of the Life of the Rev. Thomas Bradbury Chandler*; Gavin, "Rev. Thomas Bradbury Chandler in the Light of His (Unpublished) Diary"; and Warnock, "Thomas Bradbury Chandler and William Smith."
7. Will, *Conservative Sensibility*, esp. xiii–xiv.
8. Chernow, *Alexander Hamilton*, 232. For studies that describe the importance of monarchy to the colonists, see McConville, *King's Three Faces*; Nelson, *Royalist Revolution*; and Winterer, *American Enlightenments*. See also Winterer, "From

Royal to Republican". For a study that stresses the inherent conservatism of prerevolutionary society, see Wood, *Radicalism of the American Revolution*. Numerous works on the plantation South also describe the hierarchical nature of society. See, for example, Isaac, *Transformation of Virginia*; and Kulikoff, *Tobacco and Slaves*.

9. Wood, *Radicalism of the American Revolution*, 145–47; Nash, *Urban Crucible*, 303; Holton, *Unruly Americans*, 5. See also Andrews, *Methodists and Revolutionary America*.
10. Calhoon, "Afterword," 279.
11. Bailyn, *Ideological Origins of the American Revolution*, 313, 319.
12. TBC, *Friendly Address*, 5. Chandler's other two tracts were *The American Querist* and *What Think Ye of the Congress Now?*
13. Smith, *Sermon on the Present Situation of American Affairs*, 29. Strong treatments of loyalist writings include Gould, *Writing the Rebellion*; Gould, "Wit and Politics"; Potter, *Liberty We Seek*; and Crary, *Price of Loyalty*. For a look at one loyalist's mental world, see Ferling, *Loyalist Mind*.
14. Seabury, "Free Thoughts on the Proceedings of the Continental Congress," 62.
15. Smyth, "Chief Justice Frederick Smyth to the Middlesex County Grand Jury," 129.
16. Wood, *Creation of the American Republic*, viii, 6–31. Works on radical thought are too numerous to list but some of the key ones include Dworetz, *Unvarnished Doctrine*; Calhoon, *Dominion and Liberty*; Colbourn, *Lamp of Experience*; Robbins, *Eighteenth-Century Commonwealthman*; and Matters, *Citizens of a Common Intellectual Homeland*.
17. Clark, *Language of Liberty*. For an interesting take on historical memory and contemporary portrayals of history, see Black, *Charting the Past*.
18. Clark, *Language of Liberty*, 26; Seed, *Dissenting Histories*, 6–8.
19. Potter, *Liberty We Seek*, 84–106; Bannister and Riordan, "Loyalism and the British Atlantic," 10; Ingersoll, *Loyalist Problem*, 1. See also Moy, "Antiquity and Loyalist Counter-Narrative," 3. Important works on loyalism include Calhoon, *Loyalists in Revolutionary America*; Norton, *British-Americans*; Jasanoff, *Liberty's Exiles*; Nelson, *American Tory*; Calhoon, Barnes, and Davis, *Tory Insurgents*; Brannon and Moore, *Consequences of Loyalism*; Moore, *Loyalists*; Brown, *Good Americans*; Bumsted, *Understanding the Loyalists*; Calhoon, Barnes, and Rawlyk, *Loyalists and Community*; Chopra, *Choosing Sides*; Chopra, *Unnatural Rebellion*; Tiedemann, Fingerhut, and Venables, *Other Loyalists*; and Allen, *Tories: Fighting for the King*.
20. Norton, "Loyalist Critique of the Revolution," 130. Maier argues something similar in *From Resistance to Revolution*, xxi; as does Potter in *Liberty We Seek*, 10. See also Maier, "Whigs Against Whigs Against Whigs."
21. Calhoon, *Dominion and Liberty*, 24.
22. Rhoden, *Revolutionary Anglicanism*, 73.
23. These conclusions are based on a detailed analysis of Chandler's library; the catalog was published as *Catalogue of Books, for Sale by Mrs. Chandler*. It is impossible to know when Chandler bought these books and how many of them he read. For example, his wartime diary shows that he bought a significant number of books during his London exile. But I believe the evidence is overwhelming that he read widely and that he regularly borrowed books from Samuel Johnson, King's College, and other sources. His holdings at the time of his death in 1790 are ample evidence of his core intellectual interests.
24. Besides Hoyt, *Sketch of the Life of the Rev. Thomas Bradbury Chandler*, and other previously mentioned works on Chandler, see Burr, *Anglican Church in New Jersey*, 593–95.
25. For more on Chandler's relationship with Inglis, Seabury, and Cooper, see Ferguson, "Anti-Revolutionary Rhetoric." Details about Chandler's appearance are from his portrait and from Burr, *Anglican Church in New Jersey*, 595.
26. Stiles, *Literary Diary*, 3:398.
27. For a detailed analysis of Chandler's views of Hoadly and the Glorious Revolution, see Rohrer, "'Under the Claw of an Inraged Lion.'"

28. Walker, "Church Militant," 92.
29. For the importance of antiquity to loyalist thought, see Moy, "Antiquity and Loyalist Counter-Narrative"; and Winterer, "From Royal to Republican." For a good look at the views of democracy in the Western world, see Kloppenberg, *Toward Democracy*.
30. *New Whole Duty of Man*, 188.
31. Mills, "Anglican Expansion in Colonial America," 319–20; Walker, "Church Militant," 43–47. Besides Walker, "Church Militant," other good treatments of the Church of England in early America and the SPG include Bell, *War of Religion*; Bell, *Imperial Origins of the King's Church*; Thompson, *Into All Lands*; Woolverton, *Colonial Anglicanism*; Albright, *History of the Protestant Episcopal Church*; O'Conner, *Three Centuries of Mission*; Strong, *Anglicanism and the British Empire*; Pascoe, *Two Hundred Years of the SPG*; and Reeves, "John Checkley and the Emergence of the Episcopal Church."
32. Rohrer, *Jacob Green's Revolution*, 54, 115–16; Marsden, *Jonathan Edwards*, 436–46.
33. TBC to SJ, Jan. 22, 1768, in *SJ Writings*, 1:433.
34. TBC, *American Querist*, 43, 44; TBC, *Friendly Address*, 3, 5, 6.

CHAPTER 1

1. TBC, *Life of Samuel Johnson*. For details about Chandler's writing of the Johnson biography, see TBC to William Samuel Johnson, Feb. 23, 1773, and William Samuel Johnson to TBC, Dec. 21, 1785, both in *SJ Writings*, 1:490–92. The Johnson biography was first published in 1805, fifteen years after Chandler died; it was reprinted in 1824, and a modern version is available through Forgotten Books (2012).
2. SJ to the SPG, Jan. 12, 1747, SPG, image 66, vol. 15. The reference to the Latin School is from J. Wetmore to the SPG, Feb. 10, 1746/47, SPG, image 41, vol. 14.
3. The literature on Puritanism and the Great Migration is vast. Good starting points include Anderson, *New England's Generation*; Games, *Migration and the Origins of the English Atlantic World*; and Thompson, *Mobility and Migration*. See also Foster, *Long Argument*.
4. The following discussion on Chandler family history is largely drawn from *Chandler Family*. Other sources include Stearns, *Genealogical and Family History*; Larned, *History of Windham County*; Hoyt, *Sketch of the Life of the Rev. Thomas Bradbury Chandler*; and Clark, *History of St. John's Church*, 1–3.
5. Larned, *History of Windham County*, 1:385.
6. *Chandler Family*, 42–51; Stearns, *Genealogical and Family History*, 1:52.
7. *Chandler Family*, 125.
8. *Chandler Family*.
9. *Chandler Family*; TBC to SJ, Nov. 12, 1765, in *SJ Writings*, 1:357. Seabury quote is from Samuel Seabury Sr. to SPG, [n.d. visible], SPG, image 79, vol. 16.
10. TBC, *Friendly Address*, 4; Wood, *Radicalism of the American Revolution*, 18–19; Ellis, *American Dialogue*, 81.
11. Steiner, *Samuel Seabury*; Lydekker, *Life and Letters of Charles Inglis*. See also Cameron, *Seabury Among His Contemporaries*; Cuthbertson, *First Bishop*; and Hebb, *Samuel Seabury and Charles Inglis*.
12. TBC to SJ, Aug. 20, 1764, in *SJ Writings*, 1:344.
13. Conclusion is based on TBC, *Life of Samuel Johnson*; and Ellis, *New England Mind in Transition*. See also Ellis, "Puritan Mind in Transition."
14. Stiles, *Literary Diary*, 3:398.
15. To reconstruct Yale's academic life, I relied on TBC, *Life of Samuel Johnson*; Steiner, *Samuel Seabury*; Ellis, *New England Mind in Transition*; and Dexter, *Biographical Sketches of the Graduates of Yale College*. For more on books and literacy in early America, see Amory and Hall, *History of the Book in America*; and Lundburg and May, "Enlightened Reader in America."
16. Dexter, *Biographical Sketches of the Graduates of Yale College*, 2:5; Morgan, *Gentle Puritan*, 28–29; Steiner, *Samuel Seabury*, 35–37.
17. TBC, *Life of Samuel Johnson*, 63–66.
18. Good studies of the Great Awakening include Kidd, *Great Awakening*; Bushman, *Great Awakening*; Lambert, *Inventing the*

"Great Awakening"; and Noll, *Rise of Evangelicalism*.
19. Dexter, *Biographical Sketches*, 2:351; Morgan, *Gentle Puritan*, 29–33, 39.
20. TBC, *Life of Samuel Johnson*, 66.
21. TBC, 18.
22. TBC, 51, 52.
23. Marsden, *Jonathan Edwards*, 36–39.
24. For this discussion of Stiles, I have drawn on Morgan's outstanding biography, *Gentle Puritan*, esp. 26–29, 109–14, and 158–68.
25. Walker, "Church Militant," 48.
26. TBC, *Life of Samuel Johnson*, 128. See also Kinloch, "Anglican Clergy in Connecticut," which discusses Johnson's work with Yale graduates.
27. Ellis, *New England Mind in Transition*, 92–93; TBC, *Life of Samuel Johnson*, 125, 134, 145. See also Ferguson, "Anti-Revolutionary Rhetoric."
28. Ellis, *New England Mind in Transition*, 100–101; figures are drawn from Gaustad and Barlow, *New Historical Atlas of Religion*, 17, 24.
29. TBC, *Life of Samuel Johnson*, 39.
30. For general treatments of the Church of England in early America, see Mills, *Bishops by Ballot*; and Manross, *History of the American Episcopal Church*.
31. Ellis, *New England Mind in Transition*, 112–13.
32. Ellis, 93.
33. TBC, *Life of Samuel Johnson*, 120. The listing of Johnson's books can be found in *SJ Writings*, beginning on 1:497.
34. TBC to SJ, Feb. 26, 1753, in *SJ Writings*, 1:165.
35. TBC, *Life of Samuel Johnson*, 136–37.
36. Whitgift, *Works of John Whitgift*, Oct. 25, 1572, book 1, 1:61–62; Walsham, *Charitable Hatred*, 4. See also Kaplan, *Divided by Faith*; Lake, *Anglicans and Puritans*; Trevor-Roper, *Counter-Reformation to Glorious Revolution*; Weimer, *Martyrs' Mirror*; and Sowerby, *Making Toleration*. For the US perspective, see Waldman, *Founding Faith*.
37. Johnson quote is drawn from Ellis, *New England Mind in Transition*, 84–85.
38. Bushman, *Refinement of America*, xii; Hofstadter, *America at 1750*.
39. Ellis, *New England Mind in Transition*, 20–21; quote is drawn from Johnson, *Sermon on the Beauty of Holiness*.
40. Ellis, *New England Mind in Transition*, 62–63.
41. TBC, *Life of Samuel Johnson*, 23.
42. TBC, 24–25.
43. TBC, 140.
44. The most outstanding treatment of Johnson's intellectual world is Ellis, *New England Mind in Transition*. See also Fiering, "President Samuel Johnson and the Circle of Knowledge."
45. Ellis, *New England Mind in Transition*, 20–21.
46. Fiering, "President Samuel Johnson and the Circle of Knowledge," 210.
47. TBC, *Life of Samuel Johnson*, 8–9.
48. Fiering, "President Samuel Johnson and the Circle of Knowledge," 229–30; SJ, *General View of Philosophy*, loc. 53–55.
49. SJ, *General View of Philosophy*, loc. 137.
50. SJ, loc. 144, 166.
51. TBC, *Life of Samuel Johnson*, 69–70; "Samuel Johnson," Encyclopedia of Philosophy, accessed Mar. 14, 2016, http://www.americanphilosophy.net/johnson_intro.htm.
52. TBC, *Life of Dr. Johnson*, 70–71.
53. Ellis, *New England Mind in Transition*, 228.
54. TBC, *Life of Dr. Johnson*, 74–75. Johnson's account of the Hutchinson affair can be found in his autobiography, reprinted in *SJ Writings*, 1:30–31.
55. Wetmore to the SPG, Feb. 11, 1746, SPG, image 25, vol. 14; Steiner, *Samuel Seabury*, 3.
56. Samuel Seabury to SPG, Mar. 25, 1748, SPG, image 79, vol. 16; church wardens and vestry of St. John's Church to SPG, Dec. 26, 1747, SPG, image 219, vol. 1.
57. SJ to SPG, Jan. 12, 1747, SPG, image 66, vol. 15.
58. James Wetmore to SPG, Dec. 20, 1747, SPG, image 187, vol. 15.
59. TBC to SPG, May 1, 1752, SPG, image 187, vol. 20; Henry Barclay to SPG, [n.d. visible], SPG, image 201, vol. 15.
60. TBC to SPG, Jan. 5, 1762, SPG, image 193, vol. 24; TBC to SPG, Dec. 10, 1754, SPG, image 184, vol. 24.

61. "The Cambridge Platform," American Institute for Philosophical and Cultural Thought, accessed Mar. 6, 2016, http://www.americanphilosophy.net/cambridge_platform.htm; Ellis, *New England Mind in Transition*, 9.
62. Field and Wilcox, *Admonition to the Parliament*; Cartwright, *Second Admonition to the Parliament*; Hart, *Calvinism*, 19.
63. TBC, *Life of Dr. Johnson*, 21.
64. TBC, 25.
65. TBC, 45.

CHAPTER 2

1. Reverend Thomas Wood to SPG, July 30, 1750, SPG, image 315, vol. 18; TBC to SJ, Feb. 26, 1753, in *SJ Writings*, 1:166.
2. TBC to SPG, May 27, 1749, SPG, image 229, vol. 17.
3. Hawkins, "New Jersey Architecture," 78; Lundin, *Cockpit of the Revolution*, 11; McCormick, *New Jersey from Colony to State*, 84; Le Beau, *Jonathan Dickinson*, 13; Chernow, *Alexander Hamilton*, 46.
4. TBC to SPG, Dec. 20, 1749, SPG, image 244, vol. 17; Clark, *History of St. John's Church*, 61–62. The indenture is on 185–86. Details about the parsonage's history, as well as drawings of the house, can be found at "Andrew Hampton Homestead," County of Union, New Jersey, accessed Apr. 6, 2021, http://ucnj.org/parks-recreation/cultural-heritage-affairs/the-andrew-hampton-homestead.
5. Hatfield, *History of Elizabeth*, 359; Dexter, *Biographical Sketches*, 2:26. Vaughan's will can be found in Honeyman, *Documents Relating to the Colonial History of New Jersey*, 2:505.
6. Clark, *History of St. John's Church*, 192; TBC to SJ, Aug. 20, 1764, in *SJ Writings*, 1:344.
7. TBC to SJ, Aug. 20, 1764, in *SJ Writings*, 1:344; Burr, *Anglican Church in New Jersey*, 524–25.
8. TBC to SJ, Aug. 20, 1764, in *SJ Writings*, 1:344; McCormick, *New Jersey from Colony to State*, 81, 92–93.
9. Clark, *History of St. John's Church*, 192; TBC to SJ, Aug. 20, 1764, in *SJ Writings*,

1:344. For more on Jacob Green, see Rohrer, *Jacob Green's Revolution*.
10. TBC to SPG, July 8, 1764, SPG, image 205, vol. 24; TBC to SPG, July 5, 1762, SPG, image 197, vol. 24. For more on the Moravians and their missionary activities, see Rohrer, *Hope's Promise*.
11. TBC to SPG, July 8, 1764, SPG, image 205, vol. 24; TBC to SPG, July 5, 1762, SPG, image 197, vol. 24; TBC to SJ, Aug. 20, 1764, in *SJ Writings*, 1:344.
12. TBC to SPG, July 5, 1762, SPG, image 197, vol. 24.
13. Weston, *Englishman Directed*, 4.
14. Wacker, *Land and People*, 352–53.
15. Quote is from TBC, *Appeal Defended*, 142; TBC, *Free Examination*, 90.
16. Hume, *History of England*, 9.
17. Hume, 13.
18. Somerset, *Elizabeth I*, 292–301. For a recent treatment of Puritanism's founding during the Elizabethan period, see Hall, *Puritans*.
19. Hume, *History of England*, 13; Somerset, *Elizabeth I*, 296; Hart, *Calvinism*, 19, 24.
20. Field and Wilcox, *Admonition to the Parliament*; quotation is from an online version of *An Admonition* at "The First Admonition to Parliament 1572," The Reformation, accessed Apr. 7, 2021, http://www.thereformation.info/firstadmonition.htm; Hart, *Calvinism*, 19.
21. Guy, "1590s," 126–49.
22. Strype, *Life and Acts of John Whitgift*, book 1, 120–21, 125; Whitgift, *Ansvvere to a Certen Libel*, 3, 5.
23. Whitgift, *Works of John Whitgift*, 3:viii–ix; Guy, "1590s," 128–29.
24. Cartwright, *Replye to an Answere*, 122–25.
25. Whitgift, *Ansvvere to a Certen Libel*, 100–103.
26. Whitgift, 114, 119.
27. Whitgift, 75–77.
28. Whitgift, 103.
29. Somerset, *Elizabeth I*, 299–301; Collinson, *Elizabethan Puritan Movement*, 160.
30. Strype, *Life and Acts of John Whitgift*, book 3, 14–17. For more on the religious crackdowns of this era, see Walsham, *Charitable Hatred*.
31. MacCulloch, *Christianity*, 647–54.

32. Whitgift to William Burghley, July 5, 1584, Lambeth Palace Library, MS 680, fols. 87–89.
33. Whitgift to William Burghley, date unclear but likely July 17, 1584, Lambeth Palace Library, MS 680, fols. 90.
34. Whitgift, *Works of John Whitgift*, 3:586, 588.
35. Whitgift, 3:591–93.
36. TBC, *Appeal Defended*, 40.
37. Hooker, *Of the Lawes of Ecclesiastical Politie*, 175, 188. I relied on the online version available through Project Canterbury, which digitized *The Works of That Learned and Judicious Divine*, arranged by John Keble.
38. Hooker, *Of the Lawes of Ecclesiastical Politie*, 146, 147, 148, 261, 264, 267.
39. Hooker, 270, 271–74.
40. Hooker, 316–17.
41. Secor, *Richard Hooker*, 254–65.
42. TBC, *Appeal Defended*, 139.
43. TBC, 144, 146.
44. TBC, 137–42.
45. Clark, *Language of Liberty*, 13; TBC, *Friendly Address*, 20–22.
46. TBC, *Friendly Address*, 20–22.
47. For the importance of dissenter history, see Clark, *Language of Liberty*; and Seed, *Dissenting Histories*. For works on toleration, see Grell, Israel, and Tyacke, *From Persecution to Toleration*; Keeble, "Settling the Peace of the Church"; Lake, *Anglicans and Puritans*; Lake, "Anti-Puritanism"; Rhoden, "Anglicanism, Dissent, and Toleration"; and Lovegrove, *Established Church, Sectarian People*. For works on toleration and America, see Hutson, *Church and State in America*; and Martin, *Government by Dissent*.

CHAPTER 3

1. Bailyn, *Ordeal of Thomas Hutchinson*, 35–36.
2. Nash, *Urban Crucible*, 301–2.
3. TBC to SPG, Jan. 15, 1766, in *SJ Writings*, 1:357–59.
4. TBC, *Friendly Address*, 4.
5. Tyrrell, *General History of England*.
6. Size of the invasion fleet is from Vallance, *Glorious Revolution*, 113.
7. For an excellent overview of the Glorious Revolution and the historiography on the topic, see Pincus, *1688*. Other good accounts include Harris, *Revolution*; Trevor-Roper, *Counter-Reformation to Glorious Revolution*; Cruickshanks, *Glorious Revolution*; Vallance, *Glorious Revolution*; and Zook, "Violence, Martyrdom, and Radical Politics."
8. Speck, *Reluctant Revolutionaries*, 101–2; Vallance, *Glorious Revolution*, 162–74.
9. James I, *Trew Law of Free Monarchies*, 209.
10. Quote is from Hickes, *Constitution of the Catholick Church*, 14.
11. Gibson, *Enlightenment Prelate*, 14.
12. Leslie, *Constitution, Laws, and Government of England*, 4, 7–9, 88. Chandler did not own this tract but he owned the work by Higden, as well as other tracts in the controversy.
13. Leslie, 87–88.
14. Leslie, 24–26.
15. Leslie, 75–79.
16. Filmer, *Patriarcha*, 6–21.
17. Filmer, 24, 52, 53.
18. Filmer, 64, 68, 73.
19. Filmer, 73.
20. Hoadly, *Original and Institution of Civil Government*, 1, 4, 21–22.
21. Hoadly, 27, 33.
22. Locke, *Two Treatises of Government*, 1–10; quote is on p. 3.
23. Gibson, *Enlightenment Prelate*, 99–101.
24. Some recent works on toleration include Marshall, *John Locke, Toleration, and Early Enlightenment Culture*; and Sowerby, *Making Toleration*.
25. Hoadly, *Reasonableness of Conformity to the Church of England*; Gibson, *Enlightenment Prelate*, 67–72.
26. Sacheverell, *Perils of False Brethren*, 7–8, 12–13, 16; and Gibson, *Enlightenment Prelate*, 105–6.
27. Sacheverell, *Perils of False Brethren*, 7–8, 12–13, 16; Gibson, *Enlightenment Prelate*, 105–6.
28. Bonomi, *Under the Cope of Heaven*, 192–93.
29. Gibson, *Enlightenment Prelate*, 13, 110, 116, 121; Bonomi, *Under the Cope of Heaven*, 193.
30. In addition to *Reasonableness of Christianity*, Chandler owned a three-volume

collection of Locke's *Works*—this likely was a 1722 edition that reprinted Locke's major writings, including his letters on toleration. Chandler also owned separate copies of *The Limits of Human Understanding* and *An Essay Concerning Human Understanding*.
31. Gibson, *Enlightenment Prelate*, 91.
32. Gibson, 62–63, 149–50.
33. Gibson.
34. Gibson, 152–53; Snape, *Letter to the Lord Bishop of Bangor*, 30. Chandler did not have this tract but did own several others dealing with it.
35. Law, "Three Letters to the Bishop of Bangor," 1:1.
36. Law, 1:4–10; Paine, *Age of Reason*, 6; Bellah et al., *Habits of the Heart*, 221.
37. Gibson, *Enlightenment Prelate*, 174.
38. Gibson, 174–76.
39. Bailyn, *Ideological Origins of the American Revolution*, 37–38, 45, 52. For more on Atterbury, see Bennett, *Tory Crisis in Church and State*. For more on Mayhew, see Akers, *Called unto Liberty*; and Mullins, *Father of Liberty*.
40. Dellape, *America's First Chaplain*, xiii.
41. Kidd, *Benjamin Franklin*, 27, 31; Jefferson, "Notes on Virginia," 275. See also Kidd, *God of Liberty*.
42. TBC, *Sermon Before the Corporation*, 16.
43. TBC, *American Querist*, 10–11.
44. Boucher, *View of the Causes and Consequences of the American Revolution*, 528–29.
45. TBC, *Appeal Farther Defended*, 185; TBC, *What Think Ye of the Congress Now?*, 48, 6. For Chandler's earlier views of taxes, see query number 48 in *American Querist*, 28. Chandler's discussion of the colonial charters, which argued for the supremacy of the Crown and Parliament over provincial legislatures, also defended the British government's right to levy taxes; see queries 34–54.
46. Inglis, "True Interest of America Impartially Stated," 733.
47. TBC, *Free Examination of the Critical Commentary*, 64–65. For a good look at Jacobitism, see Monod, *Jacobitism and the English People*; Sack, *From Jacobite to Conservative*; Leighton, "Scottish Jacobitism"; and Lenman, "Scottish Episcopal Clergy and the Ideology of Jacobitism."
48. Kloppenberg, *Toward Democracy*, 100–109.
49. TBC, *Friendly Address*, 5.

CHAPTER 4

1. TBC, *Appeal to the Public*, 115.
2. The bishop's cause has received much attention from historians of American religion. The most comprehensive treatment remains Cross, *Anglican Episcopate*. Strong portrayals can be found in Bell, *War of Religion*; Rhoden, *Revolutionary Anglicanism*; and Walker, "Church Militant." Other works include Gerardi, "Episcopate Controversy Reconsidered"; Landsman, "Episcopate, the British Union"; and Taylor, "Whigs, Bishops, and America."
3. Steiner, *Samuel Seabury*, 102–4.
4. TBC to SJ, Aug. 20, 1764, in *SJ Writings*, 1:342; Walker, "Church Militant," 109.
5. TBC, *Life of Samuel Johnson*, 112–13; Secker, *Sermon Preached Before the Incorporated Society*, 4–6; Ingram, *Religion, Reform and Modernity*, 209–15.
6. Bell, *War of Religion*, 81.
7. TBC to SJ, Nov. 12, 1765, in *SJ Writings*, 1:356; TBC to SJ, Sept. 5, 1766, in *SJ Writings*, 1:366–69; TBC, "Summary of Address of New Jersey Convention to the Bishop of London, December 1766," sent with letter of Jan. 19, 1767, in *SJ Writings*, 1:390; Steiner, *Samuel Seabury*, 103–4.
8. Archbishop Secker to SJ, July 31, 1766, in *SJ Writings*, 3:286.
9. TBC to SJ, Sept. 5, 1766, in *SJ Writings*, 1:368.
10. TBC to SJ, Nov. 12, 1765, in *SJ Writings*, 1:356; Walker, "Church Militant," 100.
11. TBC to SJ, Nov. 12, 1765, in *SJ Writings*, 1:356; SJ to Thomas Secker, May 2, 1766, in *SJ Writings*, 1:361.
12. Samuel Auchmuty to SJ, June 12, 1766, in *SJ Writings*, 1:362, 363; Archbishop Secker to SJ, July 31, 1766, in *SJ Writings*, 3:286, 287.
13. TBC to SJ, Jan. 9, 1767, in *SJ Writings*, 1:386; Beardsley, *Life and Correspondence of*

Samuel Johnson, 316; TBC to SJ, Sept. 5, 1766, in *SJ Writings*, 1:366–69.
14. Beardsley, *Life and Correspondence of Samuel Johnson*, 316; TBC to SJ, Sept. 5, 1766, in *SJ Writings*, 1:366–69.
15. TBC, "Summary of Address of New Jersey Convention," Jan. 19, 1767, in *SJ Writings*, 1:389–91.
16. TBC to SJ, Jan. 9, 1767, in *SJ Writings*, 1:384–85; TBC to SJ, Jan. 19, 1767, in *SJ Writings*, 1:387–89.
17. TBC to SJ, June 9, 1767, in *SJ Writings*, 1:406–9; Nelson, *Blessed Company*, 124; "S-70: Coventry Parish Ruins," updated Oct. 2, 2003, https://mht.maryland.gov/secure/medusa/PDF/Somerset/S-70.pdf; Charles Inglis to SJ, Nov. 10, 1770, in Lydekker, *Life and Letters of Charles Inglis*, 117.
18. Browne, *Correspondence of Governor Horatio Sharpe*, 3:365.
19. TBC to SJ, Mar. 31, 1767, and June 9, 1767, in *SJ Writings*, 1:397, 1:406–9.
20. TBC to SJ, June 9, 1767, in *SJ Writings*, 1:406–9.
21. TBC to SJ, Aug. 20, 1767, in *SJ Writings*, 1:415–17; TBC to SJ, Mar. 31, 1767, in *SJ Writings*, 1:396; Steiner, *Samuel Seabury*, 108.
22. TBC to SJ, Dec. 14, 1770, Episcopal Church Historical Society, Francis L. Hawks Papers, box 2; Ingram, *Religion, Reform and Modernity*, 247–48.
23. TBC to the Bishop of London, Oct. 21, 1767, reprinted in Cross, *Anglican Episcopate*, 345–46.
24. TBC to the Bishop of London, Oct. 21, 1767, reprinted in Cross, 345–46.
25. TBC, *Appeal to the Public*, 6, 7, 10.
26. TBC, 12–13.
27. TBC, 14–15.
28. TBC, 15–16, 18.
29. TBC, 79, 27, 28.
30. TBC, 29–31.
31. TBC, 31.
32. TBC, 28, 33.
33. TBC, 34–36.
34. TBC, ix.
35. TBC, 113–15.
36. Harris, *Revolution*, 407, 412–15; Kidd, "Religious Realignment."
37. Chandler's eight pamphlets are bound together and can be found at the Christoph Keller Jr. Library at the General Theological Seminary in New York City. He marked them up with a pen in the margin.
38. *Late Letter Concerning the Sufferings of the Episcopal Clergy*, 8, 26, 29.
39. Morer and Monro, *Account of the Present Persecution*, 1.
40. TBC, *What Think Ye of the Congress Now?*, 2, 67.
41. TBC, *Friendly Address*, 8.

CHAPTER 5

1. TBC to SJ, Jan. 22, 1768, in *SJ Writings*, 1:432–34; Bell, *War of Religion*, 93–94; John Adams, "Sui Juris to the *Boston Gazette*," May 23, 1768, Founders Online, National Archives, https://founders.archives.gov/documents/Adams/06-01-02-0069.
2. TBC to SJ, Apr. 7, 1768, in *SJ Writings*, 1:437–38.
3. TBC to SJ, Apr. 7, 1768, in *SJ Writings*, 1:436. For more on King's College, see Gerardi, "King's College Controversy."
4. William Livingston to Noah Welles, Feb. 2, 1768, Johnson Family Papers, no. 86; Bridenbaugh, *Mitre and Sceptre*, 297.
5. Bridenbaugh, *Mitre and Sceptre*, 297–98.
6. The Timothy Tickle essays were published in the *New-York Gazette* and compiled in *A Collection of Tracts From the Late Newspapers*, accessed online at http://tei.it.ox.ac.uk/tcp/Texts-HTML/free/N08/N08490.html (updated May 1, 2011). Chandler's essay was published Apr. 18, 1768; the quote about *Whig* appeared in *A Whip for the American Whig*, no. 6 (May 9, 1768).
7. TBC to SJ, Apr. 7, 1768, in *SJ Writings*, 1:437.
8. *American Whig*, no. 1 (Mar. 14, 1768), *New-York Gazette*. For the *Whig* and *Centinel* essays, I am again relying on *A Collection of Tracts From the Late Newspapers*.
9. *American Whig*, no. 3 (Mar. 28, 1768), *New-York Gazette*.

10. *Centinel*, no. 1 (Mar. 24, 1768), *Pennsylvania Journal*.
11. *Centinel*, no. 2 (Mar. 31, 1768), *Pennsylvania Journal*.
12. *Centinel*, no. 3 (Apr. 7, 1768), *Pennsylvania Journal*.
13. *Centinel*, no. 4 (Apr. 14, 1768), *Pennsylvania Journal*.
14. *American Whig*, no. 6 (Apr. 18, 1768), *New-York Gazette*.
15. *An Advertisement to the Public*, Mar. 21, 1768, *New-York Gazette*.
16. Timothy Tickle, *A Whip for the American Whig*, no. 2 (Apr. 11, 1768), *New-York Gazette*.
17. Lippy, *Seasonable Revolutionary*, 2–3.
18. Lippy, 13, 25.
19. Lippy, 74.
20. Chauncy, *Appeal to the Public Answered*.
21. TBC, *Appeal Defended*, 2–4.
22. TBC, 15–16.
23. TBC, 16–20, 24, 25.
24. TBC, 27–31.
25. Chauncy, *Appeal to the Public Answered*, 11–12; TBC, *Appeal Defended*, 32–33.
26. TBC, *Appeal Defended*, 35–36.
27. TBC, 49–50.
28. TBC, 55.
29. TBC, 146.
30. *American Whig*, no. 12 (May 30, 1768), *New-York Gazette*.
31. *Centinel*, no. 4 (Apr. 14, 1768), *Pennsylvania Journal*.
32. TBC, *Appeal Defended*, 142.
33. TBC, 148.
34. TBC, 180.
35. TBC, 225–26.
36. Chauncy, *Reply to Dr. Chandler's Appeal Defended*, 48–49.
37. Chauncy, 56.
38. Charles Inglis to the Rev. Dr. Burton, Dec. 27, 1769, in Lydekker, *Life and Letters of Charles Inglis*, 87; TBC, *Appeal Farther Defended*, 185.
39. TBC, *Appeal Farther Defended*, 239–40; Charles Inglis to the Rev. Dr. Burton, Aug. 12, 1769, in Lydekker, *Life and Letters of Charles Inglis*, 85.
40. Charles Inglis to SJ, Nov. 10, 1770, in Lydekker, *Life and Letters of Charles Inglis*, 117–18.
41. Isaac, *Transformation of Virginia*, 181–86; Bell, *War of Religion*, 116.
42. Charles Inglis to SJ, Nov. 6, 1771, in Lydekker, *Life and Letters of Charles Inglis*, 139.
43. TBC, *Address from the Clergy of New-York and New-Jersey*, 9, 56–57, 10–31.
44. TBC, 6–7, 8–9.
45. Charles Inglis to SJ, Nov. 6, 1771, in Lydekker, *Life and Letters of Charles Inglis*, 139; Gwatkin, *Letter to the Clergy of New York and New Jersey*, 10, 11, 16.
46. Gwatkin, *Letter to the Clergy of New York and New Jersey*, 12, 14.
47. Gwatkin, 14, 15.
48. Gwatkin, 19.
49. William Smith to the SPG, 1768, in Smith, *Life and Correspondence of the Rev. William Smith*, 414; Richard Terrick, Bishop of London, to William Smith, Sept. 7, 1772, Smith MSS, Episcopal Church Historical Society, Francis L. Hawks Papers; Adams, *Works of John Adams*, 10:288; *List of Infringements and Violations of Rights*.
50. Bell, *War of Religion*, 100–103; TBC to SJ, Sept. 3, 1767, Episcopal Church Historical Society, Francis L. Hawks Papers, box 2; Ingram, *Religion, Reform and Modernity*, 97; TBC, *Free Examination of the Critical Commentary*, 53. For more on Hutchinson and his movement, see Leighton, "Hutchinsonianism."
51. Blackburne, "Critical Commentary on the Archbishop Secker's Letter," 73; Bell, *War of Religion*, 100–103. For a good recent treatment of Jacobites and the controversies surrounding them, see Parrish, *Jacobitism and Anti-Jacobitism*.
52. TBC, *Free Examination of the Critical Commentary*, 27–28, 34. See also Chandler, *Appendix to the American Edition of the Life of Archbishop Secker's Letter to Mr. Walpole*.
53. Blackburne, "Critical Commentary on the Archbishop Secker's Letter," 78–79.
54. TBC, *Free Examination of the Critical Commentary*, 29, 64–65.
55. Blackburne, "Critical Commentary on the Archbishop Secker's Letter," 65; TBC, *Free Examination of the Critical Commentary*, 90–91.
56. TBC, *Free Examination of the Critical Commentary*, 99.

CHAPTER 6

1. "Suffolk Resolves," *Essex Gazette*, Sept. 20, 1774; Middlekauff, *Glorious Cause*, 263–64.
2. The John Adams quote is from his diary, Sept. 17, 1774, available online via the Massachusetts Historical Society, http://www.masshist.org/digitaladams/archive/doc?id=D22.
3. Jefferson, "Summary View of the Rights of British Americans," 264–65; Ferling, *Leap in the Dark*, 70; Middlekauff, *Glorious Cause*, 236.
4. TBC, *American Querist*, 13, 14.
5. TBC, 18–19. According to the New-York Historical Society, Chandler at one time owned a copy of Richard Jackson and Benjamin Franklin's *An Historical Review of the Constitution and Government of Pensylvania [sic]*.
6. Phillips, *1775*, 132–50. See also Nash, *Unknown American Revolution*; and Holton, *Unruly Americans*.
7. TBC, *American Querist*, 5–10; Steiner, *Samuel Seabury*, 132.
8. TBC, *American Querist*, 43, 44; Bell, *War of Religion*, 166–67.
9. TBC, *Friendly Address*, 4.
10. TBC, 3, 6, 46.
11. TBC, 14–16.
12. TBC, 17.
13. TBC, 7, 10, 11.
14. TBC, 11.
15. TBC, 4, 48.
16. TBC, 46–47; TBC, *What Think Ye of the Congress Now?*, 12–13. Chandler appended a copy of Galloway's Plan of Union at the end of this tract.
17. TBC, *Friendly Address*, 47, 50–51.
18. TBC, 31, 33, 37, 40–41.
19. William Bradford to James Madison, Jan. 4, 1775, Founders Online, National Archives, https://founders.archives.gov/documents/Madison/01-01-02-0038; Lee, "Strictures on a Pamphlet," 385–87. Henry Barry, a lieutenant in the Fifty-Second Regiment of Foot of the British army, answered Lee in "Strictures on the Friendly Address Examined."
20. Livingston, *Other Side of the Question*, 17, 7–8; Dickinson, *Address to the Committee of Correspondence in Barbados*; Bailyn, *Ideological Origins of the American Revolution*, 184–88.
21. Livingston, *Other Side of the Question*, 9, 14, 16.
22. John Adams, "Reply to a Friendly Address," Nov. 17, 1774, Founders Online, National Archives, https://founders.archives.gov/documents/Adams/06-02-02-0060.
23. McCormick, *New Jersey from Colony to State*, 114; Rohrer, *Jacob Green's Revolution*, 130–32. See also Gerlach, *Prologue to Independence*.
24. TBC, *What Think Ye of the Congress Now?*, 48, 6. For Chandler's earlier views of taxes, see query number 48 in *American Querist*, 28. Chandler's discussion of the colonial charters, which argued for the supremacy of the Crown and Parliament over provincial legislatures, also defended the British government's right to levy taxes; see queries 34–54.
25. TBC, *What Think Ye of the Congress Now?*, 6.
26. TBC, 6, 12.
27. TBC, 13, 26–27, 30–31.
28. TBC, 30–31.
29. TBC, 46.
30. TBC, 47, 48–49.
31. TBC, 2, 49–50.
32. TBC, 52, 53.
33. Bailyn, *Ideological Origins of the American Revolution*, 95–135. In studies of the causes of the American Revolution, descriptions of the colonists' fears of a plot are standard.
34. TBC, *What Think Ye of the Congress Now?*, 55.
35. TBC, 64–65.
36. Smith, *Sermon on the Present Situation of American Affairs*, 21, 22.
37. Smith, 27, 30.
38. Smith, 21.
39. Boucher, "Letter from a Virginian," 220–21. There is some question as to whether Boucher was the author of the letter. A modern biographer, Anne Y. Zimmer, author of *Jonathan Boucher: Loyalist in Exile*, believes he was. But Gordon S. Wood, editor of the Library of America's collection of revolutionary pamphlets, is not convinced because of the letter's

moderate tone. For more on Boucher, see Zimmer and Kelly, "Jonathan Boucher"; and Clark, "Jonathan Boucher."
40. Boucher, "Letter from a Virginian," 222.
41. Boucher, 219–20.
42. Boucher, 233.
43. Calhoon, *Loyalists in Revolutionary America*, 218–19.
44. Boucher, "On Civil Liberty, Passive Obedience, and Non-Resistance," 506–8.
45. Boucher, 510, 523.
46. Boucher, 518.
47. Boucher, 529, 534.
48. Boucher, 546.
49. Boucher, 547–49, 554–60.
50. Quote is from "A New-York Freeholder," *New-York Gazette and Weekly Mercury*, Sept. 26, 1774; Inglis's other essays appeared on Sept. 12, 1774, and Oct. 10, 1774.
51. Seabury, "Free Thoughts on the Proceedings of the Continental Congress," 44, 61.
52. Seabury, "Congress Canvassed," 98.

CHAPTER 7

1. The exact date Chandler went into exile is unclear. He began a diary (Memorandums) on May 15, 1775, that opened with a short entry describing his decision to flee to New York. A letter from Jonathan Boucher to William Smith, dated May 4, 1775, described a rumor that Chandler and Myles Cooper had fled. For the Boucher letter, see Boucher to William Smith, May 4, 1775, in *Maryland Historical Magazine* 8, no. 3 (1913): 237–40.
2. "The Elizabethtown Association Resolutions," in Gerlach, *New Jersey in the American Revolution*, 97–98; "Elias Boudinot to the Morris County Committee," in Gerlach, *New Jersey in the American Revolution*, 132–34.
3. Gross, *Minutemen and Their World*, 109–32; Fischer, *Paul Revere's Ride*, 184–232.
4. Chernow, *Alexander Hamilton*, 62; Burrows and Wallace, *Gotham*, 223.
5. Boyd, *Elias Boudinot*, 24–25.
6. TBC, May 15, 1775, Memorandums; "John Tabor Kempe," Historical Society of the New York Courts, http://www.nycourts.gov/history/legal-history-new-york/legal-history-eras-01/history-era-01-kempe-john.html.
7. TBC, May 16, 1775, Memorandums; information about the *Exeter* is drawn from "British Third Rate Ship of the Line 'Exeter' (1763)," Three Decks, accessed Apr. 14, 2021, https://threedecks.org/index.php?display_type=show_ship&id=323.
8. TBC, May 17, 1775, Memorandums; information on the *Kingfisher* is drawn from "British Sloop 'Kingfisher' (1770)," Three Decks, accessed Apr. 14, 2021, https://threedecks.org/index.php?display_type=show_ship&id=4999.
9. Steiner, *Samuel Seabury*, 146, 157; Chernow, *Alexander Hamilton*, 63–64. For more on printers and the American Revolution, see Cullen, "Talking to a Whirlwind"; and Lorenz, *Hugh Gaine*.
10. Boucher, *View of the Causes and Consequences of the American Revolution*, 50; Boucher to Smith, May 4, 1775 (*Maryland Historical Magazine*).
11. Zimmer, *Jonathan Boucher*, 184–91.
12. Steiner, *Samuel Seabury*, 158–64.
13. Charles Inglis to SPG, May 30, 1775, and Oct. 31, 1776, in Lydekker, *Life and Letters of Charles Inglis*, 149, 157, 214–17.
14. William Smith to the SPG Secretary, July 10, 1775, in Smith, *Life and Correspondence of the Rev. William Smith*, 1:529; Warnock, "Thomas Bradbury Chandler and William Smith," 294–95; Byrnes, "Pre-Revolutionary Career of Provost William Smith," 249–56.
15. Norton, *British-Americans*, 29–31. See also Jasanoff, *Liberty's Exiles*; and Mason, "American Loyalist Diaspora."
16. Norton, 37.
17. TBC, May 19 and 20, 1775, Memorandums.
18. TBC, May 25 and June 10, 1775, Memorandums.
19. TBC, June 30–July 3, 1775, Memorandums.
20. TBC, July 2, 1775, Memorandums. There are no modern biographies of Josiah Tucker, but see Clark, "Josiah Tucker."
21. TBC, July 3, 1775, Memorandums.
22. TBC, July 4, 1775, Memorandums.
23. TBC, July 6, 1775, Memorandums.

24. TBC, July 7, 1775, Memorandums; Norton, *British-Americans*, 37, 67; Jasanoff, *Liberty's Exiles*, 351–58.
25. Whiteley, *Lord North*, 157.
26. TBC, July 8, 1775, Memorandums.
27. TBC, Aug. 4, 1775, Memorandums.
28. TBC, Dec. 14, 1775, Memorandums.
29. TBC, Feb. 10, 1776, Jan. 13, 1777, May 16, 1777, and July 15, 1780, Memorandums; Doll, *Revolution, Religion, and National Identity*, 212–13.
30. Paine, "Common Sense," 658–59.
31. Paine, 664–65.
32. Paine, 680. For more on Paine, see Larkin, *Thomas Paine and the Literature of Revolution*.
33. TBC to Samuel Seabury, Mar. 5, 1777, Seabury Collection.
34. TBC to Samuel Seabury, Dec. 9, 1777, Seabury Collection.
35. TBC to Samuel Seabury, June 7, 1778, Seabury Collection.
36. TBC, Feb. 10, 1776, Jan. 13, 1777, May 16, 1777, and July 15, 1780, Memorandums; Doll, *Revolution, Religion, and National Identity*, 212–13.
37. Doll, *Revolution, Religion, and National Identity*, 214–18.
38. TBC to Samuel Seabury, Mar. 5, 1777, Seabury Collection.
39. TBC to Samuel Seabury, May 16, 1777, Seabury Collection.
40. TBC, Dec. 7 and 13, 1775, and Apr. 6, 1775, Memorandums.
41. TBC, June 10, 1775, Memorandums; Charles Inglis to SPG, Oct. 31, 1776, in Lydekker, *Life and Letters of Charles Inglis*, 169–70.
42. TBC, Mar. 8, 1777, and Dec. 2, 1778, Memorandums; TBC to Samuel Seabury, May 16, 1777, and Feb. 4, 1779, Seabury Collection; TBC to Seabury, Apr. 8, 1776, reprinted in Seabury, *Memoir of Bishop Seabury*, 143. Regarding the memorials, see the entry of Mar. 22, 1784, in Memorandums, for an example.
43. Charles Inglis to SPG, Oct. 31, 1776, in Lydekker, *Life and Letters of Charles Inglis*, 160; TBC to Samuel Seabury, Feb. 4, 1779, Seabury Collection; TBC, Feb. 3, 1779, Memorandums.
44. TBC, Dec. 4, 1778, June 14, 1779, and K.1, Memorandums. Biographical information on George Panton is drawn from Weiss, *Colonial Clergy of the Middle Colonies*, 120.
45. TBC, July 17, 1781, Oct. 19, 1781, and Apr. 29, 1785, Memorandums.
46. Whitehall, to Miles [sic] Cooper and Thomas Bradbury Chandler, Apr. 5, 1775, National Archives, UK (accessed online through Adam Matthew Digital), CO5/1106; TBC, Feb. 20, 1776, and Aug. 7, 1776, Memorandums. Cooper also was awarded a £200 pension. Chandler faithfully recorded in his diary when he received his salary and pension.
47. For entries about Chandler's lodgings, see, for example, Oct. 4, 1775, Apr. 17, 1776, July 17, 1777, Apr. 18, 1778, Apr. 14, 1779, July 10, 1779, Oct. 15, 1779, Jan. 12, 1780, Apr. 13, 1780, Oct. 11, 1780; and Jan. 25, 1781, in Memorandums. The entry about him lending money to the Meyers was Nov. 17, 1784, Memorandums.
48. TBC, May 26, 1778, June 8, 1779, and G.2, C.2, and D.1, Memorandums.
49. TBC, July 21, 1775, Memorandums.
50. TBC, Aug. 14, 1775, Aug. 16, 1775, May 26, 1778, and June 8, 1779, Memorandums.
51. TBC, Nov. 10, 1775, Memorandums; Damrosch, *Club*, 71, 194.
52. For Chandler's religious activities, see entries of Sept. 17, 1775, Dec. 5, 1775, Aug. 5, 1777, Sept. 20, 1777, June 27, 1780, and Aug. 28, 1784, Memorandums; Zimmer, *Jonathan Boucher*, 199, 208–13.
53. Zimmer, *Jonathan Boucher*, 208–9; TBC to Samuel Seabury, March 5, 1777, Seabury Collection.
54. TBC, July 15, 1775, Sept. 29, 1775, and Dec. 7, 1775, Memorandums; Norton, *British-Americans*, 70–71.
55. TBC to Samuel Seabury, Feb. 4, 1779, Seabury Collection.
56. TBC to Samuel Seabury, Aug. 5, 1782, Seabury Collection.
57. TBC to Samuel Seabury, Dec. 4, 1780, Seabury Collection.
58. TBC to Samuel Seabury, Aug. 5, 1782, Seabury Collection.
59. TBC to Samuel Seabury, Mar. 15, 1783, Seabury Collection. For an interesting look at how the British and American

publics perceived war developments, see Gould, *Persistence of Empire*.
60. Lydekker, *Life and Letters of Charles Inglis*, 214, 217; Norton, *British-Americans*, 236; Inglis, *Letters of Papinian*, letters I and II, 6, 22.
61. TBC to Samuel Seabury, Mar. 15, 1783.
62. Petition of Myles Cooper, John Vardill, and Thomas Bradbury Chandler, May 12, 1777, National Archives, UK (accessed through Adam Matthew Digital), CO5/115; TBC to Seabury, Mar. 15, 1783, Seabury Collection; TBC, Aug. 17, 1784, Memorandums.
63. Norton, *British-Americans*, 242–45; "Transcript of Treaty of Paris (1783)," Our Documents, accessed Apr. 14, 2021, https://www.ourdocuments.gov/document_data/document_transcripts/document_006_transcript.html.
64. Gigantino, *William Livingston's American Revolution*, 173.
65. TBC, Oct. 22 and Oct. 29, 1784, Memorandums.
66. Samuel Seabury to Jeremiah Leaming, Sept. 3, 1783, reprinted in Seabury, *Memoir of Bishop Seabury*, 206.
67. Petitions of Mar. 26, 1783, National Archives, UK (accessed through Adam Matthew Digital), CO5/407-8, 404; Doll, *Revolution, Religion, and National Identity*, 217–20.
68. TBC, Apr. 19 and 21, 1785, Memorandums; Chandler to Samuel Seabury, July 28, 1785, Seabury Collection.
69. TBC to Samuel Seabury, July 28, 1785, Seabury Collection.
70. TBC, Apr. 29, May 6, and May 16, 1785, Memorandums.
71. Charles Inglis, Oct. 12 and 13, 1785, Journal and Letter Books, Loyalist Collection, reel 8.
72. Doll, *Revolution, Religion, and National Identity*, 229–30; Inglis, July 31, 1786, Journal and Letter Books, Loyalist Collection, reel 8.

EPILOGUE

1. Interestingly, Chandler's library catalog showed he owned at least one book on gardening, and an 1879 map depicting Elizabeth Town during the Revolution indicates that the parish grounds had an orchard and gardens. The map is available online at the Library of Congress, accessed Apr. 15, 2021, https://tinyurl.com/2wa2cecp.
2. Gigantino, *William Livingston's American Revolution*, 172. See also Macmillan, *War Governors in the American Revolution*; Bernstein, "New Jersey in the American Revolution"; and Rohrer, "Constitution and Mr. Livingston."
3. Elkins and McKitrick, *Age of Federalism*, 10; Holton, *Unruly Americans*, 5, 7. For more on the expansion of democracy in this era, see Israel, *Expanding Blaze*; Kloppenberg, *Toward Democracy*; and Cotlar, *Tom Paine's America*, as well as Israel, *Democratic Enlightenment*.
4. "The Free Citizens of the Commonwealth of Massachusetts," in Kenyon, *Antifederalists*, 103–4. For antidemocratic impulses in the 1780s, see Holton, *Unruly Americans*; Nelson, *Royalist Revolution*; Nash, *Unknown American Revolution*; and Klarman, *Framers' Coup*. See also the excellent review essay dealing with this topic, Parkinson, "Janus's Revolution."
5. For good looks at political parties in the early republic, see Elkins and McKitrick, *Age of Federalism*; Borden, *Parties and Politics in the Early Republic*; and Banning, *Jeffersonian Persuasion*. See also Allis, *Government Through Opposition*.
6. The quote on Chandler's reduced state is from his will dated Oct. 12, 1789, in NJ Wills, 7876G-7879G, Essex County, New Jersey State Archives. The will was probated in 1794.
7. For the views of young Americans who came of age after 1776, see Appleby, *Inheriting the Revolution*.
8. Scruton, *Conservatism*, 24, 16; Allitt, *Conservatives*. For an example of a work that traces modern conservatism to the 1930s and the New Deal, see Phillips-Fein, "The Roots of American Conservatism," *The Nation*, May 4, 2016, https://www.thenation.com/article/archive/the-roots-of-american-conservatism.
9. Bacevich, "Introduction," xix.

10. Will, *Conservative Sensibility*.
11. Gould, *Writing the Rebellion*, 14–15.
12. For a look at Jefferson in the 1790s and early 1800s, see Tucker and Hendrickson, *Empire of Liberty*.
13. Scruton, *Conservatism*, 24, 16, 52–53.
14. Kirk, *Conservative Mind*, 29, 34, 48; Scruton, *Conservatism*, 24.
15. Scruton, *Conservatism*, 44–45; Kirk, *Conservative Mind*, 29, 34, 48.

APPENDIX

1. *Catalogue of Books, for Sale by Mrs. Chandler*; Charles Inglis, "Catalogue of My Books," Inglis Papers, Loyalist Collection, reel 1, vol. c2; Le Beau, *Jonathan Dickinson*, 12; and Hayes, *Mind of a Patriot*, 16.
2. Fea, *Way of Improvement Leads Home*, 107; Kidd, *Benjamin Franklin*, 38.
3. Raven, "Importation of Books," 192–93; TBC to SJ, Feb. 26, 1753, in *SJ Writings*, 1:165; and TBC to SJ, July 7, 1768, in *SJ Writings*, 1:443.
4. Raven, *Business of Books*, 9, 26; Raven, "Importation of Books," 1:183–85.
5. Raven, "Importation of Books," 1:189; TBC to SJ, Mar. 14, 1771, in *SJ Writings*, 1:478.
6. The figure of twenty-two boxes is drawn from TBC to Seabury, July 28, 1785, letter 93, Seabury Collection; and TBC, June 14, 1779, and Apr. 29, 1785, Memorandums.
7. Smollett, *Adventures of Ferdinand Count Fathom*, 10.

BIBLIOGRAPHY

PRIMARY SOURCES

Adams, Charles Francis, ed. *The Works of John Adams*. Boston: Little, Brown and Company, 1856.

Barry, Henry. "The Strictures on the Friendly Address Examined, and a Refutation of Its Principles Attempted. Addressed to the People of America." In Wood, *American Revolution*, 397–410.

Beardsley, E. Edwards. *Life and Correspondence of Samuel Johnson, D.D.* New York: Hurd and Houghton, 1874.

Blackburne, Francis. "A Critical Commentary on the Archbishop Secker's Letter to the Right Honourable Horatio Walpole, Concerning Bishops in America." In *The Works, Theological and Miscellaneous—Including Some Pieces Not Before Printed—of Francis Blackburne, M.A. Late Rector of Richmond, and Archdeacon of Cleveland*. Vol. 2. Cambridge: B. Flower, 1804.

Boucher, Jonathan. "A Letter from a Virginian, to the Members of the Congress to Be Held at Philadelphia, on the First of September, 1774." In Wood, *American Revolution*, 215–36.

———. *A View of the Causes and Consequences of the American Revolution; in Thirteen Discourses, Preached in North America Between the Years 1763 and 1775: With an Historical Preface*. London: G. G. and J. Robinson, 1797.

Browne, William Hand, ed. *Correspondence of Governor Horatio Sharpe, 1761–1771*. Baltimore: Maryland Historical Society, 1895.

Cartwright, Thomas. *A Replye to an Answere Made of M. Doctor Whitgift Against the Admonition to the Parliament*. Hempstead: John Stroud, 1573.

———. *A Second Admonition to the Parliament*. Hempstead, UK: J. Stroud, 1572.

Catalogue of Books, for Sale by Mrs. Chandler, in Elizabeth-Town, New-Jersey; Being the Library of the Late Rev. Dr. Chandler, deceased. Elizabeth-Town, NJ: Shepard Kollock, 1790.

Chandler, Thomas Bradbury. *An Address from the Clergy of New-York and New-Jersey to the Episcopalians in Virginia; Occasioned by Some Late Transactions in That Colony Relative to an American Episcopate*. New York: Hugh Gaine, 1771.

———. *The American Querist: or Some Questions Proposed Relative to the Present Disputes Between Great Britain, and Her American Colonies*. New York: James Rivington, 1774.

———. *The Appeal Defended: Or, the Proposed American Episcopate Vindicated, in Answer to the Objections and Misrepresentations of Dr. Chauncy and Others*. New York: Hugh Gaine, 1769.

———. *The Appeal Farther Defended; in Answer to the Farther Misrepresentations of Dr. Chauncy*. New York: Hugh Gaine, 1771.

———. *An Appeal to the Public, in Behalf of the Church of England in America: Wherein the Original and Nature of the Episcopal Office Are Briefly Considered, Reasons for Sending Bishops to America Are Assigned*. New York: James Parker, 1767.

———. *An Appendix to the American Edition of the Life of Archbishop Secker's Letter to Mr. Walpole; Containing His Grace's Letter to the Rev'd Mr. Macclanechan, on the Irregularity of his Conduct; with an Introductory Narrative*. New York: Hugh Gaine, 1774.

———. *A Free Examination of the Critical Commentary on Archbishop Secker's Letter to Mr. Walpole: To Which Is Added, by Way of Appendix, a Copy of Bishop Sherlock's Memorial. New York: Hugh Gaine, 1774.

———. A Friendly Address to All Reasonable Americans, on the Subject of Our Political Confusions: In Which the Necessary Consequences of Violently Opposing the King's Troops, and of a General Non-Importation Are Fairly Stated. New York: James Rivington, 1774.

———. The Life of Samuel Johnson, D.D.: The First President of King's College, in New York; Containing Many Interesting Anecdotes; a General View of the State of Religion and Learning in Connecticut During the Former Part of the Last Century. New York: T. & J. Swords, 1805. Reprint, London: C. & J. Rivington, 1824.

———. A Sermon Before the Corporation for the Relief of the Widows and Children of Clergymen, in the Communion of the Church of England, in America. Burlington, NJ: Isaac Collins, 1771.

———. What Think Ye of the Congress Now? Or an Enquiry, How Far the Americans Are Bound to Abide by, and Execute the Decisions of the Late Continental Congress. New York: James Rivington, 1775.

Chauncy, Charles. The Appeal to the Public Answered, in Behalf of the Non-Episcopal Churches in America; Containing Remarks on what Dr. Thomas Bradbury Chandler has advanced, on the four following Points [...]. Boston: Kneeland and Adams, 1768.

———. A Reply to Dr. Chandler's Appeal Defended, Wherein his mistakes are rectified, his false arguing refuted, and the Objections against the planned American Episcopate shewn to remain in full force, notwithstanding all he has offered to render them invalid. Boston: Daniel Kneeland, 1770.

A Collection of Tracts From the Late Newspapers, &c., containing particularly the American Whig, A Whip for the American Whig, with some other pieces, On the Subject of the Residence of Protestant Bishops in the American Colonies, and in answer to the Writers who opposed it, &c. New York: John Holt, 1768.

Dickinson, John. An Address to the Committee of Correspondence in Barbados. Occasioned by a late letter from them to their agent in London. Philadelphia: William Bradford, 1766.

Field, John, and Thomas Wilcox. An Admonition to the Parliament. Hempstead, UK: J. Stroud, 1572.

Filmer, Robert. Patriarcha: or the Natural Power of Kings. 2nd ed. London: R. Chiswel [sic], W. Hensman, M. Gilliflower, and G. Wells, 1680.

Gwatkin, Thomas. Letter to the Clergy of New York and New Jersey, Occasioned by an Address to the Episcopalians in Virginia. Williamsburg, VA: Alexander Purdie and John Dixon, 1772.

Hickes, George. The Constitution of the Catholick Church, and the Nature and Consequences of Schism: Set Forth in a Collection of Papers, Written by the Late R. Reverend George Hickes, D.D. London, 1716.

Hoadly, Benjamin. The Original and Institution of Civil Government, Discuss'd. London: James Knapton, 1710.

———. A Preservative Against the Principles and Practices of the Nonjurors Both in Church and State. Or an Appeal to the Consciences and Common Sense of the Christian Laity. 5th ed. London: James Knapton, 1719.

———. The Reasonableness of Conformity to the Church of England, Represented to the Dissenting Ministers. In Answer to the Tenth Chapter of Mr. Calamy's Abridgement of Mr. Baxter's History of His Life and Times [...]. London: T. Childe, 1703.

Honeyman, A. Van Doren, ed. Documents Relating to the Colonial History of New Jersey: Calendar of New Jersey Wills, Administrations, etc.—1730–1750. 1st ser., vols. 1–5. Somerville, NJ: Unionist-Gazette Association, 1918.

Hooker, Richard. Of the Lawes of Ecclesiastical Politie. Vol. 7. Project Canterbury. http://anglicanhistory.org/hooker.

———. The Works of That Learned and Judicious Divine, Mr. Richard Hooker: With an Account of His Life and Death. Arranged by John Keble. Oxford: Clarendon Press, 1876.

Hume, David. The History of England, from the Invasion of Julius Caesar to the Revolution in 1688. Vol. 5. Dublin: United Company of Booksellers, 1775.

Inglis, Charles. *Letters of Papinian: In Which the Conduct, Present State, and Prospects of the American Congress Are Examined*. London: Reprinted for J. Wilkie, 1779.

———. "The True Interest of America Impartially Stated, in Certain Strictures on a Pamphlet Intitled Common Sense." In Wood, *American Revolution*, 705–70.

Jackson, Richard, and Benjamin Franklin. *An Historical Review of the Constitution and Government of Pensylvania [sic]: From Its Origin, So Far as Regards the Several Points of Controversy [. . .]*. London: R. Griffiths, 1759.

James I. *The Trew Law of Free Monarchies*, in *The Workes of the Most High and Mightie Prince, James: By the Grace of God, King of Great Britaine, France and Ireland, Defender of the Faith, &c.* London: Robert Barker and John Bill, 1616.

Jefferson, Thomas. "Notes on Virginia." In *The Life and Selected Writings of Thomas Jefferson*, edited by Adrienne Koch and William Peden, 187–292. New York: Modern Library, 1972.

———. "A Summary View of the Rights of British Americans." In *Tracts of the American Revolution, 1763–1776*, edited by Merrill Jensen, 256–76. Indianapolis: Bobbs-Merrill, 1977.

Johnson, Samuel. *A General View of Philosophy, or an Introduction to the Study of the Arts and Sciences Exhibiting a General View of All the Arts and Sciences [. . .]*. New London, CT: T. Green, 1743. Kindle.

———. *A Sermon on the Beauty of Holiness, in the worship of the Church of England. Being a very brief rationale on the liturgy*. New York: James Parker, 1761.

Kenyon, Cecelia M., ed. *The Antifederalists*. Indianapolis: Bobbs-Merrill, 1966.

A Late Letter Concerning the Sufferings of the Episcopal Clergy in Scotland. London: Robert Clavel, 1691.

Law, William. "Three Letters to the Bishop of Bangor." In *The Works of the Reverend William Law, M.A., Sometime Fellow of Emanuel College, Cambridge*, 1:3–83. London: J. Richardson, 1762.

Lee, Charles. "Strictures on a Pamphlet, Entitled a 'Friendly Address to All Reasonable Americans, on the Subject of Our Political Confusions': Addressed to the People of America." In Wood, *American Revolution*, 379–96.

Leslie, Charles. *The Constitution, Laws, and Government of England, Vindicated, in a Letter to the Reverend Mr. William Higden*. London: Booksellers of London and Westminster, 1709.

A List of Infringements and Violations of Rights Complained of by the American Colonists from the Votes and Proceedings of the Freeholders and Other Inhabitants of the Town of Boston in New England, Just Published by Order of the Town. Boston: Edes and Gill, 1772.

Livingston, Philip. *The Other Side of the Question: Or, a Defence of the Liberties of North-America, in Answer to a Late Friendly Address to All Reasonable Americans, on the Subject of Our Political Confusions*. New York: James Rivington, 1774.

Locke, John. *Two Treatises of Government: In the Former, the False Principles, and Foundation of Sir Robert Filmer Are Detected and Overthrown, 1690*. Reprint, London: Whitemore and Fenn and C. Brown, 1821.

Morer, Thomas, and Alexander Monro. *An Account of the Present Persecution of the Church in Scotland in Several Letters*. London: S. Cook, 1690.

The New Whole Duty of Man, Containing The Faith as well as Practice of a Christian; Made Easy For the Practice of the Present Age [. . .]. 11th ed. London: Edward Wicksteed, 1755.

Paine, Thomas. *The Age of Reason, in Two Parts, 1794*. Reprint, New York: G. N. Devries, 1827.

———. "Common Sense; Addressed to the Inhabitants of America, on the Following Interesting Subjects [. . .]." In Wood, *American Revolution*, 647–704.

Sacheverell, Henry. *The Perils of False Brethren, Both in Church and State: Set Forth in a Sermon Preach'd Before the Right Honorouble Lord-Mayor [. . .]*. London: H. Hills, 1710.

Schneider, Herbert W., and Carol Schneider, eds. *Samuel Johnson, President of King's College: His Career and Writings*. 4 vols. New York: Columbia University Press, 2002.

Seabury, Samuel, Jr. "The Congress Canvassed: Or, An Examination into the Conduct of the Delegates at Their Grand Convention, Held in Philadelphia [...]." In Seabury, *Letters of a Westchester Farmer*, 69–100.

———. "Free Thoughts on the Proceedings of the Continental Congress, Held at Philadelphia Sept. 5, 1774: Wherein Their Errors Are Exhibited, Their Reasoning Confuted [...]." In Seabury, *Letters of a Westchester Farmer*, 41–68.

———. *Letters of a Westchester Farmer, 1774–1775*. Edited by Clarence H. Vance. White Plains, NY: Westchester County Historical Society, 1930.

Seabury, William Jones. *Memoir of Bishop Seabury*. New York: Edwin S. Gorham, 1908.

Secker, Thomas. *A Sermon preached before the Incorporated Society for the Propagation of the Gospel in Foreign Parts; at their anniversary meeting in the Parish-Church of St Mary-Lebow, on Friday, February 20, 1740–41*. London: J. and H. Pemberton, 1741.

Smith, Horace Wemyss. *Life and Correspondence of the Rev. William Smith, D. D., with Copious Extracts from His Writings*. Vol. 1. Philadelphia: S. A. George, 1879.

Smith, William. *A Sermon on the Present Situation of American Affairs: Preached in Christ-Church, June 23, 1775*. Philadelphia: James Humphreys Jr., 1775.

Smollett, Tobias. *The Adventures of Ferdinand Count Fathom*. Self-published, CreateSpace, 2015.

Smyth, Frederick. "Chief Justice Frederick Smyth to the Middlesex County Grand Jury, April 4, 1775." In *New Jersey in the American Revolution, 1763–1783: A Documentary History*, edited by Larry R. Gerlach, 127–32. Trenton: New Jersey Historical Commission, 1975.

Snape, Andrew. *A Letter to the Lord Bishop of Bangor occasioned by his Lordship's Sermon Preached before the King*. London, 1717.

Society for the Propagation of the Gospel in Foreign Parts. Missionary Records. C Series. 24 vols. British Archives Online, London. https://www.nationalarchives.gov.uk.

Stearns, Ezra S., ed. *Genealogical and Family History of the State of New Hampshire*. New York: Lewis Publishing, 1908.

Stiles, Ezra. *The Literary Diary of Ezra Stiles, D.D., L.L.D., President of Yale College*. Edited by Franklin Bowditch Dexter. 3 vols. New York: Charles Scribner's Sons, 1901.

Strype, John. *The Life and Acts of John Whitgift, D.D.* Vol. 1. Oxford: Clarendon Press, 1822.

Tyrrell, James. *General History of England: Both Ecclesiastical and Civil; from the Earliest Accounts of Time, to the Reign of His Present Majesty, King William III*. London: W. Rogers, 1696.

Weston, Edward. *The Englishman Directed in the Choice of His Religion*. 3rd ed. London: S. Birt, 1752.

Whitgift, John. *An Ansvvere to a Certen Libel Intitled, An Admonition to the Parliament*. London: Henrie Bynneman, 1573.

———. *The Works of John Whitgift, D.D., Master of Trinity College, Dean of Lincoln, &c*. Edited by John Ayre. Cambridge: Cambridge University Press, 1852.

SECONDARY SOURCES

Akers, Charles W. *Called unto Liberty: A Life of Jonathan Mayhew, 1720–1766*. Cambridge, MA: Harvard University Press, 1964.

Allen, Thomas B. *Tories: Fighting for the King in America's First Civil War*. New York: HarperCollins, 2010.

Allis, Frederick S., Jr. *Government Through Opposition: Party Politics in the 1790s*. New York: Macmillan, 1963.

Allitt, Patrick. *The Conservatives: Ideas and Personalities Throughout American History*. New Haven, CT: Yale University Press, 2009.

Amory, Hugh, and David D. Hall, eds. *A History of the Book in America: The Colonial Book in the Atlantic World*. Vol. 1. Cambridge: Cambridge University Press, 2000.

Anderson, Virginia DeJohn. *New England's Generation: The Great Migration and the Formation of Society and Culture in the Seventeenth Century*. New York: Cambridge University Press, 1991.

Andrews, Dee E. *The Methodists and Revolutionary America, 1760–1800: The Shaping of an Evangelical Culture.* Princeton, NJ: Princeton University Press, 2000.

Appleby, Joyce. *Inheriting the Revolution: The First Generation of Americans.* Cambridge, MA: Belknap Press of Harvard University Press, 2000.

Bacevich, Andrew J. "Introduction." In *American Conservatism: Reclaiming an Intellectual Tradition,* xiii–xxi. New York: Library of America, 2020.

Bailyn, Bernard. *The Ideological Origins of the American Revolution.* Cambridge, MA: Harvard University Press, 1967.

———. *The Ordeal of Thomas Hutchinson.* Cambridge, MA: Harvard University Press, 1974.

Banning, Lance. *The Jeffersonian Persuasion: Evolution of a Party Ideology.* Ithaca, NY: Cornell University Press, 1978.

Bannister, Jerry, and Liam Riordan, eds. *The Loyal Atlantic: Remaking the British Atlantic in the Revolutionary Era.* Toronto: University of Toronto Press, 2012.

———. "Loyalism and the British Atlantic, 1660–1840." In Bannister and Riordan, *Loyal Atlantic,* 3–36.

Bell, James B. *The Imperial Origins of the King's Church in Early America, 1607–1783.* New York: Palgrave Macmillan, 2004.

———. *A War of Religion: Dissenters, Anglicans, and the American Revolution.* New York: Palgrave Macmillan, 2008.

Bellah, Robert, et al. *Habits of the Heart: Individualism and Commitment in American Life.* Berkeley: University of California Press, 2008.

Bennett, G. V. *The Tory Crisis in Church and State, 1688–1730: The Career of Francis Atterbury, Bishop of Rochester.* Oxford: Clarendon Press, 1975.

Bernstein, David A. "New Jersey in the American Revolution: The Establishment of a Government amid Civil and Military Disorder, 1770–1783." PhD diss., Rutgers University, 1969.

Black, Jeremy. *Charting the Past: The Historical Worlds of Eighteenth-Century England.* Bloomington: Indiana University Press, 2019.

Bonomi, Patricia U. *Under the Cope of Heaven: Religion, Society, and Politics in Colonial America.* Oxford: Oxford University Press, 1986.

Borden, Morton. *Parties and Politics in the Early Republic, 1789–1815.* Arlington Heights, IL: AHM Publishing, 1967.

Boyd, George Adams. *Elias Boudinot: Patriot and Statesman, 1740–1821.* Princeton, NJ: Princeton University Press, 1952.

Brannon, Rebecca, and Joseph S. Moore, eds. *The Consequences of Loyalism: Essays in Honor of Robert M. Calhoon.* Columbia: University of South Carolina Press, 2019.

Bridenbaugh, Carl. *Mitre and Sceptre: Transatlantic Faiths, Ideas, Personalities, and Politics, 1689–1775.* New York: Oxford University Press, 1962.

Brown, Wallace. *The Good Americans: The Loyalists in the American Revolution.* New York: Morrow, 1969.

Bumsted, J. M. *Understanding the Loyalists.* Sackville, NB: Mount Allison University, Centre for Canadian Studies, 1986.

Burr, Nelson R. *The Anglican Church in New Jersey.* Philadelphia: Church Historical Society, 1954.

Burrows, Edwin G., and Mike Wallace. *Gotham: A History of New York City to 1898.* Oxford: Oxford University Press, 1998.

Bushman, Richard L., ed. *The Great Awakening: Documents on the Revival of Religion, 1740–1745.* Chapel Hill: University of North Carolina Press, 1969.

———. *The Refinement of America: Persons, Houses, Cities.* New York: Vintage Books, 1993.

Byrnes, Don Roy. "The Pre-Revolutionary Career of Provost William Smith, 1751–1780." PhD diss., Tulane University, 1969.

Calhoon, Robert M. "Afterword: Loyalist Cosmopolitanism." In Bannister and Riordan, *Loyal Atlantic,* 277–87.

———. *Dominion and Liberty: Ideology in the Anglo-American World, 1660–1801.* Arlington Heights, IL: Harlan Davidson, 1994.

———. *The Loyalists in Revolutionary America, 1760–1781.* New York: Harcourt Brace Jovanovich, 1973.

Calhoon, Robert M., Timothy M. Barnes, and Robert Scott Davis. *Tory Insurgents: The Loyalist Perception and Other Essays*. Rev. ed. Columbia: University of South Carolina Press, 2010.

Calhoon, Robert M., Timothy M. Barnes, and George A. Rawlyk, eds. *Loyalists and Community in North America*. Westport, CT: Greenwood Press, 1994.

Cameron, Kenneth Walter, ed. *Samuel Seabury Among His Contemporaries: Aspects of New England Anglicanism in the Late Colonial and Early National Years*. Hartford, CT: Transcendental Books, 1980.

Chandler, George. *The Descendants of William and Annis Chandler Who Settled in Roxbury, Mass., 1637*. Worcester, MA: Press of Charles Hamilton, 1888.

Chernow, Ron. *Alexander Hamilton*. New York: Penguin, 2004.

Chopra, Ruma. *Choosing Sides: Loyalists in Revolutionary America*. Lanham, MD: Rowman & Littlefield, 2013.

———. *Unnatural Rebellion: Loyalists in New York City during the Revolution*. Charlottesville: University of Virginia Press, 2011.

Clark, J. C. D. *The Language of Liberty: Political Discourse and Social Dynamics in the Anglo-American World*. New York: Cambridge University Press, 1994.

Clark, Michael D. "Jonathan Boucher: The Mirror of Reaction." *Huntington Library Quarterly* 33 (1969): 19–32.

Clark, Samuel A. *The History of St. John's Church, Elizabeth Town, New Jersey, from the Year 1703 to the Present Time*. Philadelphia: J. B. Lippincott, 1857.

Clark, Walter Earnest. "Josiah Tucker, Economist: A Study in the History of Economics." PhD diss., Columbia University, 1903.

Colbourn, Trevor. *The Lamp of Experience: Whig History and the Intellectual Origins of the American Revolution*. Carmel, IN: Liberty Fund, 1998.

Collinson, Patrick. *The Elizabethan Puritan Movement*. Oxford: Oxford University Press, 1967.

Cotlar, Seth. *Tom Paine's America: The Rise and Fall of Transatlantic Radicalism in the Early Republic*. Charlottesville: University of Virginia Press, 2011.

Crary, Catherine S., ed. *The Price of Loyalty: Tory Writings from the Revolutionary Era*. New York: McGraw-Hill, 1973.

Cross, Arthur Lyon. *The Anglican Episcopate and the American Colonies*. New York: Longmans, Green, 1902.

Cruickshanks, Eveline. *The Glorious Revolution*. Basingstoke: Macmillan, 2000.

Cullen, George Edward. "Talking to a Whirlwind: The Loyalist Printers in America, 1763–1783." PhD diss., West Virginia University, 1979.

Cuthbertson, Brian. *The First Bishop: A Biography of Charles Inglis*. Halifax, NS: Waegwoltic Press, 1987.

Damrosch, Leo. *The Club: Johnson, Boswell, and the Friends Who Shaped an Age*. New Haven, CT: Yale University Press, 2019.

Dellape, Kevin J. *America's First Chaplain: The Life and Times of the Reverend Jacob Duché*. Bethlehem, PA: Lehigh University Press, 2013.

Dexter, Franklin Bowditch. *Biographical Sketches of the Graduates of Yale College, with Annals of the College History*. 6 vols. New York: Henry Holt, 1896.

———. "Thomas Bradbury Chandler." In *Biographical Sketches of the Graduates of Yale College, with Annals of the College History*, 2:23–29. New York: Henry Holt, 1896.

Doll, Peter M. *Revolution, Religion, and National Identity: Imperial Anglicanism in British North America, 1745–1795*. Madison, NJ: Fairleigh Dickinson University Press, 2000.

Dworetz, Steven M. *The Unvarnished Doctrine: Locke, Liberalism, and the American Revolution*. Durham, NC: Duke University Press, 1990.

Elkins, Stanley, and Eric McKitrick. *The Age of Federalism: The Early American Republic, 1788–1800*. Oxford: Oxford University Press, 1993.

Elliott, Kenneth R. *Anglican Church Policy, Eighteenth Century Conflict, and the American Episcopate*. New York: Peter Lang, 2011.

Ellis, Joseph J. *American Dialogue: The Founders and Us*. New York: Alfred A. Knopf, 2018.

———. *The New England Mind in Transition: Samuel Johnson of Connecticut, 1696–1772*.

New Haven, CT: Yale University Press, 1973.
———. "The Puritan Mind in Transition: The Philosophy of Samuel Johnson." *William and Mary Quarterly* 28, no. 1 (1971): 26–45.
Engel, Katherine Carté. "Revisiting the Bishop's Controversy." In *The American Revolution Reborn*, edited by Patrick Spero and Michael Zuckerman, 132–49. Philadelphia: University of Pennsylvania Press, 2016.
Fea, John. *The Way of Improvement Leads Home: Philip Vickers Fithian and the Rural Enlightenment in Early America*. Philadelphia: University of Pennsylvania Press, 2008.
Ferguson, Randall Lee. "The Anti-Revolutionary Rhetoric of Thomas Chandler, Myles Cooper, Charles Inglis, and Samuel Seabury: An Analysis of Metaphor." PhD diss., University of Minnesota, 1998.
Ferling, John E. *A Leap in the Dark: The Struggle to Create the American Republic*. Oxford: Oxford University Press, 2003.
———. *The Loyalist Mind: Joseph Galloway and the American Revolution*. University Park: Penn State University Press, 1977.
Fiering, Norman S. "President Samuel Johnson and the Circle of Knowledge." *William and Mary Quarterly* 28, no. 2 (1971): 199–236.
Fischer, David Hackett. *Paul Revere's Ride*. Oxford: Oxford University Press, 1994.
Foster, Stephen. *The Long Argument: English Puritanism and the Shaping of New England Culture, 1570–1700*. Chapel Hill: University of North Carolina Press, 1991.
Games, Alison. *Migration and the Origins of the English Atlantic World*. Cambridge, MA: Harvard University Press, 1999.
Gaustad, Edwin Scott, and Philip L. Barlow. *New Historical Atlas of Religion in America*. Oxford: Oxford University Press, 2001.
Gavin, Frank. "The Rev. Thomas Bradbury Chandler in the Light of His (Unpublished) Diary, 1775–85." *Church History* 1, no. 2 (1932): 90–106.
Gerardi, Donald F. M. "The Episcopate Controversy Reconsidered: Religious Vocation and Anglican Perceptions of Authority in Mid-Eighteenth-Century America." *Perspectives in American History* 3 (1987): 81–114.

———. "The King's College Controversy and the Ideological Roots of Toryism in New York." *Perspectives in American History*, no. 9 (1977): 145–96.
Gerlach, Larry R. *New Jersey in the American Revolution, 1763–1783: A Documentary History*. Trenton: New Jersey Historical Commission, 1975.
———. *Prologue to Independence: New Jersey in the Coming of the American Revolution*. New Brunswick, NJ: Rutgers University Press, 1976.
Gibson, William. *Enlightenment Prelate: Benjamin Hoadly, 1676–1761*. Cambridge: James Clarke, 2004.
Gigantino, James, II. *William Livingston's American Revolution*. Philadelphia: University of Pennsylvania Press, 2018.
Gould, Eliga H. *The Persistence of Empire: British Political Culture in the Age of the American Revolution*. Chapel Hill: University of North Carolina Press, 2000.
Gould, Philip. "Wit and Politics in Revolutionary British America: The Case of Samuel Seabury and Alexander Hamilton." *Eighteenth-Century Studies* 71 (2008): 383–404.
———. *Writing the Rebellion: Loyalists and the Literature of Politics in British America*. Oxford: Oxford University Press, 2013.
Grell, Ole Peter, Jonathan I. Israel, and Nicholas Tyacke, eds. *From Persecution to Toleration: The Glorious Revolution and Religion in England*. Oxford: Clarendon Press, 1991.
Gross, Robert A. *The Minutemen and Their World*. New York: Hill and Wang, 1976.
Guy, John. "The 1590s: The Second Reign of Queen Elizabeth I?" In *The Reign of Elizabeth I: Court and Culture in the Last Decade*, edited by John Guy, 126–49. Cambridge: Cambridge University Press, 1995.
Hall, David D. *The Puritans: A Transatlantic History*. Princeton, NJ: Princeton University Press, 2019.
Harris, Tim. *Revolution: The Great Crisis of the British Monarchy, 1685–1720*. London: Allen Lane, 2006.
Hart, D. G. *Calvinism: A History*. New Haven, CT: Yale University Press, 2013.
Hatfield, Edwin Francis. *History of Elizabeth, New Jersey: Including the Early History of*

Union County. Carlisle, MA: Applewood Books, 1868.

Hawkins, Harriet C. "New Jersey Architecture in the Revolutionary Era." In *New Jersey in the American Revolution*, edited by Barbara J. Mitnick, 77–100. New Brunswick, NJ: Rivergate Press, 2005.

Hayes, Kevin J. *The Mind of a Patriot: Patrick Henry and the World of Ideas*. Charlottesville: University of Virginia Press, 2008.

Hebb, Ross N. *Samuel Seabury and Charles Inglis: Two Bishops, Two Churches*. Madison, NJ: Fairleigh Dickinson University Press, 2010.

Hofstadter, Richard. *America at 1750: A Social Portrait*. New York: Vintage Books, 1971.

Holton, Woody. *Unruly Americans and the Origins of the Constitution*. New York: Hill and Wang, 2007.

Hoyt, Albert Harrison. *Sketch of the Life of the Rev. Thomas Bradbury Chandler, D.D.* Boston: New-England Historical and Genealogical Register, 1873.

Hutson, James H. *Church and State in America: The First Two Centuries*. Cambridge: Cambridge University Press, 2008.

Ingersoll, Thomas N. *The Loyalist Problem in Revolutionary New England*. New York: Cambridge University Press, 2016.

Ingram, Robert G. *Religion, Reform and Modernity in the Eighteenth Century: Thomas Secker and the Church of England*. Woodbridge, UK: Boydell Press, 2007.

Isaac, Rhys. *The Transformation of Virginia, 1740–1790*. Chapel Hill: University of North Carolina Press, 1982.

Israel, Jonathan. *Democratic Enlightenment: Philosophy, Revolution, and Human Rights, 1750–1790*. Oxford: Oxford University Press, 1982.

———. *The Expanding Blaze: How the American Revolution Ignited the World, 1775–1848*. Princeton, NJ: Princeton University Press, 2017.

Jasanoff, Maya. *Liberty's Exiles: American Loyalists in the Revolutionary World*. New York: Alfred A. Knopf, 2011.

Kaplan, Benjamin J. *Divided by Faith: Religious Conflict and the Practice of Toleration in Early Modern Europe*. Cambridge, MA: Belknap Press, 2007.

Keeble, N. H., ed. *"Settling the Peace of the Church": 1662 Revisited*. Oxford: Oxford University Press, 2014.

Kidd, Colin. "Religious Realignment Between the Restoration and Union." In *A Union for Empire: Political Thought and the Union of 1707*, edited by John Robertson, 145–68. New York: Cambridge University Press, 1995.

Kidd, Thomas S. *Benjamin Franklin: The Religious Life of a Founding Father*. New Haven, CT: Yale University Press, 2017.

———. *God of Liberty: A Religious History of the American Revolution*. New York: Basic Books, 2012.

———. *The Great Awakening: The Roots of Evangelical Christianity in Colonial America*. New Haven, CT: Yale University Press, 2009.

Kinloch, Hector. "Anglican Clergy in Connecticut, 1701–1785." PhD diss., Yale University, 1959.

Kirk, Russell. *The Conservative Mind: From Burke to Eliot*. Chicago: Regnery Publishing, 1953.

Klarman, Michael J. *The Framers' Coup: The Making of the United States Constitution*. New York: Oxford University Press, 2016.

Kloppenberg, James T. *Toward Democracy: The Struggle for Self-Rule in European and American Thought*. New York: Oxford University Press, 2016.

Kulikoff, Allan. *Tobacco and Slaves: The Development of Southern Cultures in the Chesapeake, 1680–1800*. Chapel Hill: University of North Carolina Press, 1986.

Lake, Peter. *Anglicans and Puritans? Presbyterianism and English Conformist Thought from Whitgift to Hooker*. London: Unwin Hyman, 1988.

———. "Anti-Puritanism: The Structure of a Prejudice." In *Religious Politics in Post-Reformation England*, edited by Kenneth Fincham and Peter Lake, 80–97. Woodbridge, UK: Boydell Press.

Lambert, Frank. *Inventing the "Great Awakening."* Princeton, NJ: Princeton University Press, 1999.

Landsman, Ned C. "The Episcopate, the British Union, and the Failure of Religious Settlement in Colonial British America." In *The First Prejudice: Religious Tolerance and Intolerance in Early America*, edited by Chris Beneke and Christopher S. Grenda, 75–97. Philadelphia: University of Pennsylvania Press, 2011.

Larkin, Edward. *Thomas Paine and the Literature of Revolution*. Cambridge: Cambridge University Press, 2005.

Larned, Ellen D. *History of Windham County, Connecticut*. Worcester, MA: Charles Hamilton, 1874.

Le Beau, Bryan. *Jonathan Dickinson and the Formative Years of American Presbyterianism*. Lexington: University Press of Kentucky, 1997.

Leighton, C. D. A. "Hutchinsonianism: A Counter-Enlightenment Reform Movement." *Journal of Religious History* 23, no. 2 (1999): 268–84.

———. "Scottish Jacobitism, Episcopacy, and Counter-Enlightenment." *History of European Ideas* 35, no. 1 (2009): 1–10.

Lenman, Bruce. "The Scottish Episcopal Clergy and the Ideology of Jacobitism." In *Ideology and Conspiracy: Aspects of Jacobitism, 1689–1759*, edited by Eveline Cruickshanks, 36–47. Edinburgh: John Donald Publishers, 1982.

Lippy, Charles H. *Seasonable Revolutionary: The Mind of Charles Chauncy*. Chicago: Nelson-Hall, 1981.

Lorenz, Alfred Lawrence. *Hugh Gaine: A Colonial Printer-Editor's Odyssey to Loyalism*. Carbondale, IL: Southern Illinois University Press, 1972.

Lovegrove, Deryck W. *Established Church, Sectarian People: Itinerancy and the Transformation of English Dissent, 1780–1830*. Cambridge: Cambridge University Press, 1988.

Lundburg, David, and Henry F. May. "The Enlightened Reader in America." *American Quarterly* 28, no. 2 (Summer 1976): 262–93.

Lundin, Leonard. *Cockpit of the Revolution: The War for Independence in New Jersey*. Princeton, NJ: Princeton University Press, 1940.

Lydekker, John Wolfe. *The Life and Letters of Charles Inglis: His Ministry in America and Consecration as First Colonial Bishop, from 1759 to 1787*. London: Society for Promoting Christian Knowledge, 1936.

MacCulloch, Diarmaid. *Christianity: The First Three Thousand Years*. New York: Viking, 2009.

Macmillan, Margaret Burnham. *The War Governors in the American Revolution*. Gloucester, MA: Peter Smith, 1965.

Maier, Pauline. *From Resistance to Revolution: Colonial Radicals and the Development of American Opposition to Britain, 1765 to 1776*. New York: W. W. Norton, 1991.

———. "Whigs Against Whigs Against Whigs: The Imperial Debates of 1765–76 Reconsidered." *William and Mary Quarterly* 68, no. 4 (Fall 2011): 578–82.

Manross, William Wilson. *A History of the American Episcopal Church*. New York: Morehouse Publishing, 1935.

Marsden, George M. *Jonathan Edwards: A Life*. New Haven, CT: Yale University Press, 2003.

Marshall, John. *John Locke, Toleration, and Early Enlightenment Culture*. Cambridge: Cambridge University Press, 2006.

Martin, Robert W. T. *Government by Dissent: Protest, Resistance, and Radical Democratic Thought in the Early American Republic*. New York: New York University Press, 2013.

Mason, Keith. "The American Loyalist Diaspora and the Reconfiguration of the British Atlantic World." In *Empire and Nation: The American Revolution in the Atlantic World*, edited by Eliga H. Gould and Peter S. Onuf, 239–59. Baltimore: Johns Hopkins University Press, 2005.

Matters, Armin. *Citizens of a Common Intellectual Homeland: The Transatlantic Origins of American Democracy and Nationhood*. Charlottesville: University of Virginia Press, 2015.

McConville, Brendan. *The King's Three Faces: The Rise and Fall of Royal America, 1688–1776*. Chapel Hill: University of North Carolina Press, 2006.

McCormick, Richard P. *New Jersey from Colony to State, 1609–1789*. Newark: New Jersey Historical Society, 1981.

McCulloch, Samuel Clyde. "Thomas Bradbury Chandler: Anglican Humanitarian in New Jersey." In *British Humanitarianism: Essays Honoring Frank J. Klingberg*, edited by

Samuel Clyde McCulloch, 100–123. Kingsport, TN: Kingsport Press, 1950.

Middlekauff, Robert. *The Glorious Cause: The American Revolution, 1763–1789*. New York: Oxford University Press, 1982.

Mills, Frederick V., Sr. "Anglican Expansion in Colonial America, 1761–775." *Historical Magazine of the Protestant Episcopal Church* 30, no. 3 (September 1970): 325–45.

———. *Bishops by Ballot: An Eighteenth-Century Ecclesiastical Revolution*. New York: Oxford University Press, 1978.

———. "The Colonial Anglican Episcopate: A Historiographical Review." *Anglican and Episcopal History* 61, no. 3 (1992): 325–44.

———. "The Internal Anglican Controversy over an American Episcopate, 1763–1775." *Historical Magazine of the Protestant Episcopal Church* 44, no. 3 (1975): 257–76.

Monod, Paul Kléber. *Jacobitism and the English People, 1688–1788*. Cambridge: Cambridge University Press, 1989.

Moore, Christopher. *The Loyalists: Revolution, Exile, Settlement*. Toronto: McClelland & Stewart, 1984.

Morgan, Edmund S. *The Gentle Puritan: A Life of Ezra Stiles, 1727–1795*. 1962. Reprint, New York: W. W. Norton, 1984.

Moy, Daniel R. "Antiquity and Loyalist Counter-Narrative in Revolutionary America, 1765–1776." PhD diss., University of Oklahoma, 2012.

Mullins, J. Patrick. *Father of Liberty: Jonathan Mayhew and the Principles of the American Revolution*. Lawrence: University Press of Kansas, 2017.

Nash, Gary B. *The Unknown American Revolution: The Unruly Birth of Democracy and the Struggle to Create America*. New York: Penguin, 2005.

———. *The Urban Crucible: Social Change, Political Consciousness, and the Origins of the American Revolution*. Cambridge, MA: Harvard University Press, 1979.

Nelson, Eric. *The Royalist Revolution: Monarchy and the American Founding*. Cambridge, MA: Harvard University Press, 2014.

Nelson, John K. *A Blessed Company: Parishes, Parsons, and Parishioners in Anglican Virginia, 1690–1776*. Chapel Hill: University of North Carolina Press, 2001.

Nelson, William H. *The American Tory*. 1961. Reprint, Oxford: Clarendon, 1992.

Noll, Mark A. *The Rise of Evangelicalism: The Age of Edwards, Whitefield, and the Wesleys*. Downers Grove, IL: InterVarsity Press, 2003.

Norton, Mary Beth. *The British-Americans: The Loyalist Exiles in England, 1774–1789*. Boston: Little, Brown, 1972.

———. "The Loyalist Critique of the Revolution." In *The Development of a Revolutionary Mentality: Papers Presented at the First Symposium, May 5 and 6, 1972*, 127–50. Washington, DC: Library of Congress, 1972.

O'Conner, Daniel. *Three Centuries of Mission: The United Society for the Propagation of the Gospel, 1701–2000*. London: Continuum, 2000.

Parkinson, Robert G. "Janus's Revolution." *William and Mary Quarterly* 76, no. 3 (July 2019): 545–61.

Parrish, David. *Jacobitism and Anti-Jacobitism in the British Atlantic World, 1688–1727*. Rochester, NY: Boydell Press, 2017.

Pascoe, C. F. *Two Hundred Years of the SPG: An Historical Account of the Society for the Propagation of the Gospel in Foreign Parts, 1701–1900*. London: SPG, 1901.

Phillips, Kevin. *1775: A Good Year for Revolution*. New York: Viking, 2012.

Pincus, Steve. *1688: The First Modern Revolution*. New Haven, CT: Yale University Press, 2009.

Potter, Janice. *The Liberty We Seek: Loyalist Ideology in Colonial New York and Massachusetts*. Cambridge, MA: Harvard University Press, 1983.

Raven, James. *The Business of Books: Booksellers and the English Book Trade*. New Haven, CT: Yale University Press, 2007.

———. "The Importation of Books in the Eighteenth Century." In *A History of the Book in America: The Colonial Book in the Atlantic World*, edited by Hugh Amory and David D. Hall, 1:183–198. Cambridge: Cambridge University Press, 2000.

Reeves, Thomas C. "John Checkley and the Emergence of the Episcopal Church in New England." *Historical Magazine of the Protestant Episcopal Church* 34, no. 4 (1965): 349–60.

Rhoden, Nancy L. "Anglicanism, Dissent, and Toleration in Eighteenth-Century British Colonies." In *Anglicizing America: Empire, Revolution, Republic*, edited by Ignacio Gallup-Diaz, Andrew Shankman, and David J. Silverman, 125–52. Philadelphia: University of Pennsylvania Press, 2015.

———. *Revolutionary Anglicanism: The Colonial Church of England Clergy During the American Revolution.* New York: New York University Press, 1999.

Robbins, Caroline. *The Eighteenth-Century Commonwealthman: Studies in the Transmission, Development, and Circumstances of English Liberal Thought from the Restoration of Charles II Until the War with the Thirteen Colonies.* Cambridge, MA: Harvard University Press, 2011.

Rohrer, S. Scott. "The Constitution and Mr. Livingston: A Study in Power, 1776–1779." Master's thesis, University of Virginia, 1985.

———. *Hope's Promise: Religion and Acculturation in the Southern Backcountry.* Tuscaloosa: University of Alabama Press, 2005.

———. *Jacob Green's Revolution: Radical Religion and Reform in a Revolutionary Age.* University Park: Penn State University Press, 2014.

———. "'Under the Claw of an Inraged Lion': Thomas Bradbury Chandler, Benjamin Hoadly, and the Meaning of the Glorious Revolution." In *Revolution as Reformation: Protestant Faith in the Age of Revolutions, 1688–1832*, edited by Peter C. Messer and William Harrison Taylor, 113–34. Tuscaloosa: University of Alabama Press, 2021.

Rudd, John C. *Historical Notices of Saint John's Church, Elizabeth-Town, New-Jersey. Contained in a Discourse, Delivered in Said Church, November 21, 1824.* Elizabeth-Town, NJ: J. and E. Sanderson, 1825.

Sack, James J. *From Jacobite to Conservative: Reaction and Orthodoxy in Britain, c. 1760–1832.* Cambridge: Cambridge University Press, 1993.

Scotland, Nigel D. *George Whitefield: The First Transatlantic Revivalist.* Oxford: Lion Books, 2019.

Scruton, Roger. *Conservatism: An Invitation to the Great Tradition.* New York: All Points Books, 2018.

Secor, Philip B. *Richard Hooker: Prophet of Anglicanism.* Kent, UK: Burns & Oates, 1999.

Seed, John. *Dissenting Histories: Religious Division and the Politics of Memory in Eighteenth-Century England.* Edinburgh: Edinburgh University Press, 2008.

Shaw, William H. *History of Essex and Hudson Counties, New Jersey.* Vol. 1. Philadelphia: Everts & Peck, 1884.

Somerset, Anne. *Elizabeth I.* New York: Anchor Books, 2003.

Sowerby, Scott. *Making Toleration: The Repealers and the Glorious Revolution.* Cambridge, MA: Harvard University Press, 2013.

Speck, W. A. *Reluctant Revolutionaries: Englishmen and the Revolution of 1688.* Oxford: Oxford University Press, 1988.

Sprague, William B. *Annals of the American Pulpit; or Commemorative Notices of Distinguished America Clergymen of Various Denominations.* Vol. 5. New York: Robert Carter & Brothers, 1861, 137–42.

Steiner, Bruce E. *Samuel Seabury, 1729–1796: A Study in the High Church Tradition.* Athens: Ohio University Press, 1971.

Strong, Rowan. *Anglicanism and the British Empire, c. 1700–1850.* Oxford: Oxford University Press, 2007.

Taylor, Stephen. "Whigs, Bishops, and America: The Politics of Church Reform in Mid-Eighteenth-Century England." *Historical Journal* 36, no. 2 (June 1993): 331–56.

Thompson, H. P. *Into All Lands: The History of the Society for the Propagation of the Gospel in Foreign Parts, 1701–1950.* London: SPCK, 1951.

Thompson, Roger. *Mobility and Migration: East Anglian Founders of New England, 1629–1640.* Amherst: University of Massachusetts Press, 1994.

Tiedemann, Joseph S., Eugene R. Fingerhut, and Robert W. Venables, eds. *The Other Loyalists: Ordinary People, Royalism, and the Revolution in the Middle Colonies, 1763–1787.* Albany: State University of New York Press, 2009.

Trevor-Roper, Hugh. *Counter-Reformation to Glorious Revolution*. Chicago: University of Chicago Press, 1992.

Tucker, Robert W., and David C. Hendrickson. *Empire of Liberty: The Statecraft of Thomas Jefferson*. Oxford: Oxford University Press, 1990.

Vallance, Edward. *The Glorious Revolution: 1688—Britain's Fight for Liberty*. New York: Pegasus Books, 2008.

Wacker, Peter O. *Land and People: A Cultural Geography of Preindustrial New Jersey: Origins and Settlement Patterns*. New Brunswick, NJ: Rutgers University Press, 1975.

Waldman, Stephen. *Founding Faith: Providence, Politics, and the Birth of Religious Freedom in America*. New York: Random House, 2008.

Walker, Peter W. "The Church Militant: The American Loyalist Clergy and the Making of the British Counterrevolution, 1701–1792." PhD diss., Columbia University, 2016.

Walsham, Alexandra. *Charitable Hatred: Tolerance and Intolerance in England, 1500–1700*. Manchester: Manchester University Press, 2006.

Warnock, James. "Thomas Bradbury Chandler and William Smith: Diversity within Colonial Anglicanism." *Anglican and Episcopal History* 57, no. 3 (September 1988): 272–97.

Weimer, Adrian C. *Martyrs' Mirror: Persecution and Holiness in Early New England*. Oxford: Oxford University Press, 2011.

Weiss, Frederick Lewis Weiss. *The Colonial Clergy of the Middle Colonies: New York, New Jersey, and Pennsylvania, 1628–1776*. Worcester, MA: American Antiquarian Society, 1957.

Whiteley, Peter. *Lord North: The Prime Minister Who Lost America*. London: Hambledon Press, 1996.

Will, George F. *The Conservative Sensibility*. New York: Hachette Books, 2019.

Winterer, Caroline. *American Enlightenments: Pursuing Happiness in the Age of Reason*. New Haven, CT: Yale University Press, 2016.

———. "From Royal to Republican: The Classical Image in Early America." *Journal of American History* 91, no. 4 (March 2005): 1264–90.

Wood, Gordon S., ed. *The American Revolution: Writings from the Pamphlet Debate, 1773–1776*. New York: Library of America, 2015.

———. *The Creation of the American Republic, 1776–1787*. New York: W. W. Norton, 1969.

———. *The Radicalism of the American Revolution*. New York: Vintage Books, 1993.

Woolverton, John Frederick. *Colonial Anglicanism in North America*. Detroit: Wayne State University Press, 1984.

Zimmer, Anne Y. *Jonathan Boucher: Loyalist in Exile*. Detroit: Wayne State University Press, 1978.

Zimmer, Anne Y., and Alfred H. Kelly. "Jonathan Boucher: Constitutional Conservative." *Journal of American History* 58, no. 4 (1972): 897–922.

Zook, Melinda S. "Violence, Martyrdom, and Radical Politics: Rethinking the Glorious Revolution." In *Politics and the Political Imagination in Later Stuart Britain*, edited by Howard Nenner, 75–95. Rochester, NY: University of Rochester Press, 1998.

INDEX

Act of Uniformity, 1559, 53, 117, 118
Adams, John, 22, 105, 124, 130, 139, 183
Adams, Samuel, 105, 153
adiaphora, 77, 80, 84, 89, 114, 118
Alison, Francis, 107
Admonition to the Parliament, 41, 53, 54, 55, 116
American Querist, 84, 130, 131–33, 135, 142, 150, 151
American Whig, 107, 108–9, 110, 112, 114, 117–18, 143–44
Ames, William, 24
Anabaptists, 56, 59
Anglicanism; Anglican Church. *See* Church of England
Anne, Queen, 82, 89
Anti-Federalists, 180
Appeal Defended, 114–15, 120
Appeal Farther Defended, 120
Appeal to the Public, 88, 90, 94, 97–103, 105, 106, 107, 108, 112, 113, 116, 121, 124, 125, 127, 164
Articles of Confederation, 179
Atterbury, Francis, 68, 79
Auchmuty, Samuel, 92, 93, 94, 122

Bacevich, Andrew J., 182
Bacon, Francis, 35, 37
Baldwin, Samuel, 50
Bancroft, Richard, 51, 61, 62, 120
Bangorian controversy, 10, 67, 79–83, 181
Berkeley, George Jr., 97, 125
Bernard, Francis, 170
Bishop of London, 93–94, 98, 113, 124, 165
Blackburne, Francis, 125–26, 127, 167
Bodin, Jean, 12
book market and trade, 169, 185–86
Boston, 65, 124, 128, 134, 139, 143, 154, 157
    Boston Massacre, 124
    Boston tea party and duty on tea, 129, 130, 134, 137, 138, 149, 150
Boucher, Jonathan, 4, 84–85, 146–49, 155–56, 170, 176, 177, 182
Boudinot, Elias, 45, 47, 153
Bradford, William, 137, 151
Bray, Thomas, 13
Bryan, George, 107
Burgoyne, John, 163

Burke, Edmund, 182, 183–84
Burnet, Gilbert, 102–3, 110, 111, 187

Calamy, Edmund, 34
Calhoon, Robert M., 4, 7
Calvin, John, 53, 59
Cambridge Platform, 41
Cambridge Platonists, 33
Carleton, Guy, 175
Carter, Robert III, 185
Cartwright, Thomas, 41, 51, 53, 54, 55, 88
Catholicism, 49, 52, 57, 63, 67, 69, 76, 78, 104, 108, 115, 143
Centinel, 107, 108, 109–11, 114, 116, 118, 119
Chandler, Jane (wife of TBC). *See* Emott, Jane
Chandler, John (grandfather), 19, 20
Chandler, Thomas Bradbury, 59, 65, 66, 70, 72, 78, 105, 182
    Awakening, views of, 12, 14, 24–26, 113
    bishop's campaign, 2, 11–12, 51, 61, 66, 85, 88–127, 152, 161–64, 175–77
    campaign for American Anglican clergy, 153, 164–66
    college years, 17, 21, 23–27
    dissenters, views of, 11, 13–14, 26, 43, 44, 48–49, 63, 64, 84, 85 (*see also* Chandler, Thomas Bradbury: political beliefs: toleration, views of)
    early years, 8–9, 18–22
    family life, 8, 47, 152, 154, 171, 174–75, 179
    Glorious Revolution, views of, 7–8, 9, 10, 12, 66, 84–87, 88, 92, 145, 181
    health of, 152, 174, 175, 176, 177, 179, 181
    Johnson, Samuel, biography of, 17, 34, 36, 37, 41, 91
    library of, 7, 9, 10, 12, 34, 44, 51, 55, 59, 64, 67, 72, 76, 77, 79, 86, 169, 185–216; selected works, 188p
    London exile, 15, 16, 152–77; Atlantic crossing, 157–58; English travels, 158–59, 168–69; final days in exile, 173–77; fleeing to New York City, 152–55; meetings with British officials, 160–61, 163, 170–71
    Maryland visit, 95–97
    military campaigns, views of, 163, 171–72

Chandler, Thomas Bradbury (*continued*)
  New England and Congregationalism, views of, 12, 13, 14, 31, 41–42, 90, 104, 129, 141–42, 181 (*see also* Puritanism)
  pastorship and missionary work, 13, 40, 43, 48
  pastorship, recruitment to, 38–40
  political beliefs, 1, 2, 14, 131–36, 144–45, 180, 182; authority, rebellion, and order, views of, 1, 3, 4, 9–10–11, 21, 23, 31, 51, 61–64, 66, 87, 101, 134–35, 180; monarchy and episcopacy, views of, 32, 40, 42, 44, 66, 84–87, 88, 116–17, 118, 153, 161, 172, 184; revolutionary movement, views of, 4, 9–11, 14–15, 87, 129, 131–32, 136, 143; toleration, views of, 15, 62–64, 85, 89, 114–15, 117, 118, 120, 182
  religious beliefs, 32, 34, 40, 41, 49, 78–79, 84–87, 118–19
  writings, political tracts, 2, 15, 21, 84, 86, 129–31, 132–37, 139–46 (see also *American Querist; Friendly Address to All Reasonable Americans*; and *What Think Ye of Congress Now?*); attacks on, 2, 15, 132, 133, 137–39, 143, 153
Chandler, Polly (daughter), 171
Chandler, William (son), 167–68, 174–75
Chandler, William, and Annis (great-great-grandparents), 18
Chandler, William, and Jemima (parents), 18, 19, 20, 22
Charles I, 62, 70, 73, 86, 125, 135, 142
Charles II, 68, 69
Church of England
  colonial church, 13, 26, 29, 48, 63, 66, 91, 101–2, 164
  state church, role of, 10, 13, 31, 32, 44, 52, 62–64, 70
  Stuart-era church, 68–70, 72, 76–79, 80–83, 117
  Tudor-era church, 52–61, 115–16
  See also high church Anglicanism
Chauncy, Charles, 62, 107, 112–14, 115, 116, 118, 119–20
Civil Wars, English, 5, 10, 70, 74, 86, 135
Clap, Thomas, 24, 25, 26, 27
Clark, J. C. D., 6
Clarke, Samuel, 34, 38
clerical conventions, annual, New Jersey, 90, 92, 94
commissaries, 90, 95, 121
Common Sense, 85, 130, 161–62
  See also Thomas Paine
comprehension, 77, 78, 79

conservatism, 2, 3, 6–7, 13, 15, 17, 126, 145, 181–82
Constitution, Laws, and Government of England, Vindicated, 72
constitution, New Jersey, 179
constitution, federal, 180, 181
Continental Association, 129, 130, 133, 137
Continental Congress, First, 128, 129, 130, 133, 136, 137, 139, 142, 144, 146
Continental Congress, Second, 139, 147, 149, 150
Cooper, Myles, 9, 47, 92, 93, 97, 107, 122, 155, 156, 158, 164, 165, 173
Cooper, Samuel, 107
Cornwallis, Charles, 171
Cornwallis, Frederick, 160
Cranmer, Thomas, 51, 115
Critical Commentary, 125
Cromwell, Oliver, 5, 86, 142

Dartmouth, Earl of, 161
Davenport, Addington, 113
Davenport, James, 25, 26, 32
Democratic-Republican Party, 181, 183
Dickinson, John, 107, 130, 131, 135, 138
Discourse Concerning Unlimited Submission, 83
Drummond, Robert Hay, 90
Duché, Jacob, 83

Edward VI, 33, 57, 115, 116
Edwards, Jonathan, 14, 26
Eikonoklastes, 86
Elizabeth, Queen, 14, 52, 53, 56–57, 108, 116, 120, 125, 159
Elizabeth Town, NJ, 15, 45, 50, 51, 127, 129, 151, 153, 154, 171, 176
Elizabethtown Association, 139, 153
Ellis, Joseph, 38
Emott, Jane, 47, 154, 167, 173
Emott, John, 45
Essex County, NJ, 50–51, 139
Exeter, 155, 157

Federalists, 181, 182–83
Field, John, 54
1563 Articles of Religion, 57
Filmer, Robert, 12, 74–75, 76, 84, 86, 87, 90, 148
Fithian, Philip Vickers, 185
Fleetwood, William, 50
France, 69, 70, 71, 91, 163
Franklin, Benjamin, 83, 185
French Revolution, 181, 183
Friendly Address to All Reasonable Americans, 86–87, 133–34, 136, 137–38, 139, 142, 153

INDEX   245

Gage, Thomas, 128
Gaine, Hugh, 122
Galloway, Joseph, 7, 129, 136
George I, 82–83, 109
George II, 109
George III, 86, 91, 93, 129
Germaine, Lord, 160
Gibson, Edmund, 102
Glorious Revolution, 7, 9, 67–79, 85, 109
Gould, Philip, 182
Great Awakening, 1, 2, 3, 12, 14, 24–25, 49
Great Migration, 18, 62
Grindal, Edmund, 56, 57
Gunpowder Plot, 67, 77
Gwatkin, Thomas, 121, 122–24

Hales, Edward, 68
Henry, Patrick, 185
Halifax, 157
Hamilton, Alexander, 3, 45, 155
Hampton, Andrew, 45
Hanoverians, 71, 82
Hay, Robert, 161
Henley, Samuel, 121
Henry VIII, 108, 115, 116, 168
high church Anglicanism, 1, 10, 15, 16, 17, 22, 24,
    31, 40–42, 49, 51, 71, 73–74, 78, 80–83, 87,
    98, 108–9
history, views of
    loyalists' views, 6–7, 10, 12, 146–48, 181
    Whigs' views, 5–6, 7, 10, 12, 63, 64, 68, 108–9,
        110–11, 144, 162
Hoadly, Benjamin, 10, 34, 67, 68, 72, 75–76, 77,
    78, 79–83, 110, 114, 187
Holland, 69, 70, 71
Hooker, Richard, 12, 51, 53, 59–61, 76, 100, 116
Horrocks, James, 121
Howe, William, 163, 165
Hume, David, 51, 52
Hutchinson, John, 37–38, 124
Hutchinson, Thomas, 170

Independent Reflector, 106
    See also Livingston, William
Inglis, Charles, 9, 22, 85, 89, 106, 120, 121, 122,
    129, 149–50, 156, 165, 171, 172–73, 176, 177,
    182, 185
Innes, Alexander, 80
Institution of a Christian Man, 115
Intolerable Acts, 128, 129, 130, 139

Jacobitism, 72, 78, 85, 125, 126, 142

James I, 71, 104
James II, 7, 10, 67, 68–69, 70, 71, 145
Jefferson, Thomas, 22, 83–84, 130–31, 138, 183, 185
Jenkinson, Charles, 160
Jewel, John, 51
Johnson, Samuel, 8, 9, 15, 17–18, 22, 23, 26, 43, 48,
    89, 92, 93, 94, 97, 102, 105, 127, 182
    New Learning, 15, 35–37, 182
    relationship with Chandler, 17, 30–32, 34–35,
        38, 44
    as teacher of ministers, 27–30, 34, 41
Johnson, William Samuel, 94, 186

Kempe, John Tabor, 154
Kennett, White, 116
Kirk, Russell, 183
Kingfisher, 155, 157
King's College, 47, 106, 155, 164
Knox, William, 164

Lambeth Palace, 66, 91, 108, 160
latitudinarians, 33, 72, 77, 78
Laud, William, 13, 62, 64, 93, 109, 113, 116, 125
Law, William, 81–82
Leaming, Jeremiah, 167
Lee, Charles, 137–38, 142
Leland, John, 50
Leslie, Charles, 72–75, 86
Letters from a Pennsylvania Farmer, 130, 131
Letter from a Virginian, 146–47, 149
Letters of Papinian, 173
Letters of a Westchester Farmer, 150
Levelers, 86
Lilburne, John, 86
Livingston, Philip, 138–39
Livingston, William, 15, 105–6, 107, 127, 139,
    179–80
Locke, John, 10, 67, 68, 73, 74, 76, 83, 139, 148, 182
London, 157, 159–60, 164, 167, 168–69
Louis XIV, 68
Lowth, Robert, 97, 125
loyalism, 4, 6–7, 9, 15, 16, 150
    loyalist exiles, 154, 157, 159–60, 173–74
    loyalist writings, 4–5, 145, 146–50, 182

Madison, James, 137, 180
Markham, William, 161
Mary (Tudor), Queen, 52, 69, 108, 116
Mary (wife of James II), 69
Mary (wife of William III, daughter of James II),
    69, 70, 71, 73, 76
Mayhew, Jonathan, 83, 113

246 INDEX

Milton, John, 73, 83, 86
Montagu, James, 155
Moore, John, 163, 175–76, 177
Moravians, 49

New Bedford, NY, 39
New York City, 65, 129, 152, 154, 172
Newton, Isaac, 38
nonjurors, 10, 67, 70–79, 81, 85, 126, 144, 181
North Castle, NY, 39
North, Lord, 160, 175
Norton, Mary Beth, 6, 159–60
Nova Scotia, 173–74, 175, 176, 177
Noyes, Joseph, 24

Of the Laws of Ecclesiastical Politie, 59–61
The Original and Institution of Civil Government, 75
Overton, Richard, 86

Paine, Thomas, 85, 161–62
Panton, George, 166–67
Parliament
    in bishop's campaign, 89, 90, 92, 94
    constitutional role, 7, 66, 69–73, 92, 133, 135, 136–37, 138, 141, 162
    disputes with American revolutionaries, 108, 124, 128, 130–31, 133, 134, 160, 172
Parker, Henry, 86
Parker, James, 97, 107
Parker, Samuel, 62
passive obedience, 7, 68, 72, 78, 85, 145, 148
Patriarcha: or the Natural Power of Kings, 74, 76, 84–85
Potter, John, 42, 100
Presbyterians, 100, 109, 114, 115
    in New Jersey, 13, 15, 40, 43, 45, 48, 132, 176
    relations with Anglicans, 6, 13, 48, 62, 64, 96, 117, 119–20, 136, 146
    views of episcopacy, 88–89, 90, 115, 117, 119
    in Scotland, 103–4
Puritanism, 31, 109, 114, 115
    in New England, 27, 41, 62, 182
    relations with Anglicans, 6, 13, 14, 23–24, 33, 44, 51, 52–57, 61, 64, 86, 136, 146
    views of episcopacy, 34, 41, 88–89, 90, 116, 181

Quebec Act, 63

Ramus, Petrus, 35
Rapin, Paul de, 117

Reasonableness of Conformity to the Church of England, 77
Rhoden, Nancy L., 7
Rivington, James, 155, 157
Rivington, John, 186

Sacheverell. Henry, 68, 77–78, 111
St. John's Church, 1, 8, 13, 39, 40, 43, 44, 45, 48, 95
    glebe and parish house, 45–47
Scotland, 12, 41, 53, 71, 89, 103–4, 110, 177
Scruton, Roger, 181, 183
Seabury, Samuel Jr., 9, 22, 47, 89, 92, 93, 97, 106, 107, 122, 129, 149, 150, 156, 164–65, 166, 170, 171, 175, 177, 182
Seabury, Samuel Sr., 21, 39, 40
Secker, Thomas, 90, 91, 92, 93, 102, 125, 126
Seed, John, 6
Seven Years' War, 91
Shays' Rebellion, 180
Shelburne, Lord, 172
Sherlock, Thomas, 50
Skinner, Cortlandt, 107
Smith, William, 4–5, 9, 90, 92, 124, 145–46, 156
Smith, William Jr., 106
Smyth, Fredrick, 5
Snape, Andrew, 80–81
Society for the Promotion of Christian Knowledge (SPCK), 13
Society for the Propagation of the Gospel in Foreign Parts (SPG), 11, 13, 27, 28, 39, 40, 43, 47, 50, 65, 66, 111, 113, 125, 156, 163–64, 165
Sons of Liberty, 15, 65, 127, 129, 133, 143, 146, 155
Southwell, Edward, 159
Stamp Act, 65, 92, 138, 144
Stiles, Ezra, 9, 23, 26, 27
Stillingfleet, Edward, 33, 34, 115
Stratford, CT, 29
Suffolk Resolves, 128, 133, 142, 144, 150
Sugar Act, 92
Sydney, Algernon, 73, 74, 83

Terrick, Richard, 124, 161
Test Act, 62, 90, 117
Thirty-Nine Articles of 1563, 57, 58, 116–17
Three Letters to the Bishop of Bangor, 81–82
Tickle, Timothy, 107, 126
Toleration Act, 76–77
Townsend, Charles, 160
Trinity College, 54, 92
Tucker, Josiah, 158–59
Tudor England, 51–61, 108, 116

Two Treatises of Government, 76
Tyrell, James, 10, 67

Uniformity Act of 1662, 62

Vardill, John, 164, 173
Vaughan, Edward, 39, 47
via media, 33
virtual representation, 135

Walpole, Horatio, 125
Walton, Izaak, 59
Washington, George, 183
Watts, Isaac, 26
Wedderburn, Alexander, 164
Welles, Noah, 24, 106
Wesley, John, 79
Weston, Edward, 50
Wetherhead, John, 155
Wetmore, James, 38, 39, 40
What Think Ye of the Congress Now?, 136, 139–45, 146

Whip for the American Whig, A, 107
Whitby, Daniel, 33, 34
White, Thomas, 71
Whitefield, George, 1, 2, 14, 25, 26, 49
Whitehall, 66, 71, 72, 175
Whitgift, John, 14, 31, 51, 53, 54, 55–56, 57, 58–59, 61, 62, 64, 88, 116, 118, 120, 125, 148
Wilcox, Thomas, 54
Will, George F., 3
William of Orange, 67, 68, 69, 70, 71, 73, 76, 77, 85, 103, 109
Wollebius, Johannes, 24
Wood, Gordon S., 5
Wood, Thomas, 43
Woodbridge, NJ, 40, 48
Woodstock, CT, 8, 18, 19

Yale Apostasy, 22, 33
Yale College, 8, 12, 17, 21, 22, 23–27, 30, 33, 35, 182

www.ingramcontent.com/pod-product-compliance
Lightning Source LLC
Chambersburg PA
CBHW022048290426
44109CB00014B/1022